ATLA Monograph Series
edited by Dr. Kenneth E. Rowe

1. Ronald L. Grimes. *The Divine Imagination: William Blake's Major Prophetic Visions.* 1972.
2. George D. Kelsey. *Social Ethics Among Southern Baptists, 1917-1969.* 1973.
3. Hilda Adam Kring. *The Harmonists: A Folk-Cultural Approach.* 1973.
4. J. Steven O'Malley. *Pilgrimage of Faith: The Legacy of the Otterbeins.* 1973.
5. Charles Edwin Jones. *Perfectionist Persuasion: The Holiness Movement and American Methodism, 1867-1936.* 1974.
6. Donald E. Byrne, Jr. *No Foot of Land: Folklore of American Methodist Itinerants.* 1975.
7. Milton C. Sernett. *Black Religion and American Evangelicalism: White Protestants, Plantation Missions, and the Flowering of Negro Christianity, 1787-1865.* 1975.
8. Eva Fleischner. *Judaism in German Christian Theology Since 1945: Christianity and Israel Considered in Terms of Mission.* 1975.
9. Walter James Lowe. *Mystery & The Unconscious: A Study on the Thought of Paul Ricoeur.* 1977.
10. Norris Magnuson. *Salvation in the Slums: Evangelical Social Welfare Work, 1865-1920.* 1977.
11. William Sherman Minor. *Creativity in Henry Nelson Wieman.* 1977.
12. Thomas Virgil Peterson. *Ham and Japheth: The Mythic World of Whites in the Antebellum South.* 1978.
13. Randall K. Burkett. *Garveyism as a Religious Movement: The Institutionalization of a Black Civil Religion.* 1978.
14. Roger G. Betsworth. *The Radical Movement of the 1960's.* 1980.
15. Alice Cowan Cochran. *Miners, Merchants, and Missionaries: The Roles of Missionaries and Pioneer Churches in the Colorado Gold Rush and Its Aftermath, 1858-1870.* 1980.
16. Irene Lawrence. *Linguistics and Theology: The Significance of Noam Chomsky for Theological Construction.* 1980.

THE RADICAL MOVEMENT
OF THE 1960's

by

Roger G. Betsworth

ATLA Monograph Series, No. 14

The Scarecrow Press, Inc.
and
The American Theological Library Association
Metuchen, N.J., & London
1980

277.3082
B465

81030324

Library of Congress Cataloging in Publication Data

Betsworth, Roger G   1933-
    The radical movement of the 1960's.

    (ATLA monograph series ; no. 14)
    Bibliography: p.
    Includes index.
    1. United States--Religion--1960-   2. Nationalism
and religion--United States. I. Title. II. Series:
American Theological Library Association. ATLA mono-
graph series ; no. 14.
BL2530.U6B46   277.3'0826   80-12534
ISBN 0-8108-1307-6

Copyright © 1980 by Roger G. Betsworth

Manufactured in the United States of America

To Joan

EDITOR'S NOTE

Since 1972, the American Theological Library Association, has undertaken responsibility for a modest dissertation publishing program in the field of religious studies. Our aim in this series is to publish two dissertations of quality each year at a reasonable cost. Titles are selected from studies in a variety of religious and theological disciplines nominated by graduate school deans or directors of graduate studies in religion. We are pleased to publish Roger G. Betsworth's study of the radical movement of the 1960's as number 14 in our series.

Following undergraduate studies at the United States Naval Academy, Mr. Betsworth studied theology at Drew University and took the doctorate in social ethics at the University of Southern California. Mr. Betsworth currently serves as Chaplain and Associate Professor of Religion in Simpson College, Indianola, Iowa.

Kenneth E. Rowe
Series Editor

Drew University Library
Madison, New Jersey 07940

ACKNOWLEDGMENTS

For many of the insights of this study I am indebted to the people of the Community Methodist Church of Huntington Beach, California and to the religion faculty of the University of Southern California. Many of the persons of the Church were vitally involved in the societal conflicts of the sixties. Some persons were establishment figures whose vocations placed them in direct conflict with sectarians; some were sectarians themselves. The faculty at USC encouraged my attempts to understand the struggles of the decade. They enabled me to think with Troeltsch, Bellah and Berger about the nature of the turmoil through which the American society had passed.

I especially appreciate the interest of Professor Jack Crossley, who first obtained a fellowship which enabled me to devote my full time to this work, and who then spent many hours reading and discussing the rough draft.

Finally, I want to express appreciation to my wife, Joan, who gave double measure of herself in teaching and home-making while I wrote; to David, who kept me playing racquetball; to Deborah, who made neat the disorder of my desk; and to Sharon, who cheered me each afternoon with stories fresh from first grade.

Roger G. Betsworth

TABLE OF CONTENTS

I

INTRODUCTION

Emile Durkheim defines religion as a unified system of beliefs and practices relative to sacred things, which unites all who adhere to them into one single moral community. For Durkheim, such an understanding of religion clarifies the necessity of a civil religion.

> There can be no society which does not feel the need of upholding and reaffirming at regular intervals the collective sentiments and the collective ideas which make its unity and its personality. Now this moral remaking cannot be achieved except by the means of reunions, assemblies and meetings where the individuals, being closely united to one another, reaffirm in common their common sentiments; hence come ceremonies which do not differ from regular religious ceremonies, either in their object, the results which they produce, or the processes employed to attain these results. What essential difference is there between an assembly of Christians celebrating the principal dates of the life of Christ, or of Jews remembering the exodus from Egypt, or the promulgation of the decalogue, and a reunion of citizens commemorating the promulgation of a new moral or legal system or some great event in the national life? [Durkheim, 1915, p427].

Robert Bellah argues that the American civil religion is a religion according to Durkheim's definition.

> What we have then, from the earliest years of the republic is a collection of beliefs, symbols, and rituals with respect to sacred things and institutionalized in a collectivity. This religion--there seems no other word for it--while not antithetical to and indeed sharing much in common with Chris-

tianity, was neither sectarian nor in any specific
sense Christian [Bellah, 1970, p175].

The sacred things of the American civil religion are
not primarily the mighty acts of God with his people Israel
nor his Word as revealed in Jesus, but the Divine or provi-
dential purpose and mission for the New Israel, the American people. The great events of Exodus and Cross-Resur-
rection are paradigmatic, but American history is the new
act of God. The widespread use of the term New Israel to
designate the American people is significant. The Scriptures,
so sacred to early American divines, are willing to speak
only of a new covenant to the old Israel. Even Paul, to
whom the meaning of Israel had become such an enigma,
could only refer to Christians as the Israel of God in the
sense of the true Israel (Galatians 6:16, cf. Conzelmann,
1962, p55).

But to Americans, God had done a new thing in this
land, a thing comparable to the establishment of a New
Covenant in Old Israel: nothing less than the founding of a
New Israel. The import of such clues as this has been
overlooked in the ongoing debate over whether the American
civil religion has its own independent source or is a watered-
down version of Protestantism. If in fact the civil religion
is merely watered-down Protestantism, such heresy would
not have been tolerated in periods of vigorous doctrinal struggle such as the Great Awakenings. The evangelical Protestantism of the Great Awakenings and the rational categories
of the Enlightenment were both able to accept the American
civil religion. The Calvinist conception of man as fallen opposed the messianic understanding of America. Yet the Calvinist also envisioned America as a people who honored and
obeyed the word of the Lord. This was the basis of the doctrine of the New Israel, a land discovered and settled by
Divine Providence.

The destiny of the American Republic to lead the world
to millenial glory emerged with the Revolution. Men under
the sway of the Great Awakening were expecting God to do a
new thing. The Revolution was therefore no mere political
convulsion. Even while the guns were still firing, sermons
and histories began to claim that the Revolution was of serious consequence for the whole Christian world. With independence such a claim became irresistible. J. F. Maclear
has suggested that

> To all these interpreters, the Revolution was the
> greatest revealing moment since the Reformation,
> illuminating the past and pointing to a future in
> which the nations would increasingly adopt "our
> wisdom, liberty and happiness, " knowledge and
> religion would be diffused throughout the earth, and
> mankind would be prepared "for the universal reign
> of the son of God in the glories of the latter day"
> [Maclear, 1971, pp184-195].

Such a doctrine could easily be expressed in a Rous-
seauean spirit by interpreting God's will in terms of democracy and liberty. Thus the Puritan conviction that they were
called to establish a new covenanted community was translated into rational categories, and received classic form in
the Declaration of Independence and the Constitution (Stark,
1966, vol. I, pp186-197).

By 1800 the collective sentiments and the collective
ideas which make the unity and personality of a society were
put to the test in America. For the first time in modern
politics an incumbent political party suffered an electoral defeat and simply turned over power to its opponents (Lipset,
1967, p50). The American civil religion had emerged, by
whose doctrine

> ... the Union was understood as a transcendent
> reality, a proper object of reverence and loyalty,
> an enduring, possibly eternal, source of moral in-
> spiration, and surely something that was far great-
> er than the individuals or the states of which it was
> composed. Its makers stood in awe of their handi-
> work and often ascribed its real authorship to a
> benevolent Deity. And even such strict Calvinists
> among them as Roger Sherman or John Witherspoon
> regarded these convictions as neither wayward nor
> idolatrous [Ahlstrom, 1972(b), pp108-109].

Sydney Ahlstrom traces the subsequent ideological
compromise between Americans committed to a universal republican model of government (which was the hope of mankind) and those loyal to an Elect Nation (which was a light
to all the nations). While on the one hand the compromise
can be seen as part of the ongoing dialogue between Puritan
theology and the rational tradition, on the other hand it was
also the steady modification of the orthodox Protestant the-
ologies by the American experience. The sense of human

progress, the doctrines of the natural rights of man, the
experience of political freedom which suggested a more profound human freedom enlarged the Puritan view of human
moral ability.   The movement can be almost personified in
the lives of Jonathan Edwards and his grandson Timothy
Dwight.   By the time Dwight became president of Yale in
1975, a fervent patriotic tradition had become an essential
part of evangelical Protestantism in America.   The civil
religion, far from being a watered-down version of mid-
eighteenth-century Protestantism, by 1800 was able to engage
and modify a vigorous Protestant evangelicalism, even while
Protestants hoped to fashion a Christian civilization.

With the Civil War the theme of sacrifice for the
nation gained a central place in the civil religion.   The paradigmatic experience was the Crucifixion, but the immediate
event of revelation was the War itself--the inflow of a history
that Americans as Americans hold in common.   It was a
history presided over by the somber figure of Abraham Lincoln, the theologian of the civil religion.   By her sacrifices,
by his sacrifice, America was to be purified for its mission
as a light to the nations.   The themes of suffering for the
right was also stressed in the South.   In fact, sacrifice for
the nation--meaning the nation as expressed in Southern tra-
ditions--became especially strong in the area of the Old
Confederacy.   The tradition of a society which had known a
landed aristocracy, slavery and defeat in war continued in
the Southern regional form of the civil religion.

The fact that leading spokesmen for the civil religion
such as Lincoln often couched their beliefs in language that
was unmistakably Protestant should not lead us to conclude
that the civil religion was merely a generalized Protestantism.
Certainly, there was much of that, and the religious references to providence and sacrifice do have their deepest source
in the biblical traditions of the churches.   Yet the national
religion and the denominations have remained distinct.   Both
Roman Catholics and Jews developed a deep faith in the destiny of America.   The differences between religious groups
were transcended at least on the plane of a national faith
where Americans held common beliefs (Cherry, 1971, pp14-
15).

The civil religion itself has changed as the American
experience has changed.   After the Civil War, the Protestant
emphasis on making the United States a world model of
humanitarian concern narrowed its focus to personal conversions, fundamentalism, temperance crusades and missions

informed by the same restricted and often nativistic theology
(Tyler, 1944). The social gospel, especially as articulated
by Walter Rauschenbusch, attempted to alleviate the suffering
engendered by rapid economic and social change. Although
the social gospel sought to give new goals to the civil religion, still the American faith found its more popular expression in the jingoism of Theodore Roosevelt and the passion of
preachers who presented arms to make the world safe for
democracy. The rush of outward events between 1876 and
1932 was more real as history to Americans than the flowering of one of the richest periods of American philosophy,
scholarship, architecture, poetry, fiction and music. Especially in the area of radical social criticism on the meaning
and purpose of America was some of the finest work done
(Abell, 1963; Bottomore, 1966; Bremner, 1956; Gabriel,
1956; Hopkins, 1940; Lasch, 1965; May, 1967; Schlesinger &
White, eds., 1963; Silverman, ed., 1970; Weinstein, 1967).
What was lacking, according to Sidney Ahlstrom,

> was the kind of political leadership which could
> mediate this greatness and deepen the popular
> understanding of the country's civic faith. So we
> have the anomaly of a great cultural flowering time
> during which the public concern for the nation's
> nature and purpose is largely given over to out-
> sized patriotic weeds [Ahlstrom, 1972(b), pp118-
> 119].

The Great Depression, the New Deal, Roosevelt, war
again, then cold war, have all left their stamp on the civil
religion. For many Americans, the Depression and the New
Deal were as cataclysmic events as the founding of the nation
and the Civil War. In the thirties, nineteenth-century individualism gave ground to a new emphasis on social security
and collective action. The individualistic twenties were
scorned as "escapist." Private experience was held to be
self-indulgent compared to the demands of public life.
Roosevelt and the New Dealers reached back to Lincoln's hope
for America, and felt themselves heirs of the Enlightenment
as well. They wanted America to be part of a broadly humanistic movement to make man's life on earth more tolerable. Roosevelt was essentially a moralist who sought certain humane reforms and who wanted to rekindle the faith of
the nation in government of, by and for the people. The
New Deal both envisioned and achieved a more just society
by including groups who had been excluded from decision
making in government and society. This was especially true

of the industrial workers.   Yet the revolution was only partial: the poor, the unemployed, the unorganized poor worker,
the black, the brown, the yellow, the red Americans were
still left outside the emerging prosperity.   Rhetoric included
them, but reality did not.   To them was born the revolutionary generation of the 1960's (Leuchtenburg, 1963).

World War II altered the civil religion in a profound
way.   The emergence of America by the end of the war as
the preeminent world power tempted the nation to seek to
order the whole society of man.   The civil religion encouraged the belief that since America is the Elect Nation
with a universal destiny, her power will always be used in
the service of virtue.   This attitude was one of the factors
which contributed to the emerging cold war.

From even this brief tracing it is clear that the
foremost institution of the civil religion has been the nation
itself.   John E. Smylie has shown that the nation gradually
assumed the traditional role of the church for Americans.
The pattern of denominationalism and disestablishment created
American "churches" rather than an American church.   Thus

> Gradually in America the nation emerged as the
> primary agent of God's meaningful activity in
> history.   Hence Americans bestowed on it a
> catholicity of destiny similar to that which theology
> attributes to the universal church [Smylie, 1963,
> pp313-317].

The public schools have served as an important sub-
institution, providing the place of instruction in the sacred
history of the civil religion.   The school has emphasized the
holy days of America's faith--Thanksgiving and the providen-
tial founding of the nation, Memorial Day and sacrificial
dying for the nation, and the birthdays of Founder and Martyr.
From kindergarten to high school, American students celebrate in literature and art the great events of the American
experience.   As the National Education Association said in
1951, the public school has taught a common faith--the supreme importance of the individual personality, common
consent, brotherhood, the pursuit of happiness, and "the
values which made America great" (Michaelsen, 1966,
pp380-400).

The civil religion as sketched above is what Stark
refers to as the established religion.   The established

religion usually expresses itself in three associated institutions and sets of ideas: a sacred ruler, a sacred nation and a sacred mission. The sacred ruler is central as long as society is communal, for the sacred ruler is society writ large. But when society becomes associational, the king is displaced, both religiously and administratively. The locus of holiness shifts from king to people. However, the sacred mission is retained. The sacred mission is retained because it expresses the basic thrust of all religion. According to Weber, the primary and perennial source of religion is the experience of suffering in human life. Where there is suffering, there is yearning for salvation, health, wholeness and rescue from the painful condition. The yearning for salvation is the heart of all faith. The sacred mission is thus at the heart of every civil religion. For example, Shinto expresses the mission thus:

> Since the foundation of the Japanese Empire it has been the yearning of all Japanese to unite all the races of the world into a happy society. We regard this as the great mission of the Japanese People. We strive also to clear away from the earth injustice and inequality and to bring everlasting happiness to all mankind [Stark, 1966, vol. II, p105].

The sacred mission is granted to the people. Therefore the historical experience of the people becomes the medium of revelation. The voice of the people is the voice of God. For the American faith, such a vox Dei is not the voice of the people expressed in any one election or vote of representatives, but the historical choices that the people make through the unfolding of the democratic process across time. In order to safeguard the established religion, the constitution under which the sacred people have chosen to live is believed to be of more than human origin. Thus the founding documents become sacred scriptures by which the sacred people hope to maintain the established tradition, the fulfillment of the sacred mission.

The mainstream of American history flows along the channel prepared by the established type of the civil religion. The nation is perceived mainly, though not wholly, through the institutions of the state, for through these institutions the sacred people choose those who are entrusted with crucial roles in fulfilling the sacred mission. It is, as Bellah, Ahlstrom, Cherry and others indicate, the ruling class that usually articulates the civil religion. Those who rise to positions of leadership in politics, economics, Church, education, indeed, in every aspect of the social order understand themselves to have been entrusted with the sacred mission. The established type of the civil religion is therefore by its nature accepting of the present order, believing what is, is ordained of God.

The established type is what is usually referred to as the American Civil religion. The apparent lack of a prophetic tradition leads to the charge that the American civil religion is a watered-down version of Protestantism. Although the established type of civil religion accepts a transcendental, universal mission for America to the world, this type seldom sees a need to criticize the present structure of American society. The dominant classes, who exercise power in society, seem to use the common American experience to praise what is, and thus themselves. The American civil religion is therefore not seen as a true religion but an idolatry. It cannot participate in a moral remaking of the nation. Herberg argues

> Civic religion is a religion which validates culture and society, without in any sense bringing them under judgement. It lends an ultimate sanction to culture and society by assuring them that they constitute an unequivocal expression of "spiritual ideals" and "religious values." Religion becomes in effect the cult of culture and society, in which the "right" social order and the received cultural values are divinized by being identified with the divine purpose [Herberg, 1960, p263].

Mead, however, argues that the American civil religion is not the American way of life as we know and understand it. Herberg is in error on that point, Mead believes. Such a conclusion is equivalent to concluding that the Christian faith is the way of life exemplified by ordinary professing Christians. Cherry suggests that Mead and Bellah are arguing there must be a distinction between religious nationalism and a national religion (Cherry, 1971, p17).

But such a distinction lends credence to a second criticism of the concept of an American civil religion: how can coherent beliefs and values be said to be drawn from the American experience? Even more devastatingly, it is asked how behavior can be said to correspond with such beliefs? While the cult of the American civil religion can be readily

outlined, for a religion to be identified as such in a modern
society, it is not enough that symbols be shared, but cult,
symbols, beliefs and behavior must cohere in a manifest way.
Therefore the diversity of the American experience, such as
the polarities of abolitionists versus slaveholders who both
appeal to paradigmatic events of American history, suggests
that the American civil religion is only a vague concept
based on a vague set of symbols, and not a reality.   Religious nationalism is evident, but a civil religion is not (Wilson, 1971, p12).

The impasse can be bridged and the reality and
strength of the American civil religion set into proper perspective by applying the church-sect typology of Ernst
Troeltsch to the civil religion.   The church type is the
established type of civil religion which is traced above, and
which is usually the focus of the civil religion discussion.

Yet there has been a persistent tradition in America
of those, who, in close connection with their current situations and concerned with the development of society, have
opposed the direction which the ruling group has chosen.
There is a continuity between the radicals of 1776 and the
radicals of 1966.   Paine, Garrison, George, Thoreau and
Debs sought a new direction for America that they believed
was truer to its revolutionary principles than the direction
the ruling class had marked out.   The radical tradition is
not only intellectual, but it is also active.   These men and
their sons translated book and pamphlet to sermon, stump
speech and political activity.   So the son of utopian socialist
Robert Owen drafted the Fourteenth Amendment and the son
of John Brown provided food for the Haymarket anarchists
as they awaited execution (Lynd, 1969, pp8-9).   But precisely
because the activity of radicals has at times been incorporated
into the political institutions (such as the Fourteenth Amendment) and at times has solidified the established civil religion in opposition (such as during the Palmer raids and Mc-
Carthy era), the established civil religion cannot be understood except in conjunction with the radical aspect of the
civil religion.   This radical tradition is the sectarian form
of the civil religion.

The thesis upon which this study rests, then, is that
both an established and sectarian form of the civil religion
are a logical result of the opening phase of the American
experience, and both have continued to the present.   Only
conjointly do they enable us to grasp the full meaning of the

American faith, and allow us to envision the new forms into which that faith is flowing today. The methodology to be used in demonstrating this thesis is the church-sect typology of Ernst Troeltsch (Troeltsch, 1960, vols. I and II).

First, Troeltsch argues that the church type accepts the present secular order, believes that the good which the church incarnates is universal, and ought to cover the whole life of humanity and dominate the masses for the sake of their own salvation. The sects, on the other hand, seek perfection, which is, of course, not yet attained. Thus they demand a reordering of the present social structure. They renounce the idea of dominating the world, and stress personal relationships that are direct and caring. Although sects are often hostile toward the present structure of state and society, they may be tolerant or indifferent toward structures. Their aim is to replace present social institutions, at least as far as their own members are concerned, and often for the whole of society.

The established type of the civil religion also believes that the present American order is good and ought to be universal, and cover the whole life of humanity, dominating the world for the sake of its own salvation. President Mc-Kinley urged the nation into the War of 1898 "for our little brown brethren for whom Christ also died." So the "Manifest Destiny" doctrine of the established civil religion moved beyond continental expansion to the task of world empire. Such a move was all but inevitable, for even in the midst of revolution Americans had believed with Timothy Dwight that the destiny of this first new nation was universal.

> As the day spring unbounded, thy splendour shall
>   flow
> And earth's little kingdoms before thee shall bow;
> While the ensigns of union, in triumph unfurl'd
> Hush the tumult of war, and give peace to the
>   world [Ahlstrom, 1972(b), p111].

The sect type of the civil religion rejects the pretensions of the present to universal goodness and rightful empire. It seeks to replace the social order by a new, purer, more just one. It sees in its own band of faithful the hope of a new society. Thoreau argues

> All men recognize the right of revolution; that is
> the right to refuse allegiance to, and resist, the

government, when its tyranny or its inefficiency
are great and unendurable.   But almost all say
that such is not the case now.   But such was the
case, they think, in the Revolution of '75 ...
but ... when a sixth of the population of a nation
which has undertaken to be the refuge of liberty
are slaves, and a whole country is unjustly overrun
and conquered by a foreign army, and subjected to
military law, I think that it is not too soon for
honest men to rebel and revolutionize.... This
people must cease to hold slaves, and to make war
on Mexico, though it cost them their existence as
a people [Thoreau, 1953, pp284-285].

Lynd persuasively argues that Thoreau's philosophy of civil
disobedience was a manifesto of a movement, rather than
merely a personal statement (Lynd, 1969, pp122-125).

Second, Troeltsch notes that while both church and
sect are in close connection with the actual situation and the
development of society, the church intertwines the institutions
of state and ruling classes with her own life.   Thus the
church becomes both part of the existing order and dependent
upon it.   The sect, however, maintains its connection with
the lower classes and those who are opposed to the state.

The established type of the civil religion has been
primarily articulated by the ruling class.   The fact that
this expression is widely accepted in a society is due to
what Amitai Etzioni refers to as a basic human need for
context.   Cognitions, emotions and beliefs are all affected
by input from a variety of societal sectors, including the
educational, economic, political and religious orders.   The
person seems to have a need to integrate the variety of inputs into one.   A contextuating orientation is costly to
establish.   In the American situation, it was established by
genuine threat to life, first in the experience of settling an
inhospitable shore and secondly in the experience of the
Revolution.   The power to interpret events and establish
contexts is not randomly distributed in a social system, but
is structured and organized, allocated and applied in much
the same ways as other kinds of power.   It is as costly to
change a contextuating orientation as it is to establish it.
Etzioni suggests that while a theory or world view is a context,
a fact or attitude is a bit.   Bits may be changed without
major social cost if the context is not challenged.   But if the
bits are seen to be challenging the context, the costs rise.

When bit replacement threatens to unseat the context, the
costs will be nearly as major as the costs which established
the original context (Etzioni, 1968, pp 158, 358, 624). Thus
once set by the ruling class, the established civil religion
continues to provide the contextuating orientation for most
Americans, especially those who feel they are fulfilling the
sacred mission.

The sect type of the civil religion is in close connection with its current situation but opposes the present social
order. Garrison is a prime example, when in 1836 he began
a series of polemics against Lyman Beecher, attacking
Beecher's defense of the established type of the civil religion. Garrison rejects the belief that the destiny of liberty
rests upon the people of the United States

> As if God has suspended the fate of all nations,
> and hazarded the fulfillment of his glorious
> promises, upon the result of a wild and cruel
> "experiment" by a landstealing, blood-thirsty,
> man-slaying and slave-trading people in one
> corner of the globe! As if God could not easily
> dash this nation in pieces, as a potter's vessel
> is broken, and thereby vindicate his eternal
> justice ... [Lynd, 1969, p132].

When Beecher heaps scorn upon demagogues who seek to
make the working man feel as if "they were despised and
wronged, and that there is oppression in the fact that others
were richer than they," Garrison attacks again.

> Is it not true that our laboring population are to an
> alarming extent, despised and wronged? ... To
> say nothing of the treatment of the Southern laboring
> population ... our Northern working men have
> every reason to be alarmed at the prospect before
> them. There is a conspiracy all over the land
> against them [ibid., p136].

Thus Garrison maintains the sectarian position of
opposition to the present social order and solidarity with the
slaves and the poor working class.

Third, for Troeltsch, the church incorporates a genuine asceticism into its structure. Asceticism is a method
of acquiring virtue and special achievements by discipline and
repression of the senses. It is on good terms with the world.

The asceticism of the sects on the other hand is denial of
worldly goods and achievements as of major worth.   This
opposition to the world and its social institutions is not
opposition to the life of the senses, nor to the average life
of humanity, but indeed emphasizes a union in love which is
not affected by the social inequalities and struggles of the
world.

The Puritan work ethic is the form asceticism takes
in the established civil religion.   The gaining of special
achievement is believed to be possible for all.   One stream
within the established civil religion sees work as a calling--
as Weber documents--and in the Gilded Age the man of money
is per se the saint of the civil religion.   The sectarian type
of the civil religion, like the sect type of the Christian religion, denies that worldly goods and achievements determine
the worth of a man.   Rauschenbusch, of all the men of
socialist persuasion, most eloquently and explicitly opposes
the civil religion of the Gilded Age.   He recites the history
of the Revolution and the Civil War, the previous understand-
ings of the Kingdom of God with their political overtones,
all with the purpose of reminding his generation that America
was founded in protest against autocracy and the Civil War
was waged to dethrone slavery.   Therefore autocracy and
slavery are not to be tolerated in the economic order.
Americans must remember, Rauschenbusch believes, that the
sacred mission may be abrogated; the sacred people dismissed from history, for

> Nations do not die by wealth, but by injustice....
> Progress slackens when a single class appropriates
> the social results of the common labor, fortifies
> its evil rights by unfair laws, throttles the masses
> by political centralization and suppression, and
> consumes in luxury what it has taken in covetous-
> ness....   Internal convulsions or external catas-
> trophes will finally reveal the state of decay
> [Rauschenbusch, 1964, p284].

Fourth, Troeltsch sees that the main stream of development flows along the church type.   Because of the
desire of the church type to establish a universal ideal, control great masses of men and to establish a world wide
Christian civilization, the church type becomes the obvious
vehicle of historical record.   The sect type is, by definition,
and often by law, outside the corporate life of the ecclesias-
tical tradition.   In view of the church, the sect is one-sided,

an exaggeration or abbreviation of churchly Christianity. In
the view of the sects, the church has fallen away from the
ideal of the Gospel and primitive Christianity. While the
sects make this claim polemically, Troeltsch believes the
freedom of the sect from the corporate structures which en-
mesh the church is important. It allows the sect to continue
its insistence upon the basic ideals of the Christian faith,
thereby representing in a very direct way much of the essential fundamental ideals of Christianity.

Clearly the main stream of development of the nation
flows along the established type of the civil religion, precisely because the nation is the institutional structure of the
civil religion. Both Lipset and Gabriel, in differing ways,
argue that the basic value system, as solidified in the civil
religion in the early days of the nation, gave shape to American society. This basic influence continued to mold the life
of the nation through changing geographical and economic
conditions (Gabriel, 1956; Lipset, 1967). The historical
record of the nation therefore reflects the sacred mission:
the concern to establish American civilization first upon the
continent and then upon the earth.

The sectarian form of the civil religion believes that
the main stream of development has fallen away from the
ideals articulated by the Founding Fathers. These ideals
are the hope of the world, but they have been betrayed by
the compromises of slavery, war, and economic exploitation.
Thus the sectarian form of the civil religion appeals again
and again to the Sacred Documents (the Declaration of Independence and the Constitution) and to the basic principles of
humanism upon which those documents are based. It is this
appeal that gains the sect a hearing as it raises its voice
against the apostasy of the establishment.

Henry George exemplifies the sectarian position when
he compares the poverty of the working man in the Gilded
Age to slavery. He opposes the established form of the
civil religion of his time because it produces inequality. He
chooses Jefferson as his patron saint and cherishes most
Jefferson's compilation of the sayings of Jesus. To George
the doctrines of the Democracy are those of the Declaration
of Independence.

> In our time as in times before creep on the insidi-
> ous forces that, producing inequality, destroy Liberty.
> On the horizon the clouds begin to lower. Liberty

> calls to us again.   We must follow her further; we
> must trust her fully.   Either we must accept her
> fully or she will not stay [Gabriel, 1956, p210].

Even a stronger appeal to the doctrines of the Declaration of Independence is made by William Hosmer, a sectarian of both Christian and civil religions, and one of the
founders of the Free Methodist Church.   In opposing slavery
he asserts

> The fact that a law is constitutional amounts to
> nothing, unless it is also pure; it must harmonize
> with the law of God, or be set at naught by all
> upright men.   Wicked laws not only may be broken,
> but absolutely must be broken; there is no other
> way to escape the wrath of God. ...   When the
> fundamental law of the land is proved to be a con-
> spiracy against human rights, law ceases to be law,
> and becomes a wanton outrage on society [Smith,
> T. L. , 1957, p206].

Fifth, Troeltsch points out that the more the church
tries to achieve its universal ideal and world wide dominance
by organization and missionary effort, the more it is forced
to make its Christian character independent of the subjective
character and actions of individual believers.   Therefore the
church focuses its attention on the objective possession of
religious truth and power which are contained in the tradition
of Christ.   The sect, however, appeals to the ever new common performance of the moral demands which rest finally
only upon the Law and example of Christ.   The life of Jesus
and the Scriptures are not the starting point of institutional
development, but are permanent ideals to which the individual
must be radically obedient.   This stress on radical obedience
to an ideal of perfect love limits the sects to groups based
on personal intimacy.   It further requires constant renewal
of the ideal, necessitates pronounced individualism and
creates the sense of solidarity with idealistic and oppressed
persons of all social classes.

The established type of the civil religion likewise
seeks to achieve the universal ideal by organized effort.
This requires faith that the character of the nation is independent of the characters of individuals or even of particular
administrations or leaders.   America is believed to be sacred
people entrusted with a sacred mission.   The actions of the
nation which suggest to some that America is imperialist,

or that she seeks her own good at the expense of others, are dismissed as aberrations or mistakes. The established type of the civil religion believes that the divine purpose will be fulfilled independent of particular policies. The American mission will be achieved in spite of seemingly contradictory policies of the nation. The faith of the established type is therefore centered on the doctrine that America is to be a light to the nations. The task of the faithful is to organize and evangelize so that that faith will be actualized in the life of the world today.

The sectarian form of the civil religion, however, appeals to ever new actions which express and demonstrate the same commitment to freedom, brotherhood and democracy that was evidenced by the Founding Fathers. They were willing to commit their lives, fortune and sacred honor. Individuals, both in and out of office, must be equally committed to freedom today. For the sectarian, democracy and freedom are inseparable from present actions. Morris Hillquit sets the tone for sectarians in a Socialist campaign speech in 1917.

> We are for peace. We are unalterably opposed to the killing of our manhood and the draining of our resources in a bewildering pursuit of an incomprehensible "democracy" ... a pursuit which begins by suppressing the freedom of speech and press and public assemblage, and by stifling legitimate political criticism [Weinstein, 1967, p151].

Finally, Troeltsch understands the essence of the church to be its objective institutional character. The individual is born into it. The church dominates society, compelling all members to come under its sphere and influence. However, her power is so great that her stability is unaffected by whether she obtains sway over all individuals. Compared to this, the sect is a voluntary community whose members join of their own free will, on the basis of a conscious conversion. The sect therefore gathers a select group of the elect, and places it in sharp opposition to the world. Rather than seeking to dominate nations in the mass, it seeks its elect from amongst each nation. Insofar as it maintains a universalism at all, it is an eschatological one based on common suffering: the Day of the Lord is at hand, when the first shall be last and the poor shall be exalted.

The established form of the civil religion is seen in the institutional character of the nation. The individual is

born into it. The nation dominates society, using the public
school as the parochial school of the civil religion, compelling all members to come under its sphere and influence.

For a person to participate in the sectarian form of
the civil religion he must be "radicalized," i. e., converted.
The very life of the sect depends on the willingness of the
individual radical to be involved in actual personal service.
The only universal is likewise the universality of oppression,
and the hope for the coming day of revolution. Eugene Debs
is one of the best examples of the sect form of the civil
religion. He stresses in his speeches what it means to him
to have become a radical. To be radicalized is to

> ... thrill with a fresh-born manhood; to feel life
> truly worth while; to open new avenues of vision;
> to spread out glorious vistas; to know that I am
> kin to all that throbs; to be class-conscious, and
> to realize that, regardless of nationality, race,
> creed, color or sex, every man, every woman
> who toils, who renders useful service, every
> member of the working class without an exception,
> is my comrade, my brother and sister--and that
> to serve them and their cause is the highest duty
> of my life [Debs, 1948, p425].

In his speeches Debs seeks conversions, even when running
for political office on the Socialist ticket. Political activity
is important, Debs believes, but getting votes is not the
primary reason for running for office. The primary reason
is to convert persons to the radical perspective.

> There would be no use getting into power with a
> people that did not understand, with a lot of
> office-holders undisciplined by service in the party,
> unpurged by personal sacrifice of the selfish spirit
> of the present system [Weinstein, 1967, p11].

Troeltsch's scheme does not provide us with a formal
theory or even a very precise typology. There is in the
civil religion, as in the Christian religion, blurring of types
and what is sectarian in one age is established in another.
Nonetheless the typology does describe two clusters of basic
properties of groups who differ in their understanding of the
past and the present (Johnson, 1971, p124). These two
clusters point to differing views of reality, to different socially constructed worlds, to differing contexts into which the

discrete experiences and meanings of individuals are ordered. This meaning orientation is both subjective and objective. Its objective character is given by language. As an event or experience is named, it is typed, removed from the chaos of happenings, and given stability as the entity named. By the process of socialization, the objective meaning of an experience becomes the subjective ordering of the individual. As language transcends the concreteness of everyday life and seeks a contextuating orientation, it uses symbols which are usually either political or religious in nature, and often both. These symbols so readily combine, because the deepest threat to both the sacred and political order is chaos (Berger & Luckmann, 1966; Berger, 1967).

Such an analysis will often seem to be at some remove from concrete events in the political life of the nation during the 1960's. However, if events are questioned on succeeding levels of generality it becomes clear how important contextual orientations are in construing the meaning of happenings. Max Heirich, in analyzing the conflicts at Berkeley during the 1960's, suggests that at the most general level emergence of conflict depends on organizational trends in a society that create a conflict setting. Physical arrangements which isolate people who share common interests and problems are important to such trends. Yet of equal import are the contextuating orientations which prevent groups who debate and negotiate over societal directions from understanding one another. Emergence of conflict is also likely where prior relationships of hostility exist and where the necessity of a single solution to the crisis is felt. Troeltsch has argued that sectarians are often hostile, and almost inevitably believe in direct solutions to widespread social problems.

On the concrete levels, any act that departs from expected activity attracts attention. It is placed in an established or sectarian context, linked with other important activities established within the context in that time, assessed in relation to the claims that result, and a direct action is proposed. The direct action both attracts attention (thus recycling concrete events) and becomes a bit in opposing contextuating orientations, very often strengthening the opposition rather than moving toward compromise (Heirich, 1971).

The church-sect typology is then a way of speaking of differing contextuating orientations. The typology is therefore able to be applied both to world-views and concrete

events. The emphasis of this study on the church-sect typology is in line with Lipset's attempt to connect studies of
historical change with basic assumptions in sociological
theory--in this case, the sociology of religion. The method,
which is a historical case study, again agrees with Lipset
that at present this must be the basic mode for the study of
national evolution (Lipset, 1967, pp8-10).

The 1960's are chosen for the period of the case study
because of the visibility of the sectarian form of the civil
religion. In other periods, such as the 1920's or the 1950's,
the sectarian form of the civil religion was not as politically
active, but appeared in the arts and social sciences. Stark
suggests that the sectarians turn to overt political activity in
seasons of hope, and in seasons of despair return to liturgi-
cal and literary works. For sectarians, the sixties began
with hope and the Freedom Rides, and ended with sectarians
involved in writing, teaching and communes. During this
period, there was not only widespread political activity on
the part of sectarians, but also a great emphasis on lifestyle.
The new lifestyle included expressiveness, sexual freedom,
drug use, casual dress and hair styles, a commitment to
community and participatory democracy, the importance of
folk and rock music, and opposition to cool, uptight, square
middle class lifestyles. In their own way such emphases
became the liturgy of the movement. The lifestyle was what
Richard Flacks characterized as existential humanism. It
was seen as necessary to the movement because of the imperative to change the way people related to one another in
the establishing lifestyle. This change was considered to be
intrinsically worthwhile.

Yet the emphasis on lifestyle was also considered a
threat to the political goal of the movement a radical trans-
formation of the social order. The danger was one of ir-
responsibility, of finding a personally satisfying lifestyle, and
over-personalizing the movement, forgetting the original concern for the exploited. The situation is then created, Flacks
argues, in which

> one's personal needs and hang-ups are increasingly
> acted out in the large arena, and attempts at solu-
> tion of these take precedence over more collective
> concerns. The necessary distinction between the
> public and private self breaks down, with the likely
> result that either the community is undermined or
> personal freedom is sacrificed to preserve the com-
> munity. It seems to me that a clear consciousness
> and commitment to political goals at least has the

>virtue of limiting the interpretation of the public
>and private. So when I say that SDS must en-
>compass both orientations I think I mean something
>like this: we must keep centrally in view that we
>are a political movement ... at the same time, we
>must remain receptive and responsible to the
>standards of existential humanism ... [Flacks,
>1965, pp164-165].

The focus of the case study will therefore be on the political
side of the movement, recognizing, however, that the concern for a lifestyle of "existential humanism" is an important
factor, both for the actors personally and for the political
goals selected.

Finally, the case study will contrast the values of the
established and sectarian types in the political arenas of
racism, the war and the university. The black freedom
movement triggered the white radical movement and was its
vanguard throughout the sixties. The fifties had been a
period of student apathy. There was an absence of uncor-
rupted models of effective political action. Faculty and other
intellectuals were cautious or cynical about political action.
The black movement, beginning with Martin Luther King, Jr.
and continuing through the sixties, provided both a model
of effective and moral political action and a demonstration
of some of the major faults of the established order. Therefore the study of the sixties will look first at the black
sectarians.

White students were radicalized by their experience in
the black freedom movement. Out of this experience grew
the white radical movement. White radicals often provided
the most dramatic examples of conversion from established
to sectarian types. The reason for this is that the white
radicals, mostly students, were the principal inheritors of
the establishment type of the civil religion. They were
largely the sons and daughters of middle class liberal
parents. The experience of these students in attempting to
require America to live up to its ideals moved them from
the established to the sectarian perspective.

The movement can be divided into phases. The latter
half of the fifties was a period of preparation for a return
to widespread political activity by sectarians. Both the peace
and civil rights movements gained widespread visibility. The
Supreme Court decision which reversed the policy of "separate but equal" in the public schools created a new awareness

of racial injustice.   The Montgomery bus boycott brought
Martin Luther King, Jr. , and his style of nonviolent resistance to racist practices to national attention.   Federal troops
intervened in Little Rock.   At the University of California,
Berkeley, student political activism revived.   In 1958 and
1959 students renewed the sectarian custom of marching on
Washington for redress of grievances.   Civil rights and peace
were the emerging themes of the period.

The years from 1960 to 1965 are the period of pacifism, protest and reform.   The student civil rights movement
began with the sit-ins and the Freedom Rides.   S. N. C. C.
and S. D. S. were formed.   Repression was localized against
civil rights workers in the South and H. U. A. C. protestors
in Berkeley.   Sectarians were more fearful of being co-opted
than repressed.   The War on Poverty and the Civil Rights
Bills raised expectations of sectarians.   But the slow pace of
progress in both areas, and the escalation of the war dashed
sectarian hopes.   The process of raising hopes and dashing
them radicalized more of the young.   The New Left grew
(Flacks, 1971, pp76-82).

The period 1965 to 1970 was a time of confrontation,
radicalization and resistance.   It is the period of the institutionalization of the movement.   Rapid growth and national
recognition were given to groups such as S. N. C. C. , S. D. S. ,
the Berkeley F. S. M. and the Resistance.   The co-optation-
repression response of the established type hastened the
black/white split in the movement.   Mass demonstrations
were common.   The black movement became more and more
a class movement, while the white movement became more
an anarchist movement, especially in the emphasis on anti-
war activity.   The theme of Thoreau, "This people must cease
to hold [economic] slaves, and to make war [on Vietnam],
though it cost them their existence as a people" was sounded
again and again.

From 1970 to the present there has been a decline of
such sectarian political activity, including the demise of such
groups as S. D. S. and S. N. C. C.   There is a return from
public to private forms of sectarian activity.   The interest
in existential humanism--women's liberation, communes,
open marriages, organic farming--is in the ascendancy.   The
new students are recruited by Christian sectarians.   Flacks,
and Oglesby are writing instead of organizing.   But
some sectarians take heart in the "new politics. "   Radicals
now serve on the city council in Berkeley.   Hundreds of

blacks have been elected to public office in the South. Sectarians, including Hayden, are participating in the reform of the Democratic party. The conclusion of this period is not yet clear, however. Therefore I will not deal with it as a separate section, but will comment on it in relation to the 1965-1970 period.

Even before the detailed examination of the periods is undertaken, three basic questions emerge. It is hoped some answers can be indicated from this analysis. First, what has been the result of the resurgence of political activity by the sectarians during the 1960's? The answer must also indicate which group was primarily accommodated by the changes.

The second question is one that has been asked since 1968. What will now become of the radical movement? Will it endure? Will it return to mass political activity?

Finally, is there a possibility of resolving the ethical conflict between the established and sectarian types? Is the choice of one perspective inherently better than the other?

Perhaps an examination of the periods outlined above from the perspective of the civil religion will make it possible to answer these questions perceptively.

II

PRELUDE

THE CIVIL RELIGION AND THE
COLD WAR: 1944-1960

The Established Type
of the Civil Religion

The radical movement of the 1960's did not just happen to emerge in that particular decade. It was not merely the reappearance of the ancient conflict of the generations nor the happenstance of students turning their attention from panty raids to more serious spring flings. The radical movement of the sixties was a response to the accelerated change in American character and national action engendered by war and cold war. As the new policies--peace-time draft, large standing armies, arms races, secrecy in government, land war in Asia and continued occupation of Europe--exaggerated traditional American imperial intentions, opposition inevitably arose. That opposition was rooted in the American tradition as surely as was the imperial intention. Russel B. Nye argues that the American national purpose has remained remarkably constant over three hundred and fifty years. It proposes

--that the United States lead others toward a
further world state of freedom and liberty
as yet unknown, and that it serve as a surrogate or agent for the rest of mankind in
achieving it.
--that the United States serve as an example to
the rest of the world of God's plan for mankind, and as proof that man can govern himself in peace and justice.
--that the United States serve as a haven for the
oppressed of the world, and as a place of

opportunity for the deserving, ambitious and
godly [Nye, 1966, p168].

Although the evangelical aim of the first purpose was
primarily understood to be fulfilled by the exemplary aim of
the second purpose, America nevertheless went to war twice
in twenty-five years to lead others toward freedom and
liberty.   In another sense, however, such war was a contradiction to America's self-understanding.   Endless war was
precisely one of the sins which Americans believed they had
left behind in the Old World.   But the Spanish American War,
WW I and WW II each eroded that conviction.   Wars do not
radically alter a society, but according to Henry Commager,
they do accelerate the changes that are already in the making.
For a particular social culture nourishes war, and war in
turn transforms the social culture.

Certainly the American culture since 1940 is in
considerable part a product of World War II, and,
even more, of the responsibilities and opportunities
created by that war, of the unique position assigned
by circumstances to the United States, of changes
in technology and in the structural relations of the
military with the economic interests that emerged
out of the war.   The postwar culture was, in turn,
the setting of the cold war and of its almost
Strangelovian by-product, the war in Vietnam
[Commager, 1972, p8].

The accelerated change in American character and
action in relation to global commitments must be examined
in the postwar period.   But also the increasing demand for
justice for black people must be taken into account.   The
established and sectarian types of the civil religion placed
Nye's formulations of national purpose in opposing contextuating orientations.   For the established form, the cold
war policies were in fact the exercise of that leadership
which would create a future world state of freedom and
liberty.   However, for the sectarian type the exemplary
task was the only permissible policy.   The United States
could exercise leadership only by providing an example that
man could govern himself in peace and justice.   To the
sectarian, cold war policies were policies which emphasized
the fear of war.   The emphasis on meeting the requirements
of war--conscription, arms, alliances, secrecy, bureaucracy
and budget--made the fear of war a reality to every American.
Such policies mocked the ideal that the United States was a

land in which man could govern himself in peace.   For the
established type, the demand for justice for black Americans
was to enhance the example of the United States.   Cold war
leadership was of greater importance than the accepted
American customs.   A secondary purpose for the established
type to be sympathetic to black demands for justice was the
cruelty of oppression itself.   But for sectarians, the civil
rights movement was the attempt to prove that man can
govern himself in peace and justice.   It was not for the sake
of cold war gamesmanship nor just the black, but for the
sake of both black and white.

      Before turning to a brief examination of these trends
in the civil religion, another aspect of the postwar period
should also be noted--the revival of traditional religion.
Membership in the Protestant churches increased twenty percent, and the Roman Catholic church experienced a forty
percent growth in this period.   The majority of the Protestant as well as the Catholic converts were from the lower
and lower middle classes.   But expanding church membership was only one indication of new concern for religion:
clerics became famous for proclaiming relief from anxiety
through religion--Peale, Graham and Sheen were the best
known.   Motion pictures such as "A Man Called Peter" and
"The Ten Commandments" broke box office records.   Hit
songs celebrated faith in faith--"The Man Upstairs" and "I
Believe. "   The acceleration of change brought on by war and
cold war added yet more tension to already disrupted lives.
Weber's thesis that suffering is the perennial source of religion was abundantly documented as a society sought to be
saved from anxiety by faith in the Man Upstairs.

      Herberg, however, argues that the widespread turn
to faith might be interpreted as the personal side of the
established type of the civil religion.   He suggests that the
religious boom was more an increase in the civil religion
than in the membership of particular bodies of Protestants,
Catholics or Jews.   The fact that so many of the new religions are of the lower and lower middle class points to the
conclusion that these were third generation immigrants
seeking belonging and self-identification in a society in the
midst of chaotic change.

            ... to religion, therefore, the men and women of
            the third generation now began to turn to define
            their place in American society in a way that
            would sustain their Americanness and yet confirm

the tie that bound them to their forbears, whom they now no longer had any reason to reject, whom indeed, for the sake of a heritage, they now wanted to remember [Herberg, 1960, p31].

The more traditional expressions to which Herberg calls attention are affirmations of faith in democracy and the American way of life.   These affirmations of public faith, like the personal ones of peace of mind, meant to assure the believer that there is indeed a rescue from the painful struggle for survival that the majority of persons in the majority of nations still suffer.   Thus it is important to see this period as a revival of the American civil religion as well as of the traditional religions.   The revival is misunderstood if it is dismissed as merely a resurgence of the superficial peace of mind cultists and Madison Avenue evangelists.   Instead, the return to religion, in its civil form (both personal and public), is the attempt by a majority of Americans to be saved from the suffering engendered by war and accelerated social change.   The majority of Americans therefore came to accept the established view that the postwar situation of America in the role of world leadership is part of America's destiny.

Acceptance of the postwar situation was partly due to the fact that the established type of the civil religion was expressed most strongly through cold war rhetoric.   As the sixties wore on, the cold war began to lose its purity of definition, and the rhetoric tended to be expressed in clichés. However, in the beginning it was not so.   The cold war language was the heartfelt affirmation of free men responding to Communist aggression.   In retrospect, it can be seen that the cold war emerged from the clash of incompatible contextual orientations.   The U. S. S. R. was wholly committed to the "sphere of influence" view of world order, whereby each great power would be assured by the other great powers of an acknowledged predominance in its own sphere of interest.   The United States, in accordance with its historic understanding of mission, was committed to the universalist tradition.   The universalist tradition affirmed the universal applicability of democratic procedures and institutions as a remedy for political ills.   By such procedures each nation ought to rule itself.   In a democratic way a universal international organization should be substituted for the dangerous play of "power politics."   Wilson, in whose sub-cabinet Roosevelt served, stated the American faith eloquently.

No peace can last, or ought to last, which does not
recognize and accept the principle that governments
derive all their just powers from the consent of
the governed and that no right anywhere exists to
hand peoples about from potentate to potentate as if
they were property.... I am proposing, as it
were, that the nations should with one accord
adopt the doctrine of President Monroe as the doctrine of the world: that no nation should seek to
extend its policy over any other nation or people,
but that every people should be unafraid, the little
along with the great and powerful [Morgenthau,
1970, p86]. *

Roosevelt, who was a Wilsonian and had campaigned
for the League of Nations in 1920, declared in 1944, "There
is in this global war literally no question, either military or
political, in which the United States is not interested" (ibid.,
p62). And in 1945, in his report to Congress on the Yalta
Conference he said

The Crimean Conference ... spells the end of the
system of unilateral action and exclusive alliances
and spheres of influence and balances of power and
all the other expedients which have been tried for
centuries--and have failed [ibid., p85].

Roosevelt was not alone in espousing the universalist doctrine. Cordell Hull, the Secretary of State, was even more
determined than Roosevelt to maintain the purity of universalism. Other figures in the State Department, including
Sumner Welles, Adolf Berle, Averell Harriman and Charles
Bohlen--all of whom were to continue to have considerable
influence on U.S. policy--were also committed to universalism. Republicans also had come to share the same
vision. John Foster Dulles argued that the great threat to
peace was the revival of sphere-of-influence thinking. He
was convinced that the United States must not permit such a
revival. America must resolutely demand participation in
all policy decisions for all territories of the world. Presumably, only through such American agency could peoples

---

*Excerpts from The Origins of the Cold War, by L. C.
Gardner, A. Schlesinger, Jr., and H. J. Morgenthau. Reprinted by permission of John Wiley & Sons, Inc.

be truly free and the world find peace.   Senator Vandenberg,
in early 1945, turned from his lifelong isolationist convictions to declare in a Senate speech

> I do not believe that any nation hereafter can im-
> munize itself by its own exclusive action. . . .   I
> want maximum American cooperation. . . .   I want
> a new dignity and a new authority for international
> law.   I think American self-interest requires this
> [Goldman, 1960, p30].

Both sides of the Senate floor burst into sustained applause
upon the completion of Vandenberg's address.

The first diplomatic summary given to President
Truman after the death of Roosevelt complained that the
Soviet government was taking a firm and uncompromising
position on Poland.   When the impasse seemed beyond the
abilities of the foreign ministers of the Big Three to resolve,
Stalin sent a message directly to Truman.

> . . . It is also necessary to take into account the
> fact that Poland borders on the Soviet Union, which
> cannot be said of Great Britain and the United
> States. . . .   You, apparently, do not agree that the
> Soviet Union has a right to make efforts that there
> should exist in Poland a government friendly toward
> the Soviet Union, and that the Soviet Government
> cannot agree to the existence in Poland of a govern-
> ment hostile toward it.   Besides everything else,
> this is demanded by the blood of the Soviet people
> abundantly shed on the fields of Poland in the name
> of the liberation of Poland.   I do not know whether
> there has been established in Greece a really repre-
> sentative government, and whether the government
> in Belgium is really democratic.   The Soviet Union
> was not consulted when these governments were
> being established there.   The Soviet Government
> did not lay claim to interference in these affairs
> as it understands the whole importance of Belgium
> and Greece for the security of Great Britain.   It
> is not clear why, while the question of Poland is
> discussed it is not wanted to take into consideration
> the interests of the Soviet Union from the point of
> view of its security [Truman, 1955, pp86-87].

Stalin concluded his message to Truman that to do other than
consider Poland a Soviet sphere of influence would be to re-

nounce the interest of the security of the U. S. S. R. and turn
against his own country. Truman was a universalist. He
was convinced that there was no political or military question
in which the United States was not vitally interested. Indeed,
had not the U. S. entered a bloody war which had begun in
the first place over the question of Poland? Stalin's espousal
of the sphere of influence orientation was to Truman "most
revealing and disquieting." He understood it to mean that
the Russians were planning world conquest. That same day
Truman met with Secretary of War Stimson to talk over the
effect of the atomic bomb on future foreign relations. With
the successful test of the bomb at Alamorgordo the day before Potsdam opened, the United States had not only a global
interest but a weapon of awesome power to back that interest. Truman did not fail to mention it to Stalin at Potsdam (ibid. , pp412-416).

The emphasis on universalism was for Troeltsch the
first indication of the established type of religion. The
opening moves in the cold war, which took place in 1943-45,
were from the United States viewpoint an affirmation of its
historic mission. Universalism was the purpose of both the
great wars of the twentieth century. The universal application of democracy to all peoples was "demanded by the blood
of the [American] people abundantly shed on the fields of
[Europe] in the name of liberation. ... " Although the meaning
of the Russian civil religion is beyond the scope of this
study, from the time of the czars Holy Russia has sought to
secure her borders from a hostile world. Roosevelt yearned
to fulfill the American mission. However, realizing the
constraints upon him, he was moving to accommodate Russian aims in Eastern Europe. F. D. R. was aware that the
American people would not accept sacrifices necessary to
enforce American hopes. Americans wanted their "boys"
home. Standing armies in Eastern Europe, which would
prolong military service for millions, would not be supported.
FDR was also constrained by the necessity to control Germany, for which he needed the cooperation of the Soviet
Union. The successful test of the atomic bomb removed both
those restraints for Truman. "I'll certainly have a hammer
on those boys!" he exulted on the eve of Potsdam (Alperovitz,
1970; Daniels, 1950, p266; Kolko, 1968).

Truman's actions were characteristic of the established
type. The President was attempting to achieve the universal
ideal by missionary and organization effort. Missionary effort had failed Wilson. Truman was apparently failing again

to convince Stalin of the basic rightness of the universalistic democratic view.   Therefore organizational effort was needed. Ironically, of course, to seek to force acceptance of freely chosen democratic policies around the world was a contra- diction in terms; it was, as Troeltsch saw, to objectify truth, and make it independent of the particular actions of the United States.   The U. S. supported its position by an appeal to the great principles of its mission: to lead others toward a future world state of freedom and liberty as yet unknown.   Both Churchill and Stalin pointed out that the United States strenuously upheld a sphere of influence in its own interest: the Monroe Doctrine.   But to American leaders, there was no contradiction between universalism and the Monroe Doctrine, for the Monroe Doctrine shared the same goal: to lead others toward a future state of freedom and liberty.   Although individual acts of particular adminis- trations might have been less than the best, the American mission would not fail.

The organizational effort undertaken was based on the power of the atomic bomb.   Gar Alperovitz has argued that the use of the bomb against Japan was largely for the purpose of demonstrating its power to the U. S. S. R.   The U. S. had broken the Japanese code and knew of Japan's surrender negotiations.   Truman had no objections to continuing the Imperial succession as a figurehead as the Japanese re- quested.   Such an arrangement would have allowed the Japanese to avoid the onus of unconditional surrender and the Allies would have an indigenous source of authority in maintaining control.   The military (Eisenhower, Spaatz, Arnold, Nimitz and MacArthur) were opposed or non-committal concerning the use of atomic weapons.   Eisenhower, in his Memoirs, recalled the day Secretary of War Stimson gave him the news of the successful test in New Mexico, the plan for using it on Japan, and his own reaction.

> During his recitation of the relevant facts, I had been conscious of a feeling of depression and so I voiced to him my grave misgivings, first on the basis of my belief that Japan was already defeated and that dropping the bomb was completely un- necessary, and secondly because I thought that our country should avoid shocking world opinion by the use of a weapon whose employment was, I thought, no longer mandatory as a measure to save Ameri- can lives.   It was my belief that Japan was, at that very moment, seeking some way to surrender

> with a minimum loss of "face." The Secretary was
> deeply perturbed by my attitude, almost angrily re-
> futing the reasons I gave for my quick conclusions
> [Eisenhower, 1963, p313].

Stimson, in his diary, made clear the basis of his agitation.
He listed the number of diplomatic issues over which the
U.S. would find it necessary to "have it out" with the Rus-
sians. He concluded

> Over any such tangled weave of problems [the
> atomic bomb secret] would be dominant.... It
> seems a terrible thing to gamble with such
> stakes in diplomacy without your master card in
> your hand [Alperovitz, 1970, p69].

With the use of the bomb, universalism, which for
Americans was morally superior, was now backed by a
superior force which could be delivered any place on the
globe. Such a combination led to the illusion of American
omnipotence. James F. Byrnes, Truman's personal representative for atomic matters and his Secretary of State, had
urged use of the bomb to impress the Russians. From 1945
through 1947 he argued that the bomb "would make Russia
more manageable," and that "the U.S. could dictate its own
terms." When in 1947 such hopes had not materialized,
Byrnes demanded "measures of last resort" to force the
Russians to yield in Europe (ibid., p73).

According to Troeltsch, the established type of religion
weaves into its own fabric the broad concern of the upper and
ruling classes. Thus Byrnes' fanatic advice was not accepted
by the U.S. Government. The broader view was that

> The objectives of peace and freedom ... are bound
> up completely in a third objective ... re-establish-
> ment of world trade. In fact, the three--peace,
> freedom and world trade--are inseparable [ibid.,
> p88].

Truman proclaimed the world could not stand another global
war, for it would mean the end of civilization. The U.S.
would avoid war.

> We are going to accept the "golden rule," and we
> are going forward to meet our destiny which I
> think Almighty God intended us to have. And we
> are going to be the leaders [Gardner, 1970, p8].

The format of leadership was the Marshall Plan.
Marshall, in a speech at Harvard in April 1947, made it
clear that the purpose of the plan was the revival of world
trade so as to permit the establishment of political and social conditions in which "free institutions can exist." The
National Association of Manufacturers, the A. F. L. , the
C. I. O. , the important farm organizations and numerous other
pressure groups threw their support behind the plan.   It
passed Congress, and between 1945 to 1958 more than $67
billion of grants, loans and credits were distributed to non-
Communist countries.   Forty-two percent of the grants were
for military procurement, which permitted the formation of
N. A. T. O. in 1949.   By 1950, even though the majority of
grants and loans were to purchase American skills and equipment, in most categories economic recovery not only attained but far exceeded the prewar levels   (Link, 1967,
pp709-711).

The mainstream of development of the postwar world
was channeled by Americans along the established form of
the civil religion.   The longing for universal meaning for
the nation, the missionary effort to ensure that democracy
and free enterprise emerge triumphant, the desire to be
included in the basic political and economic decisions everywhere in the world are characteristic of the American civil
religion.   Sadly enough, Stalin saw in these concerns impla-
cable hostility to Russia and to Communism.   Likewise,
Stalin's moves in the interests of Russia's sphere of influence were seen by Americans as diabolical confirmation
of Communism's demand for world domination.   At first,
Stalin was unconcerned as to who was in power in East
Germany, Rumania and Hungary, as long as the government
was responsive to Russian interests.   But he shortly discovered the only parties willing to serve Russian interests
in Europe were Communist parties, thus he installed them
in Eastern Europe and used them in Western Europe and
Britain.   But as Morgenthau put it

> In private conversations [Stalin] heaped scorn upon
> the fools and knaves who allowed themselves to be
> used by him, but he used them because there was
> nobody else to use.   And he was as hostile to
> Communist nationalists as he was to non-Communist
> ones.   He purged the Communists of Eastern
> Europe who refused to do his bidding; for the same
> reason he was at best indifferent to Chinese com-
> munism, he exercised and tried to bring down the
> Communist government of Yugoslavia, and he op-

posed the project of a federation of Communist
Balkan States.   For him, then, Communist orthodoxy was a means to an end, and the end was the
power of the Russian state traditionally defined ...
in retrospect one can savor the irony of the pope
of Marxism-Leninism manipulating the tenets of the
doctrine with cynical pragmatism on behalf of the
national interests of Russia, while his Western opponents, more serious about the doctrine than he,
sought the meaning of his deeds in the tenets of
his doctrine [Morgenthau, 1970, pp96-97].

The American civil religion was thus given a concrete
evil against which to define itself.   Of course, the myth of
Communism as the ultimate evil has a long history in America.   It received its content first of all from the domestic
labor struggle.   Not only were the socialists and radicals
considered sworn enemies of America, but even the conservative Gompers and the A. F. L. were viewed with suspicion.
Few voices were raised in protest during the infamous Palmer raids.   Thousands of American citizens and legal immigrants were summarily seized, and imprisoned or deported.
To "protect" the nation against Communism, even the rights
of American citizens, sacred to the civil religion, could be
suspended.   The myth was further reinforced by the dramatic
success of the industrial union organizers in 1937.   The most
radical shift of social power in America was accomplished
with unions that were willing to use Communists as organizers.

By the late 1940's Russia's sphere of influence was
firmly under her control.   Yet the U. S. still clung to its
universal mission.   Thus the rhetoric of "liberation of cap-
tive nations" from the evil of Communism was born.   The
United States did not seriously intend to clear the Red Army
from the nations it has occupied.   That was made evident
when America remained aloof from appeals by nationalist
uprisings.   Nevertheless, the rhetoric continued, and was
abundantly answered by rhetoric from Moscow.   The opposing
blocs were solidified in their self-righteous cold war.   The
Klaus Fuchs case, the Marshall Plan, N. A. T. O. , the War-
saw Pact, the Truman doctrine, the triumph of Mao Tse-tung
and the Korean War were all placed by either side into its
own contextuating orientation and hailed or decried.   The
Korean War drastically militarized the cold war, with each
side perceiving it as an attack.   Conventional and nuclear
armaments were enormously increased, alliances widely
sought and bases more extensively established.   By 1953 the

entire foreign policy of the United States was based on the
cold war, and although McCarthy was at last censured, Mc-
Carthyism influenced the domestic climate. Khrushchev,
feeling the U. S. S. R. to be at a disadvantage in a static
sphere of influence position versus the dynamic universalist
position of the U. S. , revived the Bolshevik expectation of
the Communization of the world. The new Russian policy
proclaimed support of wars of "national liberation," military
intervention, foreign aid and trade, diplomatic pressure and
subversion. The vision of the established form of the American civil religion narrowed under the impact of the Russian
policy. The vision of the world became less what it might
be and more what it must not be. As he took office, President Eisenhower told Churchill he considered it his duty to
make clear to the world the wickedness of Communist promises and to convince dependent peoples that their only hope
lay in cooperation with the Free World. In writing his
memoirs, Eisenhower said

> In other words, I believe that the great ideas of
> the West will continue their outward journey in
> concentric circles until one day they cover the
> entire globe. Our cardinal concepts of human
> dignity, of free enterprise, and human liberty as
> codified and refined in Roman law, the Magna
> Carta, the American Declaration of Independence
> and the Bill of Rights--and continuously enriched
> by the best thinking of other countries--will be-
> come so strong that as they crash against the con-
> flicting currents of Communism, they will over-
> come and demolish dialectical materialism and the
> ideology of regimentation [Eisenhower, 1965, pp657-
> 658].

Eisenhower, both at the beginning and end of his presidential career, was struggling with the common question of
the established type: how can it be that some peoples will
reject the truth? After all, Mao's victory had been in the
name of the People's Republic of China. It was clear that
he had the larger measure of support of the peasants of
China. In Vietnam, the Communists were fighting under the
name of the Democratic Republic of Vietnam, and Eisenhower
reluctantly conceded that

> . . . it was almost impossible to make the average
> Vietnamese peasant realize that the French, under
> whose rule his people had lived for some eighty

years, were really fighting in the cause of freedom,
while the Vietminh, people of their own ethnic
origins, were fighting on the side of slavery.   It
was generally conceded that had an election been
held, Ho Chi Minh would have been elected Premier [Eisenhower, 1963, pp337-338].

Troeltsch points out that Luther found himself in an analogous
situation.   He was convinced that where the Word was rightly
preached, there was the Church.   The Word would create a
common understanding of the truths of Scripture within the
church and a clear message without; therefore the Word
would also instruct the government in the proper discharge
of its duties and the laity would accept its ruling with a free
and willing obedience.

When the Word fails to do this the only conclusion
that can be drawn is that this failure "is due to the power
of sin and the Devil, as so often happens in this wicked
world" (Troeltsch, 1960, p490).   When faced with failure,
Luther, according to Troeltsch, came very close to "the
eschatological apocalyptic" point of view, believing that when
evil threatens to overwhelm one must do what is good for
his own soul rather than good for his neighbor, i. e. , the
world.

The established type of the civil religion could only
believe that rejection of the mission of America by any of
the peoples of the world was due to the wickedness and evil
of Communism.   Communism was believed to have the fatal
power to lure the masses from the transparently truthful
promises of America to vote for the Ho Chi Minh's of the
world.   In the face of such disaster, "the eschatological
apocalyptic" point of view appeared in the American civil
religion, as men such as Byrnes and Goldwater (whom
Byrnes later supported) urged the use of nuclear weapons.
The earnest explanation of an American advisor concerning
the destruction of a South Vietnamese village, "It was necessary to destroy it in order to save it, " was the same religious conviction expressed on a smaller scale.

The discovery of the power of the Devil motivated
Luther to define "the true Word rightly preached. "   Luther
was forced back a step from the beginnings of a free historical human interpretation of the Bible and the process of
"establishing the true doctrine" was completed in the subsequent period of orthodoxy.   Likewise, Americans set about

to define what was the genius of their mission. The definition was sometimes set forth in broad sweeping terms from
Roman law to the Bill of Rights, as Eisenhower did.   More
often the focus was on what was not American--certain
people, books in the library, teachers, organizations, etc.
In the field of foreign policy such negative definition continued to have dominance.   President Kennedy summed up
the constraints under which American policy labored when he
outlined the action the U. S. would take in the Dominican
Republic after the assassination of Trujillo.

> [There are] three possibilities in descending order
> of preference: a decent democratic regime, a
> continuation of the Trujillo regime, or a Castro
> regime.   We ought to aim at the first, but we
> really can't renounce the second until we are sure
> that we can avoid the third [Schlesinger, 1965,
> p769]. *

The narrowing of the American mission to "second best, "
i. e. to opposition to Communism, allowed U. S. support and
establishment of dictators such as Premier Diem in South
Vietnam in 1954.

    It is important to look briefly at the establishment of
Diem in the fifties, for as the heartfelt affirmations of the
fifties echoed more and more hollowly in the sixties, Vietnam
became the issue that fueled the radical movement.   It is a
commonplace that John Foster Dulles was gripped by a sense
of Holy mission, a crusade against Communism.   His sense
of the mission of America was one in which other interests
were submerged in order that the crusade might succeed.
Therefore economic and political pressures were put upon the
French not to acquiesce in a Communist takeover of Indochina through negotiations at Geneva.   The Eisenhower Administration considered the Geneva accords a disaster, for
even though the Joint Chiefs of Staff had stated that Indochina
was "devoid of decisive military objectives, " the Administration stated it could not accept a plan which would "sanction
putting millions of Vietnamese under 'Red Rule' " (Sheehan,
1971, pp10-18; Gravel, 1971, Vol I, pp86-107, 510, 562).

---

*Excerpts from A Thousand Days: John Kennedy in the White
House by Arthur M. Schlesinger, Jr. Boston: Houghton Mif-
flin, 1965.   Reprinted by permission of the publisher and
Andre Deutsch Ltd.

Persuasive arguments arose within the government against further action in Indochina after the Geneva accords, however. The C. I. A. warned that it was unlikely that South Vietnam would ever be able to establish a strong government, and the situation would probably continue to deteriorate. The Joint Chiefs of Staff objected to a proposal to train and equip the South Vietnamese Army in the absence of a strong effective government. Congressional leaders opposed unilateral intervention, and the French and British were determined to withdraw according to the Geneva accords. Yet Dulles held fast to the policy set forth by the National Security Council, to take all

> affirmative and practical steps, with or without its
> European allies, to provide tangible evidence of
> Western strength and determination to defeat com-
> munism, to demonstrate that ultimate victory will
> be won by the free world [ibid., pp472-476].

Against all negative reports, even the urging of General Collins, who had been given the rank of ambassador, that Diem be replaced, or plans be re-evaluated, Dulles remained firm: "We have no other choice but to continue our aid to Vietnam and support of Diem" (ibid., pp226, 227).

The fact that Dulles was able to persuade the Administration that there were no other alternatives testifies both to the power of the established type of the civil religion and its narrowed focus. It was almost as if the mission of America had become the rescue of the world from the ultimate evil of Communism. Therefore Dulles could argue that it may be futile to support Diem, it may be against U. S. interests to back a sure loser, but nonetheless, Diem must now be used to hold the dike, lest the flood of Communism sweep millions away. Dulles, like a crusader on a holy mission, did not base his action only on his own interests; he did not trim his sail to the prevailing winds of fortune, for even in the face of certain defeat he had no other choice but to continue. Ultimate issues were believed to be at stake; therefore ultimate resources had to be summoned for an ultimate effort.

Accordingly, since Ho Chi Minh was expected to win the 1956 elections, the Eisenhower Administration postponed them as long as possible. For since Communism was defined as the ultimate evil, even a Diem dictatorship was preferable to an elected Ho Chi Minh. Throughout the re-

mainder of the Eisenhower years, military assistance made
up nearly ninety percent of the aid to Diem. Thus by holding
an increasingly repressive dictator in office the U. S. sought
to demonstrate that "ultimate victory will be won by the free
world" (ibid. , pp284-346, 472-4].

By the time Kennedy entered the Presidency, the
established form of the American civil religion, defining its
mission in terms of the rescue of the world from the ultimate evil of Communism, had created South Vietnam. The
Pentagon Papers historian writes

> ... South Vietnam was essentially the creation of the
> United States. Without U. S. support, Diem almost
> certainly could not have consolidated his hold on
> South Vietnam; without threat of U. S. intervention,
> South Vietnam could not have refused to even dis-
> cuss the elections called for in 1956 without being
> immediately overrun by the Vietminh armies; with-
> out U. S. aid in the years following, the Diem
> regime certainly, and an independent South Vietnam
> almost as certainly, could not have survived
> [Gravel, 1971, Vol. II, p22].

Again, it is important to emphasize that the established form of the American civil religion saw no contradiction in America's assuming the role of the older imperial
empires while espousing anti-imperialist convictions. On
one level, the mission of America may be rooted in the
economic necessities of the nineteenth century to expand trade
through open door and anti-colonial foreign policies (Williams,
1969). Yet on another level, America's mission is still to
bring the blessings of her form of government, which includes the economic abundance of capitalism, to all. The
intention is often perceived to be on a pure religious plane,
even while the result may be on quite another level. For
example, in 1944, upon obtaining for the U. S. oil concessions formerly awarded the British, F. D. R. 's representative,
Patrick Hurley, writes that the "principles of imperialism,
monopoly and exploitation" have now been replaced with the
pure American principles of "liberty and democracy. " Hull
tells us that F. D. R. himself was excited "with the idea of
using Iran as an example of what we could do by an un-
selfish American policy" (Alperovitz, 1970, pp15 and 16).
Like Roosevelt in 1944, Eisenhower in 1954 could assume the
role of an older imperial empire while affirming anti-
imperialist convictions in the language of the American civil
religion.

The purpose of this brief tracing of the development of the established form of the civil religion in the post-war period has been to establish the basis of the radical protest of the sixties. The sixties did not just happen to be a radical era, but were a response to the accelerated change in American character and national action engendered by war and cold war. At the close of World War II, the United States strove desperately to achieve its historic mission "in this generation." It seemed as if the peoples of the world cried out for a messiah, and American leaders believed they possessed not only the truth but the power to answer the world's cry. But the universalism of the American vision clashed with the sphere of influence conviction of Russia, and the vision of the American civil religion narrowed to anti-communism. Truth was defined in orthodox, almost fundamentalistic terms.

Yet it is important to stress that the actions of America in the period were a genuine expression of the national faith. Americans from F. D. R. to Eisenhower truly believed that intention made the difference, that because America intended freedom, liberty, and free enterprise for all mankind, nations from Iran to Vietnam could move from the old imperialism to a new birth of freedom and plenty, from the threat of Communist enslavement to a free world of peace and justice. Not until the sixties did the establishment type of the civil religion recognize that U. S. policy was in fact supporting anti-revolutionary, anti-democratic regimes which had no intention of converting to the American democratic faith. By and large such a discovery only increased American determination. If the word would not bring forth faith, if as Eisenhower said, "our cardinal concepts of human dignity, of free enterprise, and human liberty" would not overcome the "ideology of regimentation," then surely more intense American organization, the quintessence of regimentation, would create the longed-for new world. The contradiction involved in such faith and action did not go unnoticed in the sixties.

The Sectarian Type of
the Civil Religion

Although the political expression of the sectarian type of the civil religion became fully evident in the sixties, it was beginning to come alive early in the postwar period. One of the principal groups that espoused the sectarian position against the cold war established type was the pacifists. The American peace movement as a political movement had been

sunk with the U. S. fleet at Pearl Harbor.   There was no
party such as the Socialists in World War I to continue a
vigorous anti-war campaign.   To be sure, a few, such as
George Houser, a Union Theological Seminary student, refused to register with the draft, were imprisoned, and
dreamed of a new America.   He wrote to A. J. Muste

> It seems to me that the time has definitely arrived
> for those of us who are opposed to war, and who
> favor the creation of a society with greater justice
> for all, to create a movement which can take us in
> that direction . . . we must raise up a movement
> based on non-violence as a method [Wittner, 1969,
> p63].

Muste, Secretary of the Fellowship of Reconciliation, replied
that he had not been impressed with the "sentimental, easy-
going pacifism" of the past fifty years, for society was in
the midst of revolution, and

> the only chance that revolution will really get some-
> where and will not simply devolute into a general
> breakup of Western civilization is that a non-
> violence movement should be built [that will] make
> effective contacts with oppressed and minority
> groups such as Negroes, share-croppers and in-
> dustrial workers [ibid. , p63].

Bayard Rustin and James Farmer served on the FDR staff
with Muste.   They spoke with A. J. Randolph, President of
the Brotherhood of Sleeping Car Porters, concerning the use
of Gandhian tactics in the burgeoning March on Washington
Movement.   Randolph was not a pacifist, but maintained
close contacts with the pacifist groups, as he found them to
be surer supporters of civil rights than non-pacifist whites.
Randolph agreed the tactics of non-violence were attractive.
However, the planned March on Washington was postponed
for twenty years due to the opposition of black newspapers
and the chilling effect of the Detroit riots, which white newspapers said were caused by too much militance in the struggle for racial equality.

Thus even while the war was raging--and to most
Americans it seemed as though the forces of good and evil
were locked in mortal combat--pacifists were opposing the
American vision of itself as The Good, and opposing the
American mission as it was seen by the established type of
the civil religion.

The sectarian type of the civil religion can be seen in precisely this opposition to the vision of America as The Good, which is leading the world by its present actions to a state of freedom and liberty. The sectarian civil religionist is deeply concerned about the purity of the nation. Purity of heart is to will one thing; if the nation is to be pure, it must choose irrevocably the one path--the path of example. It must demonstrate that man can govern himself in peace and justice. Only when this single purpose is wholly achieved will the possibility of leadership or agency come into view. In Nye's formulation, the sectarian sets his heart on the exemplary purpose

> that the United States serve as an example to the rest of the world of God's plan for mankind, and as proof that man can govern himself in peace and justice [Nye, 1966, p168].

Only by a pure fulfillment of the exemplary purpose will the evangelical purpose be good rather than evil. For if the United States seeks the role of world leadership while its own soul is afflicted with the cancer of injustice and hatred, then the nation will be an agent of evil rather than good. This understanding is pressed even at the risk of the life of the nation itself, as Thoreau said. As Garrison attacked Beecher for espousing the faith that the destiny of liberty rested upon the people of the United States, so the pacifists attack the view now that the destiny of liberty depends upon the United States going to war. It is this requirement of purity--that the United States be without remainder a society of peace and justice before she can be a light to the nations-- that is basic to the contextuating orientation for the pacifists.

The pacifists were vigorously attacked during the War, even to the extent that they were blamed for the out- break of war. Columnist Walter Lippmann expressed a wide- spread conviction when he wrote

> The preachment and the practice of pacifists in Britain and America were a cause of the World War. They were the cause of the failure to keep pace with the growth of German and Japanese armaments. They led to the policy of ... ap- peasement [Lippmann, 1942, p53].

The few who affirmed conscientious objector status during the war were sent to "civilian" service camps under the direction

of the military. Their complaints and strikes concerning
work without pay (a form of enslavement, they argued) received scant attention from the media and less sympathy
from the nation.

The use of the atomic bomb to destroy Hiroshima and
Nagasaki ignited a public controversy and revived the pacifist
movement. Methodist Bishop G. Bromley Oxnam, president
of the Federal Council of Churches, and John Foster Dulles,
chairman of the Council's Commission on a Just and Durable
Peace, called for a temporary suspension of air attacks on
Japan. Church leaders, though indignant, were still by and
large not pacifists, but a significant number became "nuclear
pacifists." John Hersey's Hiroshima, to which the New
Yorker devoted its entire issue of August 31, 1946, engendered deep feelings of guilt. The magazine sold out, the
book became a best seller, and for a decade money was
raised to help the victims of the bombing. More common
was a widespread fear that, as Gandhi put it, "Unless now
the world accepts non-violence, it will spell certain suicide
for mankind" (ibid. , p132).

The vast majority of Americans believe that there was
a real danger of most city people on earth being killed by
atomic bombs. Congresswoman Helen Douglas, Saturday
Review editor Norman Cousins and news commentator Ray-
mond Swing were typical of the new "nuclear pacifists."
Nuclear pacifists turned their attention to world government.
Although not large in number, nuclear pacifists had major
influence, for they tended to be part of the elite of opinion
makers. Atomic scientists were influential in the cause of
peace as well. They successfully opposed the May-Johnson
bill, which would have given control of atomic energy to
the military. Instead, Congress passed the McMahon Act,
establishing civilian control of atomic energy. The coalition
of pacifists and nuclear pacifists opposed Universal Military
Training as well. Four or five hundred men burned their
draft cards or mailed them back to the President during anti-
draft rallies in February of 1947. U. M. T. was opposed by
almost every major religious, labor, farm and educational
organization in the country. Muste recalled the campaign,
in which he, Rustin, Farmer and Dave Dellinger had all been
active, as being "the only case where a really effective coordination of pacifist forces and near pacifist was achieved"
(Wittner, 1969, p164).

But the pacifists and nuclear pacifists became more
and more estranged from one another during the fifties, for

the difference between them was basic.   They were on opposite sides of the established/sectarian types of the civil
religion.   Pacifists were sectarians, and therefore perceived
the world from a different perspective than the nuclear pacifists.   This difference was the significant difference of contextuating orientations.   The contextuating orientation of the
established type of the civil religion included, of course, as
does any contextuating orientation, much debate, dissension
and dissent concerning whether certain bits did or did not
fit into the context.   Certain groups emerged with their own
histories and labels--conservative or liberal--which could be
compared to Yinger's class church or denomination of the
Christian religion.   Such groups had sociologically describable
characteristics in terms of class, race and sometimes
region.   They would be in substantial--not perfect--harmony
with the power structure.   For the American civil religion,
the harmony or dissent concerning the bits was often influenced by the question of which group was in political
power, although this was not always the case.

Reinhold Niebuhr, by the 1950's a defender of established type of the American civil religion, sets the context
for the established type in the opening sentence of The Irony
of American History.

> Everybody understands the obvious meaning of the
> world struggle in which we are engaged.   We are
> defending freedom against tyranny and are trying
> to preserve justice against a system which has,
> demonically, distilled injustice and cruelty out of
> its original promise of a higher justice [Niebuhr,
> 1952, p1].

The rest of the book qualifies this obvious meaning but the
context does not change.   The mission of America is freedom against tyranny.   Therefore Niebuhr can support the
stockpiling of nuclear weapons while urging a pact not to use
such weapons between Russia and the U. S.   But the weapons
must be built, for Niebuhr believes a nation does not have
the power to say it would rather be annihilated than build
such weapons.   Therefore pacifism is an irrelevance.   The
Quaker witness, said Niebuhr, is

> most impressive in the Quaker works of mercy,
> and least impressive in all the problems of the
> political order where power must be placed in the
> service of justice [Niebuhr, 1967, pp237, 301].

Niebuhr, with all his serious and important reservations concerning the irony of American history, is still convinced that when power is placed in the service of the American universal mission, it is placed in the service of justice. This is the context of the established form of the American civil religion.

The pacifists have a radically different context.

> Our firm conviction as pacifists is that it is not possible to achieve democracy by undemocratic means, to overcome Communism by resorting increasingly to Communist methods, to save the values of Christian civilization by throwing them overboard as modern war requires us to do. On the positive side it is our conviction that love translated into concrete action for human brotherhood is the way to overcome evil ... [Muste, 1963, p105].

Muste supports this view by an appeal to Lincoln. When asked, "What constitutes the bulwark of our own liberty and independence?," Lincoln had replied

> It is not in our frowning battlements, our bristling sea coasts, our army and our navy. These are not our reliance against tyranny. All of these may be turned against us without making us weaker for the struggle.... Our defense is in the spirit which prized liberty as the heritage of all men, in all lands everywhere [ibid., p103].

The criticism most trenchantly made of pacifists by established religionists like Niebuhr is that their political effectiveness is low. The pacifist reply is, first of all, no one knows the political effectiveness of pacifism, because America does not deal with Communism other than with the "shooting-mad-dogs technique." The United States is not turning its tremendous intellectual and industrial force to caring for the needy and hungry. Instead, America merely mirrors the Communists: when they proclaim their way is better, America proclaims her way is better. Communists say they will prove their case by the good life that will come after the necessary violence of the revolution. Americans say they will prove their case in the good life that will come after the necessary force of atomic war or the threat of atomic war which forces surrender. The pacifist draws the line at this sort of "mutual insanity."

When he is asked whether this pacifism is politically
effective his reply is: If human beings do not draw
this line, then where will they draw the line? What
are they waiting for? In the great drama, Jakobowski and the Colonel, Jakobowski, the refugee, says
to the Nazi colonel who has just been engaged in
torturing certain victims: There is one advantage
that the hunted has over the hunter--namely, that
he is not the hunter. The advantage is an ultimate
one: Not to join the hunters. If a man loses it, there
is nothing to compensate for the loss [ibid. , p. 107].

The pacifists therefore strongly oppose the Truman
Doctrine, which is based on the conviction that the world
is irrevocably divided into two hostile blocs, and which provides military aid as its primary concern. Pacifists argue
that relief should be civilian in direction and character so
that it will be clear that it was given not for ideology's sake
but for the sake of the poor. The cold war perspective of
hostile blocs is not in the interest of the poor of the world,
for the poor are bound together in the common brotherhood
of want. It is the ruling classes who have imperialist
ambitions and designs. At this point the pacifists delineate
most clearly who is with them and who is against them, who
is a sectarian and who is an establishmentarian. If, for
whatever reason, a man is persuaded that when military
power is placed in the service of the American universal
mission it is placed in the service of justice, then he is on
the side of the imperialists; he aligns himself with the ruling
classes who profit from war, and sets himself against the
poor and needy of the world. Muste illustrates this position,
when, in an open letter to Reinhold Niebuhr, he observes
that Niebuhr's political position could not be distinguished
from that of John Foster Dulles.

Considered as a political phenomenon it is not an
accident that Reinhold Niebuhr, the radical, and
John Foster Dulles, the Wall Street Attorney ...
should now be virtually a team. For, if war is
"inevitable" whether on the basis of Marxist class
war ... or ... the necessity of exposing "the
pretensions of modern man, " in actuality the war
will be between Stalinist Russia and imperialist
United States, for "communism" on the one hand
and "free enterprise" on the other.... These are
the elements that have an interest in making war
and that possess the resources with which to make
war [Muste, 1967, p306].

Muste argues that war can be avoided only if those who are
not the "wise of the world" refuse to line up with one side
or the other in the cold war.

From Troeltsch's perspective, we can see the public
actions of pacifists as characteristic of the sectarian form
of the civil religion in the years immediately following World
War II.   Pacifists object to an American empire and yearn
for a social order with greater justice for all, i.e., a
society like their own small group.   They believe that in
order to create such a society, effective contact must be
made with oppressed and minority groups.   But if they reject
American imperial intentions generally, they passionately
oppose those intentions when they are based on force of arms.
Foreign policy that is implemented by threat of nuclear
weapons, enormous armed forces and the creation of client
military governments around the world is anathema to pacifists.   There is an uneasiness in joining forces with
"nuclear pacifists," on even one issue.   A sharp break appears between the two groups as the fifties proceed.   The
appeal of American pacifists is not only to the basic freedoms so valued by the Founding Fathers, but to actions of
individuals that demonstrate commitment to those freedoms.
They refuse to be coerced into lining up on either side of
the cold war.   The social ostracism, economic sanctions,
and at times legal authority of the state which are brought
into play against them only increase their appeals to ever
new actions to demonstrate their true commitment to freedom, brotherhood, peace and true democracy.

The brief public revival of the pacifist movement
was snuffed out by the increasing ideological combat between
liberal democracy and Communism.   E. J. Halle points out

> The ideological view of human affairs has always
> had an irresistible popular appeal because it con-
> forms to the child's image of a world divided be-
> tween two species, the good (we) and the wicked
> (they).   According to this image, the essence of
> life is the struggle between good and evil so
> represented. ... Similarly, to the extent that the
> Cold War was to be regarded as an ideological
> context there could be no geographical limit to it,
> and it could properly end only when one side had,
> at last destroyed the other [Halle, 1967, pp157
> and 158].

In a series of studies of the international conflict the
American Friends Service Committee compares the passions
of this ideological conflict to the struggles between Luther
and Rome in the sixteenth century.   Luther declared it was
better to be murderer than a monk, while Pope Pius V
urged Catherine de Medici to massacre all heretics, openly
and zealously, and receive divine favor.   The U. S. S. R. and
the U. S. A. anathematize each other in similar fashion,
A. F. S. C. feels.   In such an atmosphere of mutual distrust,
neither U. S. S. R. nor the U. S. will be able to establish
overwhelming military strength, the A. F. S. C. says.   Further,
the arms race will create such superpowers that ideological
conflict could destroy the world by the passionate anger of
a small group of dogmatic men.   Even where that does not
happen, civil liberties and democratic freedoms are eroded
on the one side and authoritarian rule strengthened on the
other by mutual fear (American Friends Service Committee,
1949).

In the second of the series, the A. F. S. C. examines
American involvement in light of America's historic understanding of herself and her mission.   According to the Committee, that heritage is rooted in the belief in the dignity
and supreme worth of every individual human being.   Governments are not ends, but means through which men seek to
secure their liberties and fulfill their moral purposes.
Americans love freedom, and believe everyone has a right
to choose his own form of government.   Differences can be
resolved by democratic procedures of discussion, elections,
representation, honorable compromises and voting.   Americans accept Jefferson's words, "Truth is great and will
prevail if left to herself ... errors ceasing to be dangerous
when it is permitted to contradict them. "

But, A. F. S. C. asks, is U. S. policy advancing the
cause of human freedom and welfare?   The answer is no,
because America forces the choice in so many cases between Communist dictatorship and military tyranny.   Further-
more, the U. S. dissipates her resources in military commitments, and fails to relieve the most desperate tyrannies
of hunger, poverty and disease.   Any who seek change in
the established order are labeled as Communist.   Blinded
by ideology, Americans betray their own revolution and
America's historic mission to the world.   The world is left
with the choice of one imperialism or another, both of which,
for all their lofty ideologies, are still imperialisms (American Friends Service Committee, 1951).

By 1955, A. F. S. C. could see that although it and
Muste had revived the almost forgotten art of pamphleteering,
and resolutions on peace had poured in a steady stream from
church conferences, labor and farm conventions, academic
associations, women's clubs and other groups, the overriding
reality was still preparation for the eventuality of total war.
That preparation was clearly changing the character of
American life.   The military-industrial complex was already
a fact of life: the American economy was already becoming
more and more dependent on the pump priming of the cold
war.   Worse, the stringent measures adopted for the sake
of "internal security"

> where loyalty oaths must be demanded, dissent
> becomes confused with disloyalty and orthodoxy
> is made the badge of patriotism (it) strikes at
> the very heart of our democracy.   It destroys our
> trust in one another, and without trust a free
> society cannot exist ... while the most powerful
> feeling in the United States is hatred of the Rus-
> sian totalitarian system, the most powerful process
> in the United States is its imitation [American
> Friends Service Committee, 1955, pp16-18].

A. F. S. C. was not alone in its discovery that in challenging the cold war version of America's mission it was
itself attacked for treason.   The attack was so widespread
that by the mid 1950's nearly all the pacifist groups were
involved in the defense of civil liberties.   The Fellowship
of Reconciliation believed that the aim of the "system" was
to convince the individual that he was helpless as an individual.   The system sought to meet regimentation with
regimentation.   Thus the individual was being forced to conform to the decisions of U. S. policymakers in order that
U. S. freedom might prevail over the authoritarianism of the
Communist form of government.   Precisely in such a situation we "must go back to the beginning," said Muste.

> [Man] must exercise the choice which is no longer
> accorded him by society....   As Life stated, in
> its unexpectedly profound and stirring editorial of
> August 20, 1945, its first issue after the atom
> bombing of Hiroshima: "Our sole safeguard
> against the very real danger of a reversion to
> barbarism is the kind of morality which compels
> the individual conscience, be the group right or
> wrong.   The individual conscience against the atom-
> ic bomb?   Yes.   There is no other way." [Muste,
> 1967, pp377 and 378].

Even such an eminent person as Albert Einstein, who had been active in seeking disarmament through world government, found his energies focused on civil liberties. In a letter to the New York Times of June 1, 1953, Einstein spoke against the suppression of academic freedom by the widespread investigations of "loyalty" by congressional committees and subcommittees.

> What ought the minority of intellectuals to do against this evil? Frankly, I can only see the revolutionary way of non-co-operation in the sense of Gandhi's. Every intellectual who is called before one of the committees ought to refuse to testify, i.e., he must be prepared for jail and economic ruin, in short, for the sacrifice of his personal welfare in the interest of the cultural welfare of his country. [Such refusal must be based] on the assertion that it is shameful for a blameless citizen to submit to such an inquisition and that this kind of inquisition violates the spirit of the Constitution [Einstein, 1968, p547].

The New York Times countered with an editorial stating that such civil disobedience was most unwise, for such action was to attack one evil with another. Bertrand Russell replied in a letter to the Times

> You seem to maintain that one should always obey the law, however bad. I cannot think you have realized the implications of this position ... I am compelled to suppose that you condemn George Washington and hold that your country ought to return to allegiance to Her Gracious Majesty, Queen Elizabeth II. As a loyal Briton, I of course applaud this view; but I fear it may not win much support in your country [ibid., p550].

The tactics of persecution took their toll. Fund appeals for pacifist organizations were refused because potential givers feared being thought subversive. The Socialist Party found it more and more difficult to gain requisite signatures to place the Party's name on ballots. The wide variety of self styled loyalty experts and groups branded F.O.R. as Communist. F.O.R. and A.F.S.C. members such as teachers and librarians lost their jobs. Pacifist ministers told Muste they were afraid to voice their convictions for fear of being labeled Communist and losing their pulpits. F. O. R. lost nearly 3, 000 members, a quarter of its membership. The Oppenheimer case made it clear that even eminent scientists were not safe. World Federalists and even U. N. supporters were likewise called Reds. The Catholic Worker organization became the center of a unique brand of anarchist pacifism, feeling that political action was useless or worse (Wittner, 1969, pp22, 232).

Although by the mid-fifties the repressive atmosphere of American society had reduced the peace movement to insignificance as a social and political movement, it was still vigorous as an intellectual movement. A. F. S. C. and Muste were continuing their analyses of American society and foreign policy. At Columbia University, C. Wright Mills was lecturing and writing The Power Elite. He gave formal definition to what the radicals had been groping toward.

> The shape and meaning of the power elite today
> can be understood only when these three sets of
> structural trends are seen at their point of co-
> incidence: the military capitalism of private
> corporations exists in a weakened and formal
> democratic system containing a military order
> already quite political in outlook and demeanor. ...
> The power elite is composed of political, economic
> and military men, but ... which of the three
> types seems to lead depends upon "the tasks of
> the period" as they, the elite, define them. Just
> now, the tasks center upon "defense" and inter-
> national affairs. Accordingly, as we have seen,
> the military are ascendant in two senses: as
> personnel and as justifying ideology [Mills, 1956,
> pp276-277].

Mills' conclusion, that the unity and shape of the power elite could easily be specified in this period of American history in terms of military ascendancy, was precisely the argument of the pacifist groups. Mills himself became a reluctant pamphleteer by the late fifties. He sought to present, to as wide an audience as possible, alternatives to the military definition of reality which he was convinced was at the center of American foreign policies. For Mills, such intellectual work was the politics of truth.

Thus by the mid-fifties the focus of the pacifists was largely on the repressive nature of American society. The repression was all too painfully real for thousands of obscure

pacifists. It was infinitely easier for Einstein to write to the
New York Times or Norman Cousins to fly to West Virginia
and back for a disarmament speech, than to be a known member of A. F. S. C. or F. O. R. in the reactionary towns and
villages of middle America. Public servants, such as
teachers, ministers and librarians, were especially susceptible to charges of Communist connections if they were
visible workers for peace, racial justice or the poor. The
experience of such pressures, applied by those who most
loudly proclaimed the established form of the American faith,
and who sat in the seats of power, more and more convinced the radicals of the fifties of the inherent injustice of
American society. The pacifist, grounded in a Christian
ethic, had argued that war is immoral because it is war.
But more and more the pacifist argument came to stress
the conviction that the depth of immorality was plumbed in
going to war for the sake of an unjust system. The sectarians, out of their experience, passionately rejected the
comparative argument of even the most sophisticated of the
established type, such as Niebuhr. Niebuhr would accuse
the Communists of "more extravagant forms of political injustice and cruelty out of the pretensions of innocence than
we have ever known in human history" and then admit that
the "liberal world which opposes this monstrous evil is filled
ironically with milder forms of the same pretension" [Niebuhr,
1952, p22]. The pacifists were coming to believe the pretension of the liberal world was scarcely milder. David
Dellinger, in excoriating the transgressions of Judge Kaufman
in the Rosenberg case, points out that Kaufman admitted into
evidence a collection can for the Spanish Refugee Appeal,
licensed by the City of New York.

> O sweet charity! In the United States we dare not
> solicit food and clothing for the victims of a fascist
> dictator or else the Judge will accept this as evi-
> dence that we are guilty of a crime "worse than
> murder" [Dellinger, 1971, p238].

Dellinger's long concluding paragraph is worth quoting in its
entirety, because it expresses so poignantly the manner in
which the pacifists, out of their own experiences in American
society, had come to believe that the two opposing systems
were more alike than different.

> The apathy of some, the blood lust of others, the
> scornful acquiescence in murder by socialists and
> liberals were based on the feeling that the Rosen-
> bergs were Communists. I believe that it is the

tragic error of Communists to believe that they
can advance the cause of human freedom, economic
equality and peace through the reluctant use of
deceit, violence and hatred--even as most liberal
exponents of Western democracy sanction the use
of deceit, violence, and hatred by "our" side for
similar goals. But who can read of the Rosen-
bergs--who, if not Communists, were at least
Communist-oriented--and not realize that in the
hearts of such as these is the love, the faith, and
the idealism which makes it ridiculous for us to
indulge in the current Red-baiting? To our un-
speakable shame, we murdered the Rosenbergs--
instead of finding ways to mingle the love that
slumbers in our hearts with the love that was so
nobly developed in theirs. Must we continue, on
a larger scale, to stifle our love and stockpile
our weapons of destruction toward Communists all
over the world, thereby encouraging them to stifle
their love and stockpile their atom bombs against
us? [ibid. , p243].

As the sectarians experienced political repression they
came more and more to share the perspective of those who
also experienced economic and racial repression in American
society. Thus the original pacifist opposition to empire
sought by force of arms, which was sectarian in itself, was
reinforced by the sectarian trait of connection to the lowest
classes of society, and feeling thereby that they were in
reality a part of the brotherhood of the oppressed. In such
a situation they issued the characteristic sectarian appeal to
join in ever new actions which express and demonstrate genuine commitment to freedom, brotherhood, peace and democracy. Einstein's conviction that intellectuals ought to face
economic ruin and jail for the sake of the culture is an excellent example. These sectarians carried into the sixties a
paradox--the conviction that one's society is unjust, repressive, militaristic and elitist, and the conviction that one is
thereby compelled to even greater sacrifices to redeem that
very social order.

Not only their own experience convinced the pacifists
of the disease of their society, or course. The social
science of Mills confirmed to them that it was the ruling
class for whom the cold war was waged. Also, as Bertrand
Russell's humorous aside indicates, the ideals of the Founding
Fathers and the rights of the individual conscience were important resources. Thus the pacifists, who could see no

trends as yet that the revival of the sectarian faith was about to dawn, still continued to be a "voice crying in the wilderness." They still continued to express in a very direct and characteristic way the essential fundamental ideals of the American democratic faith. For this they were honored by the sectarians of the sixties. Staughton Lynd says

> That Muste, Dellinger, MacDonald and other pacifist/resisters of the 1940's maintained their activism and devotion to principle throughout the 1950's may be one reason for the generally open, trusting, unembittered style of the draft resistance groups that flourished in the 1960's.... Draft resisters had in their midst a generation of older supporters, many of whom had undergone lonely and seemingly useless struggles without giving up; they served as models of patience and good cheer when youthful faith and exuberance flagged [Ferber & Lynd, 1971, p. 4]. *

Three signs appeared in the mid-fifties which encouraged the pacifist movement, however. First was the astonishing success of the Montgomery Bus Boycott. Bayard Rustin of C. O. R. E. and F. O. R. was involved almost immediately, and the demonstrated usefulness of non-violent tactics was heartening. Second, both the declaration of the atomic scientists and the declaration of the Nobel Laureates appeared in July, 1955. Both appealed for the abolition of war, recognizing that such abolition would require limitations of national sovereignty for the sake of humanity, a limitation which cold war ideology had not even permitted to be suggested earlier without stirring cries of treason (Einstein, 1968, pp632-634; Pauling, 1962, pp22, 223). The third ray of hope was the founding, and continued publication of Liberation.

Liberation is the voice of militant pacifists, and expresses their concerns--utopianism, anarchism, non-violent revolution, civil rights, the third world and peace. Its opening editorial deplores the gradual silencing of prophetic and radical voices. Liberalism, which emphasizes humaneness and the liberties of the individual, has never come to grips

---

*Excerpts from The Resistance, by Michael Ferber and Staughton Lynd. Copyright © 1971 by Michael Ferber and Staughton Lynd. Reprinted by permission of Beacon Press.

with war, poverty and authoritarianism, Liberation believes.
On the other hand, Marxism, which has broached the demand
for fundamental economic justice, has never faced realistical-
ly the emergence of the State as an instrument of war and
oppression.   The politics of the future are the politics which
Liberation seeks to bring to life.

> We do not conceive the problem of revolution or
> the building of a better society as one of accumu-
> lating power.   The national, sovereign, militarized
> and bureaucratic State and a bureaucratic collectiv-
> ist economy are themselves evils to be avoided or
> abolished.   [Liberation, A, 1956, pp3-5].

The emphasis of Liberation is the recovery of human decision
and action, direct participation of workers or citizens in
determining conditions of their own lives and work.   Technology is to be used for human ends, rather than humans
being subjugated by technology.   A poll of the readers of
Liberation in the fifties lists "teacher" as their largest single
occupational category, with more than half having received
one or more graduate degrees.   Most express no interest in
political parties, although the favorite is Socialist.   Readers
of Liberation tend toward radical and utopian views very different from those of the average American, especially in
terms of civil rights and pacifism.   Like the radicals of the
sixties, the poll reveals that the radical pacifists of the
fifties were the prototype middle class intellectuals (Wittner,
1969, pp232-239).

The resurgent peace movement focused its criticism
upon the atmospheric testing of hydrogen bombs.   On April
24, 1957, under the auspices of the Nobel Peace Prize Committee in Oslo, and printed in The Saturday Review of May
18, 1957, Albert Schweitzer issued "A Declaration of Conscience, " appealing to the nations to stop the testing of
nuclear weapons.   He pointed out that nuclear testing increased the general level of radiation in milk and well water.
Therefore the number of deformed and stillborn births increased, as well as the incidence of serious blood disease.
Testing continued, he concluded, because public opinion did
not demand an end to it (Pauling, 1958, pp225-237).

Linus Pauling delivered to President Eisenhower and
Secretary General Hammarskjold a petition from 9,235 scientists, with nearly 2,000 from the United States, urging the
immediate cessation of testing of nuclear weapons.   The

Senate Internal Security Subcommittee launched an investiga-
tion of Pauling, and sought to silence him or reduce his
influence by portraying him as a Communist agent. But
public opinion was aroused (Ibid., pp160-167). By November
1957, the National Committee for a Sane Nuclear Policy had
been formed. S. A. N. E. published its first advertisement in
the New York Times on November 15. In echoes of the
Declaration of Independence it proclaimed the convictions of
the sectarian type of the civil religion.

> In our possession and in the possession of the Rus-
> sians are more than enough nuclear explosives to
> put an end to the life of man on earth ... our
> response to that challenge seems out of sight. The
> slogans and arguments that belong to the world of
> competitive national sovereignties ... no longer fit
> the world of today or tomorrow. [We must go
> beyond] the national interest. The sovereignty of
> the human community comes before all others....
> In that community, man has natural rights. He
> has the right to live and to grow, to breathe un-
> poisoned air, to work on uncontaminated soil. He
> has the right to his sacred nature. [If govern-
> ment violates these rights] then it becomes neces-
> sary for people to restrain and tame the nations
> [Wittner, 1969, p243].

Although intended as only a temporary organization,
S. A. N. E. ignited a movement. Thousands of letters poured
in. People in all parts of the nation placed the full page
advertisement in local papers. By summer S. A. N. E. created
such a response because it was the first of the pragmatic, one
issue oriented groups to which a wide coalition of nuclear
pacifists, world government supporters, United Nations en-
thusiasts, radical pacifists, socialists and citizens who were
simply concerned about fall-out could give their support
(ibid., p246).

Radical pacifism also revived with the formation of
the Committee for Non-Violent Action. It was organized by
Lawrence Scott, an A. F. S. C. staff member who had been
considerably influenced by Muste. On the twelfth anniversary
of Hiroshima, after a prayer vigil, eleven members of
C. N. V. A. walked onto the A. E. C. project Mercury in Nevada
and were arrested. Early the next morning, the committee
members watched a nuclear explosion from a distance. One
of them was Albert Bigelow, a former lieutenant commander

in the U.S. Navy. He, with the others, determined to sail the Golden Rule, a thirty-foot ketch, into the Eniwetok area, where nuclear testing was scheduled in the summer of 1958 (Hentoff, 1963, p152).

Upon arrival in Honolulu, the crew of the Golden Rule was served an injunction prohibiting their sailing. When the Golden Rule sailed in defiance of the court order, the crew was arrested and jailed. In their stead sailed the Phoenix, with skipper Earle Reynolds and his family, and Mick Mikami, of Hiroshima. Reynolds was an anthropologist previously employed by A.E.C. in Japan, and was a resident of Hiroshima. He had completed the first group of studies on children affected by the atomic bomb radiation, and was on the last leg of an around the world sailing trip. He was not yet aware that his work for A.E.C., "Report on a Three-Year Study, 1951-3, of the Growth and Development of Hiroshima Children Exposed to the Atomic Bomb," had already been suppressed by the agency. The report had been removed from circulation and all references deleted from relevant indices. But Reynolds rapidly became aware that he was in sympathy with the crew of the Golden Rule. When Phoenix sailed for Hiroshima, she set her course through the forbidden test area. Reynolds was arrested. At his trial he told of his discovery that A.E.C. reports to the public were propaganda rather than science; that is, they were "clearly erroneous" in order to diminish unease over nuclear fallout dangers.

> I say this came as a shock to me.... There was no doubt in my mind that the AEC is playing false with the American public. For the first time in the history of American science, a scientist had to read the title of a report, then read who wrote it, and then try to determine where it came from, before he could properly evaluate the content of a so-called scientific paper. This is a terrible indictment of American scientists, and as a scientist I am ashamed that such a thing has crept into scientific literature ... I preferred to base my motives on scientific knowledge that anything that would stop nuclear testing is bound to be of benefit to mankind, to my belief that the freedom of the seas ... is being threatened, and to my knowledge ... that the law which prohibited me from entering that zone is unconstitutional [Reynolds, 1961, pp142-143].

The events caused a furor across the nation. Picket
lines sprang up around federal buildings and A. E. C. offices.
Signs demanded "Stop the tests, not the Golden Rule. " Out
on bail, Reynolds went on a tour of fifty-eight major talks,
twenty other meetings, twenty-one radio appearances, eight
television programs and countless newspaper interviews.
The chairman of the A. E. C. suggested it was all a Communist plot. But the simple, brave action of men in tiny ships
against the dangers of nuclear weapons and the might of the
U. S. Navy captured both newspaper headlines and the hearts
of millions. Reynolds, obviously the informed scientist,
made telling points about the effects of radiation on children
and children not yet born. Mothers were worried much more
about milk in the local store than about local Communists.
The nuclear pacifist issue soon went beyond the question of
nuclear tests. When the tests were voluntarily suspended by
both the U. S. and the U. S. S. R. , nuclear pacifists took up
the issue of thermonuclear war (Wittner, 1969, pp249-256).

Civil disobedience as a means of protesting nuclear
war was directed against the Civil Defense drills. Dorothy
Day of the Catholic Worker explained why she and others
remained outside in the parks of New York City every drill
day for five years rather than complying with the law that
required them to take shelter.

> It was not a question of obedience to the law or to
> duly constituted authority. Law must be according
> to right reason, and the law that made it compul-
> sory to take shelter was a mockery. In our dis-
> obedience we were trying to obey God rather than
> men, trying to follow a higher obedience. . . . We
> were setting our faces against things as they are,
> against the terrible injustice our basic capitalist
> industrial system perpetrates by making profits out
> of preparations for war. But especially we wanted
> to act against war and getting ready for war: nerve
> gas, germ warfare, guided missiles, testing and
> stockpiling of nuclear bombs, conscription, the col-
> lection of income tax--against the entire militarism
> of the state. We made our gesture; we disobeyed
> a law [Day, 1963, pp160 and 161].

From the parks of New York City civil disobedience
to Civil Defense drills spread to the campuses of surrounding
suburban communities. Each drill season saw increased
numbers of students demonstrate and become radicalized by
the experience of arrest, trial and jail.

Just as surely as the revival of religion could be seen
in the suburban church with its welling enrollment and new
buildings, so in ever widening circles from the seas off
Eniwetok to the parks of New York City did the sectarian
form of the civil religion experience revival. Reynolds, the
unlikely radical, harked back to the founding principles of
science, shocked that American scientists, who above all
ought to be committed to freedom on inquiry, would pervert
truth to propaganda. His concern was truly with the powerless: the children of the world, who could neither vote,
rebel, nor avoid the mothers' milk in which strontium 90
concentrates. In his specialty, until his civil disobedience,
his only hope of employment was the federal government.
Yet, quite unassumingly, he put such achievements of "the
world" behind, appealing in word and deed to that humanism
which underlies the Declaration of Independence, to his belief
that unjust laws ought to be disobeyed for the benefit of mankind. Dorothy Day affirmed the same sentiments in her
actions. She was moved more by the plight of the poor of
the world, and the grievous cruelty of making profits from
the manufacture of instruments of war. It was not enough
for such radicals to protest once. They stood in the park
year after year, until at last the Civil Defense Act was no
longer a reality.

As Troeltsch puts it, for the sectarian there must be
ever new actions which express and demonstrate commitment
to the basic moral demands of the religion. The emerging
public support for these actions was because of fear of fallout
and war, but also because Americans heard and accepted
much of the faith of the sectarians of the civil religion. The
sectarians touched "the mystic chords of memory" that bind
the nation. With their independence of outside pressures,
their continual emphasis on the rights and responsibilities of
the individual against the state, they represented in a very
direct and characteristic way what many Americans believed to
be the essential fundamental ideas of the American purpose and
mission. Somehow it seemed as though the nation has gone
fundamentally astray; no longer did the world look to America as
the herald of glad tidings, but feared the arrogance of her power
and the insensitivity of her imperialisms. Americans heard in
the call of the sectarians of the civil religion an appeal to
return to the "ancient paths," the path of freedom, individual
honor, right and responsibility. If America was again to be
a light to the nations, it would be by the goodness of her
character, not the force of her armies. Those who heard
the call of the sectarians most clearly were the young. Because they had the least stake in American society as the

sixties dawned, because they felt they had the greatest stake
in what it would become, "the torch passed to a new generation of Americans," in a way that John Kennedy had scarcely
envisioned.

THE CIVIL RELIGION AND
RACISM: 1944-1960

The Established Type of
the Civil Religion

In 1944, Gunnar Myrdal published his classic study,
An American Dilemma.   He was convinced that there was a
"negro problem" in America to the extent that Americans
were worried about the treatment of this particular minority--
it was "on their minds and consciences."   Many sectarians
thought Myrdal was being unduly optimistic, for there was
scant evidence that the conscience of the majority of Americans was troubled.   Yet it was the ferment, the disease
over the treatment of blacks that began to boil in the postwar period and in the sixties provided much of the steam
that initially propelled the radical movement.   Commager's
suggestion that war accelerates the changes that are in the
making in society was dramatically confirmed in the changing
relationship of the black minority to the white majority.

In December 1946, Harry Truman issued Executive
Order 9809, establishing the President's Committee on Civil
Rights.   Truman declared that while freedom from fear is
more fully realized in America than in any other country on
the face of the earth, yet not all Americans are free from
fear.   Democratic institutions were again under attack by
those who subvert and violate the Constitutional guarantees
of individual liberties and equal protection under the law.
Therefore the Committee was established to investigate such
violations and recommend necessary measures and legislation
to the President (The President's Committee on Civil Rights,
1947, ppvii and viii).

The opening section of the report emphasizes the
American heritage.   Basically the heritage is the conscious
recognition of the fundamental moral principle that all men
are created free and equal.

> Stemming from this principle is the obligation to
> build social institutions that will guarantee equality
> of opportunity to all men.   Without this equality

> freedom becomes an illusion.   The only aristocracy
> that is consistent with the free way of life is an
> aristocracy of talent and achievement [ibid. , p4].

Americans, according to the report, abhor totalitarian forms
of government which erase distinctions between citizens.
Religion, political views and social position are freely chosen
or achieved.   In America, men are equal in terms of opportunity and thus free to be different.   Those who would require
that men be of the same political party and social class desert the American heritage for a totalitarian pottage, the report believes.

The Founding Fathers also recognized, the authors
continue, that a democratic majority might become as tyran-
nical of the liberties of the individual as the despot.   Thus
personal liberties, the freedom of a man to manage his own
lawful affairs without interference of government, is established by the Bill of Rights and due process.   The report
states that this heritage of freedom and equality has given
America prestige among the nations of the world and national
pride at home.   But pride is no substitute for performance,
and the gulf between ideals and practice is at times wide.
The Committee believes the gap could be narrowed by a more
vigorous application of the normal processes of democratic,
constitutional government, even though the task

> . . . will require as much imagination, as much
> perseverance as anything we have ever done together.
> The members of this committee reaffirm their
> faith in the American heritage and in its promise
> [Ibid. , p10].

After reporting the results of its hearings and investigations, the Committee, under a heading of "The Time Is
Now, " sets forth its recommendations and the reasons there-
for.   First, the moral reason is argued.   No further justification is needed, said the Committee, than to reaffirm our
faith in the traditional American morality as outlined in the
American heritage.   But that reaffirmation must be done in
action, lest moral dry rot set in, and undermine democracy.

Second, the economic argument is detailed.   Basically
the Committee feels that since the principal economic problem facing the U. S. and therefore the world was full production, to discriminate against ten percent of the population, to
leave them in poverty, is to curtail both their purchasing
power and their production potential, thus weakening America.

Third, the Committee sets forth the international reason. It is affirmed that the goal of American foreign policy
is to make the United States an enormous positive influence
for peace and progress throughout the world. But America's
treatment of her black people is becoming an issue in world
politics. Communists continually point to the shabby treatment blacks receive as evidence that the American heritage
is not a true faith but a hypocrisy and a falsehood. By
publicizing oppressive actions against blacks, the U.S.S.R.
tries to prove the American democracy an empty fraud, and
a consistent oppressor of underprivileged people. This is,
of course, the Committee said, ludicrous to Americans, but
friends of America are concerned. So once again Americans
must be committed to a new birth of freedom.

> Our achievements in building and maintaining a state
> dedicated to the fundamentals of freedom have al-
> ready served as a guide for those seeking the best
> road from chaos to liberty and prosperity. But it
> is not indelibly written that democracy will encom-
> pass the world. We are convinced that our way of
> life--the free way of life--holds a promise of hope
> for all people. We have what is perhaps the great-
> est responsibility ever placed upon a people to keep
> this promise alive. Only still greater achievements
> will do it [Ibid., p148].

Among other recommendations, the Committee suggests
the outlawing of restrictive housing covenants. It urges a
renewed court attack, with intervention by the Department of
Justice, upon such covenants.

The Department of Justice responded to the Report by
intervening in the case of Shelley vs. Kraemer, and in May
1948, the Supreme Court ruled restrictive covenants unen-
forceable.

> The historical context in which the Fourteenth
> Amendment became part of the Constitution should
> not be forgotten. Whatever else the framers
> sought to achieve, it is clear that the matter of
> primary concern was the establishment of equality
> in the enjoyment of basic civil and political rights
> and the preservation of those rights from discrimi-
> natory action on the part of the States based on
> considerations of race or color [Ianniello, 1965,
> p27].

The young and idealistic civil rights advocates at the 1948 Democratic Convention in Philadelphia were determined to write the recommendations of the Committee on Civil Rights into the party platform.   Hubert Humphrey, Mayor of Minneapolis, had decided to speak for the civil rights plank, even though the "pros" told him it was political madness, and would destroy his political career.   He was, after all, opposing the majority report of the platform committee and Sam Rayburn, Chairman of the Convention and Speaker of the House.

Humphrey's speech is both deferential and bold.   He agrees that the racial problem is not sectional, but American. All America shares in the precious heritage of freedom, and all regions infringe that freedom by discrimination.   That clearly is wrong, for when Thomas Jefferson spoke of equality, he did not say all white, black, yellow or red men are equal, but all men are equal.   Each man is to be free to enjoy the blessings of America.   Humphrey believes that this is not merely an issue for the Democratic Party, but an issue for all Americans.

> Yes, this is far more than a party matter.   Every citizen has a stake in the emergence of the United States as the leader of the free world.   That world is being challenged by the world of slavery.   For us to play our part effectively we must be in a morally sound position. . . .   For all of us here, for the millions who have sent us, for the whole two billion members of the human family--our land is now, more than ever, the last best hope on earth.   I know that we can--I know that we shall-- begin here the fuller and richer realization of that hope--that promise of a land where all men are free and equal, and each man uses his freedom wisely and well [Ibid. , pp32 and 33].

Humphrey also commended President Truman for his courageous stand for civil rights.   Truman was unable to enact much of his civil rights program.   Nonetheless, in a civil rights message to the Congress in February 1948, Truman supported legislation covering ten specific objectives suggested by the Committee on Civil Rights.   By executive order the President established a civil rights division of the Department of Justice.   A Fair Employment Board within the Civil Service Commission was ordered to ensure that personnel would be hired and promoted on considerations of "merit

and fitness. " Most dramatically, as Commander-in-Chief,
Truman ordered equality of treatment and opportunity for all
persons in the armed services.   The segregated structure of
the military was ended.   Truman was convinced that all these
measures were urgent because

> The peoples of the world are faced with the choice
> of freedom or enslavement, a choice between a
> form of government which harnesses the state in
> the service of the individual and a form of govern-
> ment which chains the individual to the needs of
> the state. ...   We are striving to build a world
> family of nations--a world where men may live
> under governments of their own choosing and under
> laws of their own making.   To be effective in these
> efforts, we must protect our civil rights. ...   We
> know our democracy is not perfect.   But we do
> know that it offers a fuller, freer, happier life to
> our people than any totalitarian nation has ever of-
> fered.   If we wish to fulfill the promise that is
> ours, we must correct the remaining imperfections
> in our practice of democracy [Adler, 1969, pp314
> and 315].

The committee had also recommended that Congress
legislate the end of the strict and unyielding rules of segregation in the Nation's capital.   Hotels, theaters, movie
houses, restaurants and the "best" department stores did not
serve blacks.   No action was taken by Congress.   But in
the case of the District of Columbia vs. John R. Thompson
Co., the Supreme Court ruled that a local statute prohibiting
racial segregation, which was passed in 1872, had survived
the intervening changes of government in the District and
was currently enforceable.   Desegregation of public facilities
followed immediately (Ianniello, 1965, pp39-48).

The convictions of Truman, Humphrey, and the Committee and others who were government spokesmen for civil
rights are characteristic of the established type of the civil
religion.   First, the context into which the demand for civil
rights for the black minority is set is the universal mission
of America.   This mission in the postwar period is expressed
in cold war rhetoric.   Within this perspective Truman urges
the correction of the "remaining imperfections" of democracy.
Truman believes that although America's mission of offering
a fuller, freer and happier life to the peoples of the world is
even now being consummated, he sees that perfection still
eludes our grasp.   When the extra effort is made, then the

lamp of the light to the nations will burn even more brightly,
to the discomfiture of our Communist foes.   Humphrey does
not speak of perfection.   But he does see that in this hour
of cold war America has been challenged by the world of
slavery.   Of all the times of mission, of all the times when
the American way of life was the last, best hope for all
people, this is the most serious.   For Humphrey this is the
hour for us to be morally sound, to set our house in order,
to begin "the fuller, richer realization of that hope" which
America represents.   For the Committee, it is the time of
the greatest responsibility ever placed upon the American
people, or any people.   The promise of hope must be kept
alive for all mankind.   Only if America keeps the faith,
will the promise be fulfilled that democracy will prevail.
But such a triumph depends upon our righteousness, for "it
is not indelibly written that democracy will encompass the
world. "

        Typically, the ideal is to be universalized within the
United States itself by organizational effort.   It is simply
not enough to appeal to the Founding Fathers and the heritage
of America, but a long list of structural reforms are suggested to enforce the truth.   At once these begin to be employed, in political convention, in executive order, in government intervention in court cases and in enforcement of ancient
statutes.   The anxiety of the upper classes over loss of a
ready pool of low wage workers is eased by developing
analyses that suggest that economically the nation will be
better off without discriminatory practices.   Significantly,
while the Committee on Civil Rights contains representatives
of big business, big labor, education, Protestantism, Catholicism, Judaism, Veterans and Social Workers, there is no
representation of black or civil rights groups.   The reform
is closely contained within the state and ruling class.   Although reform engenders much conflict even within that class,
control of the issue will not pass to those outside the more
privileged positions of power.

        Finally, the work ethic is the context in which equality
is set.   The disparities that remain after equality of opportunity is achieved are to be accepted as evidence of differences in ability and willingness to work hard.   An aristocracy
of talent and achievement is still to be accepted, even urged.
This is basic to the established type of civil religion.   The
man who disciplines himself ought to receive the rewards of
success regardless of his race.   The Committee overlooked
the fact that true equality of opportunity is difficult to achieve

because of wide differences in the cultural experiences of
education and self-expectation. The more glaring examples
of inequality quite rightfully claimed their attention. Their
ability to see beyond the obvious was limited by their contextuating orientation. The equality they envisioned was an
ideal that could and should be attained by means of adjustments within the established order.

Although Truman had implemented as many of the
Committee's recommendations as he felt were politically possible, and vetoed legislation requiring segregated schools on
military bases in the South, still the reforms had not touched
the majority of Americans. The 1954 Supreme Court decision opposing school segregation was therefore revolutionary.
Men live by symbols, and symbols are grouped in contextuating
orientations that determine a way of life. The segregated
school was a "bit" in the contextuating orientation of the
Southern way of life that could not be removed without al-
tering the whole context. The removal of such crucial bits
entails social costs as expensive as their original construction.
The history of slavery, the Civil War, the Reconstruction,
the desperate poverty of the small farmer in contrast to the
aristocracy, and the establishment of apartheid constitutions,
laws and customs in the 1890's created a context which was
not to be easily dismantled. The industrialization and urbani-
zation of the South, the weakening of regional differences
through the impact of television and other mass media, required service in the formally desegregated armed forces,
and the slow increase in legal protection for blacks had been
bits whose changes had not altered the basic context of social,
political and economic discrimination. But school desegregation threatened the Southern culture. Major disruptions were
inevitable.

In Brown vs. Board of Education the court notes that
in approaching the problem of segregation in public education
the clock can not be turned back to 1868, when the Fourteenth
Amendment was adopted. Then it clearly meant, as Justice
William Strong said in 1880, that all persons stand equal before the law of the States, and no discrimination shall be
made against them by law because of color. Neither can the
Plessy vs. Ferguson case, in 1896, be considered basic, for
the issue there was transportation, which in no way could be
construed to be as central to the general welfare of citizens
as education is in the present.

> Today education is perhaps the most important
> function of state and local governments. Compulsory

> school attendance laws and the great expenditures
> for education both demonstrate our recognition of
> the importance of education to our democratic so-
> ciety.... Such an opportunity, where the state has
> undertaken to provide it, is a right which must be
> made available to all on equal terms [Ianniello,
> 1965, pp53 and 54].

The court then asks if segregation of children solely on the
basis of race in fact deprives children of the minority group
of equal educational opportunities, even when other education
criteria are equally met.

> We believe that it does.... To separate them from
> others of similar age and qualifications solely be-
> cause of their race generates a feeling of inferiority
> as to their status in the community that may af-
> fect their hearts and minds in a way unlikely ever
> to be undone [Ibid. , p55].

Reaction was mixed. In the two thirds of the nation
where compulsory school segregation based on race alone was
a thing of the past, important newspapers acclaimed the decision as a great reaffirmation of the American faith.

> New York Times: The highest court in the land,
> the guardian of our national conscience, has reaf-
> firmed its faith--and the undying American faith--
> in the equality of all men and all children before
> the law.
>
> Detroit Free Press: Those citizens of the United
> States who cherish the belief that the American
> concept of democracy is a vital, living, organic
> philosophy, slowly but inexorably advancing toward
> the ideals of the founders of the Union, will be
> heartened by the unanimous opinion of the Supreme
> Court in the historic school segregation case.
>
> San Francisco Chronicle: The majesty of the
> democratic idea that men are created equal and
> are entitled to the equal protection of the laws
> shines through yesterday's unanimous decision
> [Muse, 1964, pp18 and 19]. *

---

*Excerpts from Ten Years of Prelude: The Story of Integra-
tion Since the Supreme Court's 1954 Decision by B. Muse.
New York: Viking Press, 1964. Reprinted by permission of
Viking Penguin Inc.

The editorials of the South represented quite a different view. At first they were cautious, suggesting, as the Birmingham, Alabama, Post Herald did, that

> Acceptance of the decision does not mean that we are stopped from taking such honorable and legal steps as may be indicated to avoid the difficulties it presents to both races [ibid. , p17].

But Southern politicians were more outspoken. Senator James Eastland of Mississippi declared bluntly that the South would not abide by, or obey, such a legislative decision by a political court. Herman Talmadge, the Governor of Georgia, fiercely opposed the decision, saying that Earl Warren had made it, now he could try and enforce it in Georgia. James F. Byrnes, Governor of South Carolina had said that if the Court decided against segregation, schools would be closed in South Carolina. When the Court amplified its decision with the requirement to desegregate with "all deliberate speed," Prince Edward County, Virginia, refused to appropriate further funds for public schools. The Richmond News Leader, which became both a bellwether for Southern opinion and the most widely followed literary resister to the Brown decision, attacked the Court the following day in its lead editorial.

> In May of 1954, that inept fraternity of politicians and professors known as the United States Supreme Court chose to throw away the established law. These nine men repudiated the Constitution, spit upon the Tenth Amendment, and rewrote the fundamental law of this land to suit their own gauzy concepts of sociology. If it be said now that the South is flouting the law, let it be said to the high court, You taught us how.... Let us pledge ourselves to litigate this thing for fifty years. If one remedial law is ruled invalid, let us try another; and [a] second ... and [a] third.... When the court proposes that its social revolution be imposed upon the South "as soon as practicable," there are those of us who would respond that "as soon as practicable" means never at all [ibid. , pp20-22; 28 and 29].

The Southern Manifesto was signed by nearly the whole Congressional delegation of Alabama, Arkansas, Georgia, Louisiana, Mississippi, North Carolina, South Carolina, Tennessee, Texas and Virginia. In these delegations were the

majority of the Congress's most senior members, who controlled the committee system in both Houses, and therefore
wielded major influence in American government. The Manifesto was entered in the U. S. Congressional Record.

The argument of the Manifesto is that the Supreme
Court is guilty of clear abuse of judicial power in seeking
to legislate, thereby demeaning the Constitution, the Congress,
the States and the People.   The Constitution does not mention education, nor does the Fourteenth Amendment.   The
Manifesto points out the very Congress which proposed the
Fourteenth Amendment provided for segregated schools in the
District of Columbia.   The separate but equal doctrine is
specifically applied to public schools in Lum vs. Rice in
1927.

> This interpretation, restated time and again, be-
> came a part of the life of the people in many of
> the States, and confirmed their habits, customs,
> traditions and way of life.   It is founded on ele-
> mental humanity and commonsense, for parents
> should not be deprived by Government of the right
> to direct the lives of and education of their own
> children [Grant, 1968, p270].

The signers are further convinced that the unwarranted exercise of power by the Court is destroying the amicable relations between white and Negro races.   Relationships of
friendship and understanding are being replaced with hatred
and suspicion.   Ninety years of patient effort by the good
people of both races is being set to naught.   Nevertheless,
the signers of the Southern Manifesto reaffirm their faith in
America.

> We reaffirm our reliance on the Constitution as the
> fundamental law of the land.   We decry the Supreme
> Court's encroachments on rights reserved to the
> States and to the people, contrary to established
> law and to the Constitution. ...   Even though we
> constitute a minority in the present Congress, we
> have full faith that a majority of the American
> people believe in the dual system of Government
> which has enabled us to achieve our greatness and
> will in time demand that the reserved rights of the
> States and of the people be made secure against
> judicial usurpation [ibid. , pp270 and 271].

This sharp separation in the understanding of the American faith needs to be briefly analyzed in the light of the church-sect typology. How ought we to classify an important minority of the ruling class, which exercises both governmental and economic power in one of the major regions of the country, yet which opposes the actions of the majority in this one specific area of the relationship between black and white citizens? At first, one is tempted to classify the "Southern Way of Life" as a sectarian form of the "American Way of Life," and thereby as a sectarian type of the American civil religion. But grave problems immediately present themselves if that argument is pursued. The defenders of the Southern Way are in fact those who wield economic and political power; they are not in close connection with the lowest class, poor blacks. They very much accept the mission of America to the world. In this period of cold war rhetoric they are the most passionate denouncers of Communism and the most patriotic espousers of American empire. They are convinced believers in the work ethic. The argument of the Committee on Civil Rights to the effect that the only aristocracy that does exist in America is an aristocracy of talent and achievement is often used. Therefore the black is obviously inferior in talents, according to the perspective of the Southern Way of Life. There is a close connection between the beliefs of those who accept the Southern Way of Life and the structures of society in the South. In a word, the segregated school is an attempt to achieve within a certain region a universal ideal by organizational effort. The whole structure of Jim Crow laws means to enforce action where belief in the Southern Way of Life will not. Some persons will not remain in segregated groups unless the law requires it. Further, there is expressed the conviction that the majority of Americans believe in State's rights. Thus the main stream of the Southern Way of Life will be at last vindicated in the whole nation, not merely in one region. In every respect, then, the Southern Way of Life presents itself as an established form of the civil religion, even to the point that the mainstream of development in this area flowed along this faith even in spite of an apparently decisive defeat.

The Southern Way of Life can then be classified only as an established form of the civil religion. Obviously, it is regional in character as far as segregation of schools on the legal basis of race is concerned, and indeed, in terms of much legislation enforcing segregated public accommodations. But the Southern Way of Life is not regional in the broadest sense, because racism itself is an American custom.

Racism is enforced by a wide variety of sanctions throughout
the country, but for the majority of Americans the equality
which is basic to the American faith is a legal equality.
Americans accept the fact that although socially a black man
suffers whatever indignations are heaped upon him by the
majority, before the law he is formally equal. It is only
the South's insistence in enforcing the custom of racism by
a wide variety of legal sanctions that set the South at odds
with the broader American civil religion.

If we were to pursue the classifications of the civil
religion, it is clear that the established form of the civil
religion of the South is analogous to what J. Milton Yinger
refers to as the class church or denomination of the Christian
religion. Yinger sees the class church as a religious-type
which minimizes the sectarian tendency to criticize or withdraw from the social order, but at the same time

> ... it is also limited by class, racial and some-
> times regional boundaries. It may still be called
> a church, because it is in substantial--not perfect--
> harmony with the secular power structure [Yinger,
> 1962, p149].

So the established form of the civil religion in the region of
the Old Confederacy is in substantial--not-perfect--harmony
with the secular power structure of the nation. Nevertheless,
the point at issue--the status of the blacks--was one which
produced grave tensions. It was against this regional form
of the civil religion that the young sectarians of the sixties
first did battle. By the end of the decade, the racism of
the regional form of the civil religion--legalized racism--was
shattered. The racism of the national form of the civil religion, which still affirmed the freedom of the individual to
discriminate, had been only slightly modified.

In September 1957, President Eisenhower signed into
law the first federal civil rights law since Reconstruction.
The Civil Rights Act of 1957 provided authority for the
Justice Department to intervene in behalf of individuals in
instances of actual or threatened violations of the right to
vote, of general civil rights, such as the right to attend an
integrated school, and, further, it established a Federal Civil
Rights Commission and a Civil Rights Division within the
Department of Justice (Ianniello, 1965, pp58 and 60). Eisenhower was most interested in the right to vote and the right
of citizens to be treated equally before the law. In his
memoirs Eisenhower recalls

> Since my boyhood I had accepted without qualifica-
> tion the right to equality before the law of all
> citizens of this country, whatever their race or
> color or creed [Eisenhower, 1965, p148].

In all the debate and acrimony surrounding the civil rights
bill he held to this conviction.

> The next day I had a long talk with Senator Russell.
> I assured him of my understanding of the enormity
> of the problems facing the South and of my anxiety
> to be helpful in solving them, but told him I could
> not yield in my purpose of protecting the citizen's
> right to vote. This was the overriding provision
> of the bill that I wanted set down in law; with his
> right to vote assured, the American Negro could
> use it to help secure his other rights [ibid., p156].

With the passage of the Civil Rights Act, the established
form of the civil religion's belief that equality is equality
before the law was formally reaffirmed. The preliminary
steps were completed which led young black citizens to demand that that faith express itself in a fuller way.

The Sectarian Type of
the Civil Religion

Many groups opposed the vision of America and her
mission that was affirmed by the established type of the
civil religion. But the blacks with their rising crescendo
of protest exemplified most clearly Troeltsch's thesis that
sectarianism is united with the lowest class. Blacks were
the lowest class in American society. They had been the
most poverty stricken of the poor during the depression.
They were still seeing prosperity pass them by as the white
workers streamed to the expanding defense industries in the
early 1940's. A. Philip Randolph had proposed a mass march
of blacks on Washington to demand fair employment practices.
FDR sought to blunt the sharp demands of the March on
Washington Movement by establishing a Fair Employment
Practices Commission. Randolph postponed the march, but
attempted to keep the March on Washington Movement alive.

In an address to the Policy Conference of the March
on Washington Movement in 1942, Randolph warns against the
"empire makers." He is convinced that the established types

see in the war the opportunity for America to "relieve the watch," assume the "white man's burden," and reap the profits from the crumbling empire systems of Germany, France, Holland and England.

> Unless this war sounds the death knell to the old Anglo-American empire systems, the hapless story of which is one of exploitation for the profit and power of a monopoly capitalist economy, it will have been fought in vain. Our aim must then not only be to defeat nazism, fascism, and militarism on the battlefield, but to win the peace, for democracy, for freedom, and the Brotherhood of Man without regard to his pigmentation, land of his birth, or the God of his fathers ... [Meier & Broderick, 1965, p202].

Randolph sets forth the long range and the short range goals of black people. When he takes up the question of equality, which the established type of the civil religion saw as formal equality before the law, Randolph emphasizes an encompassing, active equality.

> Thus our feet are set in the path toward equality-- economic, political and social and racial. Equality is the heart and essence of democracy, freedom and justice. Without equality of opportunity in industry, in labor unions, schools and colleges, government, politics and before the law, without equality in social relations and in all phases of human endeavor, the Negro is certain to be consigned to an inferior status [ibid., p202].

In the established view, equality allows an aristocracy of talent and achievement, for freedom is still the essence of democracy. Equality is the step that moves us on toward perfection. But for the oppressed, without equality there is no freedom. Therefore in the name of freedom, equality and democracy Randolph urges immediate action. There must be the abolition of Jim Crow in government, armed services, defense industries, education and all fields of public service, transportation, entertainment and accommodations. The President's Committee believes that equality will move from rhetoric to reality by a more faithful application of the regular procedures of democratic government, i.e., by the action of the ruling class. Randolph knows that equality will be ushered in only by the action of the oppressed themselves.

> Therefore, if Negroes secure their goals, immediate
> and remote, they must win them and to win them
> they must fight, sacrifice, suffer, go to jail and if
> need be, die for them. The rights will not be
> given. They must be taken.... Our policy is that
> [the Movement] be all Negro, and pro-Negro, but
> not anti-white, or anti-semitic, or anti-labor, or
> anti-Catholic. The reason for this policy is that
> all oppressed people must assume responsibility
> and take the initiative to free themselves.... It
> develops the sense of self-reliance with Negroes
> depending on Negroes in vital matters ... it has
> as its major interest and task the liberation of the
> Negro people [ibid., pp203-205].

Randolph draws on the founding of the nation itself as an
example. The political royalists never meant the regular
processes of parliamentary representation to allow the
colonies the decisive voice in their own affairs. To move
equality from the realm of rhetoric to reality is to engage
in revolution, to risk jail. It is to lose a small measure
of freedom in hope of gaining a greater, or to risk even
death, thereby losing life in hope of a richer life for one's
whole race.

It is obvious that the experiences, hopes and under-
standings of the President's Committee on Civil Rights and
the March on Washington Movement were worlds apart. The
same state of affairs, which they both knew, one by investi-
gation, the other by experience, suggested to these differing
communities radically different solutions. The one meant to
recommit the ruling class to the ideals of America by organizational effort; the other meant to seize equality by whatever
means were necessary, even to the shedding of their own
blood.

Once again, the impact of war and cold war upon the
American society accelerated the change that was in the
making. The cold war dictated the need for the continuance
of the draft. Randolph, chairman of the newly created
League for Non-Violent Civil Disobedience Against Military
Segregation, was seeking to organize resistance to the draft
on the part of blacks unless Truman issued an executive
order against segregation in the armed services.

Randolph, in testimony before the Senate Armed Services Committee, restates his opposition to segregated armed

forces.   He reaffirms his commitment to oppose the entry
of blacks into a segregated structure.

> ... I personally will advise Negroes to refuse to
> fight as slaves for a democracy they cannot pos-
> sess and cannot enjoy.... I personally pledge my-
> self to openly counsel, aid and abet youth, both
> white and Negro, to quarantine any jimcrow con-
> scription system, whether it bear the label of
> UMT or Selective Service.... I feel morally obli-
> gated to disturb and keep disturbed the conscience
> of jimcrow America. In resisting the insult of
> jimcrowism to the soul of black America, we are
> helping to save the soul of America [Meier, 1971,
> pp278-280].

Senator Wayne Morse threatened that the Government
would apply the legal doctrine of treason to such conduct.
Randolph returned to Harlem for a public speech, reported
the hearing and the threat, and proclaimed he was at that
moment openly counseling, aiding and abetting youth to refuse to register and be drafted.

Bayard Rustin, of F. O. R. , in accepting a Thomas
Jefferson Award "for the advancement of democracy" given
by the Council Against Intolerance in America, supports
Randolph's view.

> ... I hold that segregation in any part of the body
> politic is an act of slavery and an act of war.
> Democrats will agree that such acts are to be
> resisted, and more and more leaders of the op-
> pressed are responsibly proposing nonviolent civil
> disobedience and non-cooperation as the means....
> Therefore in the future I shall join with others to
> advise and urge Negroes and white people not to
> betray the American ideal by accepting Jim Crow
> in any of our institutions, including the Armed
> Services [Rustin, 1971, pp50 and 51].

He challenges Senator Morse and the government to determine
if intimidation, repression, prison or death can stop the
struggle for freedom. If the government wishes to consider
such actions treason, Rustin argues, it would do well to
consider the advice that Justice Jackson gave the German
people at the opening of the Nuremberg trials.

Men are individually responsible for their acts,
and are not to be excused for following unjust
demands made upon them by governments.   Failure
of the German citizens to resist antisocial laws
from the beginning of the Hitler regime logically
ended in placing Jews in gas furnaces and lye pits
[ibid. , p52].

Here again appears the article of faith so dear to the
sectarian: the appeal to ever new personal actions which
express and demonstrate commitment to freedom, brotherhood, peace and democracy.   Senator Morse's suggestion
that the ruling class, personified by the government, is to
decide for all the question of the good of the nation, is
simply anathema to the sectarians.   (Ironically, such a position later became anathema to Senator Morse himself.)

The sectarians not only drew upon direct analogies
from the war against Hitlerism and exploited the cold war
necessities to make their case, but they also appealed to
the peacemaking body established by war: the United Nations.
To the horror of the established type who believed that to be
an American was to have faith that the United States was
already far advanced beyond other peoples in goodness and
freedom, the N. A. A. C. P. presented to the U. N. in 1947 the
document "An Appeal to the World. "   Edited by W. E. B.
Dubois, the "Appeal" was subtitled "A Statement on the
Denial of Human Rights to Minorities in the Case of Citizens
of Negro Descent in the United States of America and an
Appeal to the United Nations for Redress. "   It was a factual
study of the denial of educational, social, and legal rights to
black Americans.   In 1951 the Civil Rights Congress presented another petition, "We Charge Genocide, " which
catalogued lynchings and other acts of violence and asked redress under Article II of the U. N. Charter, the Genocide
Convention (Grant, 1968, p220).

Such actions seemed treasonous to the established type
because of the negative effect of the publicity on the mission
of America to the world.   Yet to the sectarian the appeal
was in the tradition of the American Revolution.   It was
nothing less than an attempt to use "a decent respect for the
opinions of mankind" to purify the American social structure.

During this same period James Farmer of the Fellowship of Reconciliation had founded the Congress of Racial
Equality.   The American Friends Service Committee was
invited to participate.   Farmer's dream was that C. O. R. E.

would be a mass movement seeking to mobilize all persons
who wished to see an end to racial discrimination in America.
Pacifists would serve as its nucleus and its driving force.
They would initiate small test cases of non-violent direct
action, and as discipline, training and unity increased, escalate to mass marches.   The black church was to be of
special importance, for the church was both the most effective means of reaching the black masses and a channel already sympathetic to non-violent persuasion.   In October
1942, the first direct action was taken against Stoner's
Restaurant in Chicago, which refused to serve blacks.   The
action was successful, and C. O. R. E. groups were established across the country.   By the fifties, C. O. R. E. groups
in the South were concentrating on schools, voting and public
accommodations, while those in the North focused on employment and housing.   Conscientious objectors returning from
prisons and work camps provided much of C. O. R. E. 's national and local leadership.   C. O. R. E. sponsored the first
Freedom Ride in 1946, after the Supreme Court struck down
state laws requiring segregated seating in interstate travel.
Bayard Rustin was one of the riders, who with the others,
was arrested and served a sentence of thirty days in North
Carolina (Meier, et al., 1965, pp210-226; Rustin, 1971,
pp13-49; Wittner, 1969, pp160 and 161).

The activities of C. O. R. E. received wide coverage in
the black media, but little attention in the white media.   The
mass movement did not appear as readily as Farmer had
hoped.   Nonetheless the C. O. R. E. activists did not turn back.
As true sectarians, they were convinced that their personal
actions were of ultimate importance.   They believed their
small integrated groups would overcome and replace the
large unjust American society.   Though they suffered much
in the struggle, they found a sustaining community in the
brotherhood of the oppressed.

Like the pacifists, the black sectarians were attacked
in the fifties as Communists or at lease Communist "dupes."
The experience of some of the sectarians in the thirties with
the Communist Party had been especially bitter.   Randolph
strongly believed the Communist Party was merely another
name for white exploitation.   Nonetheless, the attacks were
readily believed, sources of funds dried up, memberships
declined and to the repressive force of racism was added the
repressive force of McCarthyism.

In December 1955, the long awaited black non-violent mass movement arrived through the agency of Mrs. Rosa Parks and the black church of Montgomery, Alabama. Mrs. Parks, a black seamstress, quietly refused to stand and give her seat on the city bus to a white male passenger. As this was a violation of the city ordinance, she was arrested.

Martin Luther King, Jr. explains her action.

> It was an individual expression of a timeless longing for human dignity and freedom. She was not "planted" there by the NAACP, or any other organization; she was planted there by her personal sense of dignity and self-respect. She was anchored to that seat by the accumulated indignities of days gone by and the boundless aspirations of generations yet unborn. She was the victim of both the forces of history and the forces of destiny. She had been tracked down by the Zeitgeist--the spirit of the time [King, 1958, p44]. *

The Women's Political Council, incensed by the arrest, agreed that Negroes ought to boycott the buses. They immediately called E. D. Nixon, Alabama State President of the N. A. A. C. P. Nixon called Ralph Abernathy, pastor of First Baptist, and Martin Luther King, Jr. , pastor of Dexter Avenue Baptist. They supported the boycott idea. King offered his church as a meeting place, and the three began calling black ministers and black civic leaders. A meeting of about forty resulted from their efforts. Monday was to be the first boycott day. Sunday the ministers would explain and support the boycott; Monday evening would be the mass meeting to decide what to do next. King conceived of the movement as an act of massive non-cooperation rather than merely an economic boycott. To him, the actions of the black community were in the tradition of Thoreau, thereby proclaiming to the white community, "We can no longer lend our cooperation to an evil system, for he who passively accepts evil without protesting against it is really cooperating with it ... We would use this method," said King, "to give birth to justice and freedom. " (King, 1958, p51)

---

*Excerpts from Stride Toward Freedom by Martin Luther King, Jr. Copyright © 1958 by Martin Luther King, Jr. Reprinted by permission of Harper & Row Publishers, Inc.

The success of both the first day of the boycott and the determined cooperation of the black people of Montgomery in a non-violent mass movement astounded the black leadership. The white leadership was nonplussed.   Through the violence directed at them, the economic and legal pressures, and the almost crushing burden of decision making for an ad hoc organization, the leadership group and the followers were steadfast.   Slowly Martin Luther King, Jr. , emerged as both the formal and charismatic leader of the movement.

In Stride Toward Freedom, written after the successful conclusion of the struggle to end segregated seating on the buses, King reflects on his commitment both to justice and non-violence.   He recalls that as a student he was deeply moved by Muste's militant pacifism.   Nevertheless, King was uncertain that it was "practical" in combating injustice.   But Mordecai Johnson, president of Howard University, interested King in Gandhi's life and work.   King writes that the whole concept of Satyagraha became profoundly significant to him. Under the impact of reading Niebuhr at Boston, King attempted to develop a "realist pacifist" position.   He suggests this position does not claim to be free from the moral dilemmas the non-pacifist confronts.   It simply but profoundly chooses non-violent resistance as a lesser evil in circumstances which compel a choice.

King, like the other black sectarians, believes that

> Ever since the signing of the Declaration of Independence, America has manifested a schizophrenic personality on the question of race.   She has been torn between selves--a self in which she has proudly professed democracy and a self in which she has sadly practiced the antithesis of democracy. The reality of segregation, like slavery, has always had to confront the ideals of democracy and Christianity [ibid. , p190].

The task of the black American is to appeal to the basic principles of humanism which underlay the founding documents, that the ideals might confront the reality.   This appeal to the founding documents is basic to the sectarian position.   Secondly, King, like Troeltsch's sectarians, shares in the brotherhood of the poor around the world.   The liberals, such as the Christian Century, which supported the Montgomery Movement, see not the brotherhood of the poor but the Triumph of America.   In an editorial written after

the Supreme Court affirmed the bus segregation laws unconsti-
tutional, the Century exults

> All around the world people of color were once
> again assured that isolated sputterings do not set
> national policy, that the U.S. is officially set on
> a course, undulating perhaps, but undeviating--
> leading to complete justice for all its people [The
> Christian Century, 1956, p1426].

But King perceives that

> This determination of Negro Americans to win
> freedom from all forms of oppression springs from
> the same deep longing that motivates oppressed
> peoples all over the world. The rumblings of dis-
> content in Asia and Africa are expressions of a
> quest for freedom and human dignity by people who
> have long been the victims of colonialism and
> imperialism. So in a real sense the racial crisis
> in America is a part of the larger world crisis
> [King, 1958, p191].

Third, as Troeltsch points out, sectarians appeal for personal action to demonstrate commitment to freedom and
democracy. Like Randolph, King believes that the action of
the oppressed themselves is of the greatest importance in
bringing to pass a new birth of freedom and justice.

> Indeed, if first class citizenship is to become a
> reality for the Negro he must assume the primary
> responsibility for making it so. Integration is not
> some lavish dish that the federal government or the
> white liberal will pass out on a silver platter while
> the Negro merely furnishes the appetite [ibid.,
> p211].

Fourth, King is convinced, as all classic sectarians are,
that his group is the bearer of the new humanity.

> This is a great hour for the Negro. The challenge
> is here. To become the instruments of a great
> idea is a privilege that history gives only occasion-
> ally. Arnold Toynbee says in A Study of History
> that it may be the Negro who will give the new
> spiritual dynamic to Western civilization that it so
> desperately needs to survive. I hope this is pos-
> sible. The spiritual power that the Negro can

> radiate to the world comes from love, understanding
> good will and non-violence ... the Negro may be
> God's appeal to this age--an age drifting rapidly
> to its doom.   The eternal appeal takes the form of
> a warning: All who take the sword will perish by
> the sword [ibid. , p224].

Finally, more than any other black sectarians, King
was in close connection with the lowest class of Americans,
the poor black.

The Movement spread.   The Birmingham, Alabama,
Christian Movement for Human Rights determined to desegregate the buses of that city.   The night before the protest,
the home of the leader, Rev. Fred L. Shuttlesworth, was
bombed.   The explosion destroyed the bed in which Shuttlesworth was sleeping but spared him.   The following day, 250
persons integrated the buses.   In a statement of principles
the Movement said

> As free and independent citizens of the United States
> of America, we express publicly our determination
> to press forward persistently for freedom and
> democracy, and the removal from our society of
> any forms of second class citizenship....   America
> was born in the struggle for Freedom from Tyranny
> and Oppression ... we must, because of history
> and the future, march to complete freedom with un-
> bowed heads, praying hearts, and an unyielding
> determination [Grant, 1968, p285].

The Southern Christian Leadership Conference was
organized with King as president, and it gave its support to
the Birmingham movement, as well as to bus boycotts in
Baton Rouge, and Tallahassee.   In May 1957, about 35, 000
people attended a Prayer Pilgrimage in Washington sponsored
by civil rights leaders to press for integrated schools.
During the following two years, Bayard Rustin, who had been
in Montgomery during the bus boycott, organized youth
marches to Washington for integrated schools.

By far the most poignant example of sectarian dedication was the conviction and courage of black high school youth,
who faced jeering mobs, the threat of severe personal injury,
and even death to exercise their newly won freedom to share
in equal education.   Charlotte, Winston-Salem and Greensboro,
North Carolina desegregated their high schools with relative

calm. One girl, Dorothy Counts, was pursued by a rowdy
mob on her way home from Harding High School in Charlotte.
Her resolute dignity in the face of such provocation moved
the local white paper, the Charlotte Observer, to comment
in verse

> They spat and she was covered with it;
> Spittle dripped from the hem of her dress;
> It clung to her neck and arms and she wore it.
> They spat and they jeered and screamed;
> Debris fell on her shoulders and around her feet;
> And the posture of the head was unchanged.
> That was the remarkable thing.
> And, if her skin was brown, you had to
>   admit her courage was royal purple.
> [Charlotte Observer, September 5, 1957].

The courage to express one's own commitment to
freedom not only won reluctant accolades from the white
press but often took the parents of teenagers by surprise.
In Little Rock Governor Faubus had predicted, "Blood will
run in the streets" if the black pupils carried out their announced plan to integrate Central High School. Subsequently,
the National Guard, under the Governor's orders, refused to
protect Elizabeth Eckford from the mob outside the school.
Instead she was turned away from the doors, and forced to
face the angry mob on her own. When finally President
Eisenhower had federalized the National Guard, and sent the
regular Army to ensure the safety of the youths, a small
group of nine Negro pupils were ready for a third try. But
parents of two of the youngsters refused to allow their children to continue the attempt to integrate the high school.
Shortly, however, the two young people joined the group at
the home of the Bates, who were local N. A. A. C. P. leaders.
The students had insisted on their right to make the attempt.
At last the parents had granted them permission.

The black sectarians in the Little Rock struggle made
it clear that to be a sectarian of the civil religion one need
not be a sectarian of the Christian religion. Prior to Little
Rock, opposition to the established form of the civil religion
often drew upon specifically Christian motives and resources.
In contrast to King and his colleagues in S. C. L. C., the
Bates and their N. A. A. C. P. friends openly defended their
homes with guards carrying shotguns. They also carried
weapons whenever they left the house. Black young people
in schools returned blows and insults or remained passive

according to their own understanding of which might be most advantageous in the situation. Minnijean Brown, sixteen-year-old eleventh grader, was suspended for retaliating and reinstated only on the agreement that

> she would not retaliate, verbally or physically, to any harassment, but would leave the matter to the school authorities to handle [Bates, 1962, p120]. *

She was subsequently expelled for responding to harassment when the authorities would not protect her. Nonetheless, the black sectarians of Little Rock remained determined that they would claim full rights as American citizens, including the hallowed, and to them most sensible, right of self-defense.

The blacks struggling for freedom in Little Rock shared with King and the others the sectarian faith even though they were not bound together in the Christian faith. The sectarians of Little Rock foreshadowed the sectarians of the latter half of the sixties. There was no appeal to the Christian religion. There was only the appeal to the Founding Documents of the American faith. Bates wrote

> More than any other single event in many years, Little Rock demonstrated the gaping discrepancy between the Declaration of Independence--one of the most precious documents of American history-- and the reality of twentieth century America [ibid., p220].

There was the conviction that the oppressed must be involved personally in the battle for freedom.

> A second contribution that Little Rock made--a contribution by no means less significant or less dramatic--was its effect upon the Negro population. ... It was a fight waged with legal methods, fought in the glare of public opinion and political maneuver and a fight resulting in the complete victory of a just cause. Through the struggle and

*Excerpts from The Long Shadow of Little Rock, by Daisy Bates, Copyright © 1962 by Daisy Bates. Reprinted by permission of the David McKay Company, Inc.

victory, Negroes tested their own strength, and
won. They learned unmistakably that they possess
irresistible power if they become conscious of it
and unite to secure their inalienable rights [ibid.,
pp220 and 221].

There was the belief that America must be pure before she can pretend to lead the nations.

Only through the unbelievable outrage at Little
Rock was the world brought to a sharp realization
of the shameful discrimination that the world's
greatest democracy directs even against young
children--in a country that boasts of being the
leader of the "free world" and prides itself upon
having given mankind a Constitution based upon
individual dignity and liberty [ibid., pp219 and 220].

A sobering example of the distance between the sectarian and established forms of the civil religion is provided
by Mrs. Eleanor Roosevelt, who writes a Foreword to The
Long Shadow of Little Rock. Referring to the final chapter,
from which the above quotes are taken, Mrs. Roosevelt, one
of the most liberal and sympathetic of the established type,
says

I wish that Mrs. Bates, who suffered so much and
had such courage throughout all her difficulties,
who could bear to see with her husband their life's
work destroyed and still go on and work for the
cause she believed, had been able to keep from
giving us some of the sense of her bitterness and
fear in the end of her book [ibid., pxv].

The same event, in this case the description of the
struggle in Little Rock, is to one a sign of hope and the
other a sense of bitterness. This feeling of bitterness, according to Muse, settled over the Southern form of the
established type of civil religion. Any suggestion of support
for blacks was considered to be Communist inspired, for the
crusade for civil rights was believed to be Communist directed. Choruses from black colleges were no longer invited to sing for white audiences. Black groups, which had
formerly taken part in holiday parades and festivities, were
now excluded. White community leaders who had been active
in aiding and advising individual blacks, especially promising
young students, abandoned their activity. The Urban League,

the long-respected black assistance organization which was
not at this time involved in integration activities, was excluded from its previous position as a participant in local
Community Chest drives.   Most of its white supporters de-
serted it.   White Citizen's Councils were established and
through their meetings, speakers bureaus, publications and
activities they celebrated the Southern form of the established
type of the civil religion.   At the same time, the Citizens
Councils urged the economic and police forces to vigorously
oppose the black sectarians.

SUMMARY

        The purpose of this brief review of the post war
trends of the American civil religion has been to trace the
background of the radical movement of the 1960's.   The post
war period to 1960 was one of accelerated change in American character and national action--a change which was engendered by war and cold war.   In this period the basic
characteristics which Troeltsch described as essential to the
church and sect forms of the Christian religion have been
applied to the American civil religion, delineating its established and sectarian forms.   The cold war mission of America, which sought to dominate the whole of humanity for the
sake of its own salvation, was the dominant characteristic
of the established type.   The established concern for world
leadership motivated the attempt to end the more flagrant
examples of racism.   The established type felt that the
Communist world exploited American racial troubles in order
to demean the American mission.   Consequently, it was
time to bring such racial injustices to an end.   In contrast,
the sectarians set their hearts on a pure fulfillment of the
democratic ideal.   Only when the United States is in truth a
nation of peace and justice can it hope to be an example to
the world for good and not evil.   The pacifists concentrated
their criticisms against the cold war policy and rhetoric.
Black sectarians struggled against the racist domestic structures.

        Second, the established type of the civil religion was
seen to be in closest connection with the ruling classes, the
"power elite. "   The power elite, through the offices of the
President and the Congress established foreign policy, as the
Constitution provides.   However, the major inputs for decisions came from the military and industrial sectors of
society.   On the domestic front, the established type meant

also to keep the black civil rights reforms under its own control. In opposition, the pacifist radicals and black sectarians were in closest connection with the poor and lower classes. They continually sought and finally succeeded in developing a true mass movement of the poor.

Third, the work ethic was the form that asceticism took in the established type of the American civil religion. Under this doctrine the gaining of special positions of privilege was possible for all. The Marxist denial of the work ethic, especially its doctrine of just rewards such as property fanned the fires of opposition to Communism to a white heat. On the other hand, the sectarians denied that wordly goods or achievements determined the worth of a man. Therefore positions of privilege in the body politic ought not to be allowed, whether in decisions concerning nuclear weapons or jimcrow laws. The sense of brotherhood and equality of all men was strengthened for the sectarians by their common experience of oppression.

Fourth, the mainstream of development flowed along the established type. The desire to bear the mission of America throughout the world was the dominant political reality of American foreign policy. The conflict between universal and sphere of influence thinking, cast in cold war rhetoric, became the understanding of history both in textbooks and best selling histories, such as Samuel Morison's Oxford History of the American People (1965) and Link and Catton's American Epoch (1963). The legal modification of racist structures was according to the desire and pace of the established form. Against this reality, the sectarian form maintained a constant drumbeat, calling ever more insistently the peoples' attention to the fact that the mainstream of development had fallen away from the ideals of the Founding Fathers. Now had been established standing armies, heavy taxations to support armaments, wars without consent of Congress, secret intelligence agencies not responsible to Congress or the people and permanent conscription of the type the Fathers fled when they left Europe. The black sectarians stressed again and again the failure of America to live up to the ideals of the Declaration of Independence, and the rights guaranteed by the Constitution.

Fifth, the established form of the civil religion similarly attempted to achieve its universal ideal by organizational and bureaucratic effort. To establishmentarians the sacred mission of America was more important than the

actions of individuals or parties in power. They could fail
to meet American ideals, yet the mission would not thereby
flounder. Thus the established type could choose "second
best" in supporting dictators such as Diem, believing that
because America's mission was freedom, peace and justice
for all mankind, somehow good would come out of present
policy. On the domestic front, this same belief urged blacks
to work through the normal democratic processes of the
ruling classes to gain their freedom. All that was needed
according to the established type was a bit more time and
effort to complete the perfection of American democracy.
Opposing such arguments, the sectarians demanded ever new
actions from individuals which would express and demonstrate
the same commitment to freedom, brotherhood and democracy
that was evidenced by the Founding Fathers, who were willing
to pledge their lives, fortune and sacred honor. So the pacifists sailed into the nuclear test area, risking radiation
hazard, jail and professional loss. From Randolph to Bates
the black sectarians reiterated again and again that the force
that would free black people from their chains of oppression
was black people who were irrevocably committed to being
free.

What Troeltsch says of the Christian religion is equally
true of the civil religion. Only as we see and understand
the joint action of the two types of civil religion are we able
to understand the full force of the religion on American society. Further, only as we see these forces gathering
strength from the surging changes engendered in American
society by war and cold war, moving steadily toward their
climactic political confrontations in the sixties, are we able
to understand that the mass radical movement of the sixties
emerged from the collision of incompatible contextual orientations. As more and more Americans, primarily students
and blacks, became aware that their personal lives were
being ordered in what was to them intensely unjust ways, the
mass civil rights and peace movements rose to do battle for
Truth, Freedom, Peace and Justice.

From both the established and sectarian perspectives,
the battle that raged was a Holy War.

III

PROTEST AND REFORM

THE CIVIL RELIGION AND
RACISM: 1960-1965

The Established Type of
the Civil Religion

The Southern regional form of the established type of
the civil religion, which was being challenged by the civil
rights movement, continued in the first of the sixties to
mobilize the majority of the political, economic and social
forces of the region against the gathering strength of the
revolution.   Governors barred the doors of schools to blacks.
Police chiefs set dogs and high pressure fire hoses against
demonstrators.   White citizens' councils organized economic
retaliations.   Mad bombers murdered even little children in
Sunday School and were not apprehended.   Throughout it all,
the regional form of the civil religion insisted on the sanctity
of its way of life, the rightness of its conduct, the depravity
of those who sought change, and anathematized the supporters
of the civil rights movement.   The most bitterly scorned of
the supporters of black civil rights were John and Robert
Kennedy.   Their accent and actions epitomized for the regional form the reasons why damn yankees were, and of right
ought to be, thoroughly hated.   For a hundred and fifty years
Northerners had meddled in the affairs of the South, seeking
to overturn first its peculiar institution, and then its whole
way of life.   The Kennedys, whose very name had become a
hissing and a curse, attracted to themselves and symbolized
all the bitterness of that century and a half.

One of the popular doctrines of the regional form of
the civil religion held that the Kennedys and Communists
(between which a distinction was seldom made) were responsible for the civil rights movement.   Therefore we need to

look for a moment at the response of the established form of the civil religion to the civil rights movement. The record of the Kennedy Administration is a good place to gain a sounding. Outside the South, the majority of Americans, according to the pollsters, supported the Administration's attempts to protect the basic American right to vote. More reluctantly, Americans also agreed that de jure segregation of school systems ought to be ended, even though de facto segregated school systems were at the time on the increase in the large cities in the rest of the nation.

The Kennedy Administration placed civil rights in the same context as did the Eisenhower and Truman Administrations--the context of the cold war. Early in his Administration J. F. K. sent a telegram to the Conference of the Civil Rights Commission in Williamsburg, Virginia.

> Let me here pay tribute to ... the men and women responsible for maintaining our public schools and for carrying through the process of desegregation--principals, officers of school boards and public school teachers.... If we are to give the leadership the world requires of us, we must be true to the great principles of our Constitution, the very principles which distinguish us from our adversaries in the world [Kennedy, 1962, p135]. *

In the first major Administration address on civil rights, Robert Kennedy, in a speech in Athens at the University of Georgia Law School, argues that Americans must consider the worldwide impact of their actions.

> ... We must be quite aware of the fact that fifty percent of the countries in the United Nations are not white; that around the world, in Africa, South America, and Asia, people whose skins are a different color than ours are on the move to gain their measure of freedom and liberty. From the Congo to Cuba, from South Viet-Nam to Algiers, in India, Brazil and Iran, men and women and children are straightening their backs and listening--to the evil promises of communist tyranny and the

---

*Excerpts from To Turn the Tide, by John F. Kennedy. Copyright © 1962 by Harper & Row, Publishers, Inc. Reprinted by permission of the publisher.

> honorable promises of Anglo American liberty.
> And those people will decide not only their future
> but how the cause of freedom fares in the world
> [Golden, 1964, pp221 and 222].

Robert Kennedy argues that to this generation falls the burden
of proving to the world that Americans are serious when they
say all men are created free and are equal before the law.
Again, the context of civil rights for the established form of
the civil religion emerges: the cold war and equality as
equality before the law.

In addition to the cold war context, two other factors
influenced John Kennedy's actions on civil rights, however.
First, he had an activist view of the Presidency. Kennedy
had argued during the campaign that the President could do
much more on civil rights by executive action.

> Only a President willing to use all the resources
> of his office can provide the leadership, the de-
> termination and the direction ... to eliminate racial
> and religious discrimination from American society
> [Schlesinger, 1965, p929].

He emphasized especially that discrimination in federal
housing programs could be eliminated by the "stroke of a
pen."

Secondly, according to Sorenson, J. F. K. saw himself
as freedom's spokesman. He recognized the stain on American freedom which racism represented. Racism divided and
wasted the strength of the nation which was so needed in the
world struggle. But above all, it was an historic challenge.
Racial injustice was the nation's most critical domestic problem (though not to be compared to the severity of the international problem for J. F. K.). The President was determined
to meet every challenge (Sorensen, 1965, p472). Kennedy
often drew parallels between 1960 and 1860 as the times of
crisis for the nation. He considered Lincoln's farewell address to Springfield as he made his farewell address to the
Massachusetts State Legislature.

Using some of the phrases set aside for his Inaugura-
tion Address, Kennedy declares

> Our success or failure, in whatever office we hold
> will be measured by the answers to four questions:
> First, were we truly men of courage, with the

> courage to stand up to one's enemies, and the
> courage to stand up, when necessary, to one's as-
> sociates, the courage to resist public pressure as
> well as private greed? [Kennedy, 1962, p5].

This conviction that the President must exhibit courage--some
would call it machismo--in dealing with the affairs of state
is an important theme throughout the Kennedy Administration.
In his book Profiles in Courage (1955) Kennedy defines courage
as the most admirable of human virtues. He traces its
theme in American history in the lives of Senators that seem
to him to be notable examples of political courage.

From the Revolution to the present, both activism and
courage have been traits of the true American. A popular
broadside against the Stamp Act ran

> And raise your bold hearts to fair Liberty's call,
> Then join hand in hand, brave Americans all,
> By uniting we stand, by dividing we fall
> [Nye, 1966, p58].

Active, courageous men had settled the continent. Active,
courageous men had created a new kind of government.
Active, courageous men were called to leadership in the time
of crisis: the Revolution, the first Presidency, the Civil
War Presidency (ibid., pp. 1-43). Therefore Kennedy, in
stressing activism and courage, was responding to historic
elements in the American civil religion.

Kennedy's emphasis on activism and courage triggered
grave problems in the conduct of foreign affairs. Yet when
at last the civil rights movement had succeeded in bringing
the attention of the President to the desperate plight of black
citizens, these same traits enabled him to place the resources that he commanded into the struggle for civil rights.

Kennedy's slow start in dealing with the problem of
civil rights issued from the basic concerns of the established
type of the civil religion. First of all, the mission of America to the world was of primary importance. The internal
purity of America must take second place to her world mission, according to establishmentarians. In the first year of
the Administration, the year of the Bay of Pigs, Laos, Berlin and nuclear test resumption, the President left the action
on civil rights primarily to the Attorney General. Second,
the President considered that he had small chance of passing

a civil rights bill. He was convinced that he needed the support of the Southern ruling class, represented by the powerful committee chairmen of the Congress, to pass minimum wage and increased support for education bills which would aid blacks as well as whites. J. F. K. listened to Wilkins, King and other Negro leaders, as well as attorney Joseph Rauh, make the case for a civil rights bill. However, Kennedy refused to sponsor legislation, but urged the black leaders to be satisfied with his unprecedented number of appointments of blacks and with the Attorney General's voting rights suits. The President suggested to the civil rights leadership that there be no further pressure from the "liberal" side, but that instead he be allowed to make the progress possible at his own pace. J. F. K. stated his pace would be the most rapid feasible (Schlesinger, 1965, pp930-932).

In these actions of Kennedy can be seen the desire of the mainstream established type to control the course of events. The appointments and administrative action on the part of the Department of Justice were meant to hold the confidence of the black community. Kennedy also attempted to create a sense of movement by the seizing of a variety of small opportunities. He integrated the Coast Guard Academy by means of vigorous recruitment; he moved the Civil War Centennial Commission from segregated to integrated housing during its session in Charleston, South Carolina; he issued an executive order against discrimination in federal jobs, and increased dramatically the number of black lawyers in the Justice Department. By these smaller measures, and the work of Robert Kennedy in instituting voting rights suits under the civil rights acts of 1957 and 1960, the Administration hoped to maintain control of the movement. Surveying these actions, Schlesinger, who at that time was working in the White House and had some input in the area of civil rights, concluded

> It was not easy, however, to keep the turbulence of civil rights in the ordered channels of due process. In the spring of 1961 James Farmer and CORE sent out groups of freedom riders to challenge segregation. ... [Schlesinger, 1965, p936].

The dramatic events continued to demand action. The President sent the army to register Meredith at the University of Mississippi after a night of rioting. In a television address J. F. K. appealed to Mississippians to live up to their ideals and place the mission of America first.

> You have a great tradition to uphold, a tradition of
> honor and courage.... Let us preserve both the
> law and the peace, and then, healing those wounds
> that are within, we can turn to the greater crises
> that are without and stand united as a people in
> our pledge to man's freedom [Sorenson, 1965,
> p486].

Six hundred marshals were sent to guard the freedom
riders when the Governor of the state of Alabama refused
them protection. Still the President did not move for further
legislation in civil rights; still he did not take the major
step of eliminating racial segregation in federally financed
housing. He still hoped for Southern support. He still hoped
that belief in America, its mission, goodness, and freedom
would triumph over those actions of individuals which failed
to meet the exalted standard.

But at last President Kennedy signed the executive
order prohibiting racial segregation in federally financed
housing. As this order set the policy for F. H. A. and V. A.
insured loans as well as more directly financed government
housing, it eventually affected nearly all of the new housing
construction in the United States. Seven months later,
Kennedy sent the Civil Rights Bill to the Congress. He had
not reached these decisions easily. He opposed the publication of the Civil Rights Commission report in April 1963.
The Report criticized the President and Congress, who stood
by and did nothing while

> Citizens of the United States have been shot, set
> upon by vicious dogs, beaten and otherwise ter-
> rorized because they sought to vote. Since October,
> students have been fired upon, ministers have been
> assaulted ... children, at the brink of starvation,
> have been deprived of assistance by the callous
> and discriminatory acts of Mississippi officials
> administering Federal funds [Schlesinger, 1965,
> p952].

The President was moved to action by a number of
events. First, Robert Kennedy, seeking to extend his contacts with Negro intellectuals, had invited James Baldwin,
Kenneth Clark, Lena Horne, Harry Belafonte and others to
his New York apartment. One guest was Jerome Smith, a
young freedom rider who had witnessed the beatings of civil
rights workers while F. B. I. agents stood idly by. Smith had

himself been beaten.   When civil rights workers complained
to the F. B. I. of police brutality, the names of those who
complained were passed to the same police.   Smith said that
being in the same room with the Attorney General made him
want to vomit.   Kennedy felt he was committed to the cause
of justice and expressed resentment.   To his surprise and
anger, his guests united with Smith against him.   As the
person primarily responsible for civil rights in the Administration, R. F. K. carried to the President a new sense of
urgency.

Second, Randolph was once again organizing the March
on Washington.   But in contrast to the early forties, now a
widespread black mass movement was a reality.   Black
activists were yearning for a date to be set that they might
march together.   The march on Washington Movement was
no longer the dream of just a few, but a powerful political
reality.

Third, the events in Alabama demanded action.   In
May, the Federal Court ordered the University of Alabama
to admit two Negro applicants in June.   Governor Wallace
pledged to "stand in the schoolhouse door" to prevent the
University from being integrated.   The President federalized
the Alabama National Guard, sent units to the campus, and
the students were registered.

In a televised address that evening President Kennedy
sets forth his reasons for asking the Congress to pass civil
rights legislation.   He states that America must make a commitment not yet made in this century that "race has no place
in American life or law. "   J. F. K. asks for open public accommodations, the end of segregation in education, and
greater protection for the right to vote.   His basic reason
is that this nation

> ... was founded on the principle that all men are
> created equal, and that the rights of every man are
> diminished when the rights of one man are threat-
> ened.   Today we are committed to a worldwide
> struggle to promote and protect the rights of all
> who wish to be free.   And when Americans are
> sent to Vietnam or West Berlin, we do not ask
> for whites only....   We are confronted primarily
> with a moral issue.   It is as old as the Scriptures
> and is as clear as the American Constitution....
> One hundred years of delay have passed since

President Lincoln freed the slaves, yet their heirs,
their grandsons, are not fully free. They are not
yet freed from the bonds of injustice; they are not
yet freed from social and economic oppression.
And this nation, for all its hopes and all its boasts,
will not be fully free until all its citizens are free
[Lewis, 1971, pp167-169].

The President argues that America can scarcely preach
freedom to the world, or celebrate it at home and yet deny
freedom to Negroes. America can scarcely proclaim it has
no class system nor economic slaves, except for Negroes.
The moral crisis, J. F. K. points out, cannot be met by repressive police action, more demonstrations in the streets,
or tokenism. Only bold action by Congress, state and local
legislative bodies, and above all, the personal actions of
individuals can right the ancient wrong. Kennedy believes
the issue is a moral issue that is "as old as the Scriptures
and as clear as the American Constitution" (ibid.). It is
therefore time for the Congress to act.

Pushed by the sectarian form of the civil religion to
see the wrong as a moral issue, compelled by the historical
circumstance of a war waged against an enemy who proclaimed the doctrine of a master race and a cold war against
a foe who derided the "oppressive class system of the
capitalists, " the established form of the civil religion came
to grips with the ancient evil of racism. It must be emphasized that the issue was joined in the classic established
form. First, the context was that of the mission of America
to the world, i.e. , the cold war. Second, the reform was
to be made by the ruling class. The time for the underclass
to compete in the streets as demonstrators, white mobs and
police was over. The Congress and the President were to
effect the reform. Third, equality was to be equality of
public accommodations, education and voting rights--strictly
equality before the law. What inequality a man might make
out of that opportunity according to the work ethic was reaffirmed. Fourth, the time of fulfillment of the American
Dream was at hand for the whole of America; this would be
action of the Federal Government. The mainstream of development in this as in other areas flowed in accord with the
doctrines of the established form of the civil religion. The
regional form was to be compelled to join the mainstream.
Finally, once again, belief in America, its mission, goodness,
freedom and opportunity was invoked regardless of the failure
of the past. This organizational effort was to make clear to
all Americans and the world the truth and power inherent in
the American tradition.

J. F. K. immediately reinforced the understanding that reform was now in the hands of the established form of the civil religion by calling a meeting of the black sectarian leadership.   Randolph, King, Farmer, Wilkins and Young were included.   The President had declared in the message with which he sent the Civil Rights Bill to the Congress that demonstrations

> are not the way in which this country should rid itself of racial discrimination.   Violence is never justified; and while peaceful communication, deliberation and petitions of protest continue, I want to caution against demonstrations which can lead to violence.   This problem is now before the Congress. . . .   The Congress should have an opportunity to freely work its will [Sorensen, 1965, p499].

He reemphasized this point to the black sectarians.   Vice President Lyndon Johnson explained the resistance created in Congressional leadership by what it considered "undue" pressure.   King reminded Kennedy that demonstrations always seemed ill-timed to those who were not suffering the pains of oppression.   Randolph pointed out that the civil rights leadership also had a political problem: the Negroes were in the streets looking for leadership.   If the men present at the meeting did not provide that leadership, someone else would.   No one had an option of saying, "Go home until next year. "   At last the group agreed to disagree on "tactics, " but to try to keep lines of communications open (Schlesinger, 1965,   pp968-972).

Schlesinger, in reflecting on the March, sums up the perennial political moves of the sectarian and established types of the American civil religion from the established viewpoint.

> Every great period of social change in American history has been set off by the demand of some excluded but aggressive group for larger participation in the national democracy: in the age of Jackson by the frontier farmer, the city worker, the small entrepreneur; in the progressive era by the bankrupt farmers of the middle border and the by-passed old upper classes of the cities; in the New Deal by labor in the mass-production industries, the unemployed and the intellectuals.   The uprising of the Negroes now contained the potentiality of ushering in a new era which would not

only win Negroes their rights but renew the democratic commitment of the national community....
A generation ago Roosevelt had absorbed the energy
and hope of the labor revolution into the New Deal.
So in 1963 Kennedy moved to incorporate the Negro
revolution into the democratic coalition and thereby
help it serve the future of American freedom
[Schlesinger, 1965, pp976-977].

But the moves of Roosevelt and Kennedy, so acceptable to Schlesinger and others of his established perspective,
were greeted with suspicion and hostility by the more radical
of the sectarians.   To them, such measures were seen as
half-hearted, hypocritical attempts to avoid the depth of the
crisis.   On the night that Kennedy made what many established types call "The Second Emancipation Proclamation, "
Medgar Evers was murdered.   No attempt was made by
local authorities to find the assassin and bring him to justice.
When the F. B. I. succeeded in establishing a good case
against Beckwith, an all-white jury freed him.   In June a
group of blacks were jailed for six months in Itta Bena,
Mississippi, for peacefully asking protection against harassment during a voter registration campaign.   In September
twelve black residents of Clinton, Louisiana, were jailed for
writing letters to the mayor requesting appointment of a
biracial committee (Lewis, 1971, p241).

Before the Civil Rights Bill passed in 1964, Governor
Wallace had entered the Democratic primaries in Indiana,
Maryland and Wisconsin.   His campaign was racist, with a
thin veneer of states' rights.   He won over thirty-five percent of the vote.   In Gary, Indiana, where blacks had sued
to end racial inbalance in the public schools, Wallace carried
every white precinct.

Although a majority of Americans, according to the
polls, had approved of Kennedy's speech, the majority also
felt that "progress was too rapid" in the area of civil rights
(ibid. , p223).   The continuing repression in the South, the
success of Wallace, and the opinion polls all confirmed that
racism was still part of the fabric of American society.
The established form of the civil religion was committed to
the task of achieving equality before the law.   It was not
committed to the task of eradicating racism.   Even the nar-
rower task of achieving equality before the law was set upon
deliberately, rather than urgently.

President Johnson, after the assassination of President
Kennedy, moved wholeheartedly from his own perspective to
see a strong civil rights bill through the Congress.   When he
reflected on civil rights, he said there was no question about
what he would do.   He knew that he would use all the resources at his command--including the tremendous moral
force of the presidency--to gain justice for black Americans.

L. B. J. refused to accept compromise on the Bill.
He brought his considerable resources of pressure and persuasion to bear on the Senate, where the issue turned on the
question of cloture.   Senator Dirksen, leader of the Republican forces, which in the past had voted with their conservative colleagues of the Southern Democrats against cloture,
took the floor of the Senate to say the time had come for
equality of opportunity, and that meant cloture and enactment
of a civil rights bill.   Like Vandenberg's speech a generation
earlier, Dirksen's eloquence carried the day.   Cloture was
voted and the Bill passed.   Equality before the law, equality
of opportunity, had moved from the rhetoric of the American
civil religion to the law of the land.

After the election of 1964, President Johnson sought
to pass a Civil Rights Bill that would fully and adequately
guarantee voting rights.   Like Eisenhower and Kennedy, in
full agreement with the classic doctrine of the established
type of the civil religion, Johnson believed that legislation to
secure, once and for all, equal voting rights would be even
more central than earlier legislation.   The vote would grant
blacks the same legitimate power that other Americans
shared.   As a consequence of that power, many other barriers would fall.   Johnson used the emotional impact of the
Selma crisis to present the Civil Rights Act of 1965 to a
joint session of the Congress.

In his speech, L. B. J., whose homespun Southern manner so alienated many Northerners, especially students and
intellectuals, plainly means to touch the hearts of his fellow
Americans through the common faith of the American civil
religion.

> I speak tonight for the dignity of man and the destiny
> of democracy.... At times history and fate meet
> at a single time in a single place to shape a turning
> point in man's unending search for freedom.   So it
> was at Lexington and Concord.   So it was a century
> ago at Appomattox.   So it was last week in Selma,

Alabama. . . .   There is no constitutional issue here.
The command of the Constitution is plain.   There
is no moral issue.   It is wrong--deadly wrong--to
deny any of your fellow Americans the right to vote
in this country.   There is no issue of states' rights
or national rights. . . .   It is the effort of American
Negroes to secure for themselves the full blessings
of American life.   Their cause must be our cause
too.   Because it is not just Negroes, but really it
is all of us who must overcome the crippling legacy
of bigotry and injustice.   And . . . we . . . shall . . .
overcome [ibid. , p165].

Not only does Johnson invoke the sacred history to hallow
the present experience of Selma, but he also reaffirms that
for Americans the wide questions of morality and human
rights are settled if the command of the Founding Documents
is clear.   In the case of voting rights the command of the
Constitution is plain.   Because it not only settles political
rights but also the questions of morality and human rights,
it is obviously more than the command of a Constitution but
an ultimate command, the command of Providence or God.
The struggle for human rights is equated with the securing of
the full blessings of American life.   The full blessings of
American life mean "life, liberty and the pursuit of happiness" and "equality and justice for all. "   It is certain that
while some do not enjoy equality and justice none of us will
experience the full blessings of life, liberty and the pursuit
of happiness.   Therefore the cause of the Negro American is
the cause of all Americans.   Johnson is confident that, regardless of past failures, America in her goodness, purpose,
and mission will overcome the crippling legacy of bigotry
and injustice.

The Bill was duly passed, but the legacy was not
overcome.   Harlem, then Watts, then a whole host of American cities burned summer after summer.   Black power replaced black and white together.   White sectarians, returning
from the civil rights experience, turned their attention to
their own oppressions: the university and the war.

The Sectarian Type of the Civil Religion: The Struggle Against Racism

In the Social Teachings of the Christian Churches,
Troeltsch comes to the conclusion that

> There can be no doubt about the actual fact: the
> sects, with their greater independence of the world,
> and their continual emphasis upon the original ideals
> of Christianity, often represent in a very direct and
> characteristic way the essential fundamental ideas
> of Christianity; to a very great extent they are a
> most important factor in the study of the develop-
> ment of the sociological consequences of Christian
> thought [Troeltsch, 1960, p334]. *

As we consider this early period of the movement of the
1960's, there can be no doubt about the fact that the emphasis
sectarians place upon the principles expressed in the Declaration of Independence and the Constitution represented in a
very direct and characteristic way the essential fundamental
ideals of the American civil religion. The established type's
slow progress in exorcising the curse of racism from the
land was an expression of the necessity to maintain universal
control of the masses, rather than to recover in practice the
ideals of the Revolution. Therefore the political structures
which necessitated compromises with the ideal were willingly
used. The compromises, which made possible some movement in the direction of the ideal, were good as far as the
established type was concerned. While the ideal had not
been reached, establishmentarians believed the best possible
result for this time and this place had been achieved. The
sectarian, on the other hand, continued to appeal to the
ideal. As the conflict sharpened, more and more sectarians
were beaten and even murdered. Not only did they ridicule
the reality of freedom and justice for all, but more and more
passionately denounced the established type. At last the
sectarians became convinced that the willingness of the established type to compromise was tantamount to first, approval
of, and then criminal complicity in, murder and repression.
The mood of the sectarians shifted under the impact of brutal
conflict from "he who is not against us is with us" to "he
who is not with us is against us." This move represented
the hardening of diametrically opposed world views and the
perception of the other as enmeshed in a hopelessly evil
system. For some the trip was one from innocence to
cynicism. For others, it was a journey from romantic

*Excerpts from The Social Consequences of the Christian
Church by Ernst Troeltsch. New York: Harper & Row,
1960. (Originally published by Macmillan, 1931.) Reprinted
by permission of Macmillan and Allen & Unwin Ltd.

idealism to a stern, even rigid determination to master one's own fate and determine one's own destiny.

The opening scene of the sectarian movement of the 1960's took place in Greensboro, North Carolina. Ralph Johns, the owner of a small clothing store was offended by the segregation at the lunch counter in the nearby Woolworth's. He often suggested to students at the local North Carolina Agricultural and Technical College that a sit-in would force the lunch counter to be desegregated. On February 1, 1960, four students from the College responded to Johns' challenge.

The manager of Woolworth's immediately went to the police station. The chief of police told the manager the police would not interfere unless the store wished to issue a trespass warrant. The manager did not wish to serve the warrant, but simply "wanted the boys to leave." The chief sent officers to the store to make certain no trouble developed, and advised the manager that it would probably soon blow over. Both men were concerned for the good name of the city of Greensboro and their professional reputations. Both were considered progressive. At five o'clock, the Greensboro Evening Record and Dr. George Simkins, a black dentist and head of the Greensboro chapter of the N. A. A. C. P. were called by Johns, and told of the sit-in. The store closed at 5:15 with no incident.

The students returned at 10:00 the following day. The group of four had grown to twenty-seven men and four women. News media were on hand. Whites ate at the counter; interchanges between students and customers seemed normal, except no food was served to the blacks. In his first interview, Ezell Blair, one of the original four students, declared that black adults have been "complacent and fearful. It is time for someone to wake up and change the situation, and we decided to start here."

That night at the monthly meeting the local N. A. A. C. P. chapter voted to support the students. Dr. Simkins called C. O. R. E. to see if that organization would also be interested in helping. C. O. R. E. sent field representative Len Holt to Greensboro the following week. Martin Luther King, Jr., president of S. C. L. C., also came to encourage the students. By February 3, over sixty students were demonstrating, and white students from nearby colleges had joined the group. The College was pressured to discipline the students. However, the Dean stated students' private actions did not fall

under the authority of the College.   Groups of hostile whites
began to gather at Woolworth's, muttering threats, but police
steadfastly maintained order.   The local paper editorialized
that resentment against the dearth of facilities for blacks
was justified, but negotiation ought to be tried rather than
demonstrations.   As the situation became more tense, whites
were arrested for assault and disorderly conduct.   Several
whites were escorted from the store for using abusive language.   However, other local constables, not connected with
the Greensboro police department, began to threaten the black
students with arrest.

Woolworth's was not opposed to integration if other
local lunch counters would integrate as well.   Other merchants
refused to cooperate.   On Saturday, at a point of high tension,
a bomb threat closed the store.   The students returned to
campus, with police stopping a mob of white youths and men
who were following.   The students voted a two-week moratorium on demonstrations to allow Woolworth's time to make
a decision.

But on Monday, February 8, the movement spread.
Twenty-six miles away, in Winston-Salem, black students from
the Winston-Salem Teachers College for Negroes began sit-
ins at local variety store lunch counters.   Durham, Charlotte
and Fayetteville, all with nearby black colleges, experienced
sit-ins by Tuesday.   By the end of the week, students in six
other cities in North Carolina and five other states of the
Old South had joined the movement by sitting-in in their own
towns and cities.   Picket lines appeared in front of Woolworth's and other chain stores in the North.

At Greensboro a city councilman, Ed Zane, was appointed head of a negotiation committee.   He was opposed to
injustice, and said, "You've got to look at the nation, the
Declaration of Independence, the Constitution.   Discrimination just won't go."   He had resigned from his church over
its refusal to admit blacks.   He was also opposed to demonstration as an unfair infringement upon the rights of the
owners.   Although he gained the support of the ministerial
association most groups remained silent.   Woolworth's refused to change its policy.   Finally even the Mayor urged
the store to relent.   The sit-ins resumed at Woolworth's and
Kress's.   The lunch counters were closed.   Students began
to picket the stores.   Kress's reopened its counter on a
"guest-only" basis.   After attending the founding rally of
S. N. C. C. at Shaw University in Raleigh, students returned to

sit at the counter, be charged with trespassing, and be arrested.   But on July 25 Woolworth's changed its policy.
Five months of struggle had succeeded in desegregating the
lunch counter (Wolff, 1970).

The Greensboro experience was an unusual event in
the civil rights movement.   In many other places there was
sudden, vicious violence rather than the moderate response
of Greensboro.   Jacksonville, Florida, witnessed savage
attack, pistol whipping and murder.   Atlanta saw acid thrown
at sit-in leaders.   The black college gym in Frankfort, Ken-
tucky was burned.   In Columbia, South Carolina, a black
sit-in student was stabbed.   In Texas KKK kidnappings were
followed with floggings and brandings.   Mississippi responded
with a special savagery, a gloomy foreboding of its brutal
role as an adversary of the movement.   Clubs, tear gas,
police dogs, chain beatings, gunfire, often by police and
nearly always in their presence or purposeful absence attended attempts to secure basic rights.   In places such as
Nashville, students were summarily expelled from school for
participating (Zinn, 1965, p25).   The terror did not abate,
but increased to the point where law enforcement agencies
actively supported the planning and execution of the murder
of civil rights workers.   Had the four Greensboro students
been jailed, beaten, convicted and sentenced to the road gang
for six months and expelled from school, probably the second
day would not have happened.   Surely Greensboro would have
never reached the attention of the national news media.

At the time and place where the movement began both
the established and sectarian types seem to have been more
aware of their common bond in the American civil religion
than they were aware of the depth of difference that separated
the types.   The councilman harked back to the Founding Documents.   The Mayor and the editor of the local newspaper
argued that it was obviously unjust for merchants who depended on black trade for profit to deny those same black
citizens the full services of the store.   The indication that
this was not mere rhetoric can be seen in the actions of the
police, who clearly protected blacks from being set upon by
lawless whites.   The students pointed to the lack of action
by black adults rather than the oppressive nature of the
system.   The major point of disagreement was the method of
redress.   Even at this point, the students were amazingly
considerate.   But method was the basic difference: The
established type still argued that negotiations ought to have
started and ended the problem, thereby encapsulating it within

the state and ruling class.   The students believed they were
called to action which expressed and demonstrated their commitment to freedom, brotherhood and democracy.   Yet after
a week, they voted a two-week moratorium.   When no decision was forthcoming, they extended that two weeks five
weeks more.   Only then did they return.   They did not sit-in
fulltime, lest the merchant lose all his business, but only
filled the seats at selected times.   The administration of the
college supported the students by refusing to expel or otherwise seek to limit their freedom of action.   This took courage,
for the school came under attack from the State Legislature
which funded it.   Local black adults publicly supported the
students even though it jeopardized their jobs.   There is in
this opening scene a flexibility, an innocence, an expression
of a common faith that had not appeared in Montgomery or
Little Rock, and would not appear again in the decade of the
sixties.

Far more typical was the experience of Bob Moses in
Amite County, Mississippi.   Moses was a black born in
Harlem, educated at Harvard, and teaching at an elite school
in the Bronx.   He went South to be put to work by S. C. L. C.
S. C. L. C. had no job for him, but the Student Non-Violent
Coordinating Committee did.   S. N. C. C. had come into being
as a result of Ella Baker, the executive secretary of S. C. L. C.
She had worked for the W. P. A. , N. A. A. C. P. and Urban
League.   During the third week of February, as the movement blossomed, she had the idea that someone ought to
provide communication and coordination for the scores of
local demonstrations.   King agreed; S. C. L. C. put up the
money, and Shaw University in Raleigh agreed to host the
meeting.   Three hundred students attended.   After intense
debate, they determined not to be affiliated with S. C. L. C. ,
C. O. R. E. , N. A. A. C. P. or any other adult group.   Few of
the demonstrators had had prior contact with these groups.
Instead they decided to maintain friendly relationships, but
be independent.   An October date was set for the next meeting.
An office was to be opened in Atlanta.   Testimony to the
Democratic and Republican platform committees was to be
given that summer.

Jane Stembridge, from Virginia, describes her feelings
that first night in Raleigh.

> The most inspiring moment for me was the first
> time I heard the students sing We shall overcome....
> It was hot that night upstairs in the auditorium.

> Students had just come in from all over the South,
> meeting for the first time.   February 1 was not
> long past.   There was no SNCC, no ad hoc com-
> mittees, no funds, just people who did not know
> what to expect but who came and released the com-
> mon vision in that song.   I had just driven down
> from Union Seminary in New York--out of it, ex-
> cept that I cared, and that I was a Southerner....
> It was inspiring because it was the beginning, and
> because, in a sense, it was the purest moment.
> I am a romantic.   But I call this moment the
> one ... [Zinn, 1965].

These youth were romantics.   They were the well
scrubbed, respectable, conservatively dressed, cautious children of the white and black bourgeoisie of the South.   The
movement was a wrenching loose from everything "practical"
they had been taught by their parents and professors.   They
were converted from the vision of the practical means of
gaining success according to the American dream to the
vision of the ideal that America ought to be.

In the keynote speech, James Lawson argues that the
issue is not one of personal freedom for students (he had
been expelled for participating in the sit-ins).   It is not the
selective enforcement of the law by racist police, nor the
legal issues of segregation, nor even integration.   No, Lawson believes

> In the first instance, we who are demonstrators
> are trying to raise what we call the "moral issue."
> That is, we are pointing to the viciousness of racial
> segregation and prejudice and calling it evil or sin.
> The matter is not legal, sociological or racial, it
> is moral and spiritual.   Until America (South and
> North) honestly accepts the sinful nature of racism,
> the cancerous disease will continue to rape all of
> us [Lawson, 1960, p312].

In the second place, Lawson argues, the message of
the non-violent movement is that social change is moving far
too slowly.   At the present rate all of Africa will be free
before the American Negro attains first class citizenship.
No sin can be slowly removed.   The movement is a judgment both upon the middle-class white who screens himself
from awareness of his participation in evil and upon the
middle-class black who accepts tokenism.   Lawson concludes

The word from the lunch-counter stool demands a
sharp re-assessment of our organized evil and a
radical Christian obedience to transform that evil.
Christian non-violence provides both that re-
assessment and the faith of obedience. The extent
to which the Negro joined by many others appre-
hends and incorporates non-violence determines the
degree that the world will acknowledge fresh social
insight from America [ibid., p315].

At the outset we see the marks of the sectarian:
first of all, a pure embodiment of the ideals of the Founding
Fathers is demanded. The vaunted freedom which America
is seeking to export in fact lags behind the freedom now
being achieved by the emerging nations in Africa. If it is
to be truly free, American society must care for freedom
as passionately as does the student movement. Here is
Troeltsch's understanding of the sectarian rejection of present
society and his demand that it become like the sectarian society in order to be truly just. Secondly, the sectarians reject the present social order. The majority white order
which enforces but does not see the degradation of racist
social structures is organized evil. The social order of the
middle class black accepts that evil and protests only feebly,
without passion and risk. The students bind themselves to
the most oppressed, and are determined to renew society
now. Thirdly, the movement from the beginning rejects the
argument of both black and white middle class that the work
ethic is the form of virtue for Americans. Students reject
the belief that by personal effort one can and should seek to
get ahead, and share, even if black, some respect and status
in American society. Without freedom and justice, which are
the marks of true brotherhood, all other marks of status are
hollow, for they deny rather than affirm the true worth of
man. Fourth, there is the passionate appeal to the Founding
Documents. Marion Barry appeared for S. N. C. C. in July
at the Democratic convention and stated

... The ache of every man to touch his potential is
the throb that beats out the truth of the American
Declaration of Independence and the Constitution.
America was founded because men were seeking
room to become.... We are again seeking that
room.... We want to walk into the sun and
through the front door. For three hundred and
fifty years, the American Negro has been sent to
the back door.... We grow weary [Zinn, 1965,
p37].

Finally, as Troeltsch emphasizes, this new conviction, this new birth, this radicalization demands personal action: thus the sit-in can be only the beginning. The actions must increase in depth of meaning and even danger, in order that the commitment to freedom and democracy might likewise not stagnate, but continue to grow.

Bob Moses symbolizes those who were willing to increase the risk in order to let the oppressed go free, in order to fulfill his commitment that freedom be not just a word, but also a reality. After working in the S. N. C. C. office for a while in June, he made a field trip to Mississippi to gather people to go to the October conference. In Cleveland, Mississippi, he met Amzie Moore, head of the N. A. A. C. P. in town. Together they planned a campaign to begin registering blacks to vote the following summer. It was S. N. C. C. 's pilot project in voter registration. After returning to Mississippi in 1961 to initiate the project, Moses was severely beaten twice and jailed three times. Two other S. N. C. C. workers were badly beaten. Herbert Lee was a black farmer sympathetic to the movement, who had farmed all his life in Amite County. He was shot to death in front of the Liberty cotton gin by E. H. Hurst, a member of the Mississippi Legislature. Moses traveled from one black farm to the next all night to find witnesses. He was able to establish by three men present that it was unprovoked murder, but none would agree to testify. One of the witnesses, Louis Allen, subsequently was told to testify the murder was in self defense, and under threat did so. Later Allen told Moses he wished to reverse his testimony. Moses called the Justice Department, asking for protection for Allen, so that he might reverse his testimony before the federal grand jury. Allen was refused protection, but the F. B. I. informed the local police of the call. Allen was first beaten by a deputy sheriff who told him he knew he had contacted the Justice Department. Later Allen was found dead in front of his home, killed by three shotgun blasts.

Information that was detrimental to the life and health of S. N. C. C. workers traveled swiftly from Washington to remote Liberty. Punitive action by local authorities was even swifter. Information of violations of the civil rights of citizens traveled slowly up the chain of command. When it reached Washington, there was no action. Such realities made S. N. C. C. workers feel like vomiting when established types, like Attorney General Robert Kennedy, proclaimed they

were "wholly committed" to civil rights.   The antagonism
between the established type and the sectarian began to grow
as the sectarians came to realize the established type had
many important ties to the established regional type.   Often
those ties resulted in the death, jailing or beating of a sectarian.

Moses joined a march of 115 high school students in
McComb protesting the beatings and killings, and was arrested and jailed.   The students were expelled from school.
A Freedom School was established.   White students, such as
Paul Potter of the National Student Association and Tom
Hayden of the Students for a Democratic Society arrived to
aid the registration drive.   As they were identified, they
were dragged from their car and beaten in the street, as
were C. O. R. E. people.   The F. B. I. agents watching the
beatings filed a report.   No blacks were registered that
year.

Nonetheless S. N. C. C. continued the attempt to establish the voter registration campaign which eventuated in the
Mississippi Freedom Democratic Party.   Wherever Moses
spoke, he told the story of Herbert Lee.   Lee was memorial-
ized in a song, a dirge sung at a slow elegiac tempo, which
was the "We Shall Overcome" of the S. N. C. C. workers in
Mississippi.   The last stanza lamented

> We have hung our heads and cried
> Cried for those like Lee who died
> Died for you and died for me
> Died for the cause of equality
> No, we'll never turn back
> No, we'll never turn back
> Until we've all been freed
> And we have equality
> And we have equality.

Moses wrote from prison

> Later on, Hollis will lead out with a clear tenor
> into a freedom song, Talbert and Lewis will pro-
> vide jokes and McDew will discourse on the history
> of the black man and the Jew.   McDew--a black by
> birth and a Jew by choice, and a revolutionary by
> necessity--has taken on the deep loves and the deep
> hates which America, and the world, reserve for
> those who dare to stand in a strong sun and cast a

> sharp shadow.... This is Mississippi, in the mid-
> dle of the iceberg. Hollis is leading off with his
> tenor, "Michael row the boat ashore, Alleluia;
> Christian brothers don't be slow, Alleluia; Missis-
> sippi's next to go, Alleluia." This is a tremor in
> the middle of the iceberg--from a stone that the
> builders rejected [Newfield, 1971, pp47-49]. *

By 1965, S. N. C. C. workers had gone back to Amite County.
Even the farmers there had taken new courage. Jack Newfield described a meeting in Mount Pilgrim Baptist Church
on Steptoe's land, where Moses had conducted his first voter
registration class in 1961. Herbert Lee was buried in the
churchyard, and his son was among the fifty people present.

> The meeting began with the singing of two hymns:
> "Lord, Come by Here," and "Jesus, Hold My Hand
> While I Run This Race." Steptoe used our faces
> as his text for the evening. (Steptoe is one of the
> few local Negroes who is not religious.) ... You
> all have to go down and redish now. You should
> want to make this a better county to live in. You
> have to take that first step. You get the key to
> freedom when you redish. To be a redished voter
> means you are an American, a first-class citizen.
> It will keep bullets out of your body and clubs away
> from your head.... Then Carol Rogoff, sitting in
> the last row began to sing, "This little light of
> mine.... All over the courthouse, we're gonna
> let it shine.... All over Sheriff Jones, we're
> gonna let it shine.... All over Liberty, we're
> gonna let it shine/oh, we've got the light of free-
> dom/we're gonna let it shine." ... After a while
> Herbert Lee, Jr. began to sing: "Oh, my father
> was a freedom fighter/I'm a freedom fighter
> too ..." [ibid., pp55, 56].

It is in the singing and speaking in the public meeting
that we see the cult, the community, the church which is so
important to a Durkheimian notion of religion. As Jane
Stembridge felt the power of the community in the organizing
meeting of S. N. C. C., so are the plain farmers of Amite

---

*Excerpts from Bread and Roses, Too by Jack Newfield.
New York: Dutton, 1971. Reprinted by permission of E. P.
Dutton.

County encouraged and given new heart by the Church of the
Sectarian Type of the Civil Religion. The development of a
piacular rite in the Durkheimian sense, so necessary to the
desperately oppressed of Amite County, did indeed by 1965
serve to compensate the loss which the group felt from the
murder of Herbert Lee. By sharing that loss in the authentic tradition of American folk song, which recreated Lee as
a folk hero and enabled his son to affirm "I'm a freedom
fighter, too" the potentially isolated individuals shared a common bond. As Durkheim put it,

> Since they weep together, they hold to one another
> and the group is not weakened, in spite of the blow
> which has fallen upon it. Of course, they have only
> sad emotions in common, but communicating in
> sorrow is still communicating, and every communion
> of mind, in whatever form it may be made, raises
> the social vitality [Durkheim, 1915, p401].

As the oppression and struggle for freedom continued,
inevitably the sectarians took on the "deep loves and the deep
hates which America--and the world--reserve for those who
stand in a strong sun and cast a sharp shadow." As they
lived and worked with the lowest of classes in America, as
the sense and bond of community grew, the S. N. C. C. staff
came to love the culture which they were trying so desperately to change. Many of the Staff were complex, city-bred,
middle-class intellectuals such as Bob Moses. One of the
basic threads of the New Left, the concern for an existential
humanist lifestyle, was nurtured in the work in the rural
Amite counties of the South. The sudden departure from the
urban impersonalization and alienation of mass society to a
people who were bound together by one hundred years of
sharing a common work, a common church, a common
poverty and a common suffering because they were black was
disorienting. The fact of sharing a common oppression was
an important part of this caring society. Such a distinctive
quality of community did not exist amongst violent poor
whites of the South. At first the young vanguard of the New
Left, the S. N. C. C. workers, imagined they were bringing
freedom to Amite County. But they soon began to discover
a freedom that they had not known in an urban culture.
They agonized over the contradiction that emerged in their
work. So while "freedom" included civil rights and voting,
"freedom" also had a personal content as well--it is something relating to one's deepest hopes and desires. Freedom
is thus worth living and dying for.

In Letters from Mississippi (Sutherland, ed. , 1965) the summer workers, some of whom stayed on as S. N. C. C. staffers rather than return to school or job, reflect on the paradox that their presence represented.

> There is some strong ambivalence which goes with this work. I sometimes fear I am only helping to integrate some beautiful people into modern white society with all of its depersonalization. (I suppose that has something to do with its industrial nature.) It isn't 19th century pastoral romanticism which I feel, but a genuine respect and admiration for a culture which, for all the trouble, still isn't as commercialized and depersonalized as is our Northern mass culture [ibid. , pp47-48]. *

> I have become so close to the family I am staying with-- eleven people--that Mrs. H. finally paid me a great compliment. She was introducing me to one of her Negro women friends and said, "This is Nancy, my adopted daughter!" ... I ... have found my own inner peace by being with people who have not forgotten how to love.... When I see these simple people living lives of relative inner peace, love, honor, courage and humor, I lose patience with people who sit and ponder their belly buttons ... [ibid. , pp48-49].

> One sees a freedom here that is so much more than just the ironical fact that the enslaved people are, at least relatively, the liberated ones. Some white people sit at their feet wondering at this sorrow freed and made beautiful, sensing dimly in themselves a similar pain, but knowing, dimly, that they have bound and frustrated it by their fear of it.... I think what is at the root of what I experienced today with these black people was a sense of tragedy. And I mustn't forget how joy and deep humor are involved in that sense, how they are all one and how that is why it is the key [ibid. , p17].

---

*Excerpts from Letters from Mississippi, edited by E. Sutherland. Copyright © 1965 by McGraw-Hill. Used with permission of McGraw-Hill Book Company.

> ... And whatever small bit we did for Mississippi
> this summer, Mississippi did ten times as much
> for us.... People I knew in Mississippi could
> honestly and unselfconsciously express affection in
> a way that few people I know in the North are able
> to do.... In Mississippi I have felt more love,
> more sympathy and warmth, more community than
> I have known in my life [ibid. , p226].

Jack Newfield notes that the paradox was not exhausted
by the discovery of a freedom among Amite County blacks
that Northern intellectuals longed to experience. Ironically,
the freedom workers were more fundamentally changed than
was Amite County. For the county remained a desperately
poor place to live. The younger blacks were drafted, or
went to work for the Peace Corps somewhere else, or moved
to one of the burgeoning cities of the South or perhaps the
North. True, by 1965, 500 blacks were registered to vote,
and the iron-clad clasp of fear and submissiveness in the
black population was thereby cracked. But the bleak conditions of life were not materially altered for the blacks in
the poorest rural section of Mississippi. Yet the S. N. C. C.
workers were enriched, believing they had found a quality
of community for which they had long yearned. In this
search for an authentic lifestyle--a search which rejects the
work ethic rewards of the established type--is seen the
characteristic sectarian yearning for a true community of
man. In such a community poverty and oppression only increase the bonds of caring and love of one for the other.

While S. N. C. C. was at work in the towns and countryside, C. O. R. E. moved in a dramatic way in the urban centers, sponsoring Freedom Rides. The Freedom Rides of
1961 attracted a great deal of national publicity, largely because of the drama surrounding the courage of the Riders
and the violence of the mobs and police who opposed them.
Nevertheless, they had only secondary effects on the movement. This was because of their short duration and purpose.
The purpose, to right an ancient wrong, did not include the
development of an indigenous movement without which change
is ephemeral. But among secondary effects that were important were two: first of all, the Rides attracted about four
hundred persons, many of them active in the older pacifist-
oriented groups such as C. O. R. E. and F. O. R. Through the
Rides these people were forged into a common community
with the emerging New Left. Such a community simply could
not have emerged through the usual process of older radicals

serving as speakers at youth conventions of young radicals.
From the beginning of the sixties, only those who had participated in direct action projects now were considered as truly
committed to freedom.

Another important secondary effect was that young
radicals active in old left youth organizations, who did not
wish to invest a major portion of their time in the South,
joined the Rides.   They brought into the movement an intellectual radical critique that complemented the existential one
that was already beginning to emerge from the experiences
of the S. N. C. C. workers.   Thomas Kahn was one such
Rider.   He was at that time a student at Howard University
and a member of the executive board of the Young People's
Socialist League.

In reflecting on "The Political Significance of the
Freedom Rides" in an address given at the S. D. S. Conference
on Race and Politics at the University of North Carolina, in
1962, Kahn warns that the Kennedy Administration is more
dangerous to the movement than the Eisenhower Administration had been.   The Administration, he says, keeps telling
the movement that the most important goal is voter registration rather than direct action.   Kahn asks

> But what motivates this new interest in Negro suf-
> frage?   Certainly, foreign policy factors figure.
> The cold war integrationists are growing in influence.
> But, more than anything else, the Kennedy policy
> represents an attempt to capture the civil rights
> movement for the Democratic Party.   In itself,
> there is nothing wrong with this.   If our movement
> could become integrated into a national political
> party that genuinely had our interests at heart, then
> we could rejoice that we had found a political vehi-
> cle that would make our movement more powerful.
> But the Administration seeks to absorb us into the
> Democratic party without fundamentally changing the
> bastard character of that party [Kahn, 1962, pp63,
> 64]. *

Kahn points out that Bob Moses was already denouncing the
fact that Justice Department voting suits were aimed at areas

*Excerpts from The New Student Left, edited by Mitchell Co-
hen and Dennis Hale.   Copyright © 1966, 1967 by the Activist
Publishing Company.   Reprinted by permission of Beacon Press.

where blacks were a minority rather than a majority.   The
increase of black votes is not meant to grant black power
in local, state or national elections, but to offset the Goldwater defections by the gaining of a proportionate, but non-
threatening amount, of black votes.   The Kennedy Administration refers to such actions, in the words of Schlesinger, as
moving "to incorporate the Negro revolution into the democratic coalition and thereby help it serve the future of American freedom" (Schlesinger, 1965, p977).   Kahn is convinced
that the task of students is to consider themselves the radical
wing of the civil rights movement.   Students free of vested
interests, family obligations and economic ties, can speak
against fruitless compromises and continue to experiment with
new direct action techniques.   Secondly, Kahn argues that
students must give the movement its ideology.   That means
basically a new political alignment, a national political party
that has no vested interest in the political, economic, and
social subjugation of black people (ibid. , pp66-68).

The radically different contexts of established and
sectarian forms were becoming more apparent.   The established type moved to include blacks in registration procedures
where opposition was not as great.   The purpose was to set
precedent and to establish that some movement was being
made--in short, to do the possible.   It was a compromise
characteristic of the established type: to hold within the
power of the ruling class all the conflict--both Dixiecrats
threatening to revolt and blacks already in the streets.   But
those same actions, viewed from the perspective of the sectarian form, were simply treacherous.   They meant to co-opt
the movement.   They intended to pervert the powerful purifying thrust of the New Left to established type purposes.   The
experience of this double threat: a physical danger from the
regional established form and an attempt to capture both body
and soul by the established type hardened the sectarians
against both.   Bob Moses, in speaking of the possibility that
the murderers of Schwerner, Goodman and Chaney would be
convicted, said:

> For them to be convicted would be for society to
> condemn itself and that's very hard for society to
> do, any society.   Condemnation seems to have to
> come from outside or from the ranks within that
> are not part of it. ...   And the problem seems to
> me to be, how can a society condemn itself?   I
> think that that question is a question for the country
> in this sense.   The country refuses to look at

>Mississippi, and at the white people down there,
>as like them. So, therefore, they miss the main
>point, it seems to me, about the Deep South and
>about the people there and also about ourselves
>[Moses, 1965, pp121, 122].

James Baldwin deals with another facet of this rejection of the established type in an article in the New York
Times Magazine of March 12, 1961. Baldwin discusses the
riot by blacks at the United Nations, a disturbance triggered
by the murder of Patrice Lumumba. The suggestion that
those who rioted were all Communists is amazing to Baldwin.
A minimum of observation--that of walking through Harlem--
ought to be enough to convince anyone of the injustice that
the black suffers. But if one does not want to walk through
Harlem, he need only consider two basic moods amongst
blacks:

>At one end of the pole is the Negro student move-
>ment. The people who make up this movement
>really believe in the America of "liberty and justice
>for all." They really believe that the country is
>anxious to become what it claims to be.... The
>movement does not have as its goal the consump-
>tion of overcooked hamburgers and tasteless coffee
>at various sleazy lunch counters.... The goal of
>the student movement is nothing less than the
>liberation of the entire country from its most crip-
>pling attitudes and habits [Baldwin, 1961, p25].

The student movement therefore exercises an act of
faith to see beneath the cruelty and apathy of America a
decent, baffled and agonized soul.

But another movement, the Nation of Islam, represents
the other pole. Islam draws its vision from what is seen in
daily behavior. More and more blacks, not being Muslims,
are nonetheless convinced by the plain evidence, and are not
at all sure they wish to be integrated "into a burning
house."

>"I might," says another, "consider being integrated
>into something else, an American society more real
>and more honest--but this? No, thank you, man,
>who needs it? And this searching disaffection has
>everything to do with the emergence of Africa:
>At the rate things are going here, all of Africa

> will be free before we can get a lousy cup of
> coffee" [ibid. , p103].

Here again is the concern for "freedom" that is more than
just civil rights, but includes a personal content that relates
to one's deepest hopes and desires.   Here also is the growing
conviction that the established society--in Baldwin's examples
the established white society--is lacking the essential personal
element of freedom.   Thus even as some minor political reforms are made the concept of freedom acquires a broader
connotation which accelerates the widening gap between contexts.

The March on Washington in the summer of 1963 was
the largest demonstration of the civil rights movement.   The
March was headed by Randolph.   The Organizing Committee
was composed of Wilkins, King, Farmer, Young and Lewis
of S. N. C. C.   Bayard Rustin was chief of staff and the organizer of the March.   The four white members of the committee
were Matthew Ahmann of the National Catholic Conference for
Interracial Justice, Eugene Carson Blake of the N. C. C.,
Joachim Prinz of the American Jewish Congress, and Walter
Reuther of the U. A. W.   Farmer was in jail and did not
participate in the March.   The speeches of King and Lewis
represented the growing tensions among sectarians to which
Baldwin had pointed.   King still believed that beneath the
surface America wanted to be the home of true freedom.
The sectarianism of King remained a tolerant sectarianism.
His sectarianism fervently demanded radical change, but
King was convinced that a just society was an expression of
the true America.   Lewis was becoming more and more
estranged from the established type, in both its national and
regional manifestations.   He was convinced by events that
the true America was displaying itself in the cruelty system
of racism.   For Lewis, the conviction was growing that
perhaps the true America was not just.

King begins his address by reminding his listeners
that when the Founding Fathers wrote the Constitution and
the Declaration of Independence, they were "signing a
promissory note to which every American would fall heir. "
This note is the guarantee of unalienable rights: life, liberty
and the pursuit of happiness.   Although America has de-
faulted on this obligation and given Negroes a bad check,
King refuses to accept it.

> ... we refuse to believe that the bank of justice,
> is bankrupt.   We refuse to believe that there are

insufficient funds in the great vaults of opportunity
of this nation. So we have come to cash this
check--a check that will give us upon demand the
riches of freedom and the security of justice. We
have also come to this hallowed spot to remind
America of the fierce urgency of now [King, 1963,
p348].

King urges that blacks, in the midst of suffering, not despair
into violence, for

I say to you today, my friends, that in spite of the
difficulties and frustrations of the moment I still
have a dream. It is a dream deeply rooted in the
American dream. I have a dream that one day
this nation will rise up and live out the true meaning of its creed: "We hold these truths to be self-
evident; that all men are created equal" [ibid.,
p348].

King applies his dream to the red hills of Georgia and the
injustice of Mississippi, to his own children and the governor
of Alabama. The discords of the nation will be transformed,
he is certain, into the symphony of brotherhood.

This will be the day when all of God's children
will be able to sing with new meaning "My country
'tis of thee, sweet land of liberty, of thee I sing.
Land where my fathers died, land of the pilgrim's
pride, from every mountainside, let freedom ring!
And if America is to be a great nation this must
become true [until] all of God's children, black
men and white men, Jews and Gentile, Protestants
and Catholics, will be able to join hands and sing
in the words of the old Negro spiritual, "Free at
last! Free at last! Thank God Almighty, we are
free at last!" [ibid., pp350-351].

King's speech was one of the most eloquent of black
sectarian appeals to renew America according to the ideals
of the Founding Fathers. The speech was also a passionate
reaffirmation of the solidarity of the poor blacks of America
and an expression of their determination to enter upon ever
new actions to demonstrate their commitment to freedom.
Yet the most distinctive note is King's confidence that man
can be and at a deep, real level wants to be, brother to
man. There is in King not only the sectarian denial of

worldly goods and achievements as determining the worth of
man, but a mystic and almost saintly faith that men are ultimately lovers one of the other. In this faith King transcended both sectarian and established forms of the civil
religion. This is not to say that King was not a sectarian
of the civil religion. He was certainly almost a classic
case, amply fulfilling each of Troeltsch's categories. But
at the one point where other sectarians stressed the brotherhood of the poor and oppressed, King, believing that, yet
also continually affirmed his faith in all men. In spite of
radically different circumstances, King believes all men are
brothers one to the other.

Lewis was not so sure. He begins his speech with
an attack on the Administration's Civil Rights Bill as being
too little and too late. The Bill does nothing to protect
young children and old women from police dogs and fire
hoses, nor anything to provide for the homeless and starving
of the nation. The reason why is obvious: cheap political
leaders are still allying themselves with open forms of exploitation and oppression. The Federal Government is
amongst them. How then will the revolution succeed?

> We cannot depend on any political party, for both
> the Democrats and the Republicans have betrayed
> the basic principles of the Declaration of Independ-
> ence. We all recognize the fact that if any radical
> social, political, and economic changes are to take
> place in our society, the people, the masses must
> bring them about. ... The next time we march
> through the South, through the Heart of Dixie, the
> way Sherman did. We will make the action of the
> past few months look petty. And I say to you,
> WAKE UP AMERICA! ... The black masses in
> the Delta of Mississippi, in Southwest Georgia,
> Alabama, Harlem, Chicago, Detroit, Philadelphia
> and all over this nation are on the march [Lewis,
> 1963, pp376-377].

The vision of the black masses on the march to establish the
basic principles of the Declaration of Independence--which
will require radical social, political and economic change--
is not a vision which suggests that the speaker has confidence
in the ability of all men to be brothers one to the other.
He is confident, however, that sectarians have the ability,
to be brothers to all men.

> In the struggle we must seek more than mere civil
> rights; we must work for the community of love,
> peace and true brotherhood. Our minds, souls and
> hearts cannot rest until freedom and justice exist
> for all the people [ibid.].

Once again the lifestyle issue emerges. But more
importantly, here is the fervent faith that where the established type has failed to create justice and freedom for all
the people, the sectarian will be able to succeed. The suggestion that the image of the black masses on the march
through the South à la Sherman does not engender visions of
the community of love, peace and true brotherhood is dismissed. At present there must be bitter conflict with the
established type until the rightful power returns to the people.
Once the enemy is defeated, then the people will establish
true justice. The implication is that the enemy will then be
converted to the true understanding of brotherhood, and thus
become part of the people. In later years, when revolutionary
rhetoric became more explicit, the corollary is fearlessly
spelled out: he who will not convert will be destroyed.

King and Lewis represent the two moods of the movement that Baldwin characterized with the early civil rights
movement and the Nation of Islam. On the one hand, there
is the feeling that although there are established and sectarian types, Americans are still bound together in the American civil religion. Beneath all the forms of conflict the
basic ties which bind man to man, citizen to citizen in the
great land are yet unsundered. This faith was justified by
the opening drama in Greensboro. On the other hand, there
is a belief that even the best of the established type have
ultimately betrayed their brothers. Establishmentarians have
exchanged their birthright of brotherhood and freedom for the
cheap pottage of political, social and economic advantage.
They have cut the ties which bind man to man, brother to
brother. Each day Mississippi provided ample evidence for
this view. Oppression will end, sectarians like Lewis believe,
only when the people seize power, for only amongst "the
people" (read sectarians), does the ancient human bond still
avail. It is toward the pole represented by Lewis, rather
than that represented by King, that those active in the movement began to gravitate, even though public opinion polls
demonstrated that King was the most widely recognized and
respected of movement leaders amongst the black population
of America. This gravitation of those active in the movement toward a more radical stance stemmed from their daily

experiences with a brutal, racist social structure and their
inability to significantly alter that structure. Such failures
transform an initial hope into a deepening sense of desperation, and from desperation arises an ever more radical and
revolutionary consciousness [Debray, 1967].

Lewis is therefore also representative of the sectarians
that were beginning to stress the secular eschatology of the
movement. King still couched his eschatology in Biblical
images:

> I have a dream that one day every valley shall be
> exalted, every hill and mountain shall be made
> low, the rough places will be made plain, and the
> crooked places will be made straight, and the
> glory of the Lord shall be revealed, and all flesh
> shall see it together [King, 1963, p350].

Lewis spoke in terms of the black masses marching
and of the coming day of revolution. But obviously the black
masses were not marching; the crowd, with whites, at the
Washington March was still but the few. Fewer still were
those called to the task of S. N. C. C. worker in the fear and
brutality of the South. Troeltsch points out that this manner
of acting and speaking is characteristic of the sect:

> The sect, therefore, does not educate nations in
> the mass, but it gathers a select group of the
> elect, and places it in sharp opposition to the
> world. In so far as the sect type maintains Chris-
> tian universalism at all, like the Gospel, the only
> form it knows is that of eschatology [Troeltsch,
> 1960, p339].

To speak of the day of the black masses marching and of the
coming day of love, peace and true brotherhood was to articulate the universalism of the sectarian type of the civil religion. The established type looked to the mission of America
in the world. The sectarians came more and more to express universalism eschatologically.

By 1963 the movement was in fact becoming more and
more aware of itself as a band of the elect. The movement
had begun as a group of students, most of whom were religious, middle class reformers, seeking their rights. When
S. N. C. C. was formed the documents appealed to were the
Bill of Rights, the 13th, 14th and 15th Amendments, and the

Holy Bible. But by 1962 and 1963 another S. N. C. C. emerged.
These young people had moved into the communities of the
South and had become a nonviolent guerilla army, but one
which still believed America would honor its pledge of equality. By late 1963 and 1964, that faith was gone, replaced by
trust in the poor and oppressed, the underclass, as bringers
of the new day. The keynote words of this S. N. C. C. were
"freedom," "community" and "participatory democracy."
Martin Luther King had written his "Letter from a Birmingham Jail" expressing his disappointment in white liberals.
Over 80,000 blacks had voted in Mississippi's Freedom Ballot
in November 1963 for a black governor, but still they were
not registered to vote for the real governor. Over 700 vol-
unteers had joined S. N. C. C. and the Council of Federated
Organizations for a massive registration drive in Mississippi,
and three of them had been murdered.

From the Freedom Ballot of 1963 came the idea to
have a Freedom registration, establish a Freedom Democratic
Party, and meet in State Convention. Delegates would be sent
to the Democratic National Convention in Atlantic City to
challenge the white Mississippi delegation, which was elected
by racist regulations. The delegates were duly chosen, challenged the regular delegation at Atlantic City and were defeated in the Credentials Committee through the intervention
of L. B. J. The M. F. D. P. was offered a compromise of two
seats at large. King, Rustin and Farmer joined with white
liberals such as Humphrey, Rauh and Reuther to urge acceptance of the weak compromise. But S. N. C. C. workers,
the most numerous in Mississippi and the most numerous in
the delegation itself, were opposed to tokenism. They had
virtually risked their lives for the convention seats, and so
were adamant. After staging a sit-in in their rightful seats
in the convention, they departed to challenge the seating of
the representatives in the Congress. Again, the intense opposition of the Administration, even after the election, resulted in Congress refusing the appeal. S. N. C. C. was further
convinced that collaboration with the established type was
hopeless.

The Selma demonstrations in February and March
were the last attempt of S. N. C. C. to collaborate with the
established type. Significantly, Selma also marked the determination of King to violate a Federal Court order for the
first time, and thus to move away from a collaborationist
stance. With the passage of the Civil Rights Act of 1965,
which coincided closely with the Watts riots, much sympathy

within the established ranks for the Movement dissipated.   At
the same time, all civil rights organizations were receiving
pressure from below to speak out against the war in Vietnam.
Roy Wilkins of the N. A. A. C. P. and Whitney Young of the
Urban League easily resisted such pressures, and refused to
take a stand.   James Farmer of C. O. R. E. finally succeeded
in persuading C. O. R. E. to be silent.   S. N. C. C. workers,
however, were already distributing anti-war leaflets when
S. C. L. C. and King began to raise certain basic questions
about the direction of American policy.

> Why are there forty million poor people in a nation
> overflowing with such unbelievable affluence?   Why
> has our nation placed itself in the position of being
> God's military agent on earth, and intervened reck-
> lessly in Vietnam and the Dominican Republic?
> Why have we substituted the arrogant undertaking
> of policing the whole world for the high task of
> putting our own house in order? ... There is a
> need for a radical restructuring of the architecture
> of American society ... America must re-examine
> old presuppositions and release itself from many
> things that for centuries have been held sacred.
> For the evils of racism, poverty and militarism
> to die, a new set of values must be born [King,
> 1967, p133]. *

S. N. C. C. and S. C. L. C. scarcely were in harmony concerning
tactics, but they both clearly were sectarians.   S. C. L. C.
sought to extend its work into the North, and to focus on the
issues of poverty, education and housing.   The N. A. A. C. P. ,
the Urban League and C. O. R. E. had been so long dependent
on established type support that they felt unable to speak on
the issue of the war.   They found themselves part of the
Democratic coalition.   Some, such as Bayard Rustin, even
argued that they ought to be.   Thus once again these groups
were taken for granted by liberal politicians.   They had re-
entered that no-man's land in which Troeltsch had placed the
Evangleisch-soziale Kongress, whose supporters wanted the
social order to reflect a free Christian spirit.   Troeltsch
noted

---

*Excerpts from Where Do We Go from Here: Chaos or Com-
munity? by Martin Luther King, Jr.   Copyright © 1967 by
Martin Luther King, Jr.   Reprinted by permission of Harper
& Row, Publishers, Inc.

There is, however, no organized community in
existence which embodies this "spirit"; in reality
this spirit is always first of all produced by a
church or a sect, and it is only when it has
severed its connection with both these forms of
religious life that it becomes simply the "spirit"
of Christianity, which is a free principle, quite
subjective in character, which, in the absence of
any sociological basis of its own, finds it difficult
to do anything effective in social reform
[Troeltsch, 1960, p445].

In the history of Christianity, Troeltsch believed, no
group had been able to obtain the ethical radicalism of the
Gospel without entering upon the narrowness of the sect.
Likewise, for the major civil rights organizations there was
no hope of championing a radical reconstruction of American
society and yet at the same time maintaining broad contacts
and sympathies with the established type, especially as represented by the Administration. Without the discipline and support that the sect provided, groups found it difficult to do
much to refashion society. The sectarians had become aware
that it was not merely a question of persuading the larger
society to honor in action the values it professed, but that a
new set of values must be brought to birth. The movement
meant to father those new values. Thus the period of protest and reform merged into the time of radicalization and
resistance. White radicals were invited out of the black
movement even as their attention was being attracted by the
resistance and student movements on the campus. The black
movement became more and more a class movement, focusing
on the questions of poverty and power, while the white movement became more an anarchist movement, opposing present
values in the name of the new society that was to be.

THE CIVIL RELIGION AND
WAR: 1960-1965

The Established Type of the
Civil Religion

The Expression of the Established
Type of the Civil Religion in the
Administration of the Federal
Government

In an address in Washington on Independence Day,
1821, John Quincy Adams expressed his conviction that the

American faith was to be carried abroad only by the force of
example.   Force of arms was to be eschewed.

> Wherever the standard of freedom and independence
> has been or shall be unfurled, there will be Ameri-
> ca's heart, her benedictions, and her prayers.
> But she goes not abroad in search of monsters to
> destroy.   She is the well-wisher to the freedom
> and independence of all.   She is the champion and
> vindicator only of her own.   She will recommend
> the general cause by the countenance of her voice,
> and by the benignant sympathy of her example.
> She well knows that by once enlisting under other
> banners than her own, were they even the banners
> of foreign independence, she would involve herself
> beyond the power of extrication, in all the wars of
> interest and intrigue, of individual avarice, envy
> and ambition, which assume the colors and usurp
> the standards of freedom.   The fundamental maxims
> of her policy would insensibly change from liberty
> to force. . . .   She might become the dictatress of
> the world.   She would no longer be ruler of her
> own spirit [Steel, 1967, pxi].

This conviction was eroded in the nineteenth and
twentieth centuries.   The Mexican-American, the Spanish-
American, and the World Wars were understood by the established type to be for the purpose of making the world or the
nation safe for democracy.   The Monroe Doctrine and in-
numerable interventions by force of arms in the affairs of
Latin American states further undermined Adam's position.
Still, the exemplary understanding of the mission of America
played a major role in foreign policy until the dawn of the
cold war.   John Kennedy, in rhetoric far more eloquent than
Truman or Eisenhower, emphatically reversed Adams' understanding of the role of America in the world.   For Kennedy,
America was to be the champion and vindicator, not only of
her own liberty, but of liberty around the world.   America
was to bear this burden regardless of those costs which
convinced Adams that the price of such adventures would be
far too dear.

In his Inaugural Address, Kennedy bids his hearers
to remember their heritage, and then declares

> Let the word go forth from this time and place, to
> friend and foe alike, that the torch has been passed

to a new generation of Americans, born in this
century, tempered by war, disciplined by a hard
and bitter peace, proud of our ancient heritage,
and unwilling to witness or permit the slow undoing
of those human rights to which this nation has always been committed, and to which we are committed today at home and around the world.
Let every nation know, whether it wishes us well
or ill, that we shall pay any price, bear any burden, meet any hardship, support any friend, oppose any foe to assure the survival and success of
liberty [Kennedy, 1962, p7].

Sorensen, Kennedy's chief speechwriter, tells us that
Kennedy spent more time personally drafting and redrafting
this speech than any other.   Originally his opening phrase
was to be, "We celebrate today ... the sacrament of
democracy."   He then wished to concentrate on foreign policy.
But Kennedy was sensitive to the criticism that his emphasis
on foreign affairs might be understood as evasion on civil
rights.   Therefore, Sorensen says, at the last minute Kennedy
added the phrase, "at home, and around the world" (Sorensen, 1965, pp241-243).

Sorensen's comments underline the contrast between
Kennedy and Adams.   It is only as an afterthought that
Kennedy remembers, as he celebrates the sacrament of
democracy, to mention that America will be the champion of
the freedom of her own.   Kennedy was convinced, against
much of the American heritage, that America's raison
d'être is to pay "any price, bear any burden" to ensure the
success of liberty, not merely its survival, first around the
world, then at home.   The reason for Kennedy's opposition
to the American heritage as represented by Adams is two-
fold.   First, Kennedy's whole political career is set in the
context of the cold war.   Second, there is Kennedy's own
predilection for seeing 1960 as a crisis time for the Republic
like the crisis of 1860.   Thus special emphasis is placed on
the traditional American themes of courage and activism.

In the long history of the world, only a few generations have been granted the role of defending freedom in its hour of maximum danger.   I do not
shrink from this responsibility; I welcome it....
The energy, the faith, the devotion which we bring
to this endeavor will light our country and all who
serve it, and the glow from that fire can truly
light the world [Kennedy, 1962, p10].

But certainly most influential is the pervasiveness of the cold war form of the American civil religion. As was argued above (Chapter II), the conflict of perspectives, universalism versus sphere-of-influence, had given the established type of the American civil religion a concrete evil against which to define itself: Communism. Sorensen is convinced that in his Inaugural Address Kennedy had escaped the narrow confines of cold war rhetoric. If such be the case, Kennedy did not escape to a new perspective. Rather he escalated the expression of the mission of America as a crusade against Communism from the pedantic to the poetic. Not until nearly a year after the Cuban missile crisis, on June 10, 1963, did Kennedy seriously publicly consider a re-examination of the attitude of the United States toward the Soviet Union.

The events leading up to this change of heart were indeed perilous. Not least among the perils was the widening gap between the meaning of world events as viewed by the American government and the meaning of those same events as seen from the perspective of the governments of Russia and China.

In his State of the Union address, Kennedy looks at the issues of the economy, education, ecology and civil rights. He then warns

> But all these problems pale when placed beside those which confront us around the world. No man entering upon this office, regardless of his party, regardless of his previous service in Washington, could fail to be staggered upon learning, even in this brief ten-day period, the harsh enormity of the trials through which we must pass in the next four years. Each day the crises multiply. Each day their solution grows more difficult. Each day we draw nearer the hour of maximum danger, as weapons spread and hostile forces grow stronger. I feel ... the tide of events has been running out and time has not been our friend [ibid., p23].

J. F. K. enumerates Asia, Africa, Latin America, Cuba and Europe as problem areas which offer ample evidence that neither Russia nor China have "yielded its ambitions for world domination, ambitions which they forcefully restated only a short time ago" (ibid., p24). To meet this political challenge, Kennedy asks for a dramatic increase in the military budget, which Eisenhower had established, in order to

provide greater airlift, Polaris, and hard missile capability.
Concurrently, he suggests diplomatic moves he made to curb
the arms race.

Kennedy's perceptions of a deepening crisis were
paralleled by his actions. He approved the invasion of Cuba,
which resulted in the Bay of Pigs debacle. Kennedy did not
apologize for the action. Three days later, on April 20,
1961, in a speech to the American Society of Newspaper Editors, J. F. K. reiterated his interpretation of the Monroe
Doctrine.

> Any unilateral American intervention, in the absence
> of an external attack upon ourselves or an ally,
> would have been contrary to our traditions and to
> our international obligations. But let the record
> show that our restraint is not inexhaustible. Should
> it ever appear that the inter-American doctrine of
> non-interference merely conceals or excuses a
> policy of nonaction, if the nations of this hemisphere
> should fail to meet their commitments against out-
> side Communist penetration, then I want it clearly
> understood that this government will not hesitate in
> meeting its primary obligations which are to the
> security of our nation [ibid. , p44].

The threat was not an idle one. The U. S. had just interfered
in the internal affairs of a Latin American nation because it
disapproved its form of government. In 1965, the Marines,
rather than a ragged group of civilians, would succeed in
seizing power in a Caribbean nation.

The following week, speaking to the newspaper
publishers, J. F. K. declared that no war ever posed a greater
threat to the security of the U. S. than the cold war. Therefore newspapers ought to forego the "privileged rights of the
First Amendment"--free speech and a free press--for the
sake of national security. He urged the press of America
recommend to the Administration specific steps by which news
could be voluntarily managed by a joint effort of government
and publishers. J. F. K. concluded

> Perhaps there will be no recommendations. Per-
> haps there is no answer to the dilemma faced by a
> free and open society in a cold and secret war.
> In times of peace, any discussion of this subject,
> and any action that results, are both painful and

without precedent.   But this is a time of peace and
peril which knows no precedent in history [Kennedy,
1961, pp334ff].

Kennedy had approved invasion of a sovereign nation,
and, incensed at the unfavorable press reaction, recommended
restriction of free speech.   Yet the cold war perspective was
such that nearly eighty percent of the American public agreed
with Kennedy's strong statements.   Many thought even more
forceful action ought to have been taken against Cuba.   Demonstrations against the Administration's policy toward Cuba
did, however, break out on the campuses.   The students
formed the Fair Play for Cuba Committee.   As it became
apparent that the Administration had deceived the nation about
the role played by the U. S. Government in the invasion,
visits to Cuba began and were accelerated as travel was banned
and information concerning Cuba suppressed (Teodori, 1969,
p22).

But more important than what Kennedy said about
Cuba was the context into which he set the specifics of that
situation.   It was the universalist cold war context.   First,
J. F. K. said, the defeat in Cuba demonstrated the forces of
Communism were on the rise throughout the world.   Therefore the peril to freedom was escalating.   Second, the issue
of the survival of freedom in the western hemisphere was
now at stake.   On this issue, J. F. K. felt, there could be
no middle ground.   Those nations of this hemisphere which
did not join the U. S. crusade against Communism were to be
considered enemies.   Third, the U. S. faces a relentless
struggle, a cruel oppression and a reign of terror in every
corner of the globe.

We dare not fail to grasp the new concepts, the
new tools, the new sense of urgency we will need
to combat it--whether in Cuba or South Vietnam....
The message of Cuba, of Laos, of the rising din of
Communist voices in Asia and Latin America--these
messages are all the same.   The complacent, the
self-indulgent, the soft societies are about to be
swept away with debris of history.   Only the strong,
only the industrious, only the determined, only the
courageous, only the visionary who determine the
real nature of our struggle can possibly survive.
No greater task faces this country or this administration.   No other challenge is more deserving of
our every effort and energy [Kennedy, 1962, pp45-
47].

Obviously Kennedy continued to direct his efforts along the mainstream channeled by the established form of the civil religion. Basic to the postwar established type was the longing for universal meaning for the nation. The American mission was to see democracy and free enterprise be included in the basic political and economic decisions everywhere in the world--and emerge triumphant. In the sixties, however, beginning with Kennedy and continuing with Johnson, truth--the doctrine that it is the mission of the United States to lead others toward a future state of freedom and liberty as yet unknown--was ever more objectified. Incomprehensible amounts of military power were brought into play to force acceptance of a freely chosen democratic polity. Irony compounded irony. Kennedy, the liberal senator, forgot the maxim of the conservative George Marshall, that political problems, if thought about in military terms, become military problems. Kennedy proclaimed that the nation was engaged in a new type of war. Meanwhile, he continued to gird the nation for the old type of war. He requested greater military budgets not only in the State of the Union address, but also in special messages to the Congress in March and again in May of that year. In the May speech he urged the nation to recognize the validity of the concept of civil defense fall-out shelters. With this as preparation, Kennedy went to Vienna to meet Khrushchev in June. Khrushchev demanded talks leading to the signing of a German peace treaty and the legalization of West Berlin as a free city. Kennedy refused, certain that the guarantees of a free city would prove empty. Although Henry Kissinger and Schlesinger--who were being pressed in informal conversations with the Russians for guarantees that the U. S. would consider acceptable--urged more aggressive diplomatic action, J. F. K. turned again to military preparations. On July 25, in a report to the nation on the Berlin crisis, he announced a call-up of the reserve, a tripling of draft calls, and three billions more dollars for the defense budget. He also urged a large appropriation for civil defense, for

> In the event of an attack, the lives of those families which are not hit in a nuclear blast and fire can still be saved--if they can be warned to take shelter and if that shelter is available. . . . In the coming months, I hope to let every citizen know what steps he can take without delay to protect his family in case of attack. I know that you will want to do no less [ibid., pp67-68; 184-198].

A new bomb shelter industry sprang up, and with it both civil defense drills and protests. The Berlin wall was constructed in August. The Soviet Union began preparations for renewed nuclear testing in the atmosphere, and the tests took place in November. The U. S. felt compelled to respond, and preparation began for a series of tests which took place the following April. Kennedy agreed to begin talks concerning the German problem in September. Schlesinger felt that Khrushchev had gained his minimum objective by the wall, which was to end the flight of trained workers to the West. He concluded

> There were many ways to initiate a dialogue; and in the end the substance of negotiations turned out to matter a good deal less than the willingness to negotiate.... While inconclusive talks began, ... Khrushchev took the occasion to report ... "the western powers were showing some understanding of the situation, and were inclined to seek a solution to the German problem and the issue of West Berlin." ... The crisis was suddenly over [Schlesinger, 1965, p400].

Since the willingness to negotiate, not the substance of agreements was at issue, the crisis could have been entirely avoided if Kennedy had said in Vienna in early June what he said in Washington in late August. But courage is a more important virtue in the American experience than caution, compromise or wisdom. To Kennedy, immediate negotiation suggested lack of courage.

The Cuban missile crisis continued the classic Kennedy moves: first, the marshalling of maximum military power, both nuclear and conventional; second, the issuance of grave warnings of crisis to the American people and of threat to the Russian government; third, the solution of the problem by diplomatic agreements which were possible at the outset of the incident. According to Robert Kennedy, the tenets of the American civil religion restricted the immediate use of massive military power. (At the same time, the traits of activism and courage encouraged the moves that engendered the crisis.) Former Secretary of State Dean Acheson, famed for his "hard" stance against negotiating with the Communists, had been asked by President Kennedy to join his group of advisors seeking to formulate policy toward Cuba. He set his diplomacy in a military context: first an air attack, then an invasion. This he felt, was the only action which could protect the security of the United States.

Robert Kennedy writes

> With some trepidation, I argued that, whatever
> validity the military and political arguments were
> for an attack in preference to a blockade, America's
> traditions and history would not permit such a
> course of action. Whatever military reasons he and
> others could marshal, they were nevertheless, in
> the last analysis, advocating a surprise attack by a
> very large nation against a very small one. This,
> I said, could not be undertaken by the U.S. if we
> were to maintain our moral position at home and
> around the globe. Our struggle against Communism
> throughout the world was far more than physical
> survival--it had as its essence our heritage and our
> ideals, and these we must not destroy. We spent
> more time on this moral question during the first
> five days than on any other single matter [Kennedy,
> 1969, pp16, 17].

The attack and invasion were ultimately ruled out.
Nevertheless, the deliberations of the President and his advisors centered almost wholly on the choice of the military
means which would force the resolution of the issue in terms
favorable to America, and yet be consonant with our heritage
and ideals. The discussion apparently ignored the statement
of Cuban President Osvaldo Dorticos to the U.N. on October
8, a week before the U-2 cameras confirmed the missile
sites. Dorticos declared that Cuba now had means to defend
herself, her "inevitable weapons," and that therefore negotiations were in order. He suggested that

> ... were the United States able to give up proof,
> by word and deed, that it would not carry out ag-
> gression against our country, then, we declare
> solemnly before you here and now, our weapons
> would be unnecessary and our army redundant. We
> believe ourselves able to create peace [Walton,
> 1972, pp114-115].

Dorticos' suggestion was the basis of the agreement, with the
additional informal quid pro quo removal of U.S. missiles
from Turkey and Greece. But such flexibility did not appear
until the situation had reached the grimness evidenced by
Khrushchev's cable to Kennedy.

... Mr. President, we and you ought not to pull on
the ends of the rope in which you have tied the knot
of war, because the more the two of us pull, the
tighter the knot will be tied. And a moment may
come when that knot will be tied so tight that even
he who tied it will not have the strength to untie it,
and then it will be necessary to cut that knot, and
what that would mean is not for me to explain to
you, because you yourself understand perfectly of
what terrible forces our countries dispose [Ken-
nedy, 1969, pp67-68].

Thus John Kennedy brought the U. S. closer to a
nuclear exchange than had any President before him. For-
tunately, in the depth of the crisis, he turned back and
availed himself of the previously existing diplomatic option.
Irony did not become ultimate tragedy: the bearing of the
burden of the extinction of the nation in order to ensure the
survival and success of liberty. But the doctrine that it is
the mission of America to lead others toward freedom and
liberty had reached a new intensity under Kennedy. The mission of America, not the people of America, had come to be
his guiding image. He imagined the purpose of America was
to extend to the world that freedom which Divine Providence
had so graciously established on these shores.

The established form of religion, as Troeltsch sees it,
always seeks to make the truth objective, i. e., to bring its truth
to expression in social and political structures. (Troeltsch,
1960, p 338) Kennedy was certain that the energy, faith and devotion that was committed to the service of the mission of America
would rescue peoples everywhere from the evils of communism.
But as Adams feared, when America went abroad in search of
monsters to destroy, the fundamental maxims of her policy
insensibly changed from liberty to force.

Other elements of the established type of the civil
religion than world domination are present in the Kennedy
approach to the cold war. There is the close connection with
the ruling class. A variety of upper class non-administration
people appear in an advisory role in crucial decisions. There is
a heightened desire to control great masses of men. This
is seen most of all in the increasing role that the Secretary
of Defense McNamara came to play in the government. Roger
Hilsman has pointed out how the great management skill of
McNamara soon enabled the Department of Defense to present
to the President clear-cut options for responding to nearly
every conceivable crisis. Defense soon overshadowed State

in influence, for the solutions Defense put forth were the essence of an energetic, courageous attempt to control unwieldy events (Hilsman, 1967). In contrast, the State Department moved in the murky ambiguous world of negotiation and compromise, a world by its nature unsusceptible to control, difficult to energize to swift action, and highly enamored of caution, rather than courage. There is the emphasis on hard work as evidence of modern virtue. But the striking aspect of the opening years of the Kennedy Administration is the increased emphasis on the mission of America and the attempt to make America's truth visible in political structures.

The dramatically increased draft calls, the major increases in the military budget, the abortive invasion of Cuba, the seemingly endless sense of nuclear doom which the Berlin and Cuban missile crises engendered, the aggravation of a renewed emphasis on the building of fall-out shelters, the repetitive civil defense drills and the renewal of nuclear testing all fueled the fire of the growing student movement. Central to the student dis-ease was the sense of being managed. The ascendancy of the technological skills of McNamara was not yet visible, but it was felt. The hope that the New Frontier, whose rhetoric and very name often suggested a new involvement of the individual in his destiny, would renew American life was dimmed. Instead, the conviction grew amongst dissenting students that the seemingly grandfatherly, bumbling Eisenhower had been replaced by a team of vigorous, active managers who paid only ritual worship at the altars of freedom. Meanwhile they were ever more efficiently displacing the power of the individual to make basic decisions concerning the direction of his life or the time of his death. Yet the response of a great number of reformist students to the Kennedy Administration was ambiguous. Thousands joined the Peace Corps and thousands more hoped the stirrings of new policy directions on civil rights would presage a true effort for peace.

In the Spring of 1963, J. F. K. determined to attempt a détente with the Soviet Union. He joined Macmillan in proposing new talks on a test ban treaty. Kennedy decided the U. S. would not be the first to resume nuclear testing once the current series was ended. He hoped to succeed in reaching beyond the cold war perspectives to a new emphasis on the peaceful and the positive in the relations of the U. S. and the U. S. S. R.

In a speech given at American University in June, Kennedy urges the American people to re-examine their attitude toward the Soviet Union. He quotes a Soviet text which severely distorts American aims and purposes. J. F. K. says that while it may be discouraging to think that Soviet leaders truly believe what their propagandists write,

> it is also a warning--a warning to the American
> people not to fall into the same trap as the Soviets,
> not to see only a distorted and desperate view of
> the other side, not to see conflict as inevitable,
> accommodation as impossible, and communication
> as nothing more than an exchange of threats. No
> government or social system is so evil that its
> people must be regarded as lacking in virtue. As
> Americans, we find Communism profoundly repug-
> nant as a negation of personal freedom and dignity.
> But we can still hail the Russian people for their
> many achievements--in science and space, in
> economic and industrial growth, in culture and in
> acts of courage.... And if we cannot end now our
> differences, at least we can help make the world
> safe for diversity. For, in the final analysis, our
> most basic common link is that we all inhabit this
> small planet. We all breathe the same air. We
> all cherish our children's future. And we are all
> mortal [Kennedy, 1963, pp459-464].

Kennedy specifically disavows a Pax Americana, arguing that we must now deal with the world as it is, not as it might have been had the history of the last eighteen years been different. He closes by announcing the U.S. renunciation of nuclear tests, and he appeals for a test ban treaty to formalize the end of all such tests. Khrushchev, talking with Averell Harriman during the Moscow test ban negotiations, called it the "best speech by any President since Roosevelt" (Sorensen, 1965, p. 733).

The speech was a major reversal of form. While Kennedy had from time to time suggested such points of view, they had previously been set into a rigid cold war context. The cold war actions of the U.S. suggested such musings were for domestic political purposes. At American University Kennedy accepted a world based, at least in the West, on spheres-of-influence. Therefore it was more im-portant to make the world safe for diversity than to make the world safe for democracy, for Russia perceived that latter attempt as a mortal threat. In this recognition by Kennedy of the way the world had in fact been structured was the characteristic move of the established type to come to terms with the existing order. The first compromise was then the acceptance of spheres of influence. The second compromise was to deny that Communism was the ultimate evil, and to affirm the common humanity of American and Russian. There is here a return to the ancient paths. America can trust her mission again to the wise hand of the Providence that guides her. Men ought not to seek to force the Kingdom, for it is also good that "a man should quietly wait for the salvation of the Lord." The character of the mission of America once again is to emphasize the exemplary rather than the evangelical task. For nearly two centuries the American experiment has been the great educator of the nations, and as Troeltsch said of the Church

> like all educators she knows how to allow for various degrees of capacity and maturity, and how to attain her end only by a process of adaptation and compromise [Troeltsch, 1960, p339].

Kennedy did not live long enough to allow history to judge whether his deeds would have harmonized with his words. But Kennedy clearly saw one place where opposing forces of freedom and totalitarianism were still locked in mortal combat--in the no-man's land between the spheres of influence. The name of that land for Kennedy, Johnson, Nixon and a countless host of established types was Vietnam. The top levels of the Kennedy Administration dealt only intermittently with the question of Vietnam during 1961, according to the Pentagon Papers. A thorough review was undertaken in the Fall. The Administration decided to provide combat support but to defer the question of combat troops. No new American decisions were made until the Buddhist unrest in the last half of 1961, and no major new military policies were approved until 1965 (Gravel, 1971, p. 18).

The Buddhist protest demonstrations were profoundly political as well as religious in nature. The protests resulted from the repression of Diem's regime. The U.S. could 1) choose to support Diem, 2) support the overthrow of Diem or 3) use the instability as a reason for disengagement.

The Pentagon Papers historian writes

> In making the choice to do nothing to prevent the coup [against Diem] and to tacitly support it, the U.S. inadvertently deepened its involvement. The

inadvertence is the key factor.   It was a situation
without good alternative....   And, by virtue of its
interference in internal Vietnamese affairs, the
U.S. had assumed a significant responsibility for
the regime, a responsibility which heightened our
commitment and deepened our involvement [ibid.,
p201].

But it was not as inadvertent as the historian suggests.
The support and encouragement of the coup was in accord
with the understanding of America's mission.   For if it is
Diem who stands between the present with its cruel tyranny
and the future with its hope of liberty, then Diem must be
removed.   America is not pledged to a government.   As
J. F. K. said in his Inaugural Address, America "struggles
against the common enemies of man: tyranny, poverty,
disease and war itself."   Governments dependent upon America must join that struggle or be replaced.

The last television interview of John Kennedy on
September 30, 1963, turned to the subject of Vietnam.

Mr. Cronkite: Hasn't every indication from
Saigon been that President Diem has no intention
of changing his pattern?
President Kennedy: If he does not change it, of
course, that is his decision....   Our best judgment is that he can't be successful on this basis.
We hope he comes to see that; but in the final
analysis it is the people and the Government itself
who have to win or lose this struggle....   We ...
made this effort to defend Europe.   Now Europe
is quite secure.   We also have to participate--we
may not like it--in the defense of Asia.
Mr. Brinkley: Mr. President, have you had any
reason to doubt this so-called domino theory, that
if South Vietnam falls, the rest of Southeast Asia
will go behind it?
The President: No, I believe it.   I believe it.
I think that the struggle is close enough.   China is
so large, looms so high just beyond the frontiers,
that if South Vietnam went, it would not only give
them an improved geographic position for a guerrilla assault on Malaya but would also give the im-
pression that the wave of the future in Southeast
Asia was China and the Communists.   So I believe
it [ibid., pp827-828].

John Kennedy had accepted the spheres of influence in
Europe as the reality to which the mission of America must
adjust itself.   However, he believed that the situation in Asia
was still fluid.   From a consistent spheres-of-influence perspective, Vietnam would be as surely within the historical
and geographical sphere of influence of China as Poland was
within the sphere of influence of Russia.   Apparently the
American University speech had been directed only to Russia
and Russian Communism, and the status quo of Europe.
Where the issue was still in doubt, the cold war understanding
of the mission of America still prevailed.   "Communism as
the ultimate evil" was rewritten to read "Chinese Communism
as the ultimate evil."

The Pentagon Papers do in fact represent the policy
of the United States toward Vietnam as remaining constant
during the Kennedy Administration.   Secretaries Rusk and
McNamara presented a major memorandum to the President
in November, 1961.   They stated:

> The loss of South Viet-Nam to Communism would
> involve the transfer of a nation of twenty million
> people from the free world to the Communist bloc.
> The loss of South Viet-nam would make pointless
> any further discussion about the importance of
> Southeast Asia to the free world; we would have to
> face the near certainty that the remainder of South-
> east Asia and Indonesia would move to a complete
> accommodation with Communism.   The loss of
> South Viet-nam to Communism would not only
> destroy SEATO but would undermine the credibility
> of American commitments elsewhere.   Further,
> loss of South Viet-nam would stimulate bitter
> domestic controversies in the United States, and
> would be seized upon by extreme elements to divide
> the country and harass the Administration [ibid.,
> pp110-111].

In October 1963, at the completion of their mission to Vietnam, McNamara and Taylor recommended that the Administration reaffirm its position that the security of South Vietnam
is vital to the security of the United States (Ibid., p. 753).
The Pentagon Papers demonstrate that there were conflicting
reports from the military and diplomatic missions in Saigon
as to whether the U. S. effort was succeeding.   Kennedy, according to the Papers, postponed major decisions that seemed
either irrevocable or immensely unpopular.   Thus the policy

remained constant.   The policy was first of all an expression
of the desire of the established form of the civil religion to
be universal--to see the United States participate in, if not
control, political, economic and social decisions everywhere
in the world.   But second, and nearly as importantly, the
policy was based on the faith that the ultimate purpose of
American action--the establishment of freedom and liberty--
would inevitably be fulfilled.

Lyndon Johnson described his policy in Vietnam in
relation to Kennedy's as "Steady on Course" (Lyndon Johnson, 1971, p43).   In the sense of continuing the commitment
to universalism as the expression of the mission of America,
Johnson's perception is quite correct.   But there was a definite change in emphasis.   Part of Kennedy's indecisiveness
in ordering further military aid could be traced to the conflicting reports from civilian and military missions in Vietnam.   The fact that many of the insurgents were Diem's own
people troubled Kennedy.   Johnson immediately resolved the
dilemma in favor of the military point of view.   Two days
after the assassination, he met with the principal architects
of the Vietnam policy.   The National Security Action Memorandum, subsequently issued, clearly specified that Vietnam was
a case of aggression, and thus the purpose of the American
involvement was to enable South Vietnam to defeat the ex-
ternally directed and supported communist insurgents.   All
U. S. policies were to be judged by the effectiveness of their
advancement of this central mission.

Johnson, in The Vantage Point, reminds his readers
that while a President seeks all the information he can gain
to aid him in decision making, central to the process of
problem resolution is experience and memory.   Johnson made
his decision concerning Vietnam out of the conviction that
courageous action had always been required for the defense
of freedom.   Lack of such courage had betrayed the world
into World War II.   Munich was the code word for faint-
heartedness.   L. B. J. also remembered the actions of the
American Congress in refusing to rearm in the late thirties
and early forties.   When war did break, courage bade Americans to man the ramparts of civilization.   F. D. R. proclaimed
to Congress

> Difficult choices may have to be made in the months
> to come.   We will not shrink from such decisions.
> We and those united with us will make those deci-
> sions with courage and determination. ...   The mili-
> tarists in Berlin and Tokyo started this war, but

> the massed, angered forces of common humanity
> will finish it. ... Our own objectives are clear:
> the objective of liberating the subjugated nations--
> the objective of establishing and securing freedom
> of speech, freedom of religion, freedom from want,
> and freedom from fear everywhere in the world
> [Roosevelt, 1942, pp26-30].

Johnson had strongly supported the Eisenhower foreign
policy.   The experience of John Foster Dulles was part of
the experience of Lyndon Johnson.   Dulles saw the history of
the years since 1917 as an endless struggle of freedom
against Communism.   Johnson recalls his own speech as a
young congressman in the heat of the legislative battle over
Truman's proposal to give economic and military aid to
Greece and Turkey.

> Decisions must be made in times of danger, and I
> hope your decision will be mine. ...   I pray we are
> still a young and courageous nation; that we have
> not grown so old and fat and prosperous that all
> we can think about is to sit back with our arms
> around our moneybags.   If we choose to do that,
> I have no doubt that the smoldering fires will burst
> into flame and consume us--dollars and all [John-
> son, 1971, p47].

The courage of which Johnson speaks and which he
demonstrates in his public actions seems much less personal
than the courage which animated the charismatic Kennedy.
For Johnson, there is not the posture of the knight defending
the fair maid of freedom in the hour of her maximum danger,
and crying, "I do not shrink from this responsibility; I welcome it. "   But the conviction that courage rather than wisdom
is the essential in foreign affairs is perhaps even more sure.
Indeed, for Johnson, courage is the essence of wisdom in the
sacred task of the fulfilling of the mission of America to the
world.   He writes that he can respect courage of convictions
in those who have always argued that Vietnam is not the place
to stand, but he derides those who at first want to stand firm
but who "run for cover when a storm breaks. "   (ibid. , p50)

Johnson's worldview was one which accepted as reality
the opinion that World War II had been precipitated by the
unwillingness to name aggression as evil, and the lack of
courage to stand as granite.   Further, this worldview sup-

ported the belief that only courage had deflected Communist
designs in the postwar world.   Therefore Johnson emphasized
the character of the Vietnam war as one independent nation
attacking another.   Recognition of the war as a civil war only
led to caution and compromise, both of which had been dis-
astrous in the past.   Vietnam was then typed as a war of
Communist aggression.

Almost immediately L. B. J. ordered an elaborate program of covert military operations against the state of North
Vietnam.   As the United States found itself more and more
unable to deal with the Vietcong insurgency, attention focused
more intensively on North Vietnam as the root of the problem.   It was believed that "aggression" could be discouraged
by raising the "costs. "   The Communists were sure to retreat in face of a granite-like resolve.   This perspective
became so dominant in the Johnson Administration that opposing views were eliminated.   Arguments such as the insistence of the C. I. A. that much of the Insurgency was indigenous to South Vietnam were rejected.   The C. I. A. also
argued that the Munich-type domino theory, which suggested
that all of Southeast Asia would become Communist if South
Vietnam did, was hardly a foregone conclusion.   Neither was
this point accepted.   Instead, Johnson steadily intensified the
covert attacks against North Vietnam until the Tonkin Gulf
incident provided the justification needed for an open air war.
Meanwhile, he held firm against attempts to solve the conflict by diplomacy, discouraging attempts by the South Vietnamese government and the French to negotiate with Hanoi.
L. B. J. cabled Lodge, the Ambassador, to oppose all neu-
tralist talk and negotiations by demanding virtual surrender
as the conditions for negotiations.   This remained the U. S.
position until March 1968.   Military forces were steadily
increased.   The Pentagon historian makes it clear that the
key figure in the buildup was the President (Gravel, 1971,
Vol. III, pp106-388).

The President's public pronouncements continued to
stress the theme of courage and the concern of the U. S. that
peace be negotiated.   Following the Gulf of Tonkin incident
in August 1964, L. B. J. declared

> Aggression--deliberate, willful, and systematic
> aggression--has unmasked its face to the entire
> world.   The world remembers--the world must
> never forget--that aggression unchallenged is
> aggression unleashed. ...   The challenge we face

> in Southeast Asia today is the same challenge that
> we have faced with courage and that we have met
> with strength in Greece and Turkey, in Berlin and
> Korea, in Lebanon and in Cuba.... There can be
> no peace by aggression and no immunity from reply
> [ibid., p720].

The public statements of the Administration proclaimed
that peace was being vigorously pursued by means of all
available channels. Yet privately the instructions to Lodge
remained in force, opposing meaningful negotiations. Slowly
a "credibility gap" was created. The gap was widened by
the newspaper reports of the increasing U.S. military strength
and covert actions, both of which were denied by the Administration. Journalists such as I. F. Stone also cast doubt
on the claims of the Administration that "large and increasing
quantities of military supplies are entering South Vietnam
from outside the country, " as the State Department White
Paper said. Stone pointed out that by State's own figures,
only two and one-half percent of the captured weapons were
of Communist manufacture. The remainder were American
weapons, previously captured, stolen or purchased on the
black market by the Viet-Cong themselves (Raskin & Fall,
1967, pp. 148, 157). Such revelations only fueled the wrath
of the sectarians. They already opposed American universalism, and now it seemed to them nothing less than American imperialism. To a fundamental disagreement over policy
was added the conviction that the Administration was pur-
posely lying. Therefore it was obviously evil and morally
bankrupt. The sectarian emphasis on purity compounded this
sense of outrage.

It is important to stress that Johnson, like the Presidents before him, must be seen as an archetype of the believers in the established type of the civil religion. To him,
the calling of America is to carry the light of freedom to the
darkest corners of the globe. Where there are those who
wish to extinguish that light under the darkness of tyranny,
there must Americans call upon their own peculiar virtues.
These virtues have been wrought by conquering the nearly
overwhelming adversities of an often hostile land. They are
courage and activism. Johnson, even more than Kennedy,
appears convinced that the American mission could "make
the wrath of man praise it. " The eventual success of America in establishing freedom is so sure that the immediate
attempt to create a democratic form of government can be
postponed until the war is over. The focus can be on the

military, because the ultimate purpose is freedom and democracy, even if the means be war and suffering.   The ultimate
purpose will surely prevail.   Passionately and endlessly
Johnson, Rusk, and McNamara reiterated their faith that the
evangelical purpose of the American mission would not fail.

> Tonight Americans and Asians are dying for a
> world where each people may choose its own path
> to change.   This is the principle for which our
> ancestors fought in the valleys of Pennsylvania.   It
> is a principle for which our sons fight tonight in
> the jungles of Vietnam.   ... I wish it were possible
> to convince other men with words of what we now
> find it necessary to say with guns and planes:
> armed hostility is futile--our resources are equal
> to any challenge--because we fight for values and
> we fight for principle, rather than territory or
> colonies, our patience and our determination are
> unending [ibid., pp344, 346].

The Expression of the Established
Type of the Civil Religion in the
Administration of the University

The formulation of a normative perspective in the
American university today is pre-eminently the task of the
administration.   The larger-than-life presidents who built
the great universities early in this century are gone.   With
them has gone the fear of "presidential autocracy."   Yet
university executives find themselves required to articulate
official ideologies.   Such ideology is necessary to coordinate
broad, vague goals, ambiguous formal relationships, and the
loosely related sectors of the modern university.   A normative perspective is even more urgent in order to explain and
define the institution to the many publics which share in its
control and support.   Because the modern university administrator has only a precarious formal authority, he has
greater need for the normative power of shared ideals and
purposes in both his internal and external roles.   Yet the
administrator finds himself elaborating ideology in a context
where ideology is anathema (Lunsford, 1970, pp. 87ff).

In editing a study of Whose Goals for American Higher
Education?, Calvin Lee argues that the task of creating coherence and unity of purpose within the university is nearly
impossible.   Virtually the whole sweep of human affairs is
now the business of the American university.   The multiple

goals of the university are not only compounded by the multiple goals of its faculty members, but by the centrifugal forces of grants and support from almost every segment of society. Each segment demands that the university order itself so as to fulfill the needs of that segment. It is to this impossible task that the administrator addresses himself as he seeks to formulate a normative perspective (Dobbins & Lee, 1968). Nevertheless, it is a task which must be undertaken by the administrator.

Accepting the fact that the administrator serves as an imperfect archetype of the ideology of the university, he nevertheless provides us an important clue to the normative perspective of the modern American university. The university administrator, especially the president, is nearly always an established type, expressing his views in close consonance with the established type of the society at large. A sample of inaugural addresses of presidents of some of the major universities demonstrates this point.

> ... There are two overriding tasks confronting America and all free people: the first is to continue to build societies in which man can cultivate the full fruits of freedom, and the other is to maintain military power which will deter the enemies of freedom from attempting to destroy or overrun us. And education today is indispensable to both! [Stahr, 1962, p79]. *

> Society asks the University to be the chief bearer of our civilization, to generate our new ideas, to be the foundation of economic growth and national power, to train our public leaders and professional specialists, to inspire our young people, to be a patron of the arts, and even to entertain crowds on autumn Saturday afternoons. ... The inevitable and proper response of the University to these social changes will be growth in enrollment and expansion of function [Bowen, 1964, pp130-131].

----

*Excerpts from Builders of American Universities: Inaugural Addresses of College and University Presidents; edited by David A. Weaver. Bolivar, Mo.: Southwest Baptist College, 1969. Reprinted by permission of the author and publisher.

> ... can the free University speak to man's great
> mission of the next century? ... The university
> must try, and it will try because there is no other
> institution which can deal with these great concerns
> of modern man.   Learning, research and public
> service--these are the fundamental needs of modern
> man, and these are the fundamental missions of
> the modern university.   Need and mission have
> been joined, and it will be the overriding responsi-
> bility of the university that would lead to make
> certain that all three missions are promoted, sup-
> ported, and kept in balance [Perkins, 1963, p173].

> Maintenance of a university community based pri-
> marily upon self-directed search for truth as its
> dominant ethic necessarily excludes many other
> useful functions.   Obviously it is not the only or a
> necessary way to organize the advancement and
> transmission of learning.   Indeed, if there were
> not many institutions, including universities of the
> first rank, willing and able to organize intelligence
> to respond to practical demands, our country could
> not meet its needs for either welfare or survival.
> But the integrity of the university as a community,
> even if it seems slightly aloof, is worth preserving
> not only for the sake of the quality of learning
> which a personalized community permits, but for
> the sake of the style and character of the nation
> [Brewster, 1964, p11].

All of the addresses quoted allude to the responsibility
of the university to do its part in maintaining the strength of
the nation.   It is self evident that Troeltsch's categories of
the established type of religion apply to the ideology of American higher education.   The perception that higher education is
now universal and is no longer a possession of the elite
creates the vision of a universal mission for higher education.   That mission is to be realized through the service of
the university to the nation.   The university is to be the
"foundation of economic growth and national power. "   It is to
train the leadership of business, politics and professions.
It is to be intimately connected with and serve the elites of
society.   However, there must be balance.   Not just economic man, nor just political man, but the whole man must be
served for the good of the nation and the good of the world.

The incoming presidents believe their function is to
mediate the variety of conflicts and decision making processes
of the modern university for the good of the whole university
and the whole society.   The sectarians, of course, perceived
this mediating, balancing role as one of "control of the
masses, " to use Troeltsch's phrase.   The growth of the
university, which seemed the proper response to the demands
laid upon it, meant growth of administration beyond its proportionate share.   The purpose of such expanded staff was
to meet the ideal envisioned by organizational effort.   The
land grant universities (such as Cornell) and the state universities (such as Indiana and Iowa) did not attempt to maintain the ancient and personal tradition that called for a university to be a community of scholars in search of truth.
While Kingman Brewster at Yale suggested that such a style
still ought to be important for Yale, he recognized it was no
longer necessary to maintain that tradition to be a university
of "the first rank. "   Indeed, for the sake of the survival
and welfare of the nation, universities, Brewster says, can
no longer cling to that old pattern.   He hoped that Yale could
remain aloof, however, for the sake of the style and character of the nation.   Here is the admission that the nation
is more important than the universities within it, and that
the university serves the fundamental needs of modern man
through the mission of the nation.

A more thorough and detailed outline of the ideology
necessary to the management of the large university has
been provided by Clark Kerr, former President of the University of California, in The Uses of the University (1963).
In the introduction to The State of the University Kruytbosch
and Messinger (1970) note that Berkeley had become by the
mid-sixties the symbol of the American university and the
problems which beset it.   Likewise, the Free Speech Movement at Berkeley had become the symbol of the radical student movement.   At the same time, Kerr's analysis of the
university had become a small classic, widely and approvingly
quoted by established types in both university and national
administrations.   The Uses of the University was as widely
damned by sectarian types across the nation.   For the
established types, Kerr had described and praised the good;
for the sectarian, he had clarified the oppressive nature of
the multiversity.   Kerr himself urged that readers not con-
fuse his analysis with approval.   However, his admission
that the tone of the books was optimistic alerted the reader
to the descriptive-celebratory style--a mixture of factual nar-
ration and normative defense--which suggested that here is
indeed the model for a great university.

Kerr is convinced that the basic reality for the university is that new knowledge is recognized as the most powerful factor affecting the economic, social and cultural foundations of the nation. The modern university is therefore an expression of the age, as well as an influence operating upon it. The modern character of the multiversity is as diversified as the variety of publics as compose the society itself. This diversity, even though not a reasoned choice, is an imperative. Diversity is required by the nature of modern technological society. The multiversity is multisoul; therefore its governance is extremely precarious. The role of administration is of necessity central in reconciling the multiversity to itself. Of course the administration is the primary connector of the multiversity to the external world. By the logic of the managerial revolution going on in society at large, the locus of power in the multiversity shifts to the administration.

The president of the multiversity is to be a mediator whose first task is peace.

> Peace within the student body, the faculty, the
> trustees; and peace between and among them. . . .
> Peace between the internal environment of the
> academic community and external society that sur-
> rounds and sometimes almost engulfs it. . . .   The
> second task is progress [Kerr, 1963, pp36, 37].

Since peace and progress often conflict, the effective mediator must, at times, sacrifice peace to progress, for progress is more important than peace. The president must have an awareness of power in this process, for he must

> . . . police its use by the constituent groups, so
> that none will have too much [power] or too little
> or use it too unwisely. To make the multiversity
> work really effectively, the moderates need to be
> in control of each power center and there needs to
> be an attitude of tolerance between and among the
> power centers, with few territorial ambitions
> [ibid. , p39].

The virtues required of such a president are judgment, courage and fortitude, but "the greatest of these is fortitude" (ibid. , p40).

Kerr also accepts wholeheartedly the concept of the multiversity as a prime instrument of the national purpose. Progress is good for both the nation and the university. The university is a catalyst for national growth. This is exemplified by the fact that industries dependent on research congregate near universities. It is because California is a "center of learning," according to the Department of Defense, that forty-one percent of defense contracts for research in 1961 were concentrated in California (ibid., pp87-89). The intimate connection between national progress and multiversity progress makes it inevitable that most multiversity changes are of external origin. The directions of the multiversity have been set by its environment, "including the federal government, the foundations, the surrounding and sometimes engulfing industry" [ibid., p122].

The pressure of the environment raises grave problems.

> ... how to identify the "good" and the "bad," and how to embrace the good and resist the bad. There is also a problem of timing--how to adjust not too rapidly and not too slowly [ibid., p 107].

The ability to adjust requires above all a sense of balance.

> The essence of balance is to match support with the intellectual creativity of subject fields; with the needs for skills at the highest level; with the kinds of expert service that society currently most requires [ibid., p144].

Kerr concludes that perhaps his description is not what might be desired. Perhaps there are other visions of the university than that of the multiversity. If there is another perspective, it has not emerged in either East or West, for society and science move irresistibly forward.

> The process cannot be stopped. The results cannot be foreseen. It remains to adapt [ibid., p124].

Kerr, as an established type, accepts American society as a reality to which he must adapt. He is the expression, par excellence, of Troeltsch's conviction that educators know how to attain their ends by a "process of adaptation and compromise." Kerr does not substantially criticize the national purpose, but accepts the basic values of progress and

growth.   The enhancement of the mission of America through
the sharing of the research tasks of the Department of Defense is perceived as a good.   The multiversity as a normative model suggests also that it is good that the university
serve to the utmost of its ability the variety of economic,
political, and professional elites which support it.   This
service invests the multiversity with universal significance
as it seeks to serve all mankind.

The emphasis on the norm of control as the prime
requisite of the multiversity president, is from Troeltsch's
perspective, basic to the established type.   The president
is to control the level of conflict within and amongst the
student body, faculty and trustees, as well as to regulate
the amount of power and the manner of its use by the various
groups.   Hopefully, such control will be facilitated by the
fact that established types head each group. Compromise
amongst leaders is thus more readily achieved, for the
sectarian demand for purity of heart and action and for personal involvement of each sectarian is thereby avoided.   With
such control in hand, the president will then be able to
establish peace between the multiversity and the external
society which he cannot control, but to which he must adjust,
and to which he must seek to adapt his institution.

Kerr quite rightly perceives that victories in such a
task will be few and defeats many, and that often history will
outrun the slow pace of institutional progress.   Thus Kerr
values highly those virtues which will enable the administrator
to persevere in the attempt to achieve the ideal by organizational effort.   First is courage--the quality of mind that
enables one to face difficulty with firmness.   Second is forti-
tude--patient courage which endures under continuing affliction.

The sectarian students soon recognized not only the
identity of interest between the established type of the university and the government, but the similarity of reaction
when confronted with sectarian demands.   Sectarians soon
became aware that administrators were advocating the inter-
dependence of the national interest and the interest of the
university.   Strangely, even near the close of the sixties
faculty members of prestigious multiversities such as Berkeley
were still dismissing the sectarian criticism of that relationship as an intellectual aberration and emotional claptrap
(Searle, 1971).   However, the sectarian students and the
established types in the administration felt more surely the
reality of their opposed perspectives: for each, the other
soon became the enemy.

The Sectarian Type of the
Civil Religion

The Expression of the Sectarian
Type in the Anti-war and Anti-
poverty Emphases of the Radical
Movement

A great many of the sectarians who sought to right the
wrongs of war and poverty believed that evil exposed would be
evil destroyed. The task of the sectarian was to lay in plain
view before the American people the monstrosity of the injustice now being wrought. The mass media, by publicizing
the wrongs protested, would educate the people. The sectarians would point to what they believed was the common
faith (or ought to be the common faith) as evidenced in the
founding documents of the Republic. Galvanized, America
would then arise and right the wrong. Michael Novak suggests that such an expectation has its roots in the fact that

> From a theological point of view, Americans are
> Pelagians concerning the structure of our country.
> We tend to think that it is not and cannot be evil
> at the center. We habitually believe that American
> intentions are good ones, that America has never
> started a war, that America is always on the side
> of Democracy and justice and liberty, that American
> officials are to be trusted until proven untrust-
> worthy, and that Americans are unusually innocent,
> generous and good in their relationships with other
> people.... We believe we are free and responsible
> individuals, in command of our personal destiny
> and of our common government. We believe that
> American instincts are so sound that evils have
> only to be pointed out in order that American public
> opinion will rise up against them in outrage
> [Novak, 1969, p65].

The election of John Kennedy created a surge of
optimism amongst some sectarians. His rhetoric seemed
amenable to their concerns. They too wished to get the
country moving again. As events soon demonstrated, the
sectarians filled that phrase with quite different content than
did Kennedy. The New Frontier suggested to the activists
that once again the moral fervor of the American people
would be translated into actions that would conform the nation
to the image of freedom and justice for all. Such a hope

burst forth not only in Greensboro as young blacks demanded full recognition as citizens and persons, but a bewildering variety of places and causes across the land. To document the few is to neglect the many, yet three directions or sub-movements of the radical movement can serve as types for the whole.

First, the continuing revival of the peace movement from its postwar roots will be traced. A chronology of pertinent events will provide the context in which some of the writings of the anti-war movement can be analyzed. The opening of the air war against North Vietnam marks a new phase in the anti-war movement. The span of 1960 to 1965 is therefore the opening period in the sixties. Second, a brief word needs to be said about the anti-poverty movement, primarily in relation to S. D. S. Finally, the closing section will examine the student movement on campus. For the first half of the sixties, the Free Speech Movement at the University of California, Berkeley, is the archetype.

The Anti-war Movement. The Student Peace Union was organized in April 1959 by pacifist and socialist students in the Midwest. Groups such as T. O. C. S. I. N. at Harvard and S. L. A. T. E. at Berkeley and persons later active in S. D. S. were involved in S. P. U. By 1960 S. P. U. counted 5,000 members and 12,000 subscribers to its Bulletin. T. O. C. S. I. N., S. L. A. T. E., and the student division of S. A. N. E. rallied the peace forces on the campus. The actions of the U. S. toward Cuba, including the breaking of diplomatic relations and the Bay of Pigs invasion led to the formation of the Fair Play for Cuba Committee. C. W. Mills' Listen Yankee (1960) was widely read by students. F. P. C. C., although not pacifist, shared much of the same concern about American foreign policy as did the peace groups. Kennedy's emphasis on increased military spending and his urgings that each American be prepared for nuclear war incited the peace groups to escalate their activities. J. F. K.'s suggestion that each patriotic American would want to build his own air raid shelter and join in the civil defense as his part in the war ef-fort angered sectarians. Sectarians therefore turned Kennedy's statement to their own use. They declared that each person indeed must decide whether he would take part in the civil defense drills. By his decision, the individual would make known to the community whether he was for war or peace (Wittner, 1969, pp266-268).

The sectarian appeal was attractive to students. While
they generally rejected pacifism, students were willing to
consider seriously an alternative approach to war.   In a study
of 1200 students in sixteen colleges and universities, only
fifty-four percent believed that pacifism was "not a practical
philosophy in the world today. " Six percent favored unilateral
disarmament and seventeen percent opposed all war as being
against their moral principles.   The openness to pacifist and
anti-war arguments constituted a break with the previous
generations of college students.   The break was evidence that
cold war had begun to lose its sharpness of definition in the
political science departments of the better colleges and universities.   International politics was viewed as a power struggle.   Varying shades of gray replaced black and white convictions.   "Red or Dead" no longer seemed to be a viable
means of categorizing all of human life.   What John Kenneth
Galbraith called the "conventional wisdom" of "appeasement
or strength" was more and more called into question.   Pacifist groups noted the change immediately.   "The observers
have been wagging their heads for a long time over the
'apathy' of the 'silent generation' of college youth" remarked
a Fellowship of Reconciliation editorial in early 1960.   "But
what of now?   What has suddenly happened to this silent
generation?"   (ibid.).

In the Spring of 1960, over 2, 000 persons in New
York City resisted the yearly drill.   Included were students
at City College, Queens College, Brooklyn College and about
five hundred high school students.   Groups of students in
colleges and universities up and down the East coast joined
the protest.   S. P. U. gathered more than 10, 000 signatures on
a peace petition.   At Berkeley 3, 000 students attended peace
rallies and Harvard saw a demonstration of about 1, 000 anti-
war marchers.   While the older radical pacifists such as
Dave Dellinger and A. J. Muste were part of these demonstrations, S. P. U. , in its statement of purpose, called for a
"new and creative means of achieving a free and peaceful
society" (Teodori, 1969, p125).   The statement read

> The Student Peace Union is an organization of
> young people who believe that neither war nor the
> threat of war can any longer be successfully used
> to settle international disputes and that neither
> human freedom nor the human race can long sur-
> vive in a world committed to militarism.   Without
> committing any member to a precise statement of
> policy, the SPU draws together young people for a
> study of alternatives to war and engages in education

> and action to end the present Arms Race. The
> SPU works toward a society which will ensure both
> peace and freedom and which will suffer no individ-
> ual or group to be exploited by another ... the
> peace movement must act independently of both
> East and West, must apply the same standard of
> criticism to both ... [ibid., p125].

What was new in the statement was the willingness to
be an open group. Whoever would join in the search for
peace, regardless of past or present affiliations, would be
allowed to participate in S. P. U. The "Old Left" was rooted
in the experience of the past. It had come through the difficult struggles with the Communist Party in the twenties and
thirties. The Old Left had seen organizations destroyed by
internal wrangling, government repression and loss of public
support. Most of the New Left was not aware of this history.
Even amongst those who were, there was a weariness with the
Old Left's endless insistence on setting every criticism of American society in an anti-communist context. The Old Left was
quick to respond. Irving Howe, one of the Old Left, saw that the
young were sick to death of the mixture of chauvinism, hysteria
and demagogy created during the cold war years, and responded
by regurgitating it almost automatically. For such programmed
response, for such lack of political insight, he scorned them.

> You cannot stand the deceits of official anti-
> communism. Then respond with a rejection equally
> blatant. You have been raised to give credit to
> every American power move, no matter how re-
> actionary or cynical? Then respond by castigating
> everything American. You are weary of Sidney
> Hook's messages in The New York Times Magazine?
> Then respond as if talk about Communist totali-
> tarianism were simply irrelevant or a bogey to
> frighten infants [Howe, 1966(b) pp45, 46].

But to the New Left, whose organizations were single-issue
oriented and tended to disintegrate when the issue was no
longer an agony to the conscience of American sectarians,
talk about Communist totalitarianism was irrelevant. The
issue was American involvement in war. Only where that
issue was involved was the question of Communist countries
of import. So S. P. U. demanded

> --that America not heed the hysterical cry of those
> who would duplicate the criminal act of the Soviet
> Union by testing in the atmosphere [Teodori, 1969,
> p126].

but as important was

> --investigation of alternative use of the huge sums
> spent for ineffective "defense" measures, in order
> to cut the tie of our economy to the cold war
> [ibid.].

By 1960 S. P. U. was advocating draft resistance.   In
the Bulletin, Ken Calkins, a founder of S. P. U. , applied
Camus' famous essay "Neither Victims nor Executioners" to
the sectarian situation.

> [Camus] proposes that these rebels join together to
> form a new living society inside the corpse of the
> old.   The goal of this society will be nothing less
> than to restore sociability ("le dialogue") among
> men.   The individuals who make up this revolu-
> tionary fraternity must be prepared to resist the
> international dictatorship of violence and lies with
> their whole beings--their course will not be an
> easy one [Ferber & Lynd, 1971, p10].

Karl Meyer, perhaps the most vigorous advocate of
resistance within S. P. U. , argued that protests, petitions,
and prudent resistance were essentially worthless because
they were tolerable, even though relatively mildly repressed
by the state.   He wrote his draft board that he had come to
the conclusion he had a moral obligation to resist the draft
act.   Resistance included both personal refusal and personal
involvement in seeking to persuade others to resist.   Meyer
asserted radicals must practice what they preach.

> What we need are Christians who will practice the
> program of Jesus; individualists who will practice
> the program of Thoreau, and socialists who will
> practice the program of Debs [ibid. , pp10-11].

Meyer's passionate appeals struck a sympathetic chord
at Oberlin College.   There students began collecting signed
commitments to repudiate Selective Service registrations and
turn in draft cards.   The movement spread.   An Antioch
student, Peter Irons, made a speech urging mass draft card
turn-ins at the following S. P. U. national conference.   He had
read Muste's autobiography, Ginger's biography of Eugene
Debs, and Tolstoy's The Kingdom of God Is Within You.
He had become involved in S. N. C. C. and was arrested and
jailed for sitting-in in suburban Maryland.   In October of 1960
he sent his draft card back.   Irons argued

> I had given considerable thought to filling out the
> CO questionnaire, but my almost passionate First
> Amendment philosophy led me to reject that, since
> the religious questions were totally repugnant....
> I wouldn't fight, as a Gandhian, I felt the need to
> make a symbolic break with a country which op-
> pressed blacks, and I wouldn't apply for an exemp-
> tion based on religious grounds [ibid., p13].

Irons urged the students to resist both the moral and
physical coercion of the draft, which sought to deny freedom
not only to the body but also to the spirit. Cold war propaganda glossed over the mass destruction of war. The government urged young men to accept the murder of the innocents
in all the future Hiroshimas as the glory of patriotism. But
those who had a different view of the meaning of life, and
the meaning to America, would resist.

> If someone decides to take this stand it is because,
> in addition to the logical arguments, a responsive
> chord has been struck within, since for an argu-
> ment to take root and flower into action there must
> be fertile soil in the deepest part of the personality.
> The refusal to register or the return of the draft
> card will be but an outward manifestation of a
> basic patterning of one's life [ibid., p15].

The conference responded by seeking to stage the return of 500 draft cards, whose return had been pledged in
advance. The process of organizing was to be intensely
personal. The statement calling for the pledge to return the
draft card was not allowed to be circulated by anyone except
a "definitely affirmed signer." The pledge was not to be
circulated to a new campus unless it was signed and cared
for by at least one person on that campus.

Resistance was motivated by two basic attitudes.
First, there were the intensely committed, who saw that
resistance was but an outward manifestation of inward pat-
terning of one's life. Secondly, resistance was for the sake
of the nation. This was the larger group. For this group
the action would be considered appropriate only if enough
students joined in order to force the nation to a moral re-
examination of itself. The issue was not personal purity as
much as personal action that would restore national purity.
Thus the majority signed the pledge intending to turn in the
draft card only if a large enough number to pain the national

conscience would join them.   But not enough students to fulfill this second motive signed the pledge.   The idea lapsed
until a new organization, End The Draft, picked it up again
in 1965.   Meanwhile, S. P. U. turned to new actions.   A
group of 5, 000 students was organized in 1962 to visit con-
gressmen to lobby against nuclear testing.   A nuclear test
ban became S. P. U. 's one issue.   When the treaty was signed,
S. P. U. disintegrated.

End The Draft (E. T. D.) was formed in 1962, and took
its name from an organization called End the Draft in '63,
headed by Norman Thomas.   E. T. D. criticized Thomas'
group because Thomas opposed the draft on civil libertarian
grounds without opposing the mission of America of which
the draft is an instrument.   E. T. D. wanted to be the "subcommittee of the whole movement" on the draft.   Like
S. N. C. C. and S. P. U. , it was non-exclusionist.   It was also
non-pacifist.   E. T. D. sought to move from "symbolic resistance, " such as boarding nuclear submarines, to "politically effective action. "   David Mitchell, one of the members
of S. P. U. , was a founder of E. T. D. , and saw the purpose
of E. T. D. to be a

> program that supports and builds a movement from
> all individuals who are fighting US militarism by
> challenging the draft ... which because it is serious
> about ... US crimes, will cooperate and build a
> united front of groups and individuals to seriously
> challenge the government, instead of cooperating
> in one-shot actions, and those only when they can
> be profitable to their group [ibid. , p21].

Important to this purpose was the distinction between personal
purity and national purity.   Mitchell, in a memorable phrase
condemned those who turned the movement into a search for
personal purity as "the guards, goons and hacks of their
private churches (groups). "   The issue was the salvation of
the nation (ibid. , p. 20).   The declaration that the government is the threat to the health of the nation was emphasized
even more by such groups as the May 2nd Movement.   It
was formed by 400 students attending a Yale symposium on
the war in May, 1964.   The May 2nd Movement took an anti-
imperialist, pro-Vietcong position.

The individual moral revolt which a growing number
of students were feeling as the sixties opened was coming to
assume a wider political significance.   The concern became
to develop a politics that could express freedom and human

liberation. The desire for non-conforming lifestyles also contributed to this sense of freedom and human liberation. Gradually the isolated issues which ignited the indignation of the students--racism, war, poverty--were seen as the result of a system. Political, economic and social institutions were perceived as interconnected. This system was believed to be the major determiner of all aspects of the individual's life, trespassing on the most fundamental rights of self-realization, self-expression and personal choice. This growing recognition resulted in analyses which sought to express a different conception of the way that American society ought to be organized. To the New Left it seemed clear that the present mode of societal organization was not effecting liberty and justice for all, but power for the few over the lives of many. While the same specific issues remained the center of public action, serious thought was also being given to the structure of society itself and the means of redistributing power. The movement was evolving from protest to radicalism. One of the leading organizations in this evolution was the Students for a Democratic Society.

S. D. S. , in a formal sense, succeeded the Student League for Industrial Democracy. During the thirties, S. L. I. D. was the Socialist opposition to the Communist National Student Union. S. L. I. D. was revived after World War II by James Farmer, but dwindled again during the McCarthy era. It was revived again by the new activist radicals at the University of Michigan: Al Haber, Bob Ross and Tom Hayden, editor of the campus daily. In May of 1960, Haber organized a conference on Human Rights in the North at Ann Arbor, which was addressed by Michael Harrington and James Farmer. Some enduring relationships with S. N. C. C. people were established there. Hayden spent the summer at Los Angeles (the Democratic convention) and Berkeley, where, he says, "I got radicalized. " A group of about thirty-five met at Ann Arbor in December, 1961, to agree on a founding convention of S. D. S. (using the name by which the inactive S. L. I. D. was now called). It was agreed that Hayden would draft a manifesto. All through the spring Hayden sent out mimeographed drafts of the document for suggestions and criticisms. The founding convention was held June 11-15th at Port Huron. It was both romantic and radical. Bob Ross remembers

> It was a little like starting a journey. We all felt
> very close to each other. I remember singing
> freedom songs all night, and Casey singing "Hold
> On" so that I'll never forget it [Newfield, 1970, p96].

There was also lengthy debate over the meaning of the Port Huron Statement. It was finally agreed that it would be presented as "a document with which S. D. S. officially identifies, but also as a living document open to change with our times and experience" (ibid., p97). However, the "parent" League for Industrial Democracy was enraged by the Port Huron Statement, and the "non-exclusionary" policy of the convention. L. I. D. locked S. D. S. out of its own office, and withdrew both financial support and permission to use the S. D. S. name. Haber and Hayden were summoned to a "hearing" in July to resolve the matter. L. I. D. concluded S. D. S. was an apologist for Soviet interests. The elected S. D. S. staff was to be fired. A staff representative of L. I. D. was to be appointed. But after a summer's lobbying of the membership and arguing with the L. I. D. board, the decisions were reversed. S. D. S. began its fall work of organizing S. D. S. chapters and seeking to build campus political parties on the model of S. L. A. T. E. at Berkeley. But the bitterness between the Old and New Left remained. Tom Hayden wrote

> It taught me that Social Democrats aren't radicals and can't be trusted in a radical movement. It taught me what Social Democrats really think about civil liberties and organizational integrity [ibid., p98].

The attempt by the parent organization to replace the S. D. S. staff especially angered the new S. D. S. members, who were passionately committed to "participatory democracy." S. D. S. had expended great effort to ensure both staff and statement were truly an expression of those persons who were personally committed and involved in the movement.

In "A Letter to the New (Young) Left" in The Activist (1961), Tom Hayden sets forth his basic understanding of the need for a radical movement. The letter is an indication of his point of view as he prepared the rough draft of the Port Huron Statement. Hayden points to the several challenges confronting the peoples of the world: 1) The international situation: this includes the needs of the "underdeveloped nations" and the pervasive influence of the cold war on every private and public facet of the common life. 2) The domestic situation: most evident is the failure of nation to deal with poverty (Hayden was already strongly influenced by Harrington), the increasing influence of militarism as evidenced by Mills' power elite analysis, and the exploiting of natural

resources and the decay of the urban environment.   3) The
educational system: this crisis includes "the endless repressions of free speech and thought," the sterility of student
government, the enforcement of in loco parentis by a sti-
flingly paternalistic administration and a conspicuously
anachronistic curriculum.   Hayden sees little hope that the
older generation will provide leadership to deal with these
problems.   There is an inhibiting, dangerous conservatism
current: Niebuhr in theology; Bell, Lipset, and Kornhauser
in political science and sociology; Hofstadter and Schlesinger
in history and almost all of them liberals in the A. D. A.
They prefer "realism" to ethical thought and moral action.
Realism means the acceptance, with appropriate regrets, of
the present paralysis of will and hope.   Radicalism, on the
other hand, combines will and hope.

> Radicalism as a style involves penetration of a
> social problem to its roots, to its real cause....
> I think most persons who lean to the left political-
> ly are moved by quite important feelings of soli-
> darity for the impoverished, the oppressed, the
> debased, and all of suffering mankind; by a com-
> mitment to the general ideals of Western humanism,
> particularly to the freedoms of speech, thought
> and association.... Radicalism it seems to me,
> does not exclude morality; it invites and is given
> spirit by the quality of reflective commitment, the
> combining of our passion and critical talents into
> a provisional position.
>   Radical program is simply the radical style as
> it attempts to change the practical life [ibid.,
> pp6, 7].

The present problem with radical program, Hayden
feels, is this: moral passion is quick to know what to oppose: racism, militarism, nationalism, oppression of mind
and spirit, unrestrained capitalism and bombs; however
critical intelligence has been slower to fashion a politics
which aims at the changing of society, not merely the as-
suaging of its continuous ills.   While it is doubtful that such
a politics or such a good society can be fashioned, still

> I would suggest that it is possible and necessary to
> begin to think and act--provisionally yet strongly--
> in the midst of our doubts.   We must begin to see
> doubt, not as a reason for inaction--that way leads
> to intellectual sterility.   We must see it as a re-
> minder that infallibility is not the property of any

single man, and, moreover that compassion for
enemies is not simply a heroic show, but a manifestation of our deepest moral anxiety [ibid. , p9].

The Port Huron Statement refines and amplifies this
stance.   The statement opens with an affirmation of traditional American values--"freedom and equality for each
individual, government of, by and for the people"--these are
values by which men can live and fashion a good society.
But troubling events begin to make it clear that although
America teaches these values to her young, she does not
live by them.   First, the struggle against racism compels
students from silence to activism.   The declaration "all
men are created equal" rings hollow before the reality of
Negro life in America.   Second, the cold war, symbolized by
the bomb, diverts and compresses all of life to serve the
military-industrial interests.   America is, in the time of
mankind's great need, the hypocrite amongst the nations.   She
proclaims democracy, yet her own system is apathetic,
manipulated rather than "of, by and for the people. "   "Real-
ists, " the vast majority, accept such a contradiction as the
best possible.   The majority sees no alternative to the present.   Yet it is precisely this apathy, this despair, that grants
students a sense of urgency in their commitment to change.
This commitment is not partial, but demands and is able to
fulfill, the energies of the whole man, the whole life.

The search for truly democratic alternatives to the
present, and a commitment to social experimentation
with them, is a worthy and fulfilling enterprise, one
which moves us, and we hope, others today [Teodori,
1969, p. 165].

The Statement then considers specific areas: values, student
politics, and the university and social change.   The sections
dealing with students and the university will be dealt with
later.   But the paragraphs dealing with values and with
politics sharpen our understanding of the sectarian approach
to the issues with which the peace movement was struggling.

The Statement argues that making values explicit,
which is necessary to establish alternatives, is a task which
has been dismissed or debased.   Empiricism or sloganeering
rule in the university as well as in politics.   Brushed aside
as mere youthful idealism are the basic questions: What is
really important?   Can we live in a different and better way?
If we wanted to change society, how would we do it?   The

horror of the twentieth century destroys hope. To be idealistic, to believe that life must and can be better is thought
to be nonsense. To seek to recreate America according to
the image of the Founders who painted their hopes in such
broad strokes and vibrant colors is to be considered deluded.
The present wishes to be "toughminded," "realistic"--in
short, to have no serious aspirations. Therefore, opposing
the dominant conceptions of man as inherently incapable of
directing his own affairs, the Statement affirms

> We regard men as infinitely precious and pos-
> sessed of unfulfilled capacities for reason, free-
> dom and love. ... Men have unrealized potential
> for self-cultivation, self-direction, self-understand-
> ing, and creativity. It is this potential that we
> regard as crucial and to which we appeal, not to
> the human potentiality for violence, unreason and
> submission to authority. ... Human relationships
> should involve fraternity and honesty. Human inter-
> dependence is a contemporary fact; human brother-
> hood must be willed, however, as a condition of
> future survival and as the most appropriate form of
> social relations [ibid., pp166, 167].

These values can be actualized in a social system by
seeking

> the establishment of a democracy of individual
> participation, governed by two central aims; that
> the individual share in those social decisions
> determining the quality and direction of his life;
> that society be organized to encourage independence
> in men and provide the media for their common
> participation [ibid.].

This would mean that politics would have the function
of bringing people out of isolation into community. Politics
would also serve a meaningful function in life. Decision
making would be carried on in public groupings and channels
be made available so that private problems could be formulated as public issues. In the economic sphere major resources and means of production should be open to democratic
participation and regulation. In this as in all efforts at
change or maintenance, violence is to be abhorred because
it transforms persons from human beings into objects of
hate.

The Statement argues that the present political system
is based on power rooted in possession, privilege or circumstance rather than power rooted in love, community, reflec-
tiveness, reason and creativity. Business and politics are
militarized, affecting the whole living condition of each
American citizen. An essential part of such militarization
is propaganda, which seeks to convince the American people
that the cold war demands the sacrifice of civil liberties and
public welfare. Tremendous sums of money in both industry
and university compress the competition between alternative
social systems into a competition between missiles or armies.
As mutual nuclear destruction of the two superpowers becomes less and less an acceptable option, the doctrine of
"limited wars" arises. Protracted fighting is supported on
the soil of underdeveloped countries--a depraved sport of the
rich in the homeland of the poor.

The political system serves the economic system.
The common goal is to industrialize the world for the sake
of American profit. But sectarians believe that world industrialization must be directed toward the task of reducing
the disparity between the have and the have-not nations.
The central goal of the United States' relationship to the
rest of the world should be the elimination of hunger, poverty,
disease, violence and exploitation. Some say this is a hope
beyond all bounds. Yet

> ... it is far better to us to have positive vision
> than a "hard-headed" resignation. Some will
> sympathize, but claim it is impossible: if so,
> then we, not Fate, are the responsible ones, for
> we have the means at our disposal. We should
> not give up the attempt for fear of failure [Cohen
> & Hale, 1967, p301].

Clearly, private enterprise cannot be depended on to do the
job. The development process cannot be seen as a way of
"winning" the cold war, for it must put an end to that war.
The U.S. must aid those who need aid because it is right,
as President Kennedy said. That principle must move from
rhetoric to practice. Finally, America must accept the
right of peoples to determine their own history and social
systems. No longer may the U.S. seek to impose its own
system on others.

The religious aspect of the Port Huron Statement and
the whole radical movement in the early sixties is striking.
The collection of beliefs, symbols and rituals with which

America has celebrated the meaning of her existence is both
affirmed and criticized. It is affirmed in order to gain
leverage upon the present, to mold America more into the
image of what sectarians believe America ought to be. The
use of the language of the Founding Documents, the references
connecting American radical heroes such as Thoreau and Debs
to Jesus, and the conviction that hypocrisy--a disjunction of
belief and action--is an issue are religious in nature. The
faith is the American civil religion. The critical work is
sectarian. There is the emphasis on purity. Community has
been fractured, and it must be restored. Each individual
must express the commonly affirmed inward faith by outward
actions. The central, most important meanings must again
be searched out. Finally, these tasks are worth the whole
life of a man, for in them is the avenue of meaning, and in
their service is the human enterprise fulfilled.

Such an analysis of the movement can be extended in
terms of Troeltsch's presentation of sectarian characteristics.
First, Troeltsch suggests the sectarian renounces the idea of
dominating the world by organizational effort. The sectarian
desires that his society embody the pure truth. Therefore
he seeks to replace the current social institutions by sectarian ones. In the radical movement the rejection of the
American mission to the world in its evangelical mode appears again and again. The criticism directed against contemporary American society seeks to end the pervasive influence of the cold war. Sectarians believe the cold war
mission of America has brought an outside control over the
lives of men--a control alien to the interests of man, whether
that man is citizen of East, West, or Third World. Each
social group and society must determine its own destiny,
even as the New Left seeks to determine its own destiny
through participatory democracy of those committed and involved in the movement.

Sectarians set their doctrine of man over against the
established doctrine. The established doctrine is one which
proclaims man as depraved, as hopelessly evil, or if not a
white, anglo-protestant male American, as child-like, needing
the tutelage and guardianship of an elder brother. Man, in
this view, if not evil, is certainly weak, and inclined to evil.
Empire is therefore a good, for it preserves man from evil.
But sectarians, especially in the Port Huron Statement, affirm man's potentialities for the good. Man can be inspired;
it is a crime to seek to control him, to hold empire over
him. Since the good is the true potential of man, America

ought to turn her considerable resources to the task of making
the world safe for community and diversity.   In such a world
the good potentialities of men will succeed in establishing a
political order in which true community will flourish, even
as true community flourishes in the New Left.

The New Left recognizes how difficult such a task is.
The Old Left, so close to the New Left in so many ways, is
unable to allow the New Left the expression of its own understanding of community.   As soon as disagreement becomes
threatening, control becomes the central issue.   The liberals,
sectarians feel, practice such control on an even larger scale.
Like the Old Left, they rhapsodize concerning human potentialities, but carefully exercise control over all who disagree
with their programs.   To justify such control liberals created
the doctrine of realism.   Realism proclaims that although
man has some inclinations to the good he is evil.   Therefore
man must be controlled.   The latter part of the affirmation
is often not spoken but always expressed by action.   The appeal to empire rests, the New Left believes, on this view
of man.   Man must be controlled.

The New Left perceives that the Old Left and liberals
are unable to accept participatory democracy.   They oppose
the involvement of the committed to creating the structures
of their own lives.   The established type believes community
must be enforced rather than be allowed to emerge, which
negates the very meaning of community.   For the sectarians,
community emerges out of the participation of the members.
Bob Ross described it as the sense of sharing a common
journey.   Liberals scorn the possibility of translating such
feelings of solidarity into politics.   Radicals attempt a politics
which is expressive of the radical lifestyle.   It is the struggle to "combine passion and critical talents into a provisional
position. "   Persons in the New Left experience a closeness
which comes from a demonstrated shared commitment.   The
acts of civil disobedience, the risking of freedom and even of
life for the sake of the new society which faith envisions
builds sectarians into a community.

Second, Troeltsch sees the sectarian form of the
Christian religion as centering in those who are both connected to the lower classes but who are also in close connection with the development of society at large.   Sectarians
are not the lumpen proletariat, who have no awareness nor
concern with the direction of society.   Sectarians share with
the upper classes a common intellectual concern: the rightly

ordered society.   At the same time they feel a solidarity
with the oppressed.   The New Left, composed primarily of
student intellectuals, plainly are not the lumpen proletariat.
In fact, as Flacks points out, they are children of the middle
class.   The intellectual concern is the articulation of a
rightly ordered society.   But, as Hayden says, the New Left
is "moved by quite important feelings of solidarity for the
impoverished, the oppressed, the debased, and all of suffering mankind." These feelings, sectarians argue, are connected with a commitment to the general ideals of Western
humanism.   Troeltsch believes that the tension engendered
by holding fast to these diverse concerns produces the sectarian mentality.   In the New Left these two concerns appear
most strongly.

Third, for Troeltsch, the sectarian of the Christian
religion subscribes to an asceticism which denies that worldly
goods and achievements determine the worth of persons.   He
believes sectarians are bound together in a love which is
heightened rather than diminished by the inequalities and
struggles of the world.   Likewise, the sectarians of the civil
religion deny that worldly goods and achievements reflect the
virtue or worth of a person.   The work ethic, according to
the sectarians, is evidence of an unjust economic system
which allows one to gain not only material ease but virtue
at the expense of neighbor.   The sectarian goal is an economic system which is characterized by the participatory
democracy style of decision making.   "From each according
to his ability, to each according to his need" is the implicit
ethic.   But in contrast to Communism, decisions are to
emerge from each local economic unit, in order that work be
meaningful and the unit of production be a community.   The
Port Huron Statement proclaims that the economic sphere,
under sectarian reorganization, would have as its basis these
principles:

> --that work should involve incentives worthier than
> money or survival. It should be educative, not
> stultifying; creative, not mechanical; self directed,
> not manipulated, encouraging independence, a
> respect for others, a sense of dignity and a willing-
> ness to accept social responsibility, since it is this
> experience that has crucial influence on habits, per-
> ceptions and individual ethics;
> --that the economic experience is so personally
> decisive that the individual must share in its full
> determination;

--that the economy itself is of such social importance that its major resources and means of production should be open to democratic participation and
subject to democratic social regulation [Teodori,
1969, p168].

It must be emphasized that these principles are articulated in
a context of solidarity for the "impoverished, the oppressed,
the debased and all of suffering mankind." The perception
of work as a central, decisive experience is, of course,
shared by both sectarian and established types. But for the
established type the context is one of achievement of individual
virtue, which includes both personal economic success and
responsibility for rehabilitation of the unfortunate. But the
sense of solidarity, of community which implies common
decision making is not within the established type's horizon.
Therefore, though the established type, at its best, has expressed a deep concern that all persons have the opportunity
to share in creative work which bestows a sense of dignity,
the context has been rehabilitation of the poor rather than
solidarity with the oppressed. For the sectarian, it is the
context of solidarity that is decisive.

Fourth, Troeltsch sees that the Christian sectarians
often appeal to the primitive Church, to the New Testament
and especially to the words of Jesus. There is an attempt
to establish the sectarian church on the basis of the early
church. From this foundation, the whole church is to be
renewed. The passion of the New Left for the freedoms
espoused in the Founding Documents of the American Republic
is similar. There is confession of an "almost passionate
First Amendment philosophy," and a commitment particularly
to freedom of speech, thought and association. The Port
Huron Statement opens with a poignant reaffirmation of the
values of "government of, by and for the people" and expresses the urgent conviction that "all men are created
equal." It is the trespass of freedom and equality, the traditional American values, expressed in the founding documents,
that urges the search for "truly democratic alternatives to
the present"--a present which has betrayed those democratic
values. The sectarians seek to articulate in twentieth century
terms the vision of man that informed the Founders. This
vision is set against the pessimism of the present which is
perceived as fertile soil for the seeds of tyranny. In this
attempt to articulate anew a doctrine of man the sectarians
return to the well-springs of the faith--the humanism which
underlies the founding documents. In the light of this doctrine

the government, according to groups such as E. T. D. , is the
principal violator of the tradition.   Yet there is a clear distinction in the early sixties between the state and the nation.
There is still hope that the nation can be radically renewed,
even though the state is corrupt.

        Finally, Troeltsch emphasizes the sectarian appeal to
ever new common performances of moral demands, which are
founded on the law of Christ.   Likewise, the members of the
New Left urge one another to actions which demonstrate their
personal commitment to freedom, peace, brotherhood and
democracy.   The crisis of the nation demands personal
response: one must turn in his own draft card; one must
choose the good and shun the evil, and refuse to cooperate
with the civil defense drill.   Such actions are risky, for they
leave a person open not only to the punitive action of the
state but to the charge that personal identity crises are being
resolved through political action.   Lewis Feuer, in The Conflict of Generations, writes

> Thus, the emotion of generational struggle defined
> the direction of transition from issue to issue. . . .
> To parade, protest, to "confront" the local police
> were more of an adventure, and more satisfying to
> one's aggressive impulses.   "Confrontation" always
> has the generational overtone of the son standing
> up to the father; and if an issue, or a cause, lacked
> this element of "confrontation, " it was not emo-
> tionally satisfying.   Pure "do gooding" would never
> satisfy the student activist, because it lacked this
> element of confrontation, of conflict, of the occasion
> for aggression [Feuer, 1969, pp414, 415].

Feuer therefore concluded that the student movement was
merely an agency of generational revolt.   The aggressive
energies of youth are frustrated in such a well ordered,
well-to-do society, and emerge in generational revolt against
the System.   This is clearly the case, Feuer argues, and
the established type amongst his reviewers agrees, for
political and social problems are obviously better solved in
America through the established democratic procedures than
by the projection of adolescent rebellion on the body politic.

        The fact that lifestyle--the search for meaning and
identity--was an issue in the New Left gives a certain plau-
sibility to the psychologism of Feuer.   But the struggle to
maintain the distinction between the public and private self

was also of import.   As noted above, Flacks urged the S. D. S.
to maintain its clear consciousness as a political movement
with political goals, even though at the same time remaining
"receptive and responsible to the standards of existential
humanism. " The issue of national purity took precedence
over the issue of personal purity for the New Left, which
was politically oriented.   For the beat or hippie sub-culture,
life style was the issue, and although occasionally street
people were recruited into the political actions of the New
Left, they sought the experience of ecstasy in religious forms
other than that of the civil religion.

The personal commitment to action by the sectarians
of the civil religion grows out of the fact that the politics of
the New Left are rooted in ethical values.   Newfield suggests it is a "post-Nuremberg ethic ... which means every
individual is totally morally responsible for everything he
does" (Newfield, 1970, pp. 92, 93).   Thus the question asked
of political strategy is first of all the moral question, "Is it
right to do this?" or, "Must we not as moral men do this?"
Only after that question is answered is the pragmatic question
raised.   The person who cannot and does not discern first
the moral question, the perception of the good and the right,
is not politically able.   For the sectarians, the writers of
the Declaration of Independence demonstrate that men can take
radical political action based on moral concerns.   The inalienable right of life includes, if it means anything at all, a
man's right to choose whether he will go to war.   Liberty,
by definition, is rule over one's own life.   To abdicate that
rule to a despot, whether personal, such as King George, or
impersonal, such as The System, is not merely apathy but
immorality.   The "pursuit of happiness, " as defined by the
context of the Declaration, is not an individual matter, but
is a collective responsibility.   This is why men must make
revolution, whether in 1776 or 1962.   The inclusion of "the
pursuit of happiness" in the Declaration is evidence that the
conviction of the Founding Fathers is one with the conviction
of the New Left   individual alienations have social causes,
and thus must be addressed as social policy.   Community is
the goal of politics.   The creation of community requires a
personal commitment to brotherhood, democracy, peace and
freedom.

The Anti-poverty Movement.   The 1962-63 academic
year was relatively quiet on campuses.   S. D. S. was focusing
on organizing chapters for on-campus debates and informa-
tional activities.   The sit-ins, freedom rides and peace

demonstrations no longer seemed as dramatic. In fact, because of the Kennedy charm, rhetoric and tentative actions,
some urgency ebbed from the movement. As the nuclear test
ban treaty appeared likely, S. P. U. began to lose members
and disintegrate. Action seemed possible on the Civil Rights
Bill. Student activists planned to join the March for Jobs
and Freedom in the summer, but students were not involved
in the preparations for the March. The first generation of
student leaders, like Chuck McDew, and Tim Jenkins, were
graduating, marrying, beginning careers and thus leaving the
movement. Radical publications were folding. The alienation
of the hippie sub-culture had not yet been politicized.

But in 1963 America began to rediscover poverty.
Michael Harrington wrote The Other America in 1962. By
1963 the paperback version was being widely read. Dwight
McDonald and Bayard Rustin were also writing and speaking
about the plight of the poor. The New Yorker ran articles.
S. N. C. C. was urged to organize poor whites. Tom Hayden,
president of S. D. S., requested funds from the U. A. W. 's
Walter Reuther to organize poor whites. A five thousand
dollar grant created the Education and Research Action Project
(E. R. A. P.). S. D. S. jumped from campus to ghetto. Students
who had been South for civil rights and returned home to look
with newly opened eyes saw the same problems of poverty and
racism. E. R. A. P. was a vehicle for implementing the participatory democracy of the Port Huron Statement (Newfield,
1970, pp. 100-101).

The radical war on poverty sprang from optimistic
premises. E. R. A. P. 's purpose was to bestir the formally
democratic political institutions to act on behalf of the people.
The poor were to be organized so that they could be a new
power factor, a new insurgency. At first there was hope
that this pressure would reverse the corruption of the liberal
and trade union forces. Sectarians originally perceived
American society as a struggle between liberal-labor forces
versus corporatist and reactionary forces. Only slowly,
under the impact of both the organizing itself and the Vietnam war did liberal-labor forces emerge to the sectarian
view as hearty participants in an obviously aggressive economic imperialism.

Community organizing, as Todd Gitlin pointed out, had
many purposes, including enabling the poor to gain both decision making power and material goods. But for S. D. S.
such work had a context, an ultimate goal.

> to plant seeds that might grow into the core of a
> mass radical movement sufficiently large and serious
> and conscious and strategically placed to transform
> American institutions [Gitlin, 1965, p137].

This ultimate goal brought the S. D. S. organizers into conflict both with Alinsky's Industrial Areas Foundation and the
later War on Poverty.   Like the S. D. S. , Alinsky scorned the
War on Poverty as "political pornography." It was an attempt of the liberal-labor coalition to make political capital
of the rising urban discontent while remaining firmly in control (Alinsky, 1968, pp. 171ff).   But Alinsky was convinced
that the basic reality for the radical was the fact that the
world was an arena of power politics.   Morality was a mere
rhetorical rationale for self-interest.   The moral goal of
participatory democracy, of a reformed nation, was to Alinsky
just personal political whim.   I. A. F. focused on change
within the local community, which meant change within the
present narrow limits.   But S. D. S. sought national renewal
(Rothstein, 1969, pp. 274-275).

The theory on which E. R. A. P. was established is
articulated in "America and the New Era, " the 1963 policy
statement of the S. D. S.   This statement assumes the analysis
of "The Triple Revolution, " an article written by a coalition
of liberals and radicals, including some of the leadership of
S. D. S. (Long, 1969, pp. 339-354).   The technological militarism revolution is the first aspect of the triple revolution.
The effects are a psychological dehumanization of persons,
and societal reorganization to handle threats posed by international tensions.   This reorganization weakens individual
liberty, democratic values and the community bases of society.
A final consequence of the technological militarism revolution
is its feedback characteristic: created as a response to international tensions, it is now a major contributor to those
tensions.   It thereby creates greater dependence on military
technology to control the fears technology itself has created.

The second revolution is the cybernation revolution.
The combined efforts of computers and automated machinery
increase productive capacity and decrease need for human
labor.   Many persons face increasing prospects of life without work, or life with only meaningless work.   Cybernation
also reorganizes and centralizes economic and social life
through greater economic planning and control.   It also increases the use of technology to mold and fashion the behavior and attitudes of citizens and workers.

Third, the human rights revolution is the rising expectation of millions of persons in the United States and around the world that they will be able to claim full economic, political and social equality. This demand makes clear that present institutions have accepted and support long-lasting inequalities.

The triple revolution holds a dim promise, however. Since war is so fearful new methods of settling disputes might emerge. Blacks might be admitted to equal participation in American society. Existence might be better in material terms. But such an improbable promise is by no means a guarantee. A vision of democratic life becomes reality not by the drift of technological change but by conscious choice. Persons must create institutions which nurture the vision until it grows into reality. The heart of such a reality is a true democracy.

> Democracy, as we use the term means a community of men and women who are able to understand, express and determine their lives as dignified human beings. Democracy can only be rooted in a political and economic order in which wealth is distributed by and for people, and used for the widest social benefit. With the emergence of the era of abundance we have the economic base for a true democracy of participation, in which men no longer need to feel themselves prisoners of social forces and decisions beyond their control or comprehension [ibid. , p354].

"America and the New Era" opens by expressing again that the hope of the S. D. S. is human freedom. Freedom means the ability of men to understand, express and order their lives in fraternity. Political and economic structures must be such that power is used for the widest social benefit: the creation of community in which men can come to know each other as human beings. But instead of such hopes, the document says, the legacy has been the cold war. To it have been sacrificed the basic rights of the democratic process. The triple revolution is upon us. The "establishment" for whom "America and the New Era" means Mills' "power elite, " seeks to respond to the new era. The Kennedy Administration views its problems in a technical and administrative context, rather than a moral one. It intends to be "rational, active and adaptive, but its policies and style flow from its necessary commitment to the preservation of the

going system" (Teodori, The New Left, p. 177). Nonetheless,
particular policies do not have unanimous support within the
Establishment and are opposed by traditionalists of the Right.
But the general trend of the New Frontier is the strengthening
of general corporation power and the increase of the power
of the office of the President. There is no program for the
alleviation of poverty. Therefore for those committed to
democracy and human dignity, two emphases must be
stressed.

> First, in a world where countless forces work to
> create feelings of powerlessness in ordinary men,
> an attempt by political leaders to manipulate and
> control conflict destroys the conditions of a demo-
> cratic policy and robs men of initiative and autono-
> my. The New Frontier is engineering a society
> where debate is diminishing and the opportunities
> to express opposition and create ferment are de-
> clining.... Second, the policies of this Administra-
> tion can be characterized as "aggressive tokenism"
> [ibid., pp177-178].

It is clear to S.D.S. that the New Frontier is unable
to solve the most urgent needs of the new era: "disarmament, abundance with social justice, and complete racial
equality" (ibid.). This basic inability is seen in the continuing escalation of the U.S. involvement in the war in
Vietnam, and the lack of even minimal Administration attention to the black demand for jobs and relief from economic
distress. The decay of liberalism is evident. The major
liberal organizations, including the unions, have abandoned
the populist and progressive stands of their tradition. Liberal politics now emphasize cocktail parties and seminars,
rather than protest marches, local reform movements and
independent bases of power. A new insurgency is needed.
It is appearing in the civil rights and peace movements.
New efforts to organize the poor in radical ways must begin.
Such actions must be joined with an adequate analysis of the
American scene in order to "effectively create the impetus
for a democratic society and genuinely meet the needs of
the new era" (ibid., p182).

The hope was that such a democratic insurgency could
also provide for large numbers of the middle class a renewed and hopeful vision that might stir them out of privatism.
Therefore one of the central purposes of E.R.A.P. was to
energize the passive populists in the ranks of labor and lib-

eralism. Organization of the poor was also a means to
speak to the conscience of liberal America. The first action
of J. O. I. N. , the Chicago E. R. A. P. project, was to sell ap-
ples in the streets to symbolize the hopelessness of the unemployed.   The inclusion of a variety of labor, student,
church and professional class liberals in organizing the poor
was for the purpose of radicalizing the organizers.   S. D. S.
was certain that experiences such as the organizing of the
poor in Chester, Pennsylvania, probably meant less in the
lives of the poor of Chester than in the lives of the students
of nearby Swarthmore who were the organizers.   The inter-
dependence of issues about which S. D. S. was speaking was
amply demonstrated as students sought to modify the desperate
living conditions of Chester's slum dwellers.   Students who
became involved, out of an idealism motivated by the civil
religion, soon were "forced to face up to the realities of the
problems facing America" (ibid. , p131).   The intellectual
process of radicalization was galvanized by the emotional
impact of visiting tenements and engaging in neighborhood
meetings.

But the strict limits of changing such places as Chester
soon came into view.   The number of projects that could have
some success in Chester would soon come to an end, simply
because national unemployment was the key issue.   Sectarians
asked, "When this realization percolates through to the experience of the poor of Chester, what then?   Will the movement there, and in other places like it, simply then die?
Or will one put his hopes in a national movement to transform the nation?"   And

> ... if one puts all one's hopes in a national solution
> and therefore a national movement, how will Chester
> hook up with this national movement, and what form
> will such a movement take? ... one must make the
> jump of faith and believe that some national solution
> is possible, and that any job of radicalizing stu-
> dents, and making a local movement more sophisti-
> cated and realistic is a positive contribution toward
> that solution [Wittman, 1964, p132].

The original rationale for focusing on local issues soon
receded into the background, as E. R. A. P. found local political structures so rigid that even minor reforms could scarcely be won.   Much less was there a possibility of revolutionary
change in the national economic structure with a redistribution
of resources.   In Newark, E. R. A. P. was unable to win a

traffic light at a dangerous intersection to protect the children of the poor. Thus E. R. A. P. organizers soon began to see such confrontations as an opportunity for radicalization rather than reform. The essential ingredient in such education projects became a demand which local officials could clearly grant, but which they would probably deny. Such a confrontation

> will involve people in experiences which develop a new understanding of the society which denies them opportunities and rights; and which will open possibilities for more insurgent activity in the future [Rothstein, 1969, p279].

The radical war on poverty, although originally conceived to be directed toward the problems of the poor white, was considered from the beginning to be in close support of the civil rights movement. The first purpose was to provide blacks with white allies who were organized around their own needs. Both black and white poor obviously benefit from radical changes in the economic structure. Thus the alliance would be functional rather than charitable. A new populism was the dream.

The early organizers, such as Tom Hayden in Newark, discovered that what they had thought to be poor white neighborhoods were in fact largely black and rapidly becoming wholly black. It was clear to them that the civil rights movement had achieved little for the northern poor black. The attempt to organize both poor blacks and poor whites was then done with the purpose of seeking to stimulate the civil rights organizations to radical organizing around economic issues. Such experience would inevitably move the civil rights organizations toward radical consciousness. E. R. A. P. did play a part in influencing S. N. C. C. and C. O. R. E. to focus on such issues, although more important to such an effort was the dynamic of black power within the civil rights organization.

Tom Hayden and Carl Wittman cover such concerns in a working paper, "An Interracial Movement of the Poor" (1963). They categorize the demands of the movement. A judgment is then made as to the extent to which such demands, if enacted, would solve problems. Secondly, the effect of the demands on alliances with white groups is considered. There are four categories: 1) Demands to eliminate discrimination or de facto segregation. 2) Demands which

symbolically assert Negro dignity but neither achieve change
nor alienate whites very much.   3) Demands which are specifically racial, do not achieve very much and potentially
alienate large numbers of whites.   4) Demands for political
and economic changes of substantial benefit to the Negro and
white poor.

Hayden and Wittman favor the fourth type of demand.
The economic problems of the Negro are class problems and
cannot be solved by the elimination of discrimination.   But
the poor white and black must be improved together or there
will be violent conflict between them.   Whether the establishment chooses to leave the control of such violence to the
local police or to use troops to put it down, significant concessions to the poor would not be made.   For in either case,
"poor Negroes and poor whites will continue to struggle
against each other instead of against the power structure that
properly deserves their malice" [ibid. , p204].

What such a position implies for political work, Hayden and Wittman feel, is a new organized political presence
in society to break the problem of poverty and racism.   A
coalition of radicals and the most interested and committed
of the liberal left will be necessary.   Such liberals might
be found in some of the institutions of the church and labor.
While radical ideology would be understressed, still radicals
could make clear their commitment to

> democratic participation in a society with a publicly-
> controlled and planned economy, which guarantees
> political freedom, economic and physical security,
> abundant education, and incentives for wide cultural
> variety [ibid. , p211].

But radicals must not presume to be an elite waiting for the
masses to see the Way.   Radicals are "people who work
with people. "

> But clearly it is not an ideology that will give us a
> legitimate and radical place; rather it is the role
> we play in the community, as aides in developing a
> voice and a power among the poor.   The manner of
> this work will be basic to any change in the direc-
> tion of a new society.   The meaningful participation
> in politics, the moral reconstruction that comes
> from cooperation in positive work, and the forms
> which evolve in this struggle may be the main so-
> cial basis for a democratic America [ibid. , p213].

J. O. I. N. in Chicago demonstrated that racism could
be overcome by poor whites organized around their own demands.   J. O. I. N. worked closely with black community
groups elsewhere in the city, coordinating rent strikes and
demonstrations of black and white welfare recipients at public
aid offices.   But J. O. I. N. grew at a desperately slow pace.
By 1965 the central purposes of E. R. A. P. --addition of poor
whites to the movement, achievement of minor, though locally
important reforms, and encouragement of a coalition with the
most committed of the liberal left--were abandoned.   Only a
minuscule number of poor whites participated.   Even fewer
liberals were galvanized into action.   The local power structures were easily powerful enough to defeat challenges to
their authority.

Goals shifted.   The purpose became simply "to build
a movement. "   The movement would be one that would "end
racist exploitation and imperialism, collectivize economic
decision making, and decentralize every political, economic
and social institution in America" (Rothstein, 1969, p282).
But choice of tactics often found that such long range goals
were in inherent conflict with building a movement.   The
need to develop indigenous independent leaders conflicted with
collective decision making.   The need to dramatize the sense
of crisis in a community by such actions as rent strikes conflicted with the building of participatory democratic institutions
Residents could not easily reach a consensus on such radical
action.   Perversely, radicalization depended upon just some
such action for the experience of confrontation.

In the Spring of 1965 the E. R. A. P. structure dis-
solved.   Decisions depended too much upon local conditions
for a national organization to be effective.   Whether a given
project ought to have emphasized rent strikes or daycare
centers, community issues or the war in Vietnam could only
have been made locally and not by national or regional staff.
Each project thus became wholly self-centered, and the sense
of context was lost.   The broad vision of changing America,
of a pragmatic development of radical theory in specific
situations, narrowed to success in the particular tactic a
specific project had undertaken for the moment.

The portion of the movement that was caught up in the
organizing of the poor was perhaps the part most self-
consciously seeking to replace American society by its own.
As Troeltsch demonstrates, the method of the sectarian is
radically different from the method of the established type.

The established type seeks to cover the whole life of humanity
by organizational methods of control. The sectarian seeks to
establish a small society so pure, so attractive, that others
cannot help but be inspired by the vision of men living together in true community. It is in this eschatological hope
that E. R. A. P. entered the slums of America. There in the
most hopeless of places would be established a true community, a participatory democracy. There persons would
discover by meaningful participation in politics the "moral
reconstruction that comes from cooperation in positive work."
The small democracies so created would be the basis for a
democratic America.

The liberal left, sectarians believed, could not help
but see their own dreams come to reality in the organized
societies of the poor. The conscience of the nation would
galvanize the body politic into action. Since the liberal left
had been in the seat of power for thirty years, it possessed
the resources to renew America according to the inspiration
of the radical societies. The sectarians were sure that the
"passive populists" amongst the liberals could be energized
on behalf of the poor of America.

The other aspects of sectarian religion also appear,
of course. The very hope of inspiring the liberal left into
action expresses a deep faith. It is a faith rooted in the
American civil religion. There is the belief that America
can be the America envisioned in the Founding Documents.
There is the belief that man possesses the potential for good,
that he can create those political structures which enhance
life, that he can be inspired, that it is a crime to seek to
control him. Man is not hopelessly encased in the rigidities
of selfishness, but may be trusted to participate in the creation of the good community. The work ethic's praise of
wealth as determining man's worth is denied. Finally, the
sectarians perceive that it is personal involvement in organizing the poor that both creates and sustains radical consciousness.

The Expression of the Sectarian
Type and the Civil Religion in
the University

In the late fifties and early sixties, the University of
California at Berkeley was the leader in creating a new kind
of education system. Berkeley's system came to be characteristic of a major part of American higher education. Like-

wise, the student movement that emerged on this particular campus came to be a model for other multiversities. As a reasonably clear and compact example of the forces at work in American higher education at large, Berkeley may be used as an ideal type. In common with other great tax-supported American universities, Berkeley stands between two heritages: the academic tradition of a free unhindered search for truth and the American political tradition of balance of powers. The balance of powers tradition suggests that the university, as a public institution, does not give unfair advantage to one interest group or political party. The state university is perceived as serving not only truth but the public. Each of the various publics so served jealously strives to fashion the university in its own image of truth.

Trends at Berkeley, as elsewhere, affected the receptiveness of students to mass action that had a political focus. Campus enrollment swelled to over 26,000. The percentage of graduate students increased markedly while that of freshmen and sophomores decreased. The humanities and social sciences departments rapidly increased their share of students. Studies of Berkeley students showed that those in social sciences and humanities were much more likely to take a highly civil libertarian position than students in other departments. The time required to obtain a Ph.D. in these departments, increased to an average of five to six years. This trend created a core of students already adults, who across the years had come to know and trust one another. Finally, the policy of the University to hire prestigious scholars and grant them research time, thus decreasing their teaching time, led to widespread graduate student teaching in the humanities and social sciences. Graduate students thereby became well known to undergraduates. At the same time, graduate students did not participate in University decision making processes. Both graduate teaching assistants and undergraduates felt the faculty and administration were remote. The endless heaping of rule upon regulation, and the dehumanizing experience of an impersonal bureaucracy exercising in loco parentis control created fault lines of distrust between students and the faculty and administration (Heirich, 1971, pp50, 51).

In 1957, S. L. A. T. E. was established by an issue-oriented coalition of liberal and radical students including many graduate students. The group sponsored a slate of candidates for student government elections. Within a year S. L. A. T. E. elected the student body president and had gained

control of the student government.   Although S. L. A. T. E. 's
fortunes ebbed and flowed with the years, its style--non-
exclusionary, argumentative, issue-oriented--persisted, and
came to be characteristic of many of the organizations of the
New Left. In 1958, S. L. A. T. E. began to make criticisms of
University procedures.   Concurrently, an apolitical group of
graduate students circulated a petition asking dissociation of
graduate students from the student government and refund of
fees charged them for its support. The Administration responded
in the Spring by dissociating graduate students from student
government and <u>raising</u> the student fee over fifty percent.
Rumors were widespread as to the motives of the Administration. Distrust increased.

In the Spring of 1960, the House Committee on Un-
American Activities held a hearing in Berkeley.   The Committee was unpopular with student activists because of its
"McCarthyism. " It was seeking to establish that the Communist Party was the motivating power of the civil rights
movement, and especially of the current student sit-ins.   A
student well known to many in S. L. A. T. E. was subpoenaed
to appear before the Committee.   A group affiliated with
S. L. A. T. E. helped to organize public meetings to denounce
H. U. A. C. 's procedures as undermining the basic principles
of democracy.   Several hundred students attended the hearings.
After the students applauded H. U. A. C. 's witnesses at the
morning hearing, students were barred from the subsequent
hearings.   As the students surged, shouted, and sang in the
hall outside the hearing room, fire hoses were turned against
them.   Many were arrested.   A picket line was set up outside.   The response of the police, so obviously parallel to
the response of police against civil rights demonstrations in
the South, elicited the sympathy of a great number of students who did not march.   The subsequent dropping of all
charges, except for one student acquitted in court, further
strengthened the conviction that the students had been unjustly
oppressed by the police.   There was thereby created a core
of students, many of whom would still be at Berkeley in
1964, who considered themselves committed to direct action
for civil rights (<u>ibid.</u> , pp75-83).

During the next three years the civil rights and direct
action organizations grew.   Some of the students active in
these organizations graduated and remained in Berkeley.
Others, especially graduate students, dropped out.   The graduate drop-out rate was fifty percent.   Many "intended" to
finish, and planned to work only a year to sustain themselves

financially.   A major portion of both of these groups, seeing
themselves as alumni or students, continued to be active in
the direct action organizations.   C. O. R. E. and Friends of
S. N. C. C. were formed and became affiliated with S. L. A. T. E.
The Ad Hoc Committee Against Discrimination was created
to coordinate the efforts of activists on the many campuses
in the Berkeley area.   The A. H. C. A. D. supported the candidacy of a Berkeley professor for mayor in the Spring of
1963.   Running on a fair housing platform, the professor was
narrowly defeated.   The same Spring, James Baldwin and
Malcolm X spoke on campus to crowds estimated between
eight and nine thousand.   James Farmer gave a series of
addresses.

In the Fall, direct action projects increased, including
picketing of local merchants for discriminatory practices and
involvement in the San Francisco mayoral campaign.   Thousands of students joined in demonstrations against the racist
practices of the Sheraton-Palace Hotel in San Francisco.
Nine hundred persons were arrested, including about two
hundred Berkeley students.   The protests escalated with
demonstrations against the discriminatory practices of the
Bank of America and San Francisco's "Automobile Row. "
The massive arrests led to lengthy court cases.   Judgments
varied from months in jail to acquittal for the same offense.
Although the circumstances of each case varied somewhat,
the major difference seemed to be the jury and judge to
which the student was assigned for trial.

The inconsistent application of justice, the apparent
use of the machinery of police and courts to enforce discriminatory practices and the election of candidates opposing
fair housing and fair hiring practices created a moral crisis.
The basis of legitimacy of the political order was called into
question by the sectarians.   On the other hand, the radical
critique of American society as corrupt gained credence.
The belief that American society could be reformed by working within the "system" began to be discredited.   A substantial number of students came to believe that only direct action
could hope to overthrow the entrenched racist bureaucracy
which was making a mockery of the doctrine that "all men
are created equal" (ibid. , pp84-88).

During this period, the University sought to remain
aloof from student direct action projects.   On campus organizations were prohibited from taking positions on off-campus
issues.   Such actions were prohibited even when the University was directly involved, such as the refusal of the

S. L. A. T. E. request to hold a peace vigil against atomic testing. This regulation was applied against the students in spite of the fact that the University had substantial research contracts for the production and testing of atomic weapons. S. L. A. T. E. was subsequently stripped of on-campus status for violating this regulation. The University saw its action as an attempt to be responsible to the larger public, and not give unfair advantage to one interest group or party by allowing it use of University prestige and facilities. The students saw the University action as refusal to participate in a moral crusade to renew America. For the sectarians, this refusal was in itself evidence of lack of commitment to democracy, peace and freedom. The fact that the University also participated in weapons research while denying students the right to hold vigils for peace was to the sectarians proof that the University was not only hypocritical, but against them and their concerns. The sectarians came to agree with Kerr that the university was a prime instrument of the national purpose. Such a stance was not the good Kerr believed it to be, the sectarians argued, for the national purpose was defined by the establishment, the supporters of racism and war.

The opening move of the Free Speech Movement confrontation was the decision of the Berkeley administration to strictly enforce the Regent's policy prohibiting use of University facilities for political or religious proselytizing, including fund raising. The context for this action was the increased political activity during the 1964 presidential campaign. The specific area which was a focus of this action was a twenty-six-foot strip of brick walkway at the campus entrance on Bancroft Way, which adjoined the Berkeley public sidewalk. Small copper plaques at the edge of the sidewalk announced the walkway to be the property of the University. However, low concrete posts, placed twenty-six feet back from the sidewalk visually suggested the property line. A wide gamut of organizations had by custom recruited, raised funds, passed out literature and manned tables for petition signing, etc., in this twenty-six-foot area. It was an important source of funds for many of the student political organizations. The decision of the University Administration was solidified by the interest of the conservative Oakland Tribune in the "misuse" of University facilities. The newspaper cited as an example the twenty-six-foot strip. The day before the University published its decision to suspend political activity in the twenty-six feet, the Ad Hoc Committee to End Discrimination announced the opening of a fair hiring practices campaign

against the Oakland Tribune.   The day students began to
picket the Tribune, the University began to enforce the rule
(ibid. , pp91-102).

A coalition of radical and conservative student groups,
the United Front, was formed.   It agreed to picket, conduct
vigils and rallies and act in civil disobedience if the University stood firm on the ban.   The student paper headlined the
story, "The Fight for Free Speech Begins. "   The University
refused to modify the rules.   Picketing, vigils and rallies
began.   The Regents reinterpreted their ruling, however.
Advocacy of a position and distribution of literature on campus was allowed, but the prohibition on proselytizing, fund
raising and "political and social action" on the campus was
reaffirmed.   This reinterpretation coincided with a general
mailing by the University advocating a yes vote on a University bond issue on the November ballot.

The action suggested to the students that the University
could easily enough change its rules.   It did so to suit the
Administration's purposes, but refused student requests.   The
United Front determined to escalate the confrontation, demanding the right of "free speech, " which meant the full
range of political action, on the whole campus.   Tables were
set up for the purpose of fund raising.   Citations were handed
out by the Dean's office.   Students were suspended.   A sit-in
at Sproul Hall followed.   During the sit-in Dean Barnes defended the University policy in an impromptu debate with one
of the leaders of Friends of S. N. C. C. , Mario Savio.

Barnes sought to establish the legal distinction between
free speech and political action.   The University, he felt,
must be legally neutral.   Savio replied by stating the University was not politically neutral, but was run by the Board of
Regents, who represented the major power interests in the
State.   The blacks, the poor, the students, the advocates of
peace were not represented.   The ban on political action, on
fully free speech, served the Regents' interests.   Not only
did they turn the University to their own political purposes,
such as the building of bombs, Savio argued, but they silenced
their critics by rules.

> Consider how gross--how gross a violation of the
> spirit of the First and Fourteenth Amendments that
> is! Here's the legal principle.   I think it's more
> a moral principle.   We hold that there ought to be
> no arbitrary restrictions upon the right of freedom
> of speech [ibid. , p135].

Savio considered that the distinction between students and non-students speaking on campus was just such an arbitrary distinction. It applied most grievously against civil rights and peace movement people who wished to speak against an outrage while anger was still hot. But the Administration refused to allow such issues, the really crucial issues, to be advocated by those involved.

> Furthermore, they claim that the university is
> neutral. A lot of hogwash! It's legally neutral.
> It's the most un-politically-neutral organization
> that I've had personal contact with. It's really an
> institution that serves the interest and represents
> the establishment of the United States. And we
> have Clark Kerr's word on it in his book on the
> multiversity.... Anybody who wants to say any-
> thing on this campus, just like anybody on the city
> street, should have the right to do so--and no con-
> cessions by the bureaucracy should be acceded to
> by us, should be considered by us, until they in-
> clude complete freedom of speech! [ibid., pp134,
> 135].

The sit-in finally ended with the students determining to set up large tables for the forbidden activities, and hold a rally at Sproul Hall the following day. The students agreed not to identify themselves to the University Administration individually, which would result in individual suspensions. They wanted to force the Administration to move against them as a group. A non-student manning the C.O.R.E. table was arrested. The crowd attracted by the debate and arrest sat down around the police car. Speeches from the top of the car followed, including a review of Kerr's The Uses of the University by Hal Draper. The speakers, one of which was again Mario Savio, rehearsed the arguments of the previous evening, stressing that freedom of speech was essential if either the Nation or the University were to be true to its ideals.

The detention of the police car received wide coverage. Both the Governor of the State and the Chancellor of the University issued public statements that freedom of speech was not the issue. Governor Brown said

> This is not a matter of freedom of speech on the
> campuses. I and President Kerr and the Regents
> have long fought to maintain freedom of speech
> and an Open Forum policy on all campuses of the

University.   This is purely and simply an attempt
on the part of the students to use the campuses of
the University unlawfully by soliciting funds and
recruiting students for off-campus activities.   This
will not be tolerated.   We must have--and will
continue to have--law and order on our campuses
[ibid. , p175].

With support, the administration massed police on campus.
Negotiations were reopened.   Some members of the United
Front argued for compromise in order to avoid violence.
Kerr and the demonstrators finally agreed to end the demonstration, establish a committee to consider political freedom
on campus, and submit the cases of suspended students to
the Student Conduct Committee of the Academic Senate.

    But the fault lines of distrust between the established
type and the sectarians proved too great to overcome.   The
Free Speech Movement was formed to carry on the negotiations.   The University Administration and faculty representatives joined the F. S. M. leadership in the negotiating committee.   However, the contexts out of which the opposing
factions interpreted events were too radically different to allow true communication.   The revelation that there was no
Student Conduct Committee of the Academic Senate, and the
long delay of the Administration in recommending action on
the suspensions of the student leaders triggered angry ac-
cusations from the F. S. M.   The Administration argued, in
classic established style, that regular operation procedures
must be followed.   The justice dispensed to these students
must be the universal justice dispensed to all who offended
against University regulations.   To the Administration, authority was the paramount issue.   The F. S. M. , on the other
hand, spoke out of the sectarian context: the central issue
was the reformation of America.   The University, activists
believed, must be renewed if the nation was to be renewed.
The University was engaged in the most obvious and historic
of repressions of liberty: the denial of the right of free
speech.   Sectarians argued that since the time of the Revolution Americans have agreed with Jefferson that the right of
revolution takes precedence over the right of authority to be
respected.   The delays of the Administration were seen as an
administrative conspiracy to silence one by one those whom it
could not silence as a group.   To the students, the history of
their struggle with the Administration of the University for
free speech was an obvious parallel with the history of the
struggle of oppressed peoples everywhere, but especially with
the history of black people in America.   To the established

type of the Administration, the issue was simply one of law and order, respect for authority, and the necessity of all to follow the proper democratic procedures which made possible a peaceable resolution of disputes.

As the conflict escalated, the Regents, and the Governor, and the Oakland Herald Tribune strongly affirmed the necessity for law and order and respect for duly constituted authority. The calling of a general strike by F. S. M. in December found the majority of the general student body interpreting the conflict out of the sectarian context. The participation of the students in the strike, the anti-administration rally following the presentation of the Administration point of view at a convocation, and the election of student government officers sympathetic to the F. S. M. were all evidences of the sectarian perspective on behalf of the general student body.

Mario Savio had emerged by the time of the general strike as one of the student leaders most able to articulate the sectarian perspective. His speech at the anti-administration rally is worth analysis. Savio opened by connecting the civil rights and university struggle.

> Last summer, I went to Mississippi to join the struggle there for civil rights. This fall I am engaged in another phase of the same struggle, this time in Berkeley. The two battlefields may seem quite different to some observers, but this is not the case. The same rights are at stake in both places--the right to participate as citizens in democratic society and the right to due process of law. Further, it is a struggle against the same enemy. In Mississippi, an autocratic and powerful minority rules, through organized violence, to suppress the vast, virtually powerless, majority. In California, the privileged minority manipulates the University bureaucracy to suppress the students' political expression [Savio, 1964, p230].

Savio names the depersonalized bureaucracy as perhaps the greatest problem of the nation. The bureaucracy believes that history has come to an end. No events can now occur to change American society substantially. Everything is to be handled by the standard, universally applicable procedures. Of course these procedures are constructed first of all, to serve the bureaucrat himself, as Weber argued. But the poor, the blacks and the students do not accept the contention that history has ended, and they must be forever dispossessed. Therefore, the civil rights and student protests have a deceptively quaint ring. They demand due process of law, which simply means that the governors receive legitimation only from the consensus of the governed. This concept is historically the basis of the American experiment, but it is not being taken seriously today in America nor at Berkeley. It is so lightly regarded at Berkeley that the Administration disdains even an answer when pressed to debate the issues in the context of consent of the governed, jury of one's peers and due process. This is because the university understands itself, according to Clark Kerr, as the servant of the society. The university must therefore create a certain product. Bureaucracy, first developed in the factory, now makes of the student a factory product. Speech must therefore be censored if student speech does not serve the order of society which the university serves.

It is a bleak existence if all must participate in a game in which all of the rules have been made up, and which can no longer be changed. Yet the university, by its bureaucratic actions, seeks to fashion students to the mold that society desires for its men and women: standardized, replaceable, and irrelevant.

> It is a bleak scene ... American society in the standard conception it has of itself is simply no longer exciting. The most exciting things going on in America today are movements to change America ... an important minority of men and women coming to the front today have shown that they will die rather than be standardized, replaceable, and irrelevant [ibid. , p234].

Events now moved at a more rapid pace. Only ten percent of the more than seventeen hundred faculty members actively supported the F.S.M. Significantly, the supporters were largely drawn from those departments where the faculty had important personal contact with the sectarian point of view. These departments were those of history, mathematics and statistics. Forty percent of these departments supported the sectarians. But the majority of faculty members disliked the disruption, and as the Administration continually failed to re-establish peace, a "palace coup" resulted. The Berkeley division of the Academic Senate voted 824 to 115 to transfer responsibility from the Administration to the Academic Senate. Political activity was to be permitted, and

only its time, place and manner to be reasonably regulated.
The sole purpose of the regulation was to prevent interference with the normal functions of the University.   No
disciplinary measures were to be taken against students involved in the protest (Heirich, 1971, pp302, and 353).

The Regents rejected the Senate's actions, however,
and reaffirmed that the ultimate authority for student discipline is vested in the Regents, and delegated to the President
and Chancellor, who, however, were to seek the advice of
the faculty.   But importantly, the Regents for the first time
in the dispute took cognizance of the sectarian context,
stating

> The Regents respect the convictions held by a large
> number of students concerning civil rights and in-
> dividual liberties.   The Regents reaffirm devotion
> to the First and Fourteenth Amendments to the
> Constitution. ...   The support of all the University
> Community is essential to provide maximum indi-
> vidual freedom under law consistent with the educa-
> tional purposes of the university [ibid., p320].

On January 2, the Regents relieved Strong of his duties as
Chancellor and named Martin Meyerson, one of the more
sympathetic proponents of student concerns within the Administration, as Chancellor.

The need for protest seemed to be over.   F. S. M.
planned to disband, considering itself vindicated.   The Regents
had bound themselves to uphold the First and Fourteenth
Amendments.   The new political action rules were nearly in
accord with the policy of F. S. M.   The Academic Senate had
defended the legal position of the demonstrators.   The chief
administrative officer of the campus had been replaced by one
sympathetic to sectarian concerns, and both faculty and student body had made it clear they intended to be involved in
campus policy decisions.

But the controversy soon exploded anew.   The Administration passively accepted the obscene tone of the campus
wide Ugly Man contest.   The contest was won by "Miss Pussy
Galore," who was sponsored by one of the fraternities.
Shortly after, a single non-student was arrested for carrying
a small sign saying, "Fuck."   Faculty committees refused
jurisdiction over the incident.   Again the conflict escalated,
with the students demanding due process, jury of peers, and

consent of governed and free speech. In the midst of the
new conflict, graduate students were readmitted by vote to
the A. S. U. C.   When F. S. M. , with yet greater power, was
apparently ready to sweep the graduate representation, the
Regents voided the election.   An ad hoc faculty committee
found the students who sought to raise money for the Fuck
Defense Fund also guilty of obscenity and ordered their expulsion.   Savio led a rally repudiating the December 8 principles, and symbolically tore up a copy of the "time-place-
manner" rules for political activity.   Police were sent to
disperse the rally, but were surrounded.   Subsequently, the
Free Student Union was organized as a bargaining agent for
long-range struggle (ibid. , pp354-382).

In the second phase of the conflict, the central issue
was focused on the nature of the University itself, rather
than on the society which the University serves.   The question was whether a student has rights as a citizen of the
academic community, or only privileges granted by the patri-
archal structure as it fulfilled its in loco parentis mission.
The relationship of the Regents to the University also was
seriously debated, even by the Regents.   Are the Regents
governors not only of University property, but also of the
educational policy of the University?   Are they also the
governors of some persons within the University community
(the students)?   The conflict over this question continued to
escalate.   By the Spring of 1969, the confrontations between
students and Regents at Berkeley had reached the proportions
of war.   Pitched battles between the populace and the National Guard resulted in fatalities.

In a working paper for S. D. S. , Steven Weissman
generalizes from the Berkeley experience to campuses nationwide.   Weissman recognizes that a free university, like a
free society was a distant vision.   The belief in human dignity, freedom, democracy, and participation in decision making
is in as sad a state on-campus as off-campus.   Student
activists can radicalize students by focusing on issues that
oppress students.   When they gain a new perspective on their
own situation, students will then see society in a new way.
Four tasks are therefore before the activists: 1) Organize
and run candidates for student body offices.   Such offices
will not change the University.   But, they will be a platform
to raise the vision of student democracy (rather than student
government).   Candidates and officers can protest in loco
parentis rules, compulsory ROTC, the university keeping books
for the draft board, discriminatory admissions, housing,

hiring, and investments. Student-faculty democracy rather
than absentee government by a board of Regents ought to be
the democratic norm. 2) Free Student Unions ought to be
formed. Year round bargaining on the above issues, radical
self-education, work with the poor and in civil rights, educational reform and planning of the next campaign are all essential. 3) On-campus direct action and demonstrations
ought to be held. Activists who are serious about asserting
democratic control over their lives and education must con-
stantly affirm the right to revolt. The right must be exercised when students are affected by rules and practices in
whose formulation and administration students have no part.
4) Radicals must also organize around ideas. The radical
vision of man, society and the university must be continually
counterposed to the liberal ideology which underlies most
courses in humanities and social sciences (Jacobs & Landau,
1966, pp234-237).

It is important to underscore the fourth point. The
protest of the student sectarians is not merely the protest
of the activists against the theoreticians. The liberal doctrines are wrong, with their stress on realism, universality,
compromise and control. While it is obvious to the sectarians that man has potential for evil, it is also passionately
affirmed that if allowed to participate in the decisions structuring his own life good will emerge. The sectarian protest
arises especially within the university because the university
is to modern society what the Church was to medieval society. The university is society's spiritual center, its
source of guidance and legitimation. The dependence of state
and national governments upon academic research and advice
have changed the role and character of the university.
Michael Novak writes

> Radical students turn upon their professors as
> Protestant reformers upon complacent and powerful
> medieval churchmen. The note of disappointed in-
> nocence is poignant: how could you, you above all?
> The one hope of cutting through the American myths
> of cherry pie, virginity, self-reliance, anti-
> communism, crusades for freedom and hard work
> lies in the university. Yet university professors
> appear to prefer the comfort of their sinecures to
> preaching the original revolutionary message of
> our land, the message transmitted through our Bill
> of Rights, our Constitution, the Statue of Liberty's
> call to the oppressed and poor of the world (Novak,
> 1969, pp85-86).

As the Berkeley experience demonstrates, it is the established type of the civil religion, appearing in the university as the liberal ideology, that is finally the target of the sectarians. In the beginning, the university administration and faculty are not perceived as the enemy. But as the students enter the lists in a struggle for a new America, the sectarian perspective is fashioned. At first the aloofness of the university is scarcely remarked. The stress of the sectarian on personal action and the liberal ideology of the university suggests that the university supports the reforms. However, the university is unable to act as an institution in such events as civil rights demonstrations. But when the issues confronted begin to include those in which the university also shares directly, such as weapons research, the university comes to be perceived as part of the established type. The identification is soon made that the university is expressed by its chief administrator. Clark Kerr's book, which summarized the position of the established type, is used by the sectarians. Kerr did much to clarify the relationship of the university to the society. The doctrines of the sectarian form of the civil religion, which had been directed in debate and action against the larger society, are seen to apply as effectively against the university itself.

Once all the fervor of the sectarian commitment was brought to bear on the university, the student movement was itself transformed. First, there was provided a wedding of sectarian idealism and a student self-interest. Although student activists were but a minute fraction of a student body, a major portion of students were willing to join actions which they perceived to be in their own interest. This created a potent combination. Secondly, the public impact of such large scale demonstrations convinced the sectarians that the campus was not irrelevant to major social conflict. The oppressions faced by the poor blacks in Mississippi were common to the problems experienced by students. Further, the establishment had investments in the university. Therefore, the sectarians believed the establishment could be confronted in the university as well as in the civil rights movement. The rise of black power in the civil rights movement solidified this trend. The university was believed to have major impact not only on the war making capacity, but also on the racist structures of the larger society. University policies dealing with admissions, hiring and curriculum were more and more understood to have major impact on minority racial groups.

Above all the gap between the proclaimed ideals and actual practice yawned even wider in the university than in the society at large. The social consequences of bureaucratization were vivid in the multiversity. But even more painful was the fact that the vehement attacks on groups such as F. S. M. came from such men as Professors Feuer, Lipset and Nathan Glazer in publications like The New Leader, Commentary and The Reporter. New Left historian Jack Newfield felt Feuer typified the vituperative style and hostility when he wrote in The New Leader

> Weinberg, the police car limpnik, is a characteristic member of the student movement, that is he is a non-student. . . . The conglomeration, FSM, acts as a magnet for the morally corrupt intellectual lumpen proletarians, lumpen beatniks, and lumpen agitators wend their ways to the university campus to advocate a melange of narcotics, sexual perversion, collegiate Castroism and campus Maoism [Newfield, 1970, pp135-136].

Such attacks were especially grievous to intellectual activist students who at first hoped the university would symbolize an alternative to the prevailing culture. Instead of seeking an alternative, the university administration celebrated the wedding of national and university purpose. The university faculty attacked the erstwhile reformers or continued research as usual. Only about ten percent of the faculty supported the sectarian position.

The whole range of positions taken by the sectarian type of the American civil religion is thus a bona fide position for the student sectarian against the university. First, the national purpose as seen in the American mission is rejected. The universities' part in the cold war in terms of research and personnel training is attacked. The radical doctrine of man is set over against the liberal doctrine. The university non-community of coercion and bureaucracy is confronted with a vision of becoming a participatory democracy without which true community cannot flourish.

Secondly, the university is seen as withholding a substantial benefit from the poor, the minorities and the oppressed by its various policies. By seeking to change these policies, sectarians demonstrate their solidarity with the oppressed, even while they further their own interests. Significantly, sectarians contrive to escalate campus protest in response to the increased involvement of America in the war in Indochina. Again, both identification with the oppressed of Vietnam and self-interest in avoiding the draft are involved.

Thirdly, the work ethic is directly opposed by the demand that there be a student-faculty democracy. The work ethic decrees that privilege waits upon achievement, and structuring the university is a privilege, not a right. But students demand equal participation as a right not to be superseded by the work ethic.

Fourth, the passion of the students for free speech and student democracy emphasizes the moral rather than the legal aspect of these constitutional principles. The university is not to be administered by faceless bureaucrats carrying out decrees of absentee landlords, but is to be governed "of, by and for the people" of the university. It is the traditional American faith, expressed in the founding documents of the Republic, that urges the search for a truly democratic alternative to the present structure of the university. Again, the humanist doctrine of man which underlies the Founding Documents--the doctrine that man possesses potentialities for the good--is at the root of the passion for participatory democracy. Sectarians believe men are capable of creating for themselves more adequate structures for community, and especially for academic community, than others are able to build for them. Bureaucratic, rule-bound, moral-less, ethic-less, passion-less, realistic man is not true man. True man is found only in true community. True community is found only where each participates in the decisions that govern his own life.

Finally, like the crisis of the nation, the crisis of the university requires personal response for the sectarian. One must choose for himself whether to cooperate with the educational factory and become a faceless product, or whether he will recognize with Savio

> There is a time when the operation of the machine becomes so odious, makes you so sick at heart that you can't take part; you can't even tacitly take part, and you've got to put your bodies upon the levers, upon all the apparatus and you've got to make it stop. And you've got to indicate to the people who run it, to the people who own it, that unless you're free the machine will be prevented from working at all [Teodori, 1969, p156].

Again, this personal commitment opens the sectarian to the
ridicule or research of non-involved intellectuals such as
Feuer and Lipset. For the graduate student, who depends
upon the good graces of the faculty for placement, it jeop-
ardizes his career. But if the nation and the university
are to be renewed, the individual alienations of students
must be addressed as emerging from the policy of the university, and the university radically restructured by radical
action. The creation of the true academic community like
the true political community requires a personal commitment
to brotherhood, democracy, peace and freedom.

The escalation of the war in the Spring of 1965 had a
profound effect on the movement. As we have seen, the
escalation coincided with the last attempt of S. N. C. C. to
collaborate with the established type, and with King's move
away from the collaborationist stance. The F. S. M. became
the F. S. U. , and the major interest of the student movement
was anti-war protest. As the war demanded more and more
troops, student deferments were called into question. Increasing numbers of students were radicalized. The radicalization was hastened by the university's continued defense of
weapons research, R. O. T. C. , and industry recruitment on
campus by representatives of munitions and armament makers.
The work of the S. D. S. in the slums nearly disappeared from
public view. Instead, the media began to focus on the increasing radicalization of the students.

Radicalization meant a redefinition of the political
situation on the part of most of the movement. No longer
did the view prevail that the governing elites were open to
democratic pressure. Instead, sectarians came to believe
that the elites exercised authority illegitimately. Conventional political processes--coalition politics--were not to be
trusted. The new situation demanded new tactics. Forms
of civil disobedience were chosen that would "force the
kingdom. " The established type would be required to choose
between violent repression of dissent or acceptance of it.
Since acceptance of such action would be to abdicate rule,
sectarians believed brutal repression would be the choice.
Thus, they were sure, more and more persons would see
the true nature of the regime, and a yet larger section
of the society would be radicalized (Flacks, 1971, pp84-85).

To the tracing of this hope in action we now turn.

•

IV

RADICALIZATION AND RESISTANCE

RACISM AND THE CIVIL
RELIGION: 1965-1970

The Established Form

In June of 1965, the enthusiasm of the established type
for civil rights reached its highwater mark.   President
Johnson, speaking to the graduating class of Howard University on June 4th, selected as his theme the subject, "To
Fulfill These Rights. "   He begins by stating that the earth
was the home of revolution, where men charged with hope
contend with the ancient ways in the pursuit of justice.   The
banner of revolution that men carry around the world is the
banner of our own American revolution.   No revolution in the
world, however, touches the people of the United States more
than the American Negro revolution.   That revolution, with
the passage of the civil rights legislation of 1957, 1960, 1964,
and 1965, has seen "the end of the beginning. "   The beginning is the freedom: freedom to vote, to hold a job, to enter
a public place, to go to school (Johnson, 1967(a), pp253-260).

But a beginning is not enough, the President declares.
Not only must the gates of opportunity be opened, but all
citizens must have the ability to walk through the gates.

> This is the next and more profound stage of the
> battle for civil rights.   We seek not just freedom
> but opportunity.   We seek not just legal equity, but
> human ability, not just equality as a right and a
> theory, but equality as a fact and equality as a
> result [ibid. , p. 254].

This means that while equal opportunity is essential, it is
not enough.   Too many persons, both white and black, are

193

trapped in poverty.   Poverty is being attacked, L. B. J. states.
But, Negro poverty is not white poverty.   Its roots are more
deeply grounded, more desperate in its force.   It is the
heritage of slavery, oppression and continuing hatred and injustice.   While the influence of this heritage radiates to every
part of life, its most important effect is the breakdown of
the Negro family structure.   America must face this squarely,
the President says, for

> The family is the cornerstone of our society.   More
> than any other force it shapes the attitude, the
> hopes, the ambitions, and the values of the child.
> And when the family collapses it is the children that
> are usually damaged.   When it happens on a massive
> scale, the community itself is crippled [ibid. , p258].

Therefore, with all of the other efforts of the Great
Society, a large effort must also be made to strengthen the
Negro family.   President Johnson pledges himself to that
effort, for this is American justice--to fulfill the fair expectations of man.

> Thus, American justice is a very special thing.
> For from the first, this has been a land of towering
> expectations.   It was to be a nation where each man
> could be ruled by the common consent of all. . . .
> And all--all of every station and origin--would be
> touched equally in obligation in liberty.   Beyond the
> law lay the land . . . all were to share the harvest.
> And beyond this was the dignity of man.   Each
> could become whatever his qualities of mind and
> spirit would permit. . . .   This is American justice
> [ibid. , pp259-260].

The speech of the President was at first well received
by liberal members of both the black and white communities,
and even some sectarians approved it.   But when The Moynihan Report on The Negro Family: The Case for National
Action (1965) (Friedman, 1967, pp278-317), gained public
notice,   and with the disclosure of the fact that Moynihan had
been the original drafter of the L. B. J. speech, a controversy
erupted.   The Moynihan report attempted to establish the
thesis that the widening gap between the Negro and most other
groups in America is caused by the crumbling Negro family.
The Report argued that this was a new kind of problem, and
that a new kind of national goal was needed: the establishment of a stable Negro family structure (ibid. , p279).   Sectarian opponents perceived the thesis as racist.

L. B. J. was irritated by the uproar. To him the programs of the Great Society helped the family because they
helped the people in the family. He had moved from promise
to reality bills that created Head Start for preschoolers, Job
Corps for dropouts, Upward Bound for poor college age youth,
a domestic peace corps (VISTA), a Neighborhood Youth Corps
to provide jobs for teenagers, a Community Action program
with neighborhood centers so the poor could participate in the
identification and remediation of their needs, a new Department of Housing and Urban Development to build low cost
housing for the poor, a national health program of Medicare
and Medicaid, federal aid for schools in poverty areas, and
anti-pollution measures. Johnson remembered rural poverty
as well, and signed bills which meant to raise the standard
of living amongst migrants, American Indians and those in
Appalachia. L. B. J. also recalled that it was not only the
young who hoped for the opportunities that education and
vocational training would provide: all age groups were included in the sixty education and vocational training bills
that were passed. Although these measures were for all
the poor, a great amount of their focus was on the urban
black poor (O'Neill, 1971, pp128-131).

The sectarians were objecting to the professionalization
of reform on the part of the established type. Nathan Glazer
argued that a large body of professional persons and professional organizations had taken on themselves the concern for
the poor. As a result

> the fate of the poor is in the hands of the adminis-
> trators and the professional organizations of doctors,
> teachers, social workers, therapists, counselors
> and so forth. It is these who ... propose ever
> more complex programs which Congress deliberates
> upon in the absence of any major public interest.
> When Congress argues these programs, the chief
> pressures upon it are not the people, but the organ-
> ized professional interests that work with that seg-
> ment of the problem, and those who will benefit
> from or be hurt by the legislation [Moynihan, 1970,
> p25]. *

---

*Excerpts from Maximum Feasible Misunderstanding: Com-
munity Action in the War on Poverty by Daniel P. Moynihan.
New York: Free Press, 1970. Reprinted by permission of
Macmillan Publishing Company.

Reasonably enough, the professionals recognized that the poor needed to be involved in the wide variety of programs being funded. Yet although it was the black community that was to be deeply affected by the Community Action Program, at no time did any black have a role of any consequence in the drafting of the program's guidelines. The guidelines, drafted by Jack Conway, a labor organizer, were intended not only to include but to "arouse" the poor. The Community Action Program Guide provided that

> vital feature of every community action program is the involvement of the poor themselves--the residents of the areas and members of the groups to be served--in planning policymaking, and operation of the program [ibid., p97].

Such an effort did indeed arouse the poor, but in a different way than the professionals had hoped. The poor were aroused, not against poverty, but against those whom they perceived as being responsible for their poverty. As Moynihan puts it, over and over again the attempt to organize the poor by official agencies

> led first to the radicalization of the middle class persons who began the effort; next to a certain amount of stirring among the poor, but accompanied by heightened racial antagonism on the part of the poor if they happened to be black; next to retaliation from the larger white community; whereupon it would emerge that the community action agency, which had talked so much, been so much in the headlines, promised so much in the way of change in the fundamentals of things, was powerless [ibid., pp134, 135].

Bitterness inevitably followed. Blacks were all the more certain that whites meant to keep them down. Whites were all the more certain that blacks were ingrates and troublemakers.

The concern of the established type was to make the American ideal of justice universal yet to keep reform within the confines of the ruling class. In this effort, the professional reformers staked a great deal on unproven social theory. President Kennedy had asked a campaign associate, David Hackett, to organize the Administration's efforts against juvenile delinquency. Hackett discovered there was no con-

sensus among professionals, so he depended on Lloyd Ohlin of
the Columbia School of Social Work. Ohlin's "opportunity
theory" was a minority view amongst social scientists. However, because pilot programs based on Ohlin's theory were
already operating when the War on Poverty was initiated, the
Community Action Program became a central tenet (Sundquist,
1969, pp11, 12). Moynihan is convinced that

> This is the essential fact. The government did not
> know what it was doing. It had a theory. Or
> rather, a set of theories. Nothing more. The
> U.S. Government at this time, was not more in
> possession of confident knowledge as to how to pre-
> vent delinquency, cure anomie, or overcome that
> midmorning sense of powerlessness, than was it
> the possessor of a dependable formula for motivating
> Vietnamese villagers to fight Communism [Moynihan,
> 1970, p170].

But it is characteristic of the established type that it
will be dependent upon the upper class. In this case the
upper class was the social scientists from the best universities. Black people, and especially poor black people, were
not consulted in the fashioning of the program. Instead, in
classic established pattern, the ideal of American justice
proclaimed by President Johnson was to be attained by a truly
immense organizational effort. There was no question, but
that the established type meant to be in control of that organizational effort. As the process of radicalization began to
convert many of the lower level reformers to sectarianism
the commitment of the Administration and the Congress rapidly diminished.

The outbreak of rioting in the black ghettoes further
increased the distrust of whites and the anger of blacks.
In August of 1965, Watts erupted in flames. Five days later
thirty-four people were dead, more than a thousand wounded,
four thousand under arrest, and much of Watts in ashes.
Chief of Police William H. Parker, blamed civil rights
workers and "conspirators." Mayor Yorty blamed the Communists.

The "long hot summers" had just begun. In the summer of 1966, violence flared in the ghettoes of sixteen cities
throughout the U.S. In April of 1967, rioting broke out in
Cleveland. Several months of violence followed. Over one
hundred and fifty cities experienced conflict. In Newark, New

Jersey, twenty-six persons died and 1, 500 were injured in a
six-day period. Rioting in Detroit left forty dead, 2, 000
injured, 5, 000 homeless and required more than 12, 000 U. S.
and National Guard Troops to quell (Fogelson, 1971, pp3-5).

President Johnson established a National Advisory
Commission on Civil Disorders. The Commission was composed of a Governor, a Mayor, two Senators, two Congress-
men, a union president, a chairman of the board of a major
industry, a civil rights leader, a commissioner of commerce
and a chief of police. The civil rights leader was Roy
Wilkins of the N. A. A. C. P. , who was more of an established
type than a sectarian, although he had deep sympathies with
non-violent sectarians such as King. The Commission was
composed of persons of both parties and of both liberal and
conservative political sentiment. The staff was headed by
David Ginsburg, a Washington attorney. Much of the organizational work was done by Victor H. Palmieri, a liberal
Los Angeles attorney. The Commission was clearly representative of the established type of the civil religion.

The report of the Commission places a liberal interpretation on the disorder. The conservative interpretation,
the "outside agitator and criminal as cause" was discredited
by the F. B. I. , C. I. A. , and the findings of the Commission's
field teams (Report of the National Advisory Commission on
Civil Disorders, 1968, pp201-202). But, to fashion a consistent liberal perspective was much more difficult than to
reject the conservative view. As representative of the
established type, the Commission was convinced of the necessity that the masses be controlled. It was committed to
public order, for the Commission itself was composed primarily of persons of the state and ruling classes. A Commission of such persons was appalled by violent uprisings.
Yet those same persons were also committed to racial equality before the law. As it became more and more clear from
the investigations that blacks were subjected to unjust and
illegal discrimination across the wide spectrum of life, the
Commission sought to maintain sympathy for the oppressed
while rejecting their actions. The Commission therefore
viewed the events through the lens of "diagnostic sociology. "
From this perspective the riots were the almost inevitable
reactions of victims of intolerable conditions. The riots were
not seen as protests by demonstrators, for then the demonstrators would have to be condemned as transgressors of the
public order (Fogelson, 1971, p150).

"White racism, " the Commission said, "is essentially responsible for the explosive mixture which has been accumulating in our cities since the end of WW II" (National Advisory Commission on Civil Disorders, 1968, p10).   The mixture, the Commission felt, was compounded of pervasive discrimination and segregation in employment, education and housing, consumer exploitation, family disorganization and the increasing concentration of blacks in inner cities.   These factors were intensified by the resultant crime, drug addiction, dependency on welfare and deteriorating public services found in the ghettoes.   The bitterness of blacks was further sharpened by the double effect of the heightened expectations growing out of the civil rights movement and inability of local government to redress grievances.   The Commission felt this inability was a result of ineffective organization of local government.   A comprehensive strategy was recommended, which would meet the following goals:

> Effective communication between ghetto residents and local government; improved ability of local government to respond to the needs and problems of ghetto residents; expanded opportunities for indigenous leadership to participate in shaping decisions and policies which affect their community; increased accountability of public officials [ibid., p288].

The first phase of action to open channels of communication between government and ghetto, the Commission felt, was to establish Neighborhood Action Task Forces.   These task forces were to include a key official in the mayor's office as chairman, and the task force itself to be widely representative of both ghetto and larger community, including representatives from community organizations "of all orientations."   Grievance response mechanisms would then be established and the basic issues--legal services, joblessness, education, welfare, housing, etc.--would be attacked (ibid., pp288-301).

Such recommendations revealed the fundamental contradiction in the report of the Commission.   The analysis and recommendations were fully within the established type: the universal ideal of public order was not being met because of the apathy of the state and ruling class toward the grievances of blacks.   Blacks, being victimized by intolerable conditions, struck out in pain.   The solution, according to the Commission, was to ensure that those barriers of communica-

tion were reduced, and that government was properly organized
so that each man had equal access. The universal ideal of
equality before the law could be reached by a renewed organizational effort. Within the present system, the promises of
American democracy could still be made good to all citizens,
the tradition was still truly reflected in the present structure,
but apathy had to be replaced by determination to make the
system work.

The contradiction was in the suggestion that the barriers to access were accidental or technical rather than in-
tentional and political. The Commission had recognized at
the outset that

> What white Americans have never fully understood--
> but what the Negro can never forget--is that white
> society is deeply implicated in the ghetto. White
> institutions created it, white institutions maintain
> it, and white society condones it [ibid., p2].

But this recognition was then set aside. The Commission
turned to recommendations that were technical improvements
in institutional structures, rather than a redistribution of
political power. Indeed, as black community organizers soon
discovered, the technical changes were inimical to the development of black community political power. The fact was
that for blacks to enter the American system meant for them
to gain political control of the institutions which administer
life in the ghetto--police, education, housing, welfare, employment and transportation. For such control to be a reality, radical changes, including decentralization of control with
Federal and State revenue sharing, would be required. Technical improvements would not be enough.

At this point, the second contradiction in the report
of the Commission became clear. The Commission suggested
that white racism was responsible for the riots, and the continuing bleakness of life in the city. Inasmuch as white
racism created the climate in which institutions were closed
to black participation and control, this was true. But, as
Hannah Arendt observed, it was also misleading.

> Where all are guilty, no one is; confessions of col-
> lective guilt are always the best possible safeguard
> against the discovery of the actual culprits [Arendt,
> 1969, p28].

As subsequent struggles demonstrated, opposition to community control was not led by the ethnic groups most noted for white racism.   Such opposition was led by municipal bureaucracies and employee unions who have the greatest stake in the status quo.   The wider social support for these groups came from the commitment by business and labor to centralization, and from the commitment by liberal groups to professionalization of such social services as education, welfare, and urban planning (Fogelson, 1971, p165).

Nevertheless, by rejecting the conservative view which was probably held by the majority of Americans, and arguing that "it is time to make good the promises of American democracy to all citizens" (National Advisory Commission on Civil Orders, 1968, p2) the Commission helped create the will to close the gap between promise and performance.   The President, disappointed that the Commission did not commend his Administration for moving in the right direction and chastise Congress for refusing to appropriate adequate funds, accepted the report with little comment.   He did agree, however, that

> Until the people realized that all the riots and
> demonstrations were not the product of conspiracy,
> there was little hope of persuading them to focus
> on fundamental causes--on poverty, discrimination,
> inadequate schooling, substandard housing, slums
> and unemployment [Johnson, 1971, p173].

Martin Luther King, Jr. , was assassinated on April 4, 1968.   A shock wave of outrage, arson and rioting swept the black ghettoes.   One hundred and sixty-eight cities and towns experienced racial outbreaks.   Three days of rioting brought over 15, 000 troops to the defense of Washington, D. C.   Ten persons were killed.   Over seven hundred fires were counted (Fogelson, 1971, pp4, 5).

President Johnson, the morning after King's death, sent letters to both Speaker McCormack and Minority Leader Ford, stressing that "the time for action had come. "   It was time for the House to act on the omnibus Civil Rights Act of 1968, which had already passed the Senate.   The bill prohibited discrimination in the sale and rental of housing. L. B. J. was convinced that

> Now, in the wake of tragedy, ... housing legisla-
> tion seemed more essential than ever before.   Con-
> tinued delay and failure would be a victory for the

> forces of stalemate and repression. It would feed
> extremist charges that the "system" was no longer
> working. On the other hand, passage of the bill
> would demonstrate America's faith in its Negro
> citizens and prove the continued strength of moder-
> ate leadership, both black and white. It could be
> a new beginning [Johnson, 1971, p177].

The bill was signed into law on April 11, 1968.

In retrospect, it can be seen that Johnson continued
in his second term what was begun in the Kennedy-Johnson
Administration. After his landslide victory, L. B. J. turned
to the task with even greater enthusiasm. His proclamation
that "We seek not just legal equity but human ability, not
just equality as a right and a theory but equality as a fact
and equality as a result" broke new ground for the established type. Such a declaration suggested that compliance
with the work ethic was not after all the only prerequisite
for achievement. Johnson tempered that suggestion with his
conclusion that if the country would correct its failure to
find American justice for the black, then the work ethic
would regain its rightful place. Presumably when this special
justice was found, when this huge wrong was righted, then
America would be rediscovered anew. When America was
truly found, then the towering expectation that each man could
become whatever his qualities of mind and spirit would permit would be no longer distant hope but present reality.
But the connection between justice and the work ethic remained. When justice is flawed, the work ethic is flawed. The
conservative expression of the established type refused to accept this connection. Johnson's definition of justice was too
large. For a great many, justice was still a legal term.
But the liberal expression of the established type was dominant in 1965, for those committed to a view of justice that
was legal, equalitarian and humanitarian sat in the seats of
power.

Other classic aspects of the established type were
also seen in the work of the Johnson Administration. More
than any other president, L. B. J. sought to make his vision
of social reform a definitive doctrine of the American civil
religion. As Etzioni argued, those who exercise power in
the society also exercise power to mold contentuating orientations. By means of these perspectives men perceive and
interpret the events of their time. Johnson sought to set the
black revolution in the context of the American revolution.
His attempt failed for two reasons.

First, the concern of the established type was to make
the American ideal of justice universal yet to keep reform
within the confines of the ruling class.   This attempt found-
ered.   The "special American justice" which was expounded
by the liberal established type required a redistribution of
political power.   On the one hand, justice meant for blacks
to gain political control of the institutions which administered
their lives.   On the other hand, the established type meant
to maintain control of the center of power.   There
were numerous defectors from the established to the
sectarian type, but such defectors were only privates in the
War on Poverty--they had no major power.   The increasing
conflict moved the established type to return to the legal
understanding of justice.   The efficacy of the work ethic
within the context of a justice-before-the-law concept was
reaffirmed.

Second, and most important, the attempt to set the
black revolution in the context of the American revolution
failed because of the commitment of the established type to
the American mission.   The effort to renew America was
still set within the context of the cold war.   The mission
of America to the world continued its priority over the
inward purity of the nation.   This context had both a political
and economic effect on the attempt to reform the nation.

The political effect appeared first of all with the disaffection of the black leadership with the war in Vietnam.
The S. N. C. C. staff refused to attend the White House Conference on Civil Rights.   John Lewis, the chairman of
S. N. C. C. , was deposed for his support of the Conference.
Stokely Carmichael was elected as chairman.   S. N. C. C. then
proclaimed it could not meet publicly with the chief policy
maker of the Vietnam war to discuss the human rights of
colored people while colored people were being murdered in
Vietnam (Newfield, 1970, pp76, 77).

As noted above, Martin Luther King, Jr. , had spoken
against the war in the summer of 1965.   But at the signing
of the 1965 Civil Rights Act, Lyndon Johnson personally requested that King withhold further anti-war statements until
Arthur Goldberg could brief him.   However, King's wife,
Coretta, was active in Women's Strike for Peace and spoke
at S. A. N. E. 's summer anti-war rally.   Both Goldberg and
Humphrey assured King that serious negotiations were under-
way, peace was at hand, and anti-war statements would
hamper the cause of peace.   King remained silent until January of 1966, but then, believing himself to have been ill-used

by Johnson, began to speak more and more strongly against
the war and against the Administration. Although many other
civil rights leaders did not yet believe the conjunction of war
protest and civil rights action was wise, Floyd McKissick of
C. O. R. E. and Julian Bond of S. N. C. C. joined the list of
well known civil rights leaders who opposed the war. By the
time of the White House Conference on Civil Rights, King's
anti-war position had completely alienated Lyndon Johnson.
Martin Luther King, Jr., although attending the Conference,
was not invited to speak nor to chair one of the sections.
The President turned to leaders such as Thurgood Marshall,
who spoke enthusiastically of the legal and legislative gains
of blacks under the Johnson Administration. L. B. J. was
turning back to a more conservative expression of justice
(Lewis, 1970, pp297-312).

The political effect of the war on internal reform was
also seen in the presidential campaign of 1968. After Eugene
McCarthy had received a large vote in the New Hampshire
primary, Robert Kennedy entered the race. Jack Newfield
(1969) described Kennedy's campaign as "a politician in search
of a cause." R. F. K. went to Delano, California, and identified himself with Cesar Chavez and the grape strikers. He
visited migrant farm laborers in the Mississippi Delta and
upstate New York. He walked the streets of the slums of
New York to see at first hand the effect of the War on
Poverty. He met in stormy session with the Black Panthers
of Oakland, California. Upon hearing of the assassination
of Martin Luther King, Jr., he went directly to the ghetto
of Indianapolis, and spoke to a crowd of 600 blacks on a
street corner. He informed them King was dead, heard the
gasps and moans, and said

> ... we must make an effort, as Martin Luther
> King did, to understand with compassion and love ...
> what we need is not hatred--what we need is not
> violence, but love and wisdom, and compassion
> towards one another, and a feeling of justice to-
> wards those who still suffer within our country
> whether they be white or they be black [New-
> field, p56].

Kennedy had a special relationship with the urban
black. Surveys reported that 92 percent of the residents
of Harlem said the assassination of Robert Kennedy affected
them more than that of John Kennedy. Just 28 percent of
the whites of the Upper East Side shared that reaction. Eight

percent of New York whites visited Robert Kennedy's coffin
in St. Patrick's, while 52 percent of blacks said they filed
past. In the California Primary, many black districts with
a history of low voter turnouts saw more than 90 percent of
the registered voters give Robert Kennedy more than 90 percent of the actual vote (ibid., p74).

Kennedy openly attacked the War on Poverty as a
fraud, and promised to work for a genuine transfer of political power. Both his attacks and enthusiastic response he
received in the ghettoes eroded the Administration's commitment to obtaining the "special American justice" for blacks.
Lyndon Johnson felt those he had sought to serve so well
were ingrates. Kennedy's attacks on the war policy further
estranged the President.

Although Kennedy was opposing the president, it must
be emphasized that Kennedy's candidacy was of the established type. He was not a sectarian. In his announcement
of candidacy he argued that a new direction for America
could be achieved by changing the men who made the policies.
He did not take the sectarian position that it is the system
that must be changed. R. F. K. reviewed the inexcusable
deprivation of blacks and urged the recommendations of the
Riot Commission be implemented. Those recommendations
were fully within the established type. Kennedy emphasized
the anger of the young over the war. His candidacy, he felt,
was meant to "close the gaps between black and white, rich
and poor, young and old, in this country and around the
world" (Kennedy, 1968, pxv). Like President Kennedy,
Robert Kennedy believed it was time to end the struggle of
the sectarians in the streets. Policies must be adopted which
would encompass the needs of all people. Robert Kennedy
believed that as president he would be able to succeed in
making the American ideal of justice universal. The un-
spoken corollary was "and keep reform within the present
structures of society." It was the position taken by the
liberal established type in America ever since F. D. R.

The economic effect of the cold war was also decisive
in the failure of the Johnson Administration to attain the reform it sought. The costs of the Vietnam war far out-stripped
what the Commission on Civil Disorders had suggested
be invested in the cities. A runaway inflation had been
ignited. There was not enough money for both "guns and
butter," although the President was sure that both demands
could be met. The fact that the cold war was still the

context of the American mission was seen in the priority
that guns received over butter.   The mission of America
to the world was more important than the rescue of blacks
from the ghettoes.   The majority of Americans agreed with
the President.   The Congress appropriated endless monies
for the war, but only limited funds for the cities.

With the election of Richard Nixon the Federal Government's enthusiasm for civil rights was markedly reduced.
The conservative understanding of justice as justice before
the law was re-established.   While campaigning Nixon said
of the Report on the Commission on Civil Disorders

> One of the major weaknesses of the President's
> Commission was that it in effect blamed everybody
> for the riots except the perpetrators of the riots,
> and I think that deficiency has to be dealt with
> first.   When we talk about what we're going to do
> in the cities, we have to bear in mind that until
> we have order, there can be no progress ... the
> Commission has put undue emphasis on the idea
> that we are, in effect, a racist society ... [Con-
> gressional Quarterly, 1971, p17].

In his Inaugural Address President Nixon stated

> The laws have caught up with our conscience.
> What remains is to give life to what is the law;
> to insure at last that as all are born equal in
> dignity before God, all are born equal in dignity
> before man [ibid. , p18].

Nixon offered a set of welfare proposals more dramatic
than the previous Administration, for they included a basic
income floor for all Americans.   But the proposal attracted
much conflict, and the Administration withdrew its support.
The proposals died.   Support was also withdrawn from other
civil rights projects.   School desegregation was delayed.
Bussing to eliminate all-white schools was opposed.   Exten-
sion of the 1965 Voting Rights law was not supported by the
Administration.   As a candidate, Nixon had shown his con-
tempt for Cesar Chavez and the migrant workers by eating
grapes in public.   Under his Administration the Defense
Department purchased vast quantities of boycotted grapes.
G. Harrold Carswell, described as hostile to civil rights
causes, was nominated to the Supreme Court.   Proposals on
crime, including the D. C. crime bill, were said to prey

upon white fears of blacks (ibid., p17; O'Neill, 1971, pp396-400).

The sixties closed with Presidential advisor Moynihan recommending that

> The time may have come when the issue of race could benefit from a period of "benign neglect." The subject has been too much talked about. The forum has been too much taken over by hysterics, paranoids and boodlers on all sides [Congressional Quarterly, 1971, p24].

The N. A. A. C. P., The Urban League, the National Conference of Black Elected Officials, and the A. Philip Randolph Institute joined with nine other civil rights organizations to oppose the Moynihan memorandum. The memorandum was labeled as symptomatic of the "calculated, aggressive and systematic effort in the present administration to wipe out all the civil rights gains made in the 1950's and 60's" (ibid.).

Not surprisingly, public trust in the government dropped in the last half of the sixties. A research team from Ohio State University undertook a six-year study of the percentage of the population that had faith in American institutions. A broad segment was questioned. Twenty percent of those polled in 1964 distrusted the government, but by 1970 the number had risen to thirty-nine percent. From 1964 to 1966, the trust among blacks actually increased, while trust among whites was declining. After 1966, blacks began to lose faith in American institutions more rapidly than whites. This corresponded with the cooling of Administration enthusiasm for the "special American justice" and the increase in demands for "law and order" in response to the riots. Yet prior to 1968, a greater percentage of blacks still had faith in American institutions than whites. By 1970, however, the figures were reversed. Fifty-six percent of blacks now mistrusted government as compared to a figure of thirty-five percent mistrust among whites. Patterns of distrust were broken down into left wing and right wing. Blacks made up thirty-eight percent of all left wing cynics, and whites were more than ninety-nine percent of all right wing cynics. Whites are cynical concerning parties: to them there is little difference between Democrats and Republicans. Blacks perceive the policy gap between Republicans and Democrats as being so great that the Republican Party is not an available alternative. For both groups, a feeling of an inability to influence government was a prime cause of discontent (<u>Los Angeles Times</u>, September 21, 1972, p3).

Such loss of faith in American institutions signaled a decline in the power of the established type of the American civil religion, for the nation is the institution of the civil religion. As is so often the case, those in power in the institution seem to be the last to sense the change. Vice President Agnew stridently attacked black militants, student protesters and peace demonstrators as the few "effete snobs" who no longer believed in America. Richard Nixon referred to the sectarians as "bums." He continued to speak in 1969 and 1970 of expanding the range of opportunities for all Americans. "We can fulfill the American dream," he said, "only when each person has a fair chance to fulfill his own dreams." But the actions of the Administration brought rebuke from both the Civil Rights Commission and the moderate N. A. A. C. P. , who declared that the Nixon Administration was anti-Negro and accused it of "a calculated policy to work against the needs and aspirations of the largest minority of its citizens" (<u>Congressional Quarterly</u>, 1971, p20). Such criticism only renewed the rhetoric of the established type. Nixon summarized his oft stated convictions in his Second Inaugural.

> Above all else, the time has come for all Americans to renew our faith in ourselves and in America. In recent years, that faith has been challenged. Our children have been taught to be ashamed of their country....   America's record in this century has been unparalleled....   Let us be proud that our system has produced and provided more freedom and more abundance, more widely shared, than any other system in the history of the world [Nixon, 1973, p10].

It is not clear that the decline in the power of the established type of the American civil religion meant an increase in the power of the sectarian type. Some indications suggested this was true, especially the dramatic increase of black elected officials in the eleven states of the Old Confederacy (<u>Congressional Quarterly</u>, 1971, p69). Most of these officials, like Julian Bond, found their organizational and financial support amongst the sectarians. Yet at the same time, the more militant of the sectarian organizations were

fading: S. N. C. C. folded, C. O. R. E. was drastically diminished, and S. C. L. C. was a mere shadow of its former self.
Perhaps the power loss was of a non-zero sum nature: it
was a loss of power to the system.   Many of those who lost
faith did not become sectarians, but simply non-believers.
The American dream no longer had the power to invest their
lives with meaning and purpose.

The Nixon Administration not only has a different
stance on domestic issues, but also responds differently to
sectarian demonstrations.   The liberal response tends toward
co-opting the issue.   Reform is undertaken to make the
present system more responsive to the needs expressed in
the sectarian uprising.   The goal of the reform is often not
achieved, but the liberal wing of the established type is quick
to set reformist procedures in motion.

The conservative wing of the established type is more
likely to treat sectarian uprisings as riots.   Repressive
measures such as conspiracy trials are used.   Problem
solving is equally as important to the conservative as it is
to the liberal, but for the conservative problem solution
begins and ends within the system.   Conservatives are not
as likely to point to disruptive tactics as evidence of a need
for reform of the system.   The need to reform the individuals
causing the disruption is stressed.

The net effect of a conservative Administration being
elected to power seems to be diminishing of the sectarian
hope that America will be renewed.   As hope fades, sectarians turn from political action to other expressions of the
sectarian faith.

The Sectarian Form

In 1965, about the time that white support for the
civil rights movement was reaching its high tide, the most
militant black members of the movement felt increasingly
isolated from the American scene.   Direct action had passed
its heyday.   It had accomplished much.   Public accommodations in the South had been opened to blacks.   Retail stores
and consumer-oriented industries in the North had hired
thousands more persons of minority races.   The direct action
movement was essential to the passage of the Civil Rights
Law of 1964 and the Voting Rights Law of 1965.   Yet civil
rights workers in the South were subjected to increasing

violence and murder. In the North demonstrations against
discrimination in the building trades unions, rent strikes and
school boycotts had produced little. The progress that was
made did not keep pace with rising expectations. Non-
violent direct action began losing its appeal as an efficacious
tactic.

By 1966 the black protest movement had fragmented.
To achieve "the special American justice" for the black
urban poor was apparently an impossible task. Yet, hopes
continued to mount that some genuine equality would be
achieved. The resultant frustration divided the movement.
The left wing consisted of S. N. C. C. , the Black Panther
Party, and many individuals in C. O. R. E.; the right wing was
formed by the leadership of the Urban League and a substantial group in the N. A. A. C. P. Martin Luther King, Jr.,
attempted to maintain a centrist position, although most of
his policies were closer to the right wing. The left wing
emphasized independent politics in the style of the Black
Panther Party of Lowndes County, Alabama. This tactic
was soon applied to the urban ghettoes. The Democratic
party was considered part of the oppressive system. The
right wing, on the other hand, viewed the Democratic party
as an ally. The right wing developed a doctrine of "coalition politics" based on the direct action campaigns which led
to the 1964 and 1965 civil rights legislation (Meier, 1971,
ppxlvii-li).

The Left Wing Black Sectarians

The independent politics style was summarized in the
slogan, "Black Power. " Black Power first appeared to
public view on the occasion of James Meredith's "march
against fear" from Memphis to Jackson in June of 1966.
When Meredith was shot down, King, McKissick of C. O. R. E.,
and Stokely Carmichael, newly elected chairman of S. N. C. C.,
determined to continue the march. At Greenwood, one of
the towns on the route, where S. N. C. C. workers had organized, a rally was held. There, Carmichael, at the close of
a passionate speech, called for Black Power. Carmichael
was convinced Black Power was necessary because he felt
black people had to begin

> with the basic fact that black Americans have two
> problems; they are poor and they are black. . . .
> We had to work for power, because this country
> does not function by morality, love, and nonviolence,

> but by power. Thus we determined to win political
> power, with the ideal of moving on from there into
> activity that would have economic effects. With
> power, the masses could make or participate in
> making the decisions which govern their destinies,
> and thus create basic change in their day to day
> lives [Carmichael, 1971, pp18, 19].

Politically, Black Power meant to S. N. C. C. the coming
together of black people to elect representatives and to require those representatives to deal with the needs of the
black community that elected them. Black Power did not
inhere in the black face, but in the black community.

But, this political definition was immediately expanded,
for the popularity of the term Black Power was because it
expressed not just a form of politics, but the mood of a
people. Carmichael, within two weeks of publishing the
first definition of Black Power in the September, 1966, issue
of New York Review of Books, expanded the meaning.

> Our concern for Black Power addresses itself
> directly to this problem: the necessity to reclaim
> our history and our identity from the cultural ter-
> rorism and degradation of self-justifying white
> guilt [ibid. , p32].

A variety of Afro-American societies seized on this meaning
of Black Power and immersed themselves in African culture.

Many of the more political advocates of Black Power
were sectarians whose experiences had brought them to
despair of non-violent tactics. They hoped to reform the
nation with power, not love. They sang

> Too much love, too much love,
> Nothing kills a nigger like too much love
> [Meier, 1971, p482].

To become convinced that their experience--to have
been jailed, beaten, starved, frozen, shot at, spit upon and
at last released only to repeat the cycle--was empty of
purpose or hope was to tread the abyss of meaninglessness.
Kenneth Clark's perception of blacks as America's inner
colony was the new contextual orientation. Clark claims

> The dark ghettos are social, political, educational,
> and--above all--economic colonies. Their inhabit-
> ants are subject peoples, victims of the greed,
> cruelty, insensitivity, guilt and fear of their
> masters [Clark, 1965, p11].

Carmichael and Hamilton argue against Myrdal that there is
no real "American Dilemma" because black people in America
form a colony, and it is not in the interest of the colonial
masters to liberate them (Carmichael and Hamilton, 1967,
p5). The colonial status operates in political, economic and
social areas. With bitterness the authors trace the actions
of the established types such as Woodrow Wilson. Wilson
urged the country to war to make the "world safe for democracy." He also issued executive orders segregating most of
the public facilities for federal employees. He was convinced
that Lincoln had created a perilous state of family affairs by
emancipating Negroes too soon. Other such actions of the
established type lead to the conclusion that

> The values of this society support a racist system;
> we find it incongruous to ask black people to adopt
> and support most of those values. We also reject
> the assumption that the basic institutions of this
> society must be preserved. The goal of black
> people must not be to assimilate into middle-class
> America, for that class--as a whole--is without
> a viable conscience as regards humanity [ibid. ,
> p40].

The solution is modernization--a time of dynamism, a
time of creation of new forms and institutions to solve old
problems. The myths of coalition politics must be rejected.

> It is no good to enact an anti-poverty program
> calling for "maximum feasible participation for the
> poor" and then saddle that program with old City
> Hall and bureaucratic restrictions. The people
> will see this only as a perpetuation of the same old
> colonial situation [ibid. , p182].

Black Power advocates hope theirs will be the new American
revolution. Like Lyndon Johnson, the believers in Black
Power meant to set the black revolution in the context of
the American revolution. But their understanding of that
context was very different. It was not a matter of helping
the Negro family or of bringing the Negro up to an equal

starting point by an immense effort in social reform.   It
was much simpler, and much more difficult.   As America
was once a colony oppressed by the British Empire, so
blacks are now a colony oppressed by American imperialism.
Revolution--the seizing of power by the people so that they
could participate in making or make the decisions which
govern their destinies--was needed then.   It is needed now.

     Black Power moved north.   In 1966, the Black Panther
party was formed in Oakland, California.   Chapters soon
formed in other large black ghettoes.   The official program
of the organization formulated at the time of its founding
declared, "We want power to determine the destiny of our
black community" (Meier, 1971, p491).   A list of other
needs such as full employment, decent housing, an end to
economic exploitation of blacks by whites, jury of peers,
end to police brutality were listed.   Community organization
for control of the means of production and housing was urged.
Resistance to the draft and police brutality by self defense
groups was set forth as a policy.   To defend a racist government or to seek to implement its imperialist policies was
folly for black people.   They were themselves oppressed by
the same racism and imperialism.   The statement closed
with opening paragraphs of the Declaration of Independence.
The passages italicized by the Party are those which
declare

> that whenever any form of government becomes
> destructive of these ends, it is the right of the
> people to alter or to abolish it, and to institute
> new government, laying its foundation on such
> principles and organizing its powers in such form,
> as to them shall seem most likely to effect their
> safety and happiness [ibid. , p. 494].

The words with which the quotation closes are also emphasized:

> But when a long train of abuses and usurpations,
> pursuing invariably, the same object, evinces a
> design to reduce them under absolute despotism,
> it is their right, it is their duty, to throw off
> such government, and to provide new guards for
> their future security [ibid. , p495].

     The seventh point of the ten-point program of the
Black Panthers stated the belief that in accordance with the

Constitution of the United States, all black persons ought to arm themselves for self-defense.   This belief was acted upon by Huey Newton, Bobby Seale, and the small group that made up the early Panthers.   Conflict with the police was immediate.   Early confrontations, with the Panthers loading their weapons as soon as they emerged from their cars which the police had stopped, were shouting matches.   Police did not draw their weapons.   Officers attempted crowd control by ordering the inevitable group of onlookers to move along. Newton would object, arguing that citizens had a constitutional right to observe their police in action.   To questions such as "What are you going to do with that gun?" Newton would reply, "What are you going to do with your gun?"   Soon the conversation would reach the epithet stage: "You are a crazy nigger!" "You are a crazy racist Georgia cracker!"   But in the midst of the shouting match Newton and Seale would continually refuse to give any information but name and address, and call out to the crowd that the Constitution protected their rights to be free from harassment and to be free to bear arms.   Each such confrontation resulted in ten or twelve young black men applying at the Panther office for membership.

Newton considered the tenth objective of the Party program the most important.   It immediately preceded the quotation of the Declaration.

> We want land, bread, housing, education, clothing, justice, and peace.   And as our major political objective, a United Nations-supervised plebiscite to be held throughout the black colony in which only black colonial subjects will be allowed to participate, for the purpose of determining the will of black people as to their national destiny [Seale, 1970, p10]. *

Newton stressed that blacks ought to be perceived as a colony and the "mother country" as the oppressor.   This freed the Black Panthers from the sickness of racism.

> So we don't suffer in the hangup of a skin color. We don't hate white people; we hate the oppressor.

---

*Excerpts from Seize the Time: The Story of the Black Panther Party and Huey P. Newton. by Bobby Seale.   New York: Random House, 1970.   Reprinted by permission of the publisher.

> And if the oppressor happens to be white then we
> hate him.   When he stops oppressing us then we
> no longer hate him.   And right now in America
> you have the slave-master being a white group
> [Newton, 1968, p504].

Black Power for the Panthers was therefore described
as giving power to people who have not had power to determine their destiny.   The way for the oppressed to gain power
was outlined: 1) The black colony of America has to have
black revolutionaries who are willing to demonstrate that the
oppressed can even now begin to take control over their own
lives.   The black masses do not read.   It is action that
educates.   2) The revolution is therefore an open-ended process.   The leadership acts upon what it believes to be the
needs of the people.   The people respond.   The leadership
listens.   The next actions are in accord with what the people
now need (Newton, 1972, pp44-53).

The cultural heroes for Black Power advocates were
the revolutionaries of the world: Frantz Fanon, Mao Tse
Tung, Fidel Castro, and strangely enough, Malcolm X.
Malcolm X had not succeeded in developing either a program
or a significant following before his assassination.   He had,
however, openly and with considerable publicity argued that
violence was an acceptable method if it moved the situation
toward a solution of the black man's problem.

> I am for violence if non-violence means we continue
> postponing a solution to the American black man's
> problem--just to avoid violence.   I don't go for
> nonviolence if it also means a delayed solution.
> To me a delayed solution is a non-solution.   Or
> I'll say it another way.   If it must take violence
> to get the black man his human rights in this
> country, I'm for violence exactly as you know the
> Irish, the Poles, or Jews would be if they were
> flagrantly discriminated against [Malcolm X, 1965,
> p373].

Malcolm X was convinced that the American political, economic and social system was racist, yet a few individual
white men had the possibility of being human beings.   Therefore, black people did not need to hate white people, but only
white oppressors.   Whites who struggled against racism in
their own communities were to be respected.   Whites who
sought to struggle against racism in the black community

were to be rejected. But the few whites who struggled
against racism in their own community suggested that America's soul could be saved if the black race took a stand for
itself. Malcolm X was attempting to enable the American
black to take that stand through the development of a Black
Nationalist organization.

> Why Black Nationalism? ... in my childhood, I had
> been exposed to the Black Nationalist teachings of
> Marcus Garvey--which, in fact, I had been told had
> led to my father's murder ... the Black Nationalist
> political, economic and social philosophies had the
> ability to instill within black men the racial dignity,
> the incentive, and the confidence that the black race
> needs today to get up off its knees, and to get on
> its feet, and to get rid of its scars, and to take a
> stand for itself [ibid., p381].

Huey Newton, Bobby Seale and the Black Panthers
"related" to Malcolm X. They accepted his argument that
black people must stand up for black people. Within the
perspective of blacks as an oppressed colony who must seize
power over their own lives, they set out "to find America
for themselves, with the same immense thrill of discovery
which gripped those who first began to realize that here, at
last, was a home for freedom." Lyndon Johnson and the
established type could scarcely recognize what the Black
Power sectarians were about.

The primary reason for the rejection of the black
sectarians by the white society was the gap between the perspectives of the established type and the sectarians. Important to this rejection was the requirement of the state to
maintain a monopoly of the means of organized violence. The
self-defense of the Panthers was perceived as an attempt to
challenge the monopoly of the state. Whether organized
violence is offensive or defensive depends on the perspective
of the viewer. From the perspective of the F.B.I. and local
police, the Panthers were armed and organized for offensive
action against society.

From the standpoint of the established civil religion,
to allow an organized armed body to flourish within the state
is to allow the objective establishment of what appears to be
a competing civil religion. The established type cannot allow this. Troeltsch observed of the Christian religion

It was the aim of the leaders of the Church to
render this basis as objective as possible, by
means of tradition, priesthood, and sacrament; to
secure in it, objectively the sociological point of
contact; if that were once firmly established the
subjective influence of the Church was considered
secure; it was only in detail that it could not be
controlled. ... In this way the universalizing tendency was also made effective, since it established
the Church ... in the supreme position of power
[Troeltsch, 1960, p335].

As long as sectarians were committed to non-violence, they
could be considered as those who were wayward only in subjective
responses. Other dynamics, such as the southern form of the
civil religion, account for the murder of non-violent civil
rights workers. But once sectarians commit themselves to
the use of organized means of violence, they seek to establish an
objective civil order which challenges the power of the
established civil order.

Eldridge Cleaver moved the Black Panther Party toward organized offensive violence. Such a movement was
ultimately an act of despair. Cleaver, when he first joined
the Party, still sought to clarify for blacks that the police
were the armed protectors of society. The issue of
police brutality was set within a class rather than a race
perspective.

In Soul on Ice (1968), Cleaver says

The police are the armed guardians of the social
order. The blacks are the chief domestic victims
of the American social order. A conflict of interests exists, therefore, between the blacks and
the police. It is not solely a matter of trigger-
happy cops, of brutal cops who love to crack black
heads. Mostly it's a job to them [Cleaver, 1968,
p134].

The white power structure, Cleaver believes, seeks
to keep blacks from becoming bold and revolutionary. Revolution by blacks would likely be class revolution. Therefore
the power structure communicates in a complex way to its
army of occupation in the ghetto, the police, to control the
blacks. Blacks experience this control as madness. The
Vietnam war raises the question

> Why not die right here in Babylon fighting for a
> better life, like the Viet Cong? If those little cats
> can do it, what's wrong with big studs like us?
> A mood sets in, spreads across America, across
> the face of Babylon, jells in black hearts every-
> where [ibid. , p137].

The killing of Black Panthers by police across the
country and the arrest of Bobby Seale, Chairman of the
Black Panther Party, convinced Cleaver that blacks were
isolated. He wrote from exile, where he had fled to prevent
being returned to prison for having broken terms of his
parole

> We will not sacrifice Chairman Bobby Seale on the
> altar of interracial harmony if White people continue
> to sit back and allow this ghastly plot to go for-
> ward. So, if so-called freedom loving White people
> of America do not stand up now, while there still
> are a few moments of time left, and put an end to
> the persecution of Chairman Bobby Seale, then
> Black people will have to go it alone and step for-
> ward alone. This will mean the end of our dreams
> for the Class War which America needs and the
> beginning of the Race War which America cannot
> endure [Foner, 1970, p119].

According to Huey Newton, while Cleaver had a major
influence in the Party, the Party lost its vision and defected
from the community. The Party became a cult. No longer
was it concerned with the community. The either-or attitude
dominated: the community either picked up the gun and joined
the party or they were cowards and Uncle Toms.

> So, the Black Panther Party has reached a contra-
> diction with Eldridge Cleaver, and he has defected
> from the Party because we would not order every-
> one into the streets tomorrow to make revolution.
> We recognize that this is impossible because ...
> declaring a spontaneous revolution is a fantasy.
> The people are not at that point now [Newton, 1972,
> pp52, 53].

Newton writes that since the Cleaver phase is passed,
the Party is building the community structure which will become the true voice of the people, and promote their genuine
interest in a variety of ways. With the trials of both Newton

and Seale ending in hung juries, the Party leadership is now
free to turn to the new programs. Presently, the Panthers
are administering S. A. F. E. --Seniors Against a Fearful Environment. S. A. F. E. is a Panther service which drives
elderly, both black and white, from their homes to the downtown banks and back on the day Social Security checks arrive.
Seale now regularly visits the black churches of Oakland to
meet those who have not known Panthers. Newton is joining
with the leadership of sixteen other minority organizations to
lease cable television channels for one dollar per year to
present the Party's programs. Black Panthers sit in six of
the eighteen positions on the governing board of the West
Oakland Model Cities Governing Board. Four of the fourteen
voting members of the antipoverty board of Berkeley belong
to the Party. Panther member Elaine Brown is running for
the Oakland City Council. Chairman Bobby Seale has entered
the race for Mayor. The Party's community programs--
children's breakfast, clothing and shoes for the poor, sickle
cell anemia tests and voter registration--are once more in
full swing. More than 18,000 new voters are now on the
lists as a result of the Panther registration drive in the past
year. Thirty-five thousand persons in the Bay area are
recipients of the sickle cell anemia test. In speeches and
interviews, Newton and Seale proclaim the Party is putting down
the gun and picking up the hammer. The emphasis is on construction of a new society (Los Angeles Times, Dec. 4, 1972). *

Newton is convinced that these activities have three
purposes: 1) Survival is the most important. Food, clothing
and health are basic to the people. Police have more guns
than the Panthers, which fact demonstrates the gun is not
revolutionary, but may threaten the survival of the revolution.
2) Another purpose is to pressure the present order of government to serve the people. In the past, the Party despaired
and said the present system absolutely could not serve the
people at all. This is now seen as wrong. The Party is
now interested in forcing the system to correct itself as
much as it can. 3) These things are all done to organize
the people politically, in order to help them make the revolution. The leadership of the Party doubts that the system
will ever truly serve the people, but until the people feel the
same way, the Party works within the system. It is arrogant
and foolish for the leadership to declare the time is come for
the revolution. The people make the revolution. If the
system cannot be forced to serve them, they will tell the Party
when they are ready for the revolution (Newton, 1972, pp66-69).

---

*The Panther S. A. F. E. service is no longer active.

The left wing sectarians also attacked the prison
system.   At the close of the sixties, the sectarians attempted
to establish the class of "political" prisoner.   The reforms
enacted in the sentencing of prisoners in states such as California lent credence to such claims.   Prisoners were sentenced for indefinite terms, such as two to fifteen years.
The interest of liberals in pressing for such reforms had
been that parole boards could then release a prisoner as soon
as he had been rehabilitated.   Since rehabilitation rather than
punishment was said to be the primary purpose of the prison
system, it was argued that a prisoner ought to be returned
to society when the purpose of his incarceration was complete.
Parole boards, however, were usually made up of conservative, white, established types.   For an increasing number of
blacks, prison was a radicalizing experience.   Statements by
prisoners such as George Jackson scarcely recommended
their authors to the parole board as men who were rehabilitated.   Jackson wrote

> We can attempt to limit the scope and range of
> violence in revolution by mobilizing as many parti-
> sans as possible at every level of socioeconomic
> life, but considering the hold that the ruling class
> of this country has on the apolitical in general and
> its history of violence, nothing could be more
> predictable than civil disorders, perhaps even civil
> war.   I don't dread either ... [Jackson, 1971,
> p159].

Parole boards therefore used the reformed laws to maintain
the revolutionaries in prison for years beyond the limit for
their offenses under the older, more "rigid" laws.   To the
parole boards it was obvious such persons were not rehabilitated to the perspective of the established type.

The distinction is further made between the breaking
of the law for the individual self-interest or a violation in
the interest of the black community according to Angela
Davis.   The legal system does not acknowledge such a difference.   The person stands trial for a specific criminal offense, not a political act.   But, because the action was taken
for the sake of reformist or revolutionary social change, the
person is a political prisoner.

> The offense of the political prisoner is his political
> boldness, his persistent challenging--legally or
> extra-legally--of fundamental social wrongs fostered

> and reinforced by the state. He has opposed unjust
> laws and exploitative, racist social conditions in
> general, with the ultimate aim of transforming
> these laws and this society into an order harmonious
> with the material and spiritual needs and interests
> of the vast majority of its members [Davis, 1971,
> p31].

Davis lists Nat Turner and John Brown as historical examples
of political prisoners. A contemporary example was the New York
Panther 21 trial, where the prosecutor entered as evidence of
criminal intent literature which represented the political
ideology of the Party.   The court admitted the evidence, but
continued to insist the trial was not political (ibid. , p33).

The District Attorney's office also informed the press,
prior to the selection and sequestering of the jury, that the
Black Panthers were funded by the governments of China and
Cuba.   The office further implied that the seizure of the
Party members took place while they were on the way to
commit arson and bombings.   A year later, the defendants
were acquitted on all 156 counts.   But during the stay in
prison, a series of prison rebellions erupted in an attempt
to focus attention on the conditions in the state prison system,
including the length of confinement of prisoners before trial.
To the black sectarians, the political nature of these police
attacks and the subsequent year's imprisonment was apparent.
The success of the Panthers in radicalizing the inmates of
the New York prison system made it clear that other prisoners quickly accepted the perspective of the sectarians
(Balagoon, 1971, pp269-364).

Of all the sectarians discussed thus far, the left wing
black sectarians of the latter sixties most vehemently opposed
the doctrine of the mission of America to the world.   The
perception of black ghettoes as colonies and the nation at
large as the oppressive "mother country" filled the concept
of imperialism with bitter reality.   For black sectarians to
rail against America's imperialist foreign policy is not empty
rhetoric, but it is the expression of hostility to a policy
which also victimizes them.   The endless repetitions of the
Federal Government that the war was caused by the "invasion"
of the South by the North is compared to the endless repeti-
tion of Southern politicians that "our Negroes have been
stirred up by Northern agitators. "   The increasing understanding that the war was being waged against all the Vietnamese people in free fire zones or Viet Cong controlled

areas led to the bitter designation of the ghetto as a "free
fire zone." The fact that the vast majority of those killed
in Vietnam were non-white, and whether military or civilian,
were killed by Americans leads to the American mission being
perceived as genocide against non-whites, in Asia and in the
colonies of the mother country. The invasion of the Dominican Republic is likened to the invasion of Watts and the other
riot torn inner cities by the army. The urban riots are
therefore referred to as rebellions against the established
order. The sectarians warn that next time the rebellions
will be organized rather than spontaneous.

The heroes of left wing sectarians are the makers of
revolution, who are believed to have helped their people gain
control over their own lives. The cold war understanding of
the American mission to the world musters the full strength
of America's economic, political, and where feasible, military might against the revolutions such men have led. Black
sectarians perceive this effort to be one with the effort of
the police to kill the Panthers, and the Army and the police
to occupy the ghettoes. Therefore the idea of America having
a mission to the world is utter anathema. It is rejected with
all the passion that Christian sectarians once rejected the
worldliness of the Church. Left wing black sectarians are
opposed to the American mission to the world because they
believe it is the same imperialism they experience. Therefore, they are hostile toward the social institutions which
perpetuate that mission. Although the first concern of black
sectarians is to organize their own community to "serve the
people," a secondary interest in eventually replacing the
present social institutions of the "mother country" with institutions like those which are now being created is apparent.

Second, black, left wing sectarians are also most
marked for their concern for solidarity with the lowest class.
They argue as Huey Newton, that it is the jobless blacks of
the ghetto that are "the people" that must take control of the
institutions that control their own lives. Sophisticated
Marxists such as Angela Davis remind the sectarians that

> With the declassed character of lumpen proletarians
> in mind, Marx had stated that they are as capable
> of "the most heroic deeds and the most exalted
> sacrifices, as of the basest banditry and the dirtiest
> corruption." Too many Marxists have been in-
> clined to overvalue the second part of Marx's ob-
> servation ... while minimizing or indeed totally

> disregarding his first remark, applauding the lumpen
> for their heroic deeds and exalted sacrifices [Davis,
> 1971, p35].

She goes on to point out that especially today when so many
blacks are jobless, the role of the unemployed, which includes the lumpen proletariat, in the revolutionary struggle
must be taken seriously.   This intellectual recognition is
being put into practice in the Black Panther Party.   When
"the people" were not willing to follow the leadership into
armed revolution, the leadership declared armed revolution
is wrong, for the task of the Party is "to serve the people."
The types of programs subsequently administered--S. A. F. E. ,
free shoes and clothing, the breakfast program, and political
involvement on poverty boards--scarcely seem radical.   Yet,
they are the felt needs of the ghetto dweller, and therefore
are the programs now pursued.

However, in contrast with a host of other agencies
pursuing like programs, the sectarians use the programs as
a means of political education.   Here is seen the close connection that sectarians classically maintain between develop-
ments in society and the lowest class.   The actions of the
sectarians in serving the people are not for charity's sake,
but for the sake of aiding the people in gaining control of
their own lives.   The first step in such aid is to ensure
survival, but it is considered only the first step.

Third, the Marxist critique of capitalism which appears so often in the black sectarian literature is an explicit
denial of the work ethic.   Ghetto blacks are not considered
evil because of their poverty.   Rather it is the capitalist
system which is considered evil for enforcing such degradation upon the people.   Newton writes

> We declare that our goal is to destroy all elements
> of the oppression.   We pledge ourselves to end
> imperialism and distribute the wealth of the world
> to all the people of the world.   We foresee a sys-
> tem of true communism where all people produce
> according to their abilities and all receive ac-
> cording to their needs. ...   When we have developed
> a system that functions in the true interests of the
> people and established it in full, then the word
> "work" will be re-defined as meaningful play.   We
> will have eliminated the cause of all our problems
> ... [Newton, 1972, pp42, 43].

Yet, there is an asceticism that fits the revolutionary style. It is perceived as a giving of oneself to the people, thereby expressing and demonstrating anew the reality of a person's commitment to freedom and democracy. The Black Panther Party does not pay a salary; only basic necessities are taken care of. Yet,

> A true revolutionary will get up early in the
> morning and he'll go serve the Free Breakfast for
> Children. Then when that's done he'll go and he'll
> organize a boycott around a specific issue, to sup-
> port Breakfast for Children or support any other
> kind of program. He'll do revolutionary work in
> the community. He'll propagandize the community;
> he'll pass out leaflets. As a citizen in the com-
> munity and a member of the Black Panther Party,
> he'll go to the firing range and take firing practice,
> but he'll follow all the gun laws and he won't con-
> ceal his weapon, or other jive stuff. He'll follow
> the rules and be very dedicated [Seale, 1970, p380].

Fourth, the left wing black sectarians appeal most strongly to the Founding Documents. The Declaration of Independence is part of the Black Panther Party program. Bobby Seale understands his refusal to accept William Kunstler as his lawyer in the trial of the Chicago Eight as a Constitutional question. Since the Party is convinced black men must vigorously defend their rights, the fact that Kunstler is competent to defend a revolutionary is beside the point.

The appeal is also made to the basic principles of humanism which underlie the Founding Documents. Jefferson's original draft of the Declaration which contained a disavowal of slavery, is often quoted. The fact that Jefferson and Washington themselves owned slaves even though expressing reservations about the injustice of the system is also often cited. The point of the argument is that the economic system of capitalism repressed the full expression of humanity which these men were striving to make concrete in political institutions.

Finally, this revolutionary humanism must be fresh every morning--it must be lived. Not only do the sectarians demand the personal commitment that is seen in rising early every morning to undertake the Free Children's Breakfast and other revolutionary tasks, but as old life styles come to

be perceived as oppressive, they too must be changed for the
sake of freedom.   The most striking example is the inclusion
of the women's liberation movement as part of the revolutionary framework.   Seale remembers that in the earlier years
in the Party the men saw the women as secondary and rele-
gated them to the roles of child care and man care.   But
"we finally all had to purge our souls and purge our minds
in relation to the old environmental conditioning" (ibid., p399).
Such an effort is not possible within the capitalist system in
spite of the attempts of some women's organizations.   That
is a contradiction in itself, for

> ... the very nature of the capitalistic system is to
> exploit it and enslave people, all people.   So we
> have to progress to a level of socialism to solve
> these problems.   We have to live socialism....
> A lot of black nationalist organizations have the
> idea of relegating women to the role of serving
> their men, and they relate this to black manhood.
> But real manhood is based on humanism, and it's
> not based on any form of oppression [ibid., p403].

Such a determination to live the revolution in both
political act and personal life style requires more dedication
than the majority is able to muster.   S. N. C. C. declined by
the end of the sixties to a handful of organizers.   The Black
Panther Party, which is in a way the reincarnation of
S. N. C. C. in the northern ghetto, turned to purges of those
who would not be faithful to the rigorous Party discipline.

> If someone who is actually a Black Panther Party
> member is cussing people out or intimidating
> people or something like that, then ... they won't
> be in the Party long, because we'll expel them, and
> expose them for exactly what they are.   Generally
> we keep the Party very well disciplined.   Party
> members respect the people in the community, and
> work to serve the people in the community [ibid.,
> p340].

Members who are expelled have their picture along
with the reasons for expulsion printed in the Party Paper.
Over a thousand have been purged.   Only the most sincere
repentance and faithful work will suffice to allow a member
expelled to be once again considered for membership.   The
parallel to discipline in Christian sectarian groups such as
the eighteenth-century Methodists is striking.   But the disci-

pline also makes clear that although there is much discussion
of the whole society being replaced by a social structure like
the Party, the primary concern is the sectarian passion for
purity rather than the established type's interest in universality.

A basic question that arises out of consideration of the
left wing black sectarian experience is this: What are the
common points of contact between the vision of the truth and
the understanding of the way to the truth between these sectarians and those more obviously identified as within the
faith context of the American civil religion?   If the American
civil religion is defined too narrowly, the answer to such
questions must be that points of contact are few indeed.
Black left wing sectarians would reject the theological expression of the American ideal as Sydney Mead puts it:

> It is here suggested that for Americans the ideal
> was defined in terms of "destiny under God," and
> the way that of what Lincoln called "a constitution
> republic or democracy--a government of the people,
> by the same people."   America was to fulfill her
> destiny, under God, by working out in practice and
> demonstrating for all the world to see, the true
> possibilities of such government.   The ideal and
> the way were inseparable--that is inherent in the
> ideal of destiny [Mead, 1963, p74].

But Mead broadens that specific understanding to a wider
horizon which does then include the more radical sectarians.

> But the important thing is the interpretation of the
> experiences--that subtle combination of insight into,
> and articulation of, the meaning of the experience
> that is so deeply persuasive and widely accepted
> that it becomes a part of the common consciousness
> and passes into the realm of motivational myths
> [ibid., p75].

In this sense the radical sectarians are bound into the American experience in important ways.   Mead goes on to speak
of fundamental beliefs upon which the experience rests.

First, Americans believe in God of will and purpose,
which is equivalent to the "assertion that there is order and
ultimate meaning in the universe which is discoverable at
least in part by man" (ibid., p80).   Black left wing sec-

tarians do not by and large believe in God, but they do assert
there is order and ultimate meaning in the universe. Indeed,
the Marxist analysis which is so rigorously used invests all
events with historical significance. The thought that events
might be random, meaningless and absurd is not entertained.
Perry Miller argues that the early Americans understood by
the doctrine of providence that God

> governed the universe not only in space but also in
> time, and as there was an intelligent purpose in
> each enactment, so all events were connected in a
> longrange program which men call history [ibid. ,
> p77].

In this sense, the Marxist perspective becomes a providence
without God.

Second, Americans believe in the people. "The
people" is beyond all individuals and groups. The concept
seeks to grasp history itself--"the massive, unbroken stream
of human life with its tremendous inertia and momentum"
(ibid. , p81). Therefore, in the long run there is no higher
court of appeal than the will of "the people. " The American
civil religion usually expresses the faith that the people is
the agency of God. So Lincoln affirms, "I must trust in that
Supreme Being who has never forsaken this favored land,
through the instrumentality of this great and intelligent people"
(Wolf, 1963, p151). The black sectarians also affirm their
belief in the people as the agency of history. For them as
for the established type there is no higher court of appeal
than the people.

Third, Americans believe that the will of the people
"can really be known only when all the channels of communication and expression are kept open" (Mead, 1963, p81).
Lincoln's First Inaugural Address expresses this conviction.

> A majority held in restraint by constitutional checks,
> limitations, and always changing easily with delib-
> erate changes of popular opinions and sentiments,
> is the only true sovereign of a free people. Who-
> ever rejects it does, of necessity, fly to anarchy or
> to despotism.... Why should there not be a
> patient confidence in the ultimate justice of the
> people? Is there any better or equal hope in the
> world? [Wolf, 1963, p152].

As we have seen, the black sectarians believe also that the will of the people can be known only when the channels of communication are kept open. Thus, Huey Newton believes the Party was wrong when it sought to force the community to pick up the gun. Such attempts are arrogant, for they close off communication, and the Party no longer serves the people. The people make the revolution, and they will tell the Party when they are ready.

This belief in the necessity of open communication clarifies why the revolution urged by sectarians is not primarily a revolution which aims to replace the Constitution and its Bill of Rights, but one which aims to replace the present economic and social system. Indeed, the sectarians use their Constitutional rights to force the established type to listen to "the people." The coercive power of the Constitutional system has been the primary coercive power available for the American sectarian revolution.

The fourth fundamental belief of Americans is, as Jefferson puts it,

> that truth is great and will prevail if left to herself; that she is the proper and sufficient antagonist to error, and has nothing to fear from the conflict unless by human interposition disarmed of her natural weapon, free argument and debate; errors ceasing to be dangerous when it is permitted freely to contradict them [ibid., p82].

Jefferson was convinced that truth emerged from the conflict itself. Jefferson made this argument in the course of establishing religious freedom for Virginia. Madison expanded it in the Federalist papers to cover civil rights.

> ... in a free government the security for civil rights must be the same as that for religious rights. It consists in the one case in the multiplicity of interests, and in the other in the multiplicity of sects [ibid., p83].

The emphasis on open conflict between opposing factions as the vehicle for truth is, by its nature, not as widely honored. Each faction believes its position to be the truth. But, as they view their history, Americans believe that truth emerges out of the struggle.

The black sectarians also affirm that truth emerges
from the struggle.   The language in which this affirmation
is made is Marxist.   According to Newton

> We realized at a very early point in our develop-
> ment that revolution is a process. ...   This proc-
> ess moves in a dialectical manner and we under-
> stand the struggle of the opposites based upon their
> unity [Newton, 1972, p47].

Because of the nature of sectarianism, the internal struggles
of sectarians are not open ended.   The demand for purity
usually forecloses extended conflict.   Once the truth has been
defined in a particular situation, sects require of their members adherence to the true doctrine.   It is only later, from
the vantage point of historical perspective, that the dialectic
can be discerned.

In these important ways black left wing sectarians are
bound into the American experience.   Some of the major
figures, such as Eldridge Cleaver, do express the belief that
America must be reformed for the sake of the whole world
which suffers under her oppression, and that black people
are the only hope of reform.   Yet on the other hand, Cleaver
despairs of America and the black revolution and flees to
exile.   Stokely Carmichael reflects this same ambivalence.
The tragedy is that between the millstones of exalted hopes
and bitter experience the lives of such men are crushed.

The Right Wing Black Sectarians

In his first book following the Meredith march through
Mississippi, Martin Luther King, Jr. , devotes an extended
section to outlining his reasons for opposing the use of the
slogan Black Power.   For King, Black Power is a cry of
disappointment.   For centuries, the black man has been
caught in the tentacles of white power.   Many of the younger
blacks proclaiming Black Power are those who have labored
courageously against racism by means of non-violent direct
action.   But the experience convinced them of the brutality
of some whites and the indifference of the rest.   When Jimmy
Lee Jackson and James Reeb are both killed, the President
immediately calls Mrs. Reeb and remembers James Reeb in
a civil rights speech before Congress, but white America
does not mention Jimmy Lee Jackson.   Blacks are not recognized as real persons.   They are expected to be killed
(King, 1967, pp32-34).

The timidity of the federal government in implementing the civil rights laws, and the desperate condition of the black ghettoes resulting from the refusal of local authorities to maintain equitable law enforcement, education and social services increases the appeal of Black Power. The hypocrisy of the federal government in urging blacks to practice non-violence while slaughtering men, women, and children in Vietnam with weapons such as napalm, fuels despair. The spectacle of an Administration more concerned about the war in Vietnam than the war on poverty is nauseating (ibid., pp34-36).

But, Black Power has also broad and positive meaning. It signifies the necessity of black people to unite for political action. The problem of power in America is that it is unequally distributed. Power is necessary for black people in order to implement the demand of love and justice.

> Power at its best is love implementing the demands of justice. Justice at its best is love correcting everything that stands for love [ibid., p37].

Black Power is therefore also a call for the pooling of black economic resources and a psychological proclamation of manhood.

Even though the reasons for the emergence of Black Power and its positive features are clear, still King believes that

> Beneath all the satisfaction of a gratifying slogan, Black Power is a nihilistic philosophy born out of the conviction that the Negro can't win. It is, at bottom the view that American society is so hopelessly corrupt and enmeshed in evil that there is no possibility of salvation from within. Although this thinking is understandable ... it nonetheless carries the seeds of its own doom [ibid., p44].

Black Power's rejection of hope has planted those seeds of doom. Revolution demands hope. In place of hope Black Power puts the violence of retribution. While self-defense is the type of violence advocated, "the line of demarcation between defensive violence and aggressive violence is very thin" (ibid., p56). King believes the futility of violence in the struggle for racial justice can be seen in the riots. The riots only produced more effective police action and a few fireplug sprinklers for ghetto children to play in in the summertime.

In his last article, written for Look shortly before he was assassinated, King argues that it is time for a massive non-violent campaign to dramatize the problem of the poor. Neither riots nor talk of Black Power had moved the nation to seek a solution for the most crucial problem of black people and many white people as well: poverty. An Economic Bill of Rights to guarantee a job to all people who want to work, and an income for all who are not able to work is an absolute necessity if political freedom in America is to have meaning. The nation must be forced to face the consequences of its Vietnam policies here at home.

> We'll focus on the domestic problems, but it's inevitable that we've got to bring out the question of the tragic mix-up in priorities ... when a nation becomes involved in this kind of war, when the guns of war become a national obsession, social needs inevitably suffer. And we hope that as a result of our trying to dramatize this and getting thousands and thousands of people moving around this issue, that our government will be forced to reevaluate its policy abroad in order to deal with the domestic situation [King, 1968, p589].

King did not believe there would be a prompt response from the federal government for such an Economic Bill of Rights. The movement knows from bitter experience that the government does not move to open the doors of opportunity for blacks until it is confronted directly and dramatically.

> That really means making the movement powerful enough, dramatic enough, and morally appealing enough, so that people of goodwill, the churches, labor, liberals, intellectuals, students, poor people themselves begin to put pressure on congressmen to point that they can no longer elude our demands [ibid., p588].

King is certain that another "luminous moral chapter in American history" could be written with the leadership of black people committed to non-violent, direct action. The great dream is still possibility, for

> To end poverty, to extirpate prejudice, to free a
> tormented conscience, to make a tomorrow of
> justice, fair play and creativity--all these are
> worthy of the American ideal [ibid. , p595].

It is the willingness of King to work within the system
in the sense of depending ultimately upon a coalition that
marks the right wing of the black sectarian movement. The
black movement is, of course, incredibly complex, and
Black Power was soon widely accepted in the right wing.   But
Black Power to the right wing sectarian tends to Black reformism while Black Power to the left wing sectarian tends
to mean black revolution.   Part of the difference is rhetorical.
It is difficult to see black revolution rather than black reformism in a children's free breakfast program.   But the
left wing consistently interprets such reformist moves within
the context of Marxist dialectic, arguing the purpose is not
reform but revolution.   The right wing, accepting Black
Power by the end of the sixties even more than King did in
1968, still meant black reformism within the context of the
American constitutional and economic system.

Floyd McKissick, who had been chairman of C.O.R.E.,
accepts the perspective that perceives black people as a
colony.   In Three-fifths of a Man (1969) he writes

> Black People in the United States live in a state of
> de facto nationhood. We are a nation within a nation
> .... Black People across America have responded
> to the conspiracy of white racism in ways very
> much alike.   Today, as in slavery, they share the
> bonds of oppression and the bonds of race [ibid. ,
> p145].

But in contrast, to the left wing black sectarians, McKissick
argues that the Constitution is a document born of a valid
revolution.   Even though those who created it were racists

> If interpreted justly, in full awareness of today's
> conditions and if applied in a consistent fashion,
> the Constitution can be converted into a document
> of liberation for Black America [ibid. , p55].

McKissick makes it clear that when he is talking about power,
he is not talking about some undefined call to manhood or far
off revolution, but to the present ability to make black people's will effective in social decisions against opposition.   The

coercive power that inheres in Black Power is the power of
the Constitutional system.   While black people must be free
to choose, McKissick estimates that only about 4 percent of
black people really wish to integrate with white America.
The black middle class moves to white America to escape the
degradation of the ghetto.   Therefore blacks ought to take
advantage of the power available to them in the Constitutional
system and migrate toward the states already primarily black.
Once there, as the majority, black people could control the
political system.   The black community could then proceed
through the legal steps of public authorities and condemnation
proceedings to secure economic control.   Once such a process
is in motion, it will be so powerfully attractive to blacks
across the nation that such a state will receive a tremendous
influx of black people desiring to build a new society.   Likewise, white people who are racists would leave.   Only those
willing to join in creating a just society will remain.   But
this vision is not separatism, for

> When Black People are in control of at least a few
> American states, they will be able to exert enough
> influence within the federal system to affect the
> treatment of their Black brothers in America's
> urban centers, as well as the exercise of American
> foreign policy [ibid. , p164].

To the objection that this would be creating a nation within a
nation, McKissick replies that such a nation already exists,
but now it is powerless.   The Constitutional system provides
the avenue to power for black people, if they will but use it.
The power has been partially appropriated by use of the legal
aspect.   But the political aspect of the Constitutional system
is much more potent for black people.   Therefore McKissick
concludes that

> There are two essential instruments that if used
> together, if used to complement each other, could
> save America from destruction.   They are the
> Constitution of the United States, which necessarily
> includes the Declaration of Independence, and the
> doctrine of Black Nationalism [ibid. , p101].

McKissick perceives Black Power positively.   He is
less optimistic than King concerning the possibility of an
integrated coalition attacking the problems of black America.
But, like King, McKissick's hope rests ultimately upon a
coalition between blacks and whites.   King's coalition is

formed by the "men of goodwill," which means the resources
of the Christian religion are called into play.   McKissick's
appeal is more exclusively based upon the civil religion.   He
believes Americans are so committed to the vision of America
that is enshrined in the Founding Documents that that commitment will overcome even the evil of racism.   Because of
their faith in the Constitutional system, white Americans,
McKissick believes, will accept and enforce Constitutional
guarantees even if those guarantees result in the creation of
a black state.

Julian Bond had been refused his seat in the Georgia
legislature because of his endorsement of the S. N. C. C. statement against the war in Vietnam.   In 1966, after Stokely
Carmichael was elected chairman of S. N. C. C. , he was at
the scene of the shooting of a black man by police.   Carmichael was involved in the subsequent riot.   In the wake of
the riot, Bond resigned from S. N. C. C. , stating

> There are things I want to do, and Snick is doing
> some things I don't want to do.   But primarily it's
> because I'm twenty-six years old now and it's time
> to find out if there's anything I can do [Neary, 1971,
> p146].

In mid-1966, Bond helped found the National Conference for
New Politics, which was aimed at raising money to back
antiwar candidates for Congress and the Presidency.   By
order of the Supreme Court, Bond was finally seated in the
Legislature.   He became involved in the Forum, an ad hoc
group of Georgia Democrats challenging the delegation to the
1968 Democratic convention, which had been hand picked by
Governor Maddox.   The subsequent floor fight gave Bond
even more national publicity as one of the challenge leaders.
The compromise of half the delegation seats was accepted,
in contrast to the rejection by the S. N. C. C. delegates of
compromise in 1964.   Bond seconded the McCarthy nomina-
tion and was himself nominated for Vice President, but withdrew because he had not attained the legal age.

In A Time to Speak, A Time to Act The Movement
In Politics (1972), Bond argues that it is imperative for black
people to weld together a strong black electorate.   The mass
of American people simply do not care whether the poor or
the blacks, most of whom are poor, rise or fall, live or die.
Black people are the ones who must fight the evil, racism,
poverty and violence that suppresses them and scars all

Americans.   First of all the movement must act politically.
It can do this, for Black Americans are from 20 to 70 percent of the voters in 173 of the country's 435 Congressional
districts.   But not just political offices must be sought, for
young black people

> are desperately needed for struggles in welfare
> offices, in labor halls, in political wards and
> precincts, in poverty ridden communities, in
> courtrooms, and in the streets.   They are not
> going to be needed in some titanic confrontation
> in a visionary future; they are needed now, today
> [Bond, pp144-145].

Like the left wing black sectarians, Bond believes
blacks are a colonized people.   He agrees much of America
is lacking a conscience.   Only thirty-six members of the
House of Representatives could be found to support the recommendations of the President's Commission of Civil Disorders.   Thirty billion dollars per year are spent to interfere
with the lives of eighteen million Vietnamese while twenty-
two million black people in this country received only a pit-
tance in comparison.   But in some senses the American
mission is alike, at home and abroad.

> First one tries a little economic aid, urges local
> authorities to give the peasants a bone of reform.
> In Vietnam this is called pacification; at home it
> is the poverty program.   Next, when trouble
> erupts, counterinsurgency is used; in Vietnam, the
> local militias; in America, the police.   When the
> peasants shoot back, we bomb the hell out of them.
> Following this thought to a logical and local ending,
> we might next expect to see in America the "re-
> settlement" of Negroes into well-policed villages.
> In fact, that resettlement has already begun.   We
> do live in villages and compounds within the city,
> policed well when police action is aimed against us,
> policed poorly to contain the violent and criminal
> forces that operate in our lives daily [ibid. , p70].

Bond decries the fact that this revolutionary nation has become counterrevolutionary.   It is time for blacks to reverse
the direction by returning the control of the resources and
institutions of the black community to the community.   Such
a reversal must draw on the commitment of the disillusioned
civil rights veteran.   The movement must become powerfully
political.

> If we put this new political force together, then we
> can build the kind of world the silent Statue of
> Liberty seems to be seeking as she stands in New
> York Harbor and asks:
> Give me your tired, your poor,
> Your huddled masses yearning to breathe free,
> The wretched refuse of your teeming shore,
> Send these, the homeless, tempest-tossed, to me ..
> Sweetheart, here we are! [ibid., pp42-43].

Like McKissick, Bond is convinced that the political
system is the avenue of relief for the oppression of black
Americans. He does not advocate the Black Nationalist
viewpoint, but instead a coalition with whites in the 173
Congressional districts where blacks have significant voting
power. Although Bond is appreciative of King and his non-
violent confrontations, he believes political organization to be
a more effective method of righting the ancient wrongs, now
that the vote has been won for black people. Bond differs
from the left wing black sectarians in that he does not focus
on organizing the black community. His elections depend
primarily on his own hard work in campaigning, and the help
of a few activist friends. The Marxist perspective is not
used, and there is not the effort to raise the political consciousness of the local people. Therefore, although many of
the positions which Bond takes are in agreement with the
Panthers, there is not the call for revolution. There is
considerably more confidence that blacks will be able to
significantly improve their lot by channeling the radical commitment of the veterans of the direct action movement into
building a political force. Bond aligns himself with Charles
Evers, and quotes him approvingly.

> Help elect Negroes and change that rotten system.
> Don't become a racist. Talk about the issues and
> the problems of the Negroes and what you are
> going to do to change them.... If Negroes can get
> together they can control and rule something ... :
> My advice is to control something, control the
> economics of the county, control the ballot of the
> county, control the politics of the county.... We
> don't holler black power ... but watch it [ibid.,
> p30].

Bayard Rustin is also a right wing sectarian. He
continues to urge coalition politics and offer the most tren-
chant criticisms of Black Power. In Down the Line (1971),

he writes that although the Black Power slogan is over four
years old, its meaning is still obscure. Rustin argues that
for C. O. R. E. Black Power means a separate capitalist black
economy; for S. N. C. C. it means a politically united black
community; the Black Panthers seek a black nationalism
based on the philosophies of Marx, Lenin and Mao. Yet,
Rustin says, these differing perceptions barely begin the list.
Rustin believes the common theme in all the varieties of
Black Power is that black action must spring from the perception of blacks as a separate race. But black America is
full of divisions. According to Rustin, the suggestion that
there is an undifferentiated black community is the notion of
whites which some blacks have exploited in order to act as
spokesmen. Like every other ethnic group in America,
blacks are divided by age, class and geography. But blacks
who see race as central ignore differences and select the
ghetto experience as a common theme. Self-help projects
for the ghetto are urged, either to develop black capitalism
or revolutionary consciousness. These gain the support of
the white upper class in many ways, Rustin says, for "they
involve no large scale redistribution of resources, no infla-
tionary government spending, and above all, no responsibility
on the part of whites" (ibid., p296).

Community control is as futile as black capitalism,
Rustin feels. In a complex technological society there is
no autonomous community in large metropolitan areas.
Employment, transportation to that employment, utilities,
financial support for education and social services all lie
outside the ghetto. Thus

> Assuming that there were a cohesive, clearly identi-
> fiable black community (which, judging by the fac-
> tionalism in neighborhoods like Harlem and Ocean
> Hill-Brownsville, is far from a safe assumption)
> and assuming that the community were empowered
> to control the ghetto, it would still find itself with-
> out the money needed in order to be socially crea-
> tive. The ghetto would still be faced with the same
> poverty, deteriorated housing, unemployment, ter-
> rible health services and inferior schools--and this
> time perhaps with the exacerbation of their being
> entailed in local struggles for power [ibid., p297].

Community control must be seen as a conservative and
provincial idea in a modern society, Rustin says. It is unable to deal with the social and economic causes of black

unrest. It is an adjustment to inequality rather than a protest against it. Social change will come about only by the
commitment of all levels of government to that change. That
means a majority movement. Therefore, blacks must abandon once and for all the idea that they, as the ten percent of
the society, can effect basic changes in the structure of
American life.

> It must once more come to be clearly understood
> among those who favor social progress that the
> Democratic party is still the only mass-based
> political organization in the country with the poten-
> tial to become a majority movement for social
> change.... The political reality is that without a
> coalition of Negroes and other minorities with the
> trade union movement and with liberal groups, the
> shift of power to the Right will persist and the
> democratic Left in America will have to content
> itself with well nigh permanent minority status
> [ibid., pp307-308].

The arguments of Roy Wilkins and the late Whitney
Young are similar. But they were never as deeply involved
as Rustin in the direct action tactics of the civil rights
movement, suffering, as he did, beatings, jailings and time
on a chain gang in the South. It almost seems as if Rustin
has moved slowly to the right, and is now an established
type, urging the faithful to support the Democratic Party and
the A. F. L.-C. I. O. While there is considerable uncertainty
as to the position of men like Rustin, the historical analogy
he uses suggests that he is still sectarian at heart. To him,
the period 1968 to the present is analogous to the Reconstruction. The true radical, as far as Rustin is concerned, is a
political creature. He asks, "What can possibly be done to
reform this nation?" Yesterday what could be done was
mass demonstrations to awaken the conscience of liberals in
power. Today what must be done is coalition politics to stay
the hand of the reactionaries, who under the guidance of
President Nixon are already turning the clock of racial justice
backward. There is no point in appealing to the conservative
conscience, Rustin says, for the conservative devoutly believes most of the remaining problems of the black people
are a result of their own inadequacies. Rustin argues that
the passion for renewing America has not diminished since
1968, but the tactics which are effective in such a renewal
are radically different [ibid., 327-349].

Like all sectarians, the right wing black sectarians oppose the cold war version of the American mission to the world. But some, such as Rustin, were reluctant to connect that opposition to the black struggle. He was at last persuaded that the issues of war and poverty and race were inextricably intertwined. King, on the other hand, was one of the first voices raised in fervent opposition to the war. Left wing black sectarians complained that King's opposition was not political enough, but merely moral. President Johnson was much more concerned about the political impact of King's opposition than that of S. N. C. C. or the Black Panthers, however.

The stance taken on the war clarifies the issue of coalition politics for the right wing sectarians. King means mostly coalition with white sectarians and the left wing established types who agree on certain issues. The main line liberals who exercise major political and economic power are the architects of the cold war version of the American mission to the world. They therefore reject those who strongly criticize their creation. Rustin sees this, and because he wants to gain access to power for black people in this country, he mutes his criticism of the Vietnamese war. Out of his conviction that the cause of black people in America is more important than any other cause, Rustin opposes the war privately but is silent publicly. Of those who are oriented to working within the system, only Young and Wilkins agree with Rustin. They desire coalition with power, which Staughton Lynd derided as "coalition with the Marines." King, Bond, Evers, McKissick, Farmer and the groups they represent oppose the war publicly as well as privately. To them there is no point in gaining access to a society which has lost its own soul.

The right wing black sectarians are marked by a sense of solidarity with the lowest class. King's last project was the Poor People's March, and he was killed seeking to dramatize the plight and rights of garbage workers. Bond continues to live in the poor district out of which he was elected, and walks the district personally, talking with people who have concerns that a legislature can remedy. Evers wants to gain political strength in the poor black counties of Mississippi in order to elect black sheriffs and improve the roads and schools for the rural poor. Rustin focuses much of his effort on the reform of labor unions that poor blacks might have access to good jobs.

But again a difference appears between the left wing and right wing sectarians. Huey Newton and Bobby Seale are at home with "the brothers off the block." The lumpen proletariat of the ghetto are the people the left wing sectarians socialize with as well as organize. The right wing sectarians are more clearly middle class persons whose sympathies are with the oppressed.

The work ethic is denied amongst right wing black sectarians in a more muted way than amongst left wingers. The right wing opposes the notion that black people are the creators of their own poverty, but indict the larger society for locking them out of prosperity. However, there is acceptance of the capitalist system if it is an open system. Left wingers do not believe that that is a possibility. To them, capitalism is by nature oppressive. There is not among the right wingers the marked commitment to live in poverty that left wingers reveal, who work without salary and accept only the basic necessities for the sake of the revolution.

The right wing sectarians appeal directly to the Founding Documents. Their faith that the American system can be made to serve even the poor black is more steadfast than the faith of the left wingers. There is less appeal by right wingers to the principles of humanism and revolution that underlie the Founding Documents. The left wing sectarians make such an appeal, but the right wing depends on the documents themselves. They are confident that when the values of racism and faithfulness to the Constitution and Declaration conflict, Americans will choose the latter.

Finally, the right wing black sectarians express the conviction that black people must personally be involved in seeking a more just social order. But more than that, black people are in a peculiar sense the yeast that leavens the lump, the salt that gives taste to the whole. In Black Power and Urban Unrest, Nathan Wright, Jr., proclaims

> The Negro people of America want far more desperately than any other Americans for this nation to come into its own. This means that the black people of this land, are like Jews of old, a people peculiarly elected to transmit and to perform no less than a sacred trust. It is for us as black people to take the initiative in calling this nation as a whole to maturity.... It is for us who

> are black people to take the initiative in saving this
> nation of which we are an inextricable part [Wright,
> 1971, p373].

Wright is convinced that Black Power speaks to the plight and
needs of all Americans, who, he feels, need the prophetic
mission of black people in this hour (ibid. , p. 374).

The evidence shows that the black movement maintained
its sectarian stance throughout the latter half of the sixties.
Rustin, who was so suspect in 1963 that Wilkins and Young
refused to allow him to be named Director of the March on
Washington, moved right. Wilkins and Young moved somewhat
left, accepting demonstrations as a tactic.   King fell from
Presidential favor by opposing the war.   L. B. J. continued to
work with only those blacks who were silent about the war.
King was a sectarian moving slowly left during the period.
He was overwhelmingly the choice of urban blacks.   Eighty-
eight percent of urban blacks perceived King as the man who
had done the most to help black people.   On a separate
question, 48 percent of urban blacks disapproved of Malcolm
X in 1964, while only 1 percent disapproved of King (Marx,
1967, pp. 26, 27).   King's opposition to the war led to a
coalition with white radicals on the war issue, and King
spoke at antiwar rallies.   The Poor People's March was an
attempt to broaden this coalition to include the white
poor, thereby creating a genuine radical populist movement.

The left wing sectarians demonstrate most clearly
the ongoing conflict between established and sectarian types.
As black sectarians were perceived as a mortal threat to
the established way of life in the early sixties, the left wing
sectarians were perceived as a mortal threat to the established way of life in the whole nation in the latter sixties.
The climate of fear produced by the riots summer after
summer led to F. B. I. and police attacks on black left wing
sectarians.   Conspiracy and murder charges were lodged
against the sectarian leadership, even when authorities
admitted that such charges were likely not to be upheld by
court or jury.   Police gunned down black sectarians while
they slept in Chicago.   When, at the beginning of the
seventies, black left wing sectarians moderated their rhetoric,
the deadly actions of the established type also moderated.
This was one of the most dramatic examples of the sectarian
versus established type dynamic at work.   Rhetoric was

treated as reality.   Doctrine was not "mere" doctrine, but
was cause for armed ambush by police tactical units.

The emergence of Black Power and the subsequent
revival of Black Nationalism is a manifestation of the condition foreseen by the President's Commission on Civil Disorders: the United States is moving in the direction of two
separate societies based on race.   Of the sectarians, the
Black Panthers and Bayard Rustin oppose this movement most
strongly, as did King.   But as black trust in government
declines, the appeal of Black Nationalism grows.   Nationalists
do not seek confrontations with constituted authority nor white
opponents.   There is less of an urge to renew the nation
although renewal is a secondary goal.   Nationalists retreat to
their own enclaves, such as McKissick's all black Soul City
in North Carolina.   Ross K. Baker believes that the Nixon
Administration's

> official denunciations of busing, presidential phil-
> lipics against permissiveness, encomiums to the
> work ethic and public anger over welfare are mes-
> sages to the black community that challenge is no
> longer condoned and confrontation is untimely
> [Baker, 1973, p6].

Such a judgment indicates that to be a black sectarian,
determined to reorient the nation's racist attitudes and actions,
is still a decision fraught with conflict.

THE CIVIL RELIGION AND THE WAR

The Established Type

The Expression of the Established
Type in the Administration of the
Federal Government

> "We are the number one nation, " President Lyndon
> B. Johnson told the National Foreign Policy Con-
> ference at the State Department at a crucial mo-
> ment in the Vietnam War, "and we are going to
> stay the number one nation. "   There has never
> been a more succinct definition of the American
> national interest [Barnet, 1972, p3].

The definition is rooted in the American civil religion.
Johnson went on to quote Lincoln: "With firmness in the
right, as God gives us to see the right, let us finish the
work we are in" (Hoopes, 1969, p206).   America's Manifest
Destiny is to be the number one nation.   Until late in the
Vietnam war the vast majority of Americans believed that a
quarter century of war and cold war was forced upon America
by those countries unwilling to accept peace.   The militarization of the means by which America would fulfill her destiny
seemed to the majority a natural and necessary response.
In August of 1965, a year after the Tonkin Gulf incident and
six months after major escalation of the war had begun, only
24 percent of Americans believed the American involvement
in the war in Vietnam was wrong.   Not until 1970, when it
was clear that America could not win, did 56 percent of the
American people express the feeling that the war had been
a mistake (Cooper, 1970, p452).

     While the war in Vietnam was surely a mistake, it
was not an accident.   Richard Barnet argues that "foreign
policy is more an expression of our own society than programmed response to what other nations do" (Barnet, 1972,
p6).   David Halberstam, agonized by the war, set out to
discover why "the best and the brightest" had made such poor
decisions.

> [But] it became very quickly not a book about Viet-
> nam, but a book about America, in particular,
> about power and success in America, what the
> country was, who the leadership was, how they got
> ahead, what their perceptions were about them-
> selves, their country and their mission [Halberstam,
> 1972, p668].

The decision makers, Halberstam says, were confident of the
ability of able, rational men such as themselves to control
even irrational events such as war.   Being supreme rational-
ists, they did not take into account non-rational factors such
as the civil religion, of either the Vietnamese or the Americans.

     As the war in Vietnam escalated and U. S. policy
began to be described as imperialist by the sectarians, the
established type reaffirmed again that the mission of America
is not imperialism.   The U. S. seeks no bases, no territory,
no colonies.   It is historical necessity, a sense of mission
and an evangelical passion that was the motivation.   George
Ball declares

> Never before in human history has a nation under-
> taken to play a role of world responsibility except
> in defense and support of a world empire.... We
> find ourselves in a position unique in world history
> [Barnet, 1972, p20].

President Johnson articulates the sense of necessity and mission in a Lincoln Day speech, saying, "History and our own
achievements have thrust upon us the principal responsibility
for the protection of freedom on earth" (ibid., p19). Secretary of State Dean Rusk feels that the United States is "criticized not for sacrificing our national interests to international
interests, but for endeavoring to impose the international
interest upon other nations" (ibid., p21). Eugene Rostow
suggests America's responsibility had fallen upon her because
of the basic nature of man.

> The Utopians have always imagined that the world
> is naturally harmonious, and that the freedom of
> every man to do as he pleases would lead naturally
> to a peaceful order ... on the real front, however,
> we quickly learn the lesson of High Noon--that
> without organized power to maintain the law, free-
> dom is impossible [Rostow, 1968, pxviii].

And who will be the sheriff? Barnet asks. The
answer is cast in terms of the work ethic. The best are
those to whom power is given to maintain the law that freedom might flourish. The best are easily identified: they are
those whose virtue has been certified by worldly success.
What other nation can compare with America in terms of
achievements to boast of as outward symbols of inward grace?
Thus America as the elect nation is elected by her very success to be the bearer of responsibility for freedom on the
earth (Barnet, 1972, p70).

Under the pressures of losing the war, the unity of
the established type began to fracture. In spite of domestic
power struggles, foreign policy had proceeded under the cold
war consensus. Liberals were sometimes considered "soft, "
but the issue was largely for domestic consumption. Men
like Dean Acheson, whose professional diplomacy was un-
erringly hard line, were attacked by politicians like the late
Senator McCarthy as sympathetic to Communism. Such attacks did not reflect a true division of the established type
on foreign policy. Indeed, they tended to confirm the unity
of both liberals and conservatives in a doctrinaire cold war
attitude.

The division was within the liberal faction.   The
liberals had held power while the cold war perspective was
fashioned, and the "progressive conservatism" of the Eisenhower Administration continued the policy.   Indeed, between
1940 and 1967, all the first and second level posts in the
huge national security bureaucracy were held by fewer than
four hundred persons who rotated through a variety of key
posts.   Dean Acheson began his career in the State Department in 1941.   In 1968, he was one of the important figures
in persuading Lyndon Johnson to de-escalate the war in Vietnam.   Clark Clifford, the chief persuader of Johnson and his
Secretary of Defense, was Counsel to the President in 1946.
As such, he had drafted one of the major cold war planning
documents.   Such men continuously served as unofficial con-
sultants and certified younger men who had served them well,
such as Dean Rusk, for high office (Barnet, 1972, pp48-49).

The Pentagon Papers reveal the intensity of the internal debate, and the shift of the mood of such men as Mc-
Namara from optimism to pessimism concerning the ultimate
outcome of the war.   Finally, a man "goes dovish. "   This
usually signals a new understanding of the mission of America.   No longer is the cold war mission of America accepted.
The mission is no longer believed to be primarily evangelical,
and effected through force of arms, but more example-setting,
and effected by means other than arms.   Unless a person was
unusually skilled and experienced in the art of advocacy, as
was Clark Clifford, the shift of perspective meant the man
resigned, or as in the case of McNamara, was dismissed.

The commitments of President Johnson and his style
of consensus politics complicated the conduct of the war.
The President was committed to the Great Society.   He
called upon all the resources of the civil religion to sanctify
his effort to open wide the doors of opportunity, and if possible, achievement, to the poor as well as the middle class,
the Black, Chicano, and Indian as well as the white.   He
sought to avoid creating coalition between economic conservatives and conservatives committed to the Southern Regional
form of the civil religion.   He was certain that such a coalition would defeat his Great Society program.   Therefore, he
did not permit a long range planning, both military and fiscal,
for the Vietnam war.   The money required for the war would
have been granted, he felt, but economic conservatives would
have immediately joined the coalition to shut off the flow of
funds to the Great Society.   So during a June 1965 planning
meeting, when Clark Clifford summarized the discussion by

stating the escalation would require 750,000 troops and seven
years of war at that troop level, the President grew angry,
and said such figures were ridiculous.   Clifford turned to
General Wheeler, who confirmed the figure.   Clifford then
asked Wheeler if we won,

> "What do we do?   Are we still involved?   Do we
> still have to stay there?"   And Wheeler answered
> yes, we would have to keep a major force there,
> for perhaps as long as twenty or thirty years [Hal-
> berstam, 1972, pp596-597].

But the President did not want to accept that kind of decision
because of its effect on the Great Society.   Yet at the same
time, the cold war mission of America was not to be denied.
Caught between two issues of great import to him, the President dissembled.   He ordered 125,000 troops to Vietnam, but
decided he would make public only an increase of 50,000.
The true size of the increase was to be withheld from the
public by all staff members.   The credibility gap was born.

The gap was created within the government as well
as without.   L. B. J. met with members of the House Ways
and Means Committee, which was not informed of the projected costs of the war.   They recommended against a tax
increase.   Had the Committee known of the war budget, a
tax hike would have been recommended.   A debate between
funding the Great Society or the war would have ensued.   By
concealing the extent of the military commitment, President
Johnson was able to proceed with a consensus of his own
advisors, the Congress and the people (ibid., pp607-610).

The grip of the cold war version of the mission of
America was apparent in the statements by the President and
Secretaries Rusk and McNamara in announcing the troop
buildup.   President Johnson recalled that three times in his
lifetime Americans had gone to far lands to fight for freedom.
Now great stakes were again in the balance.   First of all,
the non-communist nations of Asia needed to be rescued from
the grasping ambition of Asian Communism.   Secondly, confidence in the word of America had to be maintained.

> We did not choose to be the guardians at the gate,
> but there is no one else.   Nor would surrender in
> Viet-Nam bring peace, because we learned from
> Hitler at Munich that success only feeds the appe-
> tite of aggression.   The battle would be renewed in

one country, and then another country, bringing
with it perhaps even larger and crueler conflict,
as we have learned from the lessons of history
[Gravel, 1971, Vol. IV, pp632-633].

In an interview on CBS television Rusk and McNamara
defended the decision to send more troops. McNamara
emphasized that South Vietnam was a test case. The Communists were attempting to discover if wars of national liberation could be the method by which they could extend their
control over independent peoples throughout the world in the
undeveloped areas of Asia, Africa and Latin America. While
the battle in Vietnam was in one sense a struggle "for the
hearts and the minds of the people of South Viet-nam," the
prerequisite to winning that battle was to guarantee the physical security. The world was watching and waiting, knowing
that in Vietnam the issue hung in balance. "If the special
warfare that the United States is testing in South Vietnam is
overcome," said McNamara, "then it can be defeated anywhere in the world" (ibid., p635). Thus it was clear, Mc-
Namara felt, that the security of the United States is "involved in those rice paddies and remote villages."

Rusk believed that the honor of the United States was
at stake. He argued that when we speak of honor, we are
not just using some empty phrase of eighteenth-century diplomacy, but we are talking "about the life and death of the
Nation." To Rusk, essential facts were clear. North
Vietnam has invaded South Vietnam with men and arms. The
U.S. was committed under the S.E.A.T.O. treaty. The
South Vietnamese, the Communists and the world all knew of
this commitment before the invasion began.

Now, this means that the integrity of the American
commitment is at the heart of this problem. I
believe that the integrity of the American commitment is the principal structure of peace throughout
the world. ... Now, if our allies, or, more particularly, if our adversaries should discover that
the American commitment is not worth anything,
then the world would face dangers of which we have
not yet dreamed [ibid., p636].

Under questioning, Rusk denied that his concept of honor was
too broad and costly. He agreed that honor did indeed have
a high cost, but he argued that it had also a great reward.
"At the very heart, gentlemen," Rusk said, "of the mainte-

nance of peace in the world is the integrity of the American
commitment under our alliances. " McNamara agreed that
the question could not be properly limited to the question of
whether we were placing too much importance upon Vietnam.

> I think the question is really more fundamental
> than are we overcommitted. The question is, what
> kind of world would we and our children live in if
> we failed to carry out the commitments we have or
> sought to reduce them? [ibid. , p638].

In the statements of Johnson, Rusk, and McNamara
can be seen the continuing belief that the mission of America
is universal. The United States is to be involved in political
decisions everywhere in the world, because upon the
American commitment rests the structure of peace in the
world. The concern of China to be preeminent in her sphere
of influence is interpreted as a direct challenge to the mission of America. Spheres of influence are not compatible
with universalism. The manifest destiny of America is to
lead all peoples toward a future state of freedom and liberty
as yet unknown. Thus, every individual, even those within
spheres of influence of other nations, are to be compelled to
come under the benevolent sphere and influence of the saving
grace of the American experiment.

By 1965, the United States had already accepted the
spheres of influence in Europe. America did not react
strongly to the Russian interventions in Hungary and Czecho-
slovakia. Yet, in Asia the doctrine of universalism held
sway. Doubts began to emerge with escalation of the war
in Vietnam. But from the escalation in the summer of 1965
until the winter of 1967, the President and most of his advisors believed that American ability, her "can-do spirit, "
matched the breadth of her mission to the world.

McNamara became progressively more disillusioned
that the war could be won. He recognized that a stalemate
could be reached by the application of American military
power, but that the stalemate would continue to escalate.
With each successive visit to Vietnam he discovered that not
only was the President deceiving the American people but the
military was also deceiving him. In April of 1965, Army
intelligence indicated that the North Vietnamese were able to
move an astonishing number of first line regiments into the
South regardless of the bombing. By November, it was
clear that the North Vietnamese meant their elite units to

neutralize the American units in order that the Viet Cong
might continue its guerrilla and political warfare.   Such
reports were not forwarded to McNamara.   The presence
of North Vietnamese units was cited as the reason for yet
more U.S. troops.   The basis of the escalation, as far as
the President and McNamara were concerned, was that it
would be brief.   Westmoreland knew better.   Being an
astute politician of the establishment, he requested only
small increases.   The increases were granted, the war was
escalated, the public deceived, and only stalemate
achieved.

By the fall of 1966, McNamara was recommending to
L. B. J. that he accept the fact the war was going to be a
long one, and set firm limits on the escalation.   With an
eye toward the Presidential election, which was only twenty-
four months away, McNamara wrote

> The prognosis is bad that the war can be brought
> to a satisfactory conclusion within the next two
> years. . . .   The solution lies in girding, openly, for
> a longer war and taking actions immediately which
> will in 12 to 18 months give clear evidence that
> the continuing costs and risks to the American
> people are acceptably limited, that the formula for
> success has been found, and that the end of the
> war is merely a matter of time [ibid. , p353].

But escalation could not be so easily limited.   An American
army in the field developed a new rationale for an ever increasing military commitment: "Our boys are there, we
must not let them down. "   The increasing numbers of American airfields needed increasing numbers of troops to protect
from rocket and sapper attacks.   The increasing number of
troops needed increasing numbers of air strikes against the
enemy.   The tremendous logistic support needed a static
defense force in addition to the units assigned to search and
destroy.   Needs spiraled upward.   A sense of America's
mission to the world motivated the original commitment, but
a sense of loyalty to those who were staking their lives to
fulfill that mission became as important as the mission itself.
The success of American troops in winning individual battles
was cited as proof that these men were the flower of America.   Thus, with the American troops in Vietnam, other facets
of the civil religion than the mission were brought into play.
McNamara's recommendations were ignored.

McNamara sought to outline a new position in a speech to the American Society of Newspaper Editors in Montreal in May of 1966. He rejected military power as the essence of security. He pointed out that there was a direct link between poverty and violence. Among the thirty-eight poorest nations of the world, thirty-two had suffered significant conflicts in an eight-year period. Therefore, the United States must recognize that its role must be this:

> to help provide security to those developing nations which genuinely need and request our help and are willing and able to help themselves.... Military force can help provide law and order, but only to the degree that a basis for law and order already exists in the developing society, a basic willingness on the part of the people to cooperate. Law and order is the shield behind which development, the central fact of security, can be achieved [Trewhitt, 1971, p268].

McNamara became increasingly appalled by the effect of the war on civilians. He closely followed Harrison Salisbury's reports from Hanoi in The New York Times. He remained close to Robert Kennedy, and they reinforced one another's dissent. Out of frustration over the war, McNamara ordered a massive study of all the papers on Vietnam, going back to the 1940's, which Daniel Ellsberg released for publication as The Pentagon Papers. Systems analysis, which was hated by the military, was applied to the bombing. It demonstrated that the bombing resulted in a fourfold net increase in 1966 in military equipment for North Vietnam due to increased support from Russia and China. It predicted more of the same in 1967 while generating for the U.S., 230 aircraft losses at a cost of 1.1 billion dollars. McNamara entered a powerful official argument against the bombing in testimony before the Senate Armed Services Committee. The President was furious, and the Joint Chiefs publicly opposed the Defense Secretary. Halberstam reported that

> Without checking with McNamara, Johnson announced in November, 1967, that his Secretary of Defense was going to the World Bank. The move came as a surprise to the Secretary, and he did not know whether or not he had been fired. The answer was that he had been [Halberstam, 1972, p645].

Other major figures of the established type, who were not susceptible to being fired by the President, were also speaking against the war.

Senator Fulbright, who had steered the Tonkin Gulf Resolution through the Senate, was one of the established type who turned against the war. The hearings of his Foreign Relations Committee legitimized dissent. In 1966, the Johns Hopkins School of Advanced International Studies invited Fulbright to deliver the Christian A. Herter lectures. He chose to speak on "The Arrogance of Power."

Fulbright argues that the war in Vietnam is a civil war. America is not there because one country has invaded another, thus threatening the freedom of the world. No,

> When all the official rhetoric about aggression and the defense of freedom and the sanctity of our word has been cited and recited, we are still left with two essential reasons for our involvement in Vietnam: the view of communism as an evil philosophy and the view of ourselves as God's avenging angels, whose sacred duty it is to combat evil philosophies [Fulbright, 1966, p107].

Communism is a distorting prism through which we Americans see projections of our own rather than reality, Fulbright asserts. We see Ho Chi Minh as a despised dictator, but Ky as the defender of freedom; the Viet Cong are mere puppets of Hanoi, while the Saigon government is America's stalwart ally; China, with no armies in Vietnam, is the true aggressor, while we, with hundreds of thousands of troops, are fighting for freedom against foreign intervention. Fulbright concludes

> These perceptions are not patently wrong, but they are distorted and exaggerated. It is true that whatever the fault may be on our side, the greater fault is with the Communists, who have indeed betrayed agreements, subverted unoffending governments, and generally done a great deal to provoke our hostility [ibid., p108].

But America's shortcoming is that while she is able to take the initiative and show magnanimity, she is not doing so. Rather, the administration has embarked on a course that is unprecedented in American history, because it has in effect proclaimed a Monroe doctrine for Asia.

Fulbright believes the American involvement in Vietnam is rooted in the arrogance of power. Power confuses itself with virtue. Thus, a great nation comes to believe it has a special destiny to refashion the world in its image. The world will be juster, wiser, richer and happier once the process is completed. Since the good is so great, all power, including the sword, may be legitimately marshalled to complete the task.

Historically, Fulbright argues, America has sought to fulfill its mission in one of two ways: she has regarded herself as friend, counselor and example for those who desire freedom and wish her help, or she has understood herself to be God's avenging angel, the appointed missionary of freedom in a darkened world. The first view is dominant in American history. It is exemplified by men like Lincoln and Adlai Stevenson. It is rich in decency and humanity, and tempered by the knowledge of human imperfection. The second view, however, has appeared all too often, in men such as Theodore Roosevelt and Lyndon Johnson. It is marked by an absolute self-assurance fired by the crusading spirit, which like all crusades, does not hesitate to reform by the sword. Fulbright concludes by urging a return to the first view.

> America, in the words of John Quincy Adams, should be "the well-wisher to the freedom and independence of all," "but the champion and vindicator only of her own." If we can bring ourself so to act, we will have overcome the dangers of the arrogance of power. It would involve, no doubt, the loss of certain glories, but that seems a price worth paying for the probable rewards, which are the happiness of America and the peace of the world [ibid., p258].

Senator Eugene McCarthy, like Fulbright, dismayed by the war, determined to enter the Democratic primaries against Lyndon Johnson. He meant his entry to be an opportunity to both speak to the people concerning the war and to allow the people to register their response by means of the vote. To McCarthy, this was a practical political challenge. He was convinced that the Democratic party was already grievously divided over the war. If this division could be dramatically exposed by means of the primaries, the Administration would be forced to change the Indochina policy or suffer defeat. A deeply divided party would be unlikely to

win in November.   McCarthy considered that Robert Kennedy
would be the best challenger for such an effort, but when
Kennedy refused to enter the race, McCarthy declared.

In his book, The Year of the People (1969), McCarthy
includes his first speech following the announcement of his
candidacy.   He declares that central to all of the problems
of America is the war in Vietnam.   It is a war of question-
able legality and constitutionality.   It is diplomatically inde-
fensible.   It scorns the decent opinions of mankind.   It is a
war which is being presented in the context of a past era.
Munich appears to be the starting point of history for the
Administration.

> What is necessary is a realization that the United
> States is a part of the movement of history itself;
> that it cannot stand apart, attempting to control the
> world by imposing covenants and treaties and by
> violent military intervention; that our role is not to
> police the planet, but to use military strength with
> restraint and within limits while at the same time
> we make available to the world the great power of
> our economy, of our knowledge, and of our good
> will [McCarthy, p286].

Finally, the war is morally wrong because the Administration
has set no limits on the price it will pay and demand in
blood for a military victory empty of purpose.   McCarthy
declares that therefore, it is time to test the mood and
spirit of America.

By the time the campaign trail brought him to California, McCarthy tells us that he had become convinced that
persons such as himself, his supporters and the Senate Foreign Relations Committee were not the dissenters: the dissenters were the Administration.   The position is similar to
that which Luther took in his debates with Rome; it is the
Pope and His Administration that have left the Church.

McCarthy documents this conviction by outlining what
are to him the great principles of foreign policy.   First,
America accepts the hardship of war when liberty is truly at
stake, but does not war against poor and underdeveloped
nations.   Second, foreign policy is based primarily on political rather than military solutions.   Third, the United States
seeks to build world order and peace by working in concert
with an ever widening group of nations; "going it alone" is
the definition of isolationism.   Fourth, the ability of America

to shape the kind of world we shall live in depends not on the size of its arsenal but on the ideals America embodies and as Jefferson wrote, by the "decent respect" she pays to the opinions of mankind. Fifth, the leaders of government accept the responsibility to be truthful with the Congress and the people in foreign as well as domestic affairs, and thus Administrations ask for major commitments openly and without ruse (ibid., p157).

Although the assassination of Kennedy and the bitterness of the Democratic Convention depressed McCarthy, he was convinced that in spite of it all, 1968 revealed there is still a great deal of goodwill as well as ability in America. He closes with the reflection

> We have always done best for our country and for the world when we were prepared to make mistakes, if we had to make them, on the side of an excess of trust rather than on the side of mistrust or suspicion; ... when we were prepared to make mistakes because of an excess of hope rather than an excess of fear.... "America is hard to see," as Robert Frost has written, but if one looks hard and long one will see much that is good [ibid., p261].

Like McNamara, Robert Kennedy had been enamored of counterinsurgency warfare in the early sixties. It was a style of warfare that appealed to the New Frontiersmen as tough and practical; it did not require that nuclear brinkmanship be the only military option. R. F. K. visited Southeast Asia in 1962, and declared that the solution in Vietnam was in winning the war. Not until just before the overthrow of Diem, after President Kennedy had publicly stated that the South Vietnamese government must seek to win popular support, did Robert Kennedy begin to modify his views. He suggested American withdrawal be considered as an option. He did not argue for it, however. His first cautious, public doubts about the war did not appear until 1965. In February of 1966, at the close of the Vietnam hearings by the Senate Foreign Relations Committee, Kennedy argued that a reasonable compromise in Vietnam meant that the Vietcong must have a share of the power and responsibility in the political life of South Vietnam. But for the rest of the year he evaded any further statements on Vietnam. On March 2, 1967, after a week of buildup in the press, Kennedy spoke against the war from his seat in the Senate. He argued for an uncon-

ditional bombing halt and negotiations.   Slowly in the next
year Kennedy escalated his remarks against the war.

Kennedy collects his thoughts on Vietnam in 1968 in
his book, To Seek a Newer World (1968).   In the opening of
the section on Vietnam, Kennedy accepts his share of the
responsibility for arguing for the initial involvement.   But he
describes those decisions as tragic, and urges their reversal.

> Tragedy is a tool for the living to gain wisdom, not
> as a guide by which to live.   Now as ever, we do
> ourselves the best justice when we measure our-
> selves against ancient tests, as in the Antigone of
> Sophocles: "All men make mistakes, but a good
> man yields when he knows his course is wrong,
> and repairs the evil.   The only sin is pride" [ibid.,
> p162].

The tragedy consists in the fact that the astounding might of
American military power now falls upon the people of a remote and unknown land.   Death by fire falls upon a mother
and child from an improbable machine sent by a country they
barely comprehend.   Refugees wander homeless from villages
now obliterated.   An unending crescendo of violence, hatred
and fury devour the familiar life of village and family.   It is
we who live in abundance and send our chemicals to scorch
the children and our bombs to level the villages.   Although
freedom and security must sometimes be purchased by blood,
we must feel as men the anguish of what we are doing (ibid.,
pp164-165).

In his last speech on the floor of the Senate, Kennedy
passionately challenged the moral right of America to continue
the war.

> Moreover there is the question of our moral re-
> sponsibility.   Are we like the God of the Old
> Testament that we can decide in Washington, D. C.,
> what cities, what towns, what hamlets in Vietnam
> are going to be destroyed?...   Do we have that au-
> thority to kill tens and tens of thousands of people
> because we say we have a commitment to the South
> Vietnamese people?   But have they been consulted--
> in Hue, in Ben Tre, in other towns that have been
> destroyed? ... What we have been doing is not the
> answer, it is not suitable, and it is immoral, and
> intolerable to continue it [Newfield, 1969, pp140-
> 141].

Kennedy concludes his discussion of Vietnam in To Seek a Newer World by arguing that the pursuit of a military victory is damaging to America's national interest. The faith of people in America is being drastically eroded both at home and around the world. The world's resolve to work together for freedom and peace is weakened. The means employed in Vietnam have outrun the purposes. The pursuit of military victory is not in the interest of either the people of America or Vietnam. The national interest and the human anguish of the war combine to demand it be ended (Kennedy, 1968, pp216-229).

It is not as though McNamara, Fulbright, McCarthy and Kennedy had moved from an established perspective to a sectarian perspective. Rather, they were still established types, who continued to believe in the mission of America to the world. But, Vietnam was seen as a tragic mistake because the means had outrun the ends. The costs and risks, as McNamara put it, must be "acceptably limited." The U.S. must recognize development of the poor nations of the world is the central fact of the American mission. Fulbright deplored the cold war mission of America that insisted upon the U.S. being the avenging angel of God, smiting all who will not be refashioned in America's image. But he did not reject the rightness of the American mission, only its hot war form. By returning to the wisdom of men like John Quincy Adams, America's mission can indeed ensure the "happiness of America and the peace of the world."

McCarthy urges the recognition that the mission of America cannot succeed by force of arms, but only by our making available to the world "the great power of our economy, of our knowledge, of our good will." This has been the historic path of the American mission to the world. Vietnam was a mistake springing from an excess of mistrust, suspicion, and fear. Much better are the mistakes made out of an excess of hope and trust as America seeks to be the bearer of good to the world.

Kennedy pressed the moral issue most passionately. But again, the mission was not to be abandoned because the means were immoral. Rather were the means to be seen as wrong and the evil repaired.

These four men are dramatic examples of the conviction of the established type that the goodness of America is independent of particular actions of Administrations that can

fail, and do evil. The truth that is contained in the American tradition is objective truth--truth which will weather the
evil that men do in the present. America will yet be a
blessing to mankind.

The established types who turn against the war are
also those who see the necessity of redefining the doctrines
of the civil religion through political and intellectual effort.
Therefore, it must be revised by the political process.
There must be a return to an earlier, more basic understanding. But this return will not be made by those who
march in the streets. It will be made by the established
type. Those of the established type who oppose the war
will legitimize dissent, but only their style of dissent. They
will strongly urge the marchers to leave the streets for the
sidewalks, there to ring the doorbells of political campaigns.
To this faction of the established type, Vietnam is then not
evidence that the nation is morally bankrupt, but Vietnam is
a mistake. It is a mistake that can be righted by means of
the traditional political process. The nation does not need
to be fundamentally renewed; if one looks hard and long he
will still see much good. It is the Administration that needs
to be replaced.

The Tet offensive of 1968, the appointment of Clifford
as the new Secretary of Defense, and the request by Generals
Westmoreland and Wheeler for 206, 000 additional troops triggered an agonizing reappraisal of the Vietnam policy within
the Johnson Administration. Clifford was appointed chairman
of an ad hoc task force to review the request and consider
the alternatives. Clifford had made recent trips to Asia at
Johnson's request, to seek additional help for the fighting
forces in Vietnam. The casual, unconcerned attitude that the
Asian governments expressed toward the "aggression" in
Vietnam impressed Clifford. Their perception of danger was
in sharp contrast to U. S. statements. With great uneasiness
Clifford recommended a small troop increase to meet immediate needs, but it seemed as if it were a purchase of
disaster on the installment plan. On the day Kennedy entered
the Presidential race, L. B. J. declared to his advisors he was
not going to stop the bombing, and was not interested in
further discussion.

Yet Johnson was uneasy, in spite of his strident
declarations. He consulted Dean Acheson. Acheson declared
he would give his advice only if he were free to make his
own inquiry. The freedom was granted, and Acheson as-

sembled a group of knowledgeable people on the lower levels of State, Defense and the C. I. A.   He reported to the President that the J. C. S. were leading him down the garden path, that what was required for victory was unlimited resources and five years.   He added that no one believed the President's speeches about the war, and that the country no longer supported it.   While L. B. J. did not like the advice, he respected Acheson.

Clifford, who sensed now a major change in the Senior Advisory Group, a body of former public officials whose informal advice Johnson greatly respected, suggested the group be convened for a post-Tet evaluation.   Clifford was in the minority amongst official advisors.   But the majority of the "Wise Men, " as the group was called, opposed the present policy.   The President was shaken, and asked the junior officers who had briefed Acheson and the Senior Advisory Group to brief him.

L. B. J. selected Sunday, March 31, as the date for his major speech to the country on Vietnam.   Two drafts of the speech were prepared, one defiant, bellicose, and reflecting the views of the J. C. S. and the advisors who were committed to continuing the same policy.   The other was drafted by McPherson and Clifford, and represented the views of those who wished to disengage.   After reading both speeches, Johnson selected the peace speech (Hoopes, 1969, pp177-224).

L. B. J. writes in The Vantage Point that his decision to de-escalate was based primarily on two factors: first, he was concerned about the divisiveness and pessimism of the American people.   But, secondly, he had become confident that the South Vietnamese could carry a heavier share of the war.   Tet had demonstrated that the majority of South Vietnamese supported their government.   The U. S. role could now be diminished in a patient, measured way without jeopardizing the peace, progress, and stability of that vital part of the world (Johnson, 1971, pp422-423).

The "Wise Men" and Clifford felt the country had overextended itself.   Vietnam was a mistake.   Their arguments made less use of moral categories than those of Fulbright, McCarthy and Kennedy, and there was no suggestion that the cold war mission of America was fundamentally wrong.   Rather, the United States found itself in a situation where the costs were outrunning the benefits, so it was time to write off the losses and withdraw.

Although Lyndon Johnson was affected by their argument and reversed the flow of men to Vietnam, he did not accept their reasoning. To him, the mission of America to the world was still paramount. Only if that mission would permit a change in policy would he change the policy. He believed that there was evidence that the policy could be changed without disrupting the mission.

The vision of L. B. J. prevailed. Richard Nixon's secret plan to end the war was to continue the Johnson policy of a patient, measured withdrawal.

Henry Kissinger makes an elegant argument for the new understanding of American mission in American Foreign Policy (1969). No longer must America offer altruism as a guarantee of reliability. Other nations believe that a disinterested policy is precisely one that is likely to be unreliable. Altruism leads to an undifferentiated globalism. The U. S. must think in terms of power and equilibrium. The new administration must relate commitments to interests and obligations to purposes. Since the United States can no longer operate global programs, imposing its own solutions, it must encourage and evoke programs which coincide with its interests. Such encouragement should be offered not where it is the principal effort, but where it will make the difference between success and failure. This does not mean the mission of America is abandoned. No, for

> A sense of mission is clearly a legacy of American history; to most Americans, America has always stood for something other than its own grandeur. But a clearer understanding of America's interests and of the requirements of equilibrium can give perspective to our idealism and lead to humane and moderate objectives, especially in relation to political and social change [ibid. , p94].

President Nixon in a speech in November 1969 makes it clear that he believes that precipitate withdrawal of American forces from Vietnam would threaten the peace of the world. Instead, a policy of Vietnamization is to be followed. This means that the primary mission of U. S. troops will be to enable the South Vietnamese Army to assume the active combat role, and that U. S. troop strength will be slowly reduced month by month. To ensure no more Vietnams, Vietnamization will be extended by means of the "Nixon Doctrine." Thus, while the U. S. will keep its treaty commitments, and provide a nuclear defense for its allies, no longer will American troops supply the manpower for nations whose freedom is threatened. That will be their responsibility.

Nixon closed by speaking of the national destiny. When the nation was weak and poor, America was the hope of the world.

> Today we have become the strongest and richest nation in the world, and the wheel of destiny has turned so that any hope the world has for the survival of peace and freedom will be determined by whether the American people have the moral stamina and the courage to meet the challenge of free-world leadership. Let historians not record that, when America was the most powerful nation in the world, we passed on the other side of the road and allowed the last hope for peace and freedom of millions of people to be suffocated by the forces of totalitarianism [Nixon, 1969].

Vietnamization did not mean that U.S. troops would not be involved in offensive actions, however. Convinced that Communist sanctuaries in Cambodia were an intolerable threat to both the remaining American forces and the South Vietnamese forces, Nixon ordered that the sanctuaries be attacked in May 1970. The President explained his actions to the American people in a television address.

In the address, President Nixon speaks of the stepped-up attacks against both South Vietnamese and American units. Such threat is intolerable. American men must be protected. While the United States is willing to be conciliatory at the conference table it "will not be humiliated." Attacks from privileged sanctuaries will not be permitted. Such attacks while negotiations are in progress are evidence of the anarchy that threatens abroad. The destruction of the universities is the same anarchy unleashed at home. It is a time for those who believe in America to be strong, for

> If, when the chips are down, the world's most powerful nation, the United States of America, acts like a pitiful, helpless giant, the forces of totalitarianism and anarchy will threaten free nations and free institutions throughout the world. It is not our power, but our will and character that is being tested tonight [Nixon, 1970].

In early 1971, Nixon ordered U.S. units to support a coordinated attack against the Ho Chi Minh trail, in Laos. The Laos incursion exhausted the last of the patience of the country with the war. The President's popularity plummeted. For the first time, the Congress seriously considered setting a date for withdrawal of American troops. The attacks on the sanctuaries did not prevent the North Vietnamese from launching the largest offensive of the war, in March of 1972. It dwarfed the Tet attack of 1968. Mining of North Vietnamese harbors and the heaviest bombing of the North followed. Just before the elections, Kissinger announced peace was at hand, but talks deadlocked. Bombing, which had been halted on October 24, was renewed even more intensively. Finally, on January 23, 1973, a cease fire, withdrawal of U.S. troops and prisoner exchange was agreed to. President Nixon, in a speech to the American people, announced the achievement of "peace with honor."

To Nixon, peace with honor means that "the people of South Vietnam have been guaranteed the right to determine their own future without outside interference" (The Los Angeles Times, Jan. 24, 1973, p11). The United States, however, recognizes only the Republic of Vietnam as the legitimate government, even though it does not represent all the people of South Vietnam.

The accord itself, however, explicitly affirms that "The United States and all other countries respect the independence, sovereignty, unity and territorial integrity of Vietnam...." The political future of South Vietnam is to be decided through "genuinely free and democratic general elections." Reunification of North and South Vietnam is to be achieved step by step through peaceful agreement. The United States is not to "continue its military involvement nor intervene in the internal affairs of South Vietnam." Both the agreement and Henry Kissinger's admission at a news conference that the Vietnamese struggle has been a civil war suggests a reevaluation of three decades of U.S. policy in Indochina (Fitzgerald, 1973, p13).

The basic principles of the Geneva accords of 1954, which the U.S. refused to sign, are affirmed in the present agreement. Yet, according to The Pentagon Papers, in 1954 both the Viet Minh and the United States were displeased with the agreement. Ho Chi Minh believed, and no French authority in Geneva doubted him, that a complete military victory could be won against the French. However, both China and

Russia feared U. S. intervention, and pressured Ho for the
settlement. He declared that the Viet Minh did not agree to
the permanent division of Vietnam.

> ... North, Central and South Viet Nam are terri-
> tories of ours. Our country will certainly be uni-
> fied, our entire people will surely be liberated.
> Our compatriots in the South were the first to wage
> the war of Resistance. ...   I am confident that they
> will ... join their efforts with the entire people in
> strengthening peace, achieving unity, independence
> and democracy all over the country ... [Gravel,
> Vol. I, p172].

The United States set itself to the task of opposing the Viet
Minh.   Leslie Gelb, the director of The Pentagon Papers
study and the writer of the "Analysis" sections, concludes
that

> ... the Administration, convinced that any attrition
> of what had been regarded as "Free World" terri-
> tory and resources was inimical to American global
> interests, could only view the settlement as the
> acceptance of terms from the Communist victors.
> The task in Vietnam ... was therefore to work
> with what had been "retained" in hope, by no means
> great, that the Diem government could pull the
> country up by its bootstraps in time to present a
> meaningful alternative to Ho Chi Minh's DRV [ibid.,
> p178].

Again in 1973, after nineteen more years of war, the
parties agree to return to the political struggle for South
Vietnam and renounce the military struggle.   But since the
South Vietnamese government is primarily prepared for
military action while the Vietcong are primarily able to
continue political action, the accord is extremely precarious.
The political and military can scarcely be separated.   Henry
Kissinger, writing of "The Vietnam Negotiations," attempts
to limit the perception of American interests.

In terms of the American mission, the agreement with
the North Vietnamese is an acceptance of the fact that the
U. S. can no longer operate global programs, imposing its
own solutions.   But the U. S. mission is still to the whole
world.   While the U. S. now recognizes that other nations
have spheres of influence contiguous to their own borders,

the U. S. sphere of influence is not so limited. But that influence will be the force of example. America will only be the "well wisher to the freedom and independence of all," except--and this is a large and perilous exception--where American military effort "will make the difference between success and failure."

The American civil religion provided motivation first for the entry into Vietnam and then for disengagement. The sense of mission, and the passion of the established type to achieve the universal ideal by organizational effort, led America into the quicksand that was Vietnam. But, after 1965, as the war continued to escalate, the actions of America no longer seemed consonant with her character, at least to the left wing established types. They believed that America had universal meaning, and that meaning was expressed in actions that were clearly for the good of all mankind. The enormous military power of America destroying the hapless peasants and countryside of a small agricultural nation was not consonant with the character of America as understood by the civil religion. America was elected to lead the nations to a more abundant life, not to rain death upon them from the skies.

For the majority of the established type, however, the war was wrong because it was a failure. It required a means disproportionate to the ends. Here the work ethic came into play. Worldly success had long been accepted by the established type as the certification of virtue. It is the very success of America herself that is a sign of her election to be the bearer of responsibility for freedom on the earth. But the war in Vietnam was not a success. Freedom was no closer in 1968 than in 1960. America was suffering grievous divisions. The war-fueled inflation threatened the dollar. Lack of success made it evident that the policy was not virtuous, did not belong amongst those efforts which America ought to enshrine in history.

It was the work ethic that led the Senior Advisory Group to suggest that L. B. J. withdraw. He could not accept his own failure. (Who can agree he is amongst the damned?) As he wrote his memoirs, L. B. J. therefore interpreted his change of policy both to himself and to his public in the context of change of mission.

Henry Kissinger and Richard Nixon understood the meaning of the change of policy, however. The left wing

established type urged a return of the mission of America to
more exemplary roles.   A move has been made in that direction.   The left wing established types were still in favor of
a mission carried out by economic, political and educational
persuasions.   The right wing types heartily agreed.   But
Kissinger and Nixon do not eschew military force.   "No more
Vietnams!" on the lips of Richard Nixon means "No more
failures!"   No more interventions in America's global sphere
of influence when the intervention is not decisive.   Our intervention can be meaningful only if it makes "the difference
between success and failure."

So, the American involvement in the war in Vietnam
ends as it began--slowly moving from a peripheral concern
to center stage and back again to the periphery.   The struggle between the Vietnamese for political and military control
goes on.   But the U. S. is not likely to intervene militarily
again.   Lyndon Johnson, a man possessed by a vision of the
glory of America, carried away by the faith that there is
nothing America cannot do at home and abroad, is dead.
His dream for America and for Vietnam is dead, too.   Not
that America is willing to settle down to the traditional
spheres of influence.   She still has a mission.   But she is
now behaving toward the world with more restraint.   Kissinger summarizes it:

> Thus our conception of world order must have
> deeper purposes than stability, but greater re-
> straints on our behavior than would result if it
> were approached only in a fit of enthusiasm
> [ibid.].

Ironically enough, the very men who at the opening of the
sixties believed that above all they were rational men con-
trolling rational events are perceived, at the close of the
decade, to have been acting out a last fit of religious enthusiasm.

The Expression of the Established
Type in the Administration of the
University

The leadership of the university continued, throughout
the sixties, to argue that the multiversity was to serve the
public good.   The public good was largely identified with the
national interest.   To be sure, the action of sectarians stim-
ulated a great deal of discussion within the established type

in the university.   Robert Nisbet, Professor of Sociology and
Vice Chancellor of the University of California, Riverside,
sums up the images of the university that were urged as
normative by the close of the sixties: 1) The university as
capstone of the research establishment; 2) The university as
adjunct to the establishment; 3) The university as the micro-
cosm of culture; 4) The university as humanitarian-in-chief;
5) The university as radical social critic and 6) The university as therapeutic community (Nisbet, 1971, pp171-196).
The established type argued for the first four visions as
constituting the university, while the sectarians argued that
the latter four visions constituted the university.

        Nisbet does not accept any of the six as constitutive
of the university.   He believes that

> the university's most feasible function for the future
> is in essence what it has been in the past: that of
> serving as a setting for the scholarly and scientific
> imagination [ibid., p207].

Central to achieving such a function is the restoration of
authority.

> Nothing else can be achieved until the university is
> able to create again a system of recognized author-
> ity such as it had down until a decade or two ago
> [ibid., pp213-214].

To Nisbet, the faculty's authority must be central in the
appointment and promotion of professors, admissions, grant-
ing of degrees and curricular matters.   Administrators are
to be responsible for the multitude of other ancillary areas
of the university.   Students are to be students.

> It is utter nonsense to suppose that students, none
> of them likely to be present on the campus for
> more than four or five years at most, their re-
> sponsibility for the campus accordingly diminished,
> should participate at high and crucial levels in the
> formal government of the university, either within
> administrative or within faculty councils [ibid.,
> p219].

        But if students are to be students, then teachers must
be teachers.   The importance of teaching must be reinstated.
Therefore, there must be a clearing of the vast majority of

the institutes, centers, bureaus and consultantships. Research must again be for the sake of the scholarly and scientific imagination, not for the government nor for industry. Needless to say, the university must also be depoliticized.

> It will suffice to say that one of the highest of all priorities for rehabilitation of the university as the setting for ideas, as the scene of teaching and scholarship in the learned disciplines, is abandonment of the present limitless, boundless, Faustian conception of the university and its relation to man and society [ibid., p233].

Nisbet's argument is typical of senior faculty. It is long past time to reverse the trends and get back to being the university as defined and managed by the senior faculty. But Clark Kerr, surveying the scene from the more detached (and peaceful) vantage point of the Chairman of the Carnegie Commission on Higher Education points out that the question, still unresolved at the end of the sixties, is "Who governs?" (Kerr, 1970). There are more claimants for power and no more power to be distributed. It is a zero-sum game. The main transfer of power has been from the administration, including the board of trustees, especially in public universities. State executives and legislatures have become interested in the appropriateness of the relationships of students and faculties to political issues and action. Domination of the budget is shared with the state house, thus the Administration has lost much of its principal lever of control. The legislators and governors, concerned with re-election as well as education, ask how the university can best serve the needs of their constituents. The university will recover this power only when it sets its house in order and it is no longer politically advantageous to be visibly involved in governing the university (Kerr, 1970, pp108-118).

Meanwhile, within the university Kerr largely agrees with Nisbet. The faculty ought to deal with educational matters and the administration with all others, including ordering the life of the university community. However, students must be involved in democratic ways in both endeavors. They obviously are central in ordering the life of the community. Students also ought to share importantly in the discussion of pre-professional curricula matters, especially in the liberal arts colleges. With such working relationships established, perhaps authority would again appear secure on campus and power begin to flow back from the state house to the university (ibid.).

One of the best known of besieged campus presidents in the latter half of the sixties was S. I. Hayakawa of San Francisco State College. Hayakawa was resolute in restoring authority. To him the functional division of the university so elegantly argued by Kerr and Nisbet was obvious. Students were to learn, faculty to teach and make educational decisions, and the administration to administer all else. For those who opposed authority, the police were to police. To depart from the traditional structure was to invite chaos.

In a speech to the San Francisco Commonwealth Club in January of 1969, Hayakawa praises the university for its great contributions to the life of the nation and the world. The great work going forward in the sciences, social sciences and humanities makes the university one of the great nerve centers of modern society. The university is perhaps as important to society today as the medieval church was to the middle ages. For the bulk of the speech Hayakawa suggests ways in which the state college may extend its service to the society by becoming more involved with the basic needs of people. Both the educational services and the location of these services ought to be more diversified (Hayakawa, 1969, pp198-212).

Yet, for all its service to the people, institutions of higher learning are being threatened by internal disorder, faculty disaffection and violence. The obvious question is why? Hayakawa believes higher education is threatened by a planned attack by the revolutionary movement.

> It seems to me that there is a systematic plan to bring this college to a halt, as there was to bring Berkeley to a halt or Columbia to a halt, as a prelude for an attack on all higher education. ... It isn't just student disaffection [ibid., p199].

Hayakawa recognizes that the rapidity of social change creates demand, especially by students, for rapid adjustments in the life of institutions. But the disruption of the university goes beyond this. It is the attempt "to destroy one of the nerve centers of our culture, namely the universities" (ibid.).

The President's Commission on the Causes of Campus Unrest disagreed. The Commission found that while the tactics of campus confrontations escalated in the latter half of the sixties, the causes remained much the same. The new youth culture, rejecting what it sees to be the operational

ideals of American society, is "the cause of student protest
against the war, racial injustice and the abuses of the
multiversity" (The President's Commission on Campus Unrest, 1970, p52). The new tactics of terrorism, bombings,
arson and property destruction are a result of a mix of
increased commitment to change, frustration, and response
to the action of police or national guard units. As far as
the Commission is concerned, dissent, within the limits of
law is not a problem, but a right protected by the First
Amendment. This is true when the dissent outrages reason,
as well as when it is responsible. But the university must
recognize

> its responsibility to protect itself, its values, and
> human life in the event of disorder. The univer-
> sity must honestly and forcefully reiterate its first
> principles and must clearly distinguish between
> those forms of protest which it will permit and
> defend and those it will prohibit [ibid., p145].

While universities need to be reformed to allow more participation of faculty and students in decision making, universities
cannot be run on a "one man one vote basis with participation of all members on all issues" (ibid., p14). Students
often believe that because they hold their views with great
moral intensity they have a right to determine national and
university policy. But

> the rhetorical commitment to democracy by students
> must be matched by an awareness of the central role
> of majority rule in a democratic society and by an
> equal commitment to techniques of persuasion within
> the political process [ibid., p15].

The established type that emerges in the university
administration in the latter half of the sixties is the left
wing established type. There is a great sympathy with those
who oppose the war in Vietnam, and university administrations often facilitate campus wide teach-ins. This was
especially true at the time of the military strike against the
Cambodian sanctuaries. There is also recognition of and
sympathy with the new youth culture, and the demand to
implement racial justice. The university even recognizes
the ponderousness of its own procedures, and the anger that
students feel in being reduced to the status of computer
punch cards. The idea of a more democratic society, including a more democratic university, is largely accepted.

While many senior faculty might share Nisbet's feelings that it is utter nonsense to allow students to participate in the crucial formal government of the university, more universities are following Kerr's advice. At least token democracy, such as graduate student representatives to Department and Academic Senate meetings, is attempted.

But there is no doubt that such student participation will be within the context of a resurgent authority of the established type. The struggle for power is between the political powers outside and administrative and faculty functions within the university. As the campuses quiet, and other issues attract the politicians, the faculty seems to have emerged with a greater increase of power on campus. But that is likely to last only as long as faculty attention is focused on faculty prerogatives. Regardless of whether faculty or administration gains, student participation is exercised within the confines of established authority. The faculty and administration define the meaning of the university, and control, insofar as possible, the mainstream of its development. The work ethic is reasserted. Those who have not yet obtained the certification of success by means of proper degrees ought not participate in important decisions regarding the university. The transience of students, the fact that the university is not the life's work of many of them, is another argument in excluding them from the decision making process. Nevertheless, the university commits itself once again to the unfettered search for truth. This search will be conducted by the proper organizational effort, however. The university will still be a critical force in society, but criticism will be responsible. This means it will be generated by faculty, not students, except within the educational structures.

The major remaining effect of the turmoil of the sixties on campus was increase in enrollment of black students. The percentage of blacks in colleges and universities increased from 4. 6 percent in 1965 to 9. 0 percent in 1971. The percentage of black graduate students jumped an impressive 38 percent in 1971 over the 1970 figure. Nearly one-half of the 1971 class of black students were from families earning under $6,000 per year, and only 14 percent from families earning over $12,000 (Shafer, 1972, p6).

But it was this vigorous recruitment of poor blacks that had opened the doors to much violence and, ironically, those white universities which recruited most strongly

amongst poor blacks were scenes of the most violence. The
best example is Cornell. When James Perkins came to
Cornell as President in 1963 there were few blacks enrolled.
He began vigorous recruiting, and soon a militant group of
blacks was formed on campus. Their demands continually
escalated. When they barricaded a building, they were
armed with rifles and ammunition belts. Perkins was forced
to resign. The president of Swarthmore died of a heart attack during a confrontation with the black students he had
helped recruit. For the black poor, the violent lifestyle of
the ghetto continued on the campus. It also had certain rewards. The Urban Research Corporation of Chicago revealed
that as a rule the more violent a protest, the more likely it
was to succeed. Black demands were twice as likely to be
granted as other kinds of demands (O'Neill, 1971, p190).

Norman Mailer, in Miami and the Siege of Chicago,
writes that as he waited for Ralph Abernathy to appear at a
news conference, suddenly he was tired of black demands.
Mailer wonders if this is racism or just ordinary weariness.
He suspects racism. Whatever, by the seventies the established type on the campus was also tired of black demands.
Black recruitment would continue, but the authority of the
institution would be reaffirmed. Nonetheless, the established
type could point with pride to the increase in black enrollment as
the fruit of the sixties. Recruitment of the black poor had
been the universities' response to the black revolution. The
university has weathered the storm, authority has been reasserted, but blacks are still being recruited. From the
established perspective, on this point at least, all seems
well as the seventies unfold.

The Sectarian Type

In his discussion of the Hussites and Peasant Uprisings
Troeltsch argues that the tendency toward violence was the
new element. Such a tendency could not be supported by
appealing to the New Testament and the Law of Christ, so
sectarians turned to the Old Testament and the "Holy Wars."
Sects separated most sharply from one another: on the one
hand were the passive, communist style groups which withdrew from the world; on the other hand were the aggressive
sectarians proclaiming the revolutionary right of resistance
and holy war. The only universalism these sectarians knew
was the Chiliastic form, the belief that all those who have
been oppressed in this world will see their wrongs righted at

the Last Judgment.   The aggressive sectarians believed,
Troeltsch says, that the End of the World had already come,
and thus the Holy War of the Last Days was waged with the
authority of the Scriptural Apocalypse.   Thus the demand of
the Gospel for unconditional brotherly love could be seen to
move through a cycle:

> At first men hoped that this ideal would be realized
> naturally, as soon as the relatively corrupt Church
> was reformed; then arose the hope of a miraculous
> Divine intervention and the Chiliastic dream; then,
> with the appeal to the Old Testament, men took to
> violence and brought in a Christian communism by
> force; ultimately these idealists withdrew once more
> from the world as a religious community which set
> up the Christian law in the center of its own life,
> and tolerated secular institutions as the results of
> sin and as an alien environment, waiting for their
> hour of doom to strike [Troeltsch, 1960, p380].

Troeltsch observes that the sect vacillates between seeking
to restore universal purity by force, which is a contradiction,
and renouncing universalism or taking refuge in eschatology.

The first half of the sixties saw the opening moves of
the cycle: there was first the hope that American society
would be reformed naturally.   This was followed by the
belief that once "the people" realized how truly repressive
the rulers were, then they would rise up and cast them out.
But slowly through the latter half of the sixties, there was a
growing disillusionment with this hope, and violence was
more and more accepted if the ideals of the sect were to be
universal.   But amongst some of the sectarian perspective
violence was also rejected almost immediately, and the withdrawal began to take place.

The escalation of the war early in 1965 affected the
antiwar movement in a variety of ways.   Most obviously,
the movement expanded far beyond the activist groups themselves.   The intensity of antiwar feeling amongst a major
segment of younger persons granted the activist sectarians
a great mobilizing ability.   But with the involvement of the
increasingly wide sectors of the population came a greater
diversity amongst the sectarians, and increasing conflicts
over positions and tactics.   Finally, the breadth and intensity of the antiwar movement had a serious impact both
upon national politics and upon the sectarian groups themselves (Teodori, 1969, p56).

The first anti-war teach-in was conducted at the University of Michigan on March 24, 1965. As the Greensboro sit-in was an inspiration for the early civil rights movement, so the Michigan teach-in fired the imagination of the anti-war movement. Without an organized political force to oppose the war, the anti-war movement seemed impotent. But the use of the university was a rare stroke of political genius. Regardless of the stance of the administration, the university was understood by the media and the public to oppose the war. Teach-ins took place in hundreds of universities across the spring of 1965, reaching thousands of students and faculty members. More importantly, the media, especially television, carried the message of the teach-ins to the entire society. The May 22 teach-in at the University of California at Berkeley was the zenith of the teach-ins. More than 35, 000 persons attended. Speakers included Senator Gruening, A. J. Muste, I. F. Stone, Norman Mailer, Staughton Lynd and Mario Savio. Nearly the whole spectrum of anti-war activists participated.

The April S. D. S. March on Washington was joined by pacifist organizations, such as the Committee for Non-Violent Action, the traditional left, such as the W. E. B. DuBois Clubs and the New Left, such as S. N. C. C. In August, Robert Moses, Staughton Lynd and Dave Dellinger organized the Assembly of Unrepresented People in Washington, D. C. to declare peace with the people of Vietnam. Out of that gathering emerged the National Coordinating Committee to End the War in Vietnam. The Committee organized the International Days of Protest, which were held in about one hundred cities the following October (ibid. , pp56-57).

Carl Oglesby was the first president of S. D. S. who had not been at the founding convention, but had become politically active only with the anti-war movement. He spoke at the November anti-war rally in Washington. Over 40, 000 persons attended.

In his speech, Oglesby (1965) states that the men who now engineer the war are not moral monsters. Bundy, McNamara, Rusk, Lodge, Goldberg, the President himself are all honorable men. "They are all liberals. " Since this is true, it is necessary to take a closer look at American liberalism. There are perhaps two quite different liberalisms: one that is authentically humanist; the other not so human at all.

Oglesby lists the parallels between the American revolution and the Vietnamese revolution. Our present leaders cannot see them because

> Their aim in Vietnam is ... to safeguard what they take to be American interests around the world against revolution or revolutionary change, which they always call communism--as if it were that [ibid., p314].

Those who cannot understand Watts or Mississippi without a devil theory can scarcely be expected to understand Vietnam. A devil theory twists all truth: we cry that Communism is about to take over the world, but take pride in our six thousand military bases on foreign soil; we officially deplore racism, but strongly support the economics of Rhodesia and South Africa to keep them from going Communist; we are puzzled by the tendency of Latin American states to become embroiled in left wing revolutions, for we believe that

> the world is coming our way, that change from disorder can be orderly, that our benevolence will pacify the distressed, that our might will intimidate the angry ... these are quite unlikely fantasies ... because we have lost that mysterious social desire for human equity that from time to time has given us genuine moral drive [ibid., p315].

This is evidenced by the fact that we can send 200,000 men to Vietnam to kill and die and not get 100 voter registrars to Mississippi.

No, the men who guide the nation are not evil. But they have been divided from their compassion by the institutional system that inherits us all. The name of that system is corporate liberalism. His enemy is change, which it gives the religious name of Communism. Corporate liberalism now functions for the corporate state as the Church once performed for the feudal state. It justifies its burdens and protects it from change. So now the time of decision is upon us.

> Corporatism or humanism: which? For it has come to that. Will you let your dreams be used? Will you be a grudging apologist for the corporate state? Or will you help try to change it--not in the name of this or that blueprint or ism, but in the

name of simple human decency and democracy and
the vision that wise and brave men saw in the time
of our own Revolution? [ibid. , p320].

The sectarian perspective is apparent in Oglesby's
appeal to the American Revolution and to the "true humanism"
which, he believes, is its foundation. There is also the
call to personal action and the expression of solidarity with
the lowest class that is typical of sectarians. But Oglesby
also recognizes the new situation in which the activists find
themselves. The movement no longer includes only the committed few; thousands are responding to anti-war sentiment.
Oglesby shares his faith that radicals are the true liberals,
the true humanists, and the true Americans and that corporate
liberalism and the corporate state have departed from the way
of true democracy. It is not the men who are evil, but the
system. The purpose of this argument is to bring those who
are focused on just one issue--anti-war or anti-draft--to the
radical perspective which argues that the war is not just a
mistake but a logical outcome of the established order. The
sectarians hope to harness the passion of the anti-war movement to pull for change in all of society, not just one policy.

In the furor that arose over the representations by
the media that S. D. S. had been responsible for nationwide
outburst against the war (whereas ad hoc student groups
were attempting to coordinate a plethora of local activities),
S. D. S. issued a statement which expressed most clearly its
radical commitment.

> The commitment of SDS, and of the whole genera-
> tion we represent, is clear: we are anxious to
> build villages; we refuse to burn them. We are
> anxious to help and change our country; we refuse
> to destroy someone else's country. We are anxious
> to advance the cause of democracy; risk our lives--
> we have been risking our lives in Alabama and
> Mississippi, and some of us died there. But we
> will not bomb the people, the women and children,
> of another country [Newfield, 1970, p107].

Although the S. D. S. was not of one mind as to whether
to make the anti-war movement its priority issue, it did urge
all young men to apply for C. O. status. This was meant to
be both a way to avoid the war for those who succeeded in
gaining C. O. classification and a protest for those who did
not. But the decision of the Selective Service to schedule

examinations to rank students academically and draft the least
successful engendered a storm of protests against the examinations, the university for cooperation and the draft itself.
Three arguments were raised against the examinations: 1)
Students were forced to compete with one another to keep
from being killed.   The analogy with Nazi death camps was
drawn.   2) In the words of protesters at City College of New
York,

> there are other young men who cannot take this
> test.   Many Negroes, Puerto Ricans and other
> poor guys who do not have the opportunity to go
> to college. ...   We ask for an end to this system
> which discriminates between rich and poor, black
> and white [Ferber and Lynd, 1971, p40].

3) The Oberlin S. D. S. stated simply: "The war in Vietnam
is the most important reason why we oppose college cooperation with the S. S. S. " (ibid.).

The debate raged over whether the S. D. S. ought to
oppose the draft completely, even a draft for C. O. or humanitarian causes.   Finally in a statement to the House Armed
Services Committee drafted jointly by Oglesby and Carmichael,
the position was taken that the government had no right to
draft persons for any purpose, military or otherwise.

But in spite of the publicity given by the media,
S. D. S. leadership in the anti-war movement was an uncertain
trumpet.   Therefore, other groups in the white radical movement attempted to build and coordinate draft resistance.   In
the latter half of 1966 draft calls rose as high as 46, 000 in
one month.   As anti-draft sentiment grew, the work of the
organizers gained enough momentum to make the hope of a
genuine mass movement of draft resisters realistic.   A. J.
Muste, David Dellinger and the traditional pacifist groups
with which they were affiliated supported noncooperation.
Six young men, who were non-cooperators, called a conference
in the fall of 1966, to further noncooperation.   Over two
hundred attended.   The atmosphere was serious.

> The six men who called it were themselves non-
> cooperating which gave an element of seriousness
> to the affair.   It began with each of them telling
> us why he chose this path.   Speaking to others out
> of one's own personal life, rather than in political
> abstractions, eventually became the Resistance way

of organizing, and this was one of the early examples of it [ibid., p49].

The Marxist groups, such as the Progressive Labor Party, followed the Leninist policy of entering military service and seeking to radicalize the troops. Such a tactic had no appeal beyond the minute cadres of committed Marxists, because it moved altogether outside the framework of American civil religion.

Most young men were neither pacifist nor Marxist, and since S.D.S. was not offering leadership, other groups began to form. In July 1966, a group of young men met in New Haven and drew up a statement which said

> We men of draft age disavow all military obligations to our government until it ceases wars against peoples seeking to determine their own destinies. On November 16, we will return our draft cards to our local boards with a notice of our refusal to cooperate until American invasions are ended [ibid., p52].

The group became known as the We Won't Go. They followed the Resistance mode of organizing, rejecting, with a dig at S.D.S., "the type of organizing that issues calls to do something, writes magazine articles and prints newspaper ads, and then expects people to act" (ibid., p54). In late August, after two months of traveling the country and involving hundreds of uneasy young men in intense discussion, the group from New Haven met with an expanded group of activists in Des Moines, Iowa. The argument centered on whether to allow each local troupe to "go public" in its own way and in its own community, or to focus all groups on a big draft card turn-in in November. It was decided to leave the decision to the groups themselves. The tension continued in the Resistance for the next two years between these two approaches. Some groups, such as the one in Detroit, gained considerable publicity by holding city wide meetings on the draft. Others worked quietly. But the movement grew.

By the end of the year, S.D.S. had finally issued a militant anti-draft resolution. Anti-draft unions were formed from coast to coast. Induction centers and draft boards were picketed. Early in 1967, the anti-draft group at Cornell moved directly into mass civil disobedience. The personal Resistance method of organizing was used. By March enough

men had been radicalized that the Cornell group went public,
issuing a call to publicly destroy draft cards at the Spring
Mobilization.

In the call, the Cornell group argues that although
they have demonstrated to stop the destruction of the lives
and consciences of millions of Americans and Vietnamese by
the military of the U.S., still the draft and the war go on.
In Vietnam, the war machine is directed against all, young
and old, soldiers and civilians.   In America, the

> war machine is directed specifically against the
> young, against blacks more than against white,
> but ultimately against all.   Body and soul, we
> are oppressed in common.   Body and soul, we
> must resist in common [ibid., p72].

The plan was that five hundred would burn their cards
at once, but by the time of the Mobilization, only one hundred and twenty had pledged to do so.   At a meeting on
April 14, the day before the Mobilization, the group decided
that fifty would be enough to make the card burnings a genuine political act.   Fifty-seven agreed to burn their cards, but
in the actual moment between one hundred fifty and two hundred burned their cards.

Tom Bell records that he could not shake his reservations concerning either the pledges to burn or the burnings,
for perhaps later the resisters could not hold their commitment.

> I am afraid for many of them the decision comes
> from the emotionalism of the moment.   The ses-
> sions in the student union are very much like
> revival services (including some of the rhetoric at
> times).   We have speeches, a collection for the
> anti-war office and on the spot conversions--signing
> pledges, plus alot of personal witness [ibid., p73].

But Bell goes on to say that although he doesn't want to
manipulate anyone, it is essential for the sake of both the
persons involved and all humanity that America change.   The
religiousness of the means bothers Bell, but the purpose is
so important that these means can be accepted.   He does not
reflect upon the fact that personal and social salvation is a
religious purpose for which religious expressions are quite
apt.

The public burning and the following march was indeed
a religious exercise.   The serious intensity of the crowd as
the burners lighted their cards in Sheeps Meadow, the rush
of others to join in the symbolic act, and then

> the Cornell contingent, numbering in the thousands,
> was led by its "We Won't Go" organization and
> draft card burners under a large banner, "We
> Won't Go" emblazoned in the school colors.   Locked
> arm in arm they were literally dancing down the
> street, joyful, defiant, irresistible.   "Hell, No,
> We Won't Go, " their words vibrated between the
> sterile buildings on Madison Avenue and echoed up
> and down the canyonlike side streets [ibid. , p76].

The Resistance, which at Stanford had as its nucleus
David Harris and a small group of fellow undergraduates
gained strength from the Spring Mobilization.   Sixty-five
thousand had gathered in San Francisco and 200,000 in New
York.   Prominent persons such as Martin Luther King, Jr.,
were now speaking at anti-war rallies.   The leading colum-
nists, including James Reston of the New York Times, specu-
lated that the government was deeply concerned about the
spread of the movement.   Perhaps up to twenty-five percent
of college youth would refuse to cooperate.   A Vietnam Summer Project to raise money for anti-war groups was supported by major gifts from those close to the Kennedy family.
A Stop The Draft Week was scheduled for October.   Important
Resistance groups grew in Chicago and Boston.

A mass draft card turn-in was planned by the New
England Resistance in the Arlington Street Church.   Michael
Ferber, one of the organizers, was enthusiastic about holding
the turn-in in a church.

> What better way to underscore the moral gravity
> of the act we were embarking on than to hold it
> in a place of worship?   It was a little like con-
> firmation or baptism: a rite of passage into man-
> hood, from slavery and a "channeling" to the
> promised land of peace and freedom.   True, most
> potential resisters were not religious, but then
> neither was I in the usual sense, and I found the
> idea compelling [ibid. , p109].

Both William Sloane Coffin, chaplain of Yale University, and
Ferber spoke.   About five thousand people attended the rally
and service.

In his speech, "A Time to Say No," Ferber opens by affirming that the basis of unity for those assembled is the "no" expressed in the act of burning or returning the draft card. But what is the "yes"? The Resistance disagrees about many things. Many despise the very tradition of the church in whose building the multitude has assembled. But there is within the church a radical tradition that has always struggled against the conservative and worldly forces in control.

> This tradition in modern times has tried to recall us to the best ways of living our lives: the way of love and compassion, the way of justice and respect, the way of facing other people as human beings and not as abstract representatives of something alien and evil. ... The radical tradition is still alive: it is present here in this church. ... This tradition is something to which we can say Yes [Ferber, 1967, p109].

But radicals, both political and religious, often make the mistake of dwelling too much on Utopia or the Apocalypse. Neither the Revolution nor the Revelation is at hand. All radicals tend to be apocalyptarians. Therefore, those who gather as a community must recognize that the bombing, the killing, the draft, and the racism that America sponsors will go on. This is not the end but the beginning. It is not going to be easy to change America. It will require that Resisters work hard and long with each other to build a community; to let others know they can be depended upon. Only then can the Resistance make it difficult and politically dangerous for the government to prosecute Resisters. Only as the Resistance says Yes to these things can it step forward together to say No to the United States Government.

For his sermon Coffin (1967) chooses the text, "We must obey God rather than men." He rehearses the heritage of radicals in America. The men who are honored today are those who of old refused to surrender their consciences to the state. The roll call is impressive: the Puritans, the Quakers in Boston, John Woolman in Pennsylvania, Washington, Hamilton, Jefferson, Adams, the Abolitionists, and Thoreau. If Americans would remember their heritage, they would applaud those who today refuse to surrender their consciences to the state.

> The issue is one of conscience. Let us be blunt. To us the war in Vietnam is a crime. And if we

> are correct, if the war is a crime, then is it
> criminal to refuse to have anything to do with it?
> Is it we who are demoralizing our boys in Vietnam,
> or the Administration which is asking them to do
> immoral things? [ibid., p264].

Coffin concludes by noting that it is almost the 450th Celebration of the Reformation. What is needed today is a new
reformation, a reformation of conscience.

> You stand now as Luther stood in his time. May
> you be inspired to speak, and we to hear, the
> words he once spoke in conscience and in all
> simplicity: "Here I stand, I can do no other.
> God help me" [ibid., p267].

S. N. C. C. and much of S. D. S. still opposed the Resistance philosophy through 1967. Revolutionaries who see themselves fighting against the system rather than appealing to the
conscience of society argued against letting the "enemy put
me away." An amazing number of the S. N. C. C. staff,
determined to keep working for S. N. C. C., and not to go to
jail, not to be drafted, not to leave the country, succeeded
in their fight against the system. They used series of appeals, court cases, C. O., physical exemptions, bad security
risks, homosexuality and anything imaginable. S. D. S., on
the eve of the anti-war actions of October 16, affirmed its
support of the Resistance, but still expressed criticism.

> SDS recognizes the validity of all direct challenges
> to illegitimate authority, but seeing the insufficiency
> and misdirection of symbolic-confrontation-oriented
> movements, urges members of "the Resistance" to
> involve themselves in local community organizing
> projects aiming to build a powerful insurgent white
> base inside the United States [Ferber & Lynd, 1971,
> pp129-130].

Yet many S. D. S. leaders as well as the men active in the
Resistance understood personal liberation and political effectiveness not as opposites, but as part of a single process.
When persons share with one another about the way in which
their deepest longings are frustrated by the society in which
they live, the personal becomes political. The rediscovery
of community becomes the rediscovery of the levers of political power. Yet the tension grew between the factions in the
movement. Former S. N. C. C. worker Julius Lester wrote of
the difference in protesting and resisting.

> To protest is to speak out against.   To let it be
> known that you do not like a certain action of
> another. ...   To protest is to play a game.   You
> go to a demonstration, listen to speeches, wave
> signs, and go home to see if you got on television.
> To resist is to pit Life as you define it against
> Life as they define it and to do all that is necessary
> to see that their definition is destroyed in all of its
> parts. ...   To resist is to make the President afraid
> to leave the White House because he will be spat
> upon wherever he goes to tell his lies. ...   Have
> we forgotten?   The man is a murderer. ...   One
> does not protest murder.   One apprehends the
> murderer and deals with him accordingly [ibid.,
> p135].

The tension between the S. D. S. style of resistance and the
protest of The Resistance was acted out at the Pentagon and
on the streets.   Some of the sectarians despaired more and
more of renewal, reform, or change.   Their apocalypticism
grew.   To them the revolution was at hand.   But others still
hoped against hope, and sought to reform American society.

At the Pentagon demonstration, the S. D. S. contingent
sprinted ahead of the 35, 000 marchers, and sought to enter
the building.   They were thrown back by troops.   When the
main march arrived, the mood changed.   There was an attempt to communicate with the soldiers.   A shock of recognition had passed between both sides, that here were age mates.
Flowers, songs, cheers, chants, talk were offered to the
troops, who were commanded to be silent.   The feeling of
the demonstrators that they were one with the soldiers grew.

> And again, absolutely spontaneously, a great chant,
> "We love you!   We love you!   We love you!"   It is
> impossible to convey the sound of this chant to
> those who did not hear it. ...   By sound I mean its
> real meaning. ...   Our sense of ourselves as a
> community--the community that could be, the one we
> felt had to be (and deeply American one at that) was
> acute.   And there before us--one would say in panic
> might--was the vast engine that is in fact destroying
> the modern world [ibid., p139].

But as Mailer reports, later in the night the young troops
were replaced by Vietnam veterans.   Suddenly the soldiers
formed a wedge, and began to beat and arrest the demonstra-

tors. S. D. S. leaders pleaded with the demonstrators to withdraw, for the beatings and arrests were senseless. But the
sense of community held the crowd.

> To leave was to leave one's brothers and sisters to
> get clubbed, yet to passively remain in the locked
> chain was also to participate in the senseless bru-
> tality. . . .   One cannot articulate the agony of those
> who sat and watched this go on slowly for hours
> amidst the songs, the pleas, the tears and the
> impotent curses . . . [Mailer, 1968, p273].

In Oakland, the split between the pacifists and Resistance on the one hand and the Marxists and S. D. S. on the
other became much more marked.   Demonstrations were
therefore divided, with pacifists taking Monday, Wednesday,
and Thursday of Stop the Draft Week and militants demonstrating on Tuesday and Friday.   The pacifist sit-ins were
the normal non-violent protests, with the demonstrators being
arrested for disturbing the peace at the Oakland induction
center.   On Tuesday, three thousand demonstrators furiously
battled police for half an hour, resulting in a score of injuries and arrests.   On Friday, ten thousand demonstrators
surrounded the induction center.   Using mobile tactics, they
ran when police advanced, but formed behind police lines,
blocking intersections and keeping military buses from getting
through.   The heady experience of effectively, though tem-
porarily, stopping a small portion of the war machine while
avoiding arrest impressed all but the staunchest of pacifists.
The tactic was much discussed, admired, and urged throughout the rest of the movement.

In one sense, the anti-war movement covered the
ground in two years that the civil rights movement covered
in seven.   The cycle that Troeltsch describes was compressed.
Already by the close of 1967 the hope of a great reformation
of America was fading, and men were taking to violence to
bring in the new day by force.   The classic sectarian faith
had also been embraced by a bewildering variety and number
of young persons.   They saw themselves as the oppressed,
not because of their poverty, but because they were of draft
age.   Those who were students recognized that the poor and
black amongst them who were of draft age were even more
oppressed, for they could not avail themselves of student
deferments nor glibly recite their theological reasons for
claiming C. O. status.   The draft was often compared to the
slavery of totalitarian systems.   Indeed, a government memo-

randum arguing that the draft served the beneficial effect of
"channeling" young men into useful vocations (those with a
draft deferment) was widely quoted.   American pretensions
to world hegemony were scorned.   America could scarcely
be light to the nations while she countenanced such abominable
practices at home, and napalmed babies in Vietnam.

         The anti-war movement also appealed strongly to the
Founding Fathers as Carl Oglesby's speech demonstrates.
The humanism which underlay the Founding Documents was
appealed to both as a witness against the draft and a witness
against the atrocities that the war was afflicting on the Vietnamese people.   But perhaps most striking in the 1965-1967
period is the sense of community that emerges in the Resistance.   Community is expressed in many ways: in the personal style of organizing, in the emphasis on consensus and
participatory democracy in group decision making, in the
seriousness of the early public demonstrations, in the abandoned celebration of the marches, in the chants of "we love
you" to the troops, and in the common pledge to one another
to renew the life of the nation and in the sense of being a
part of the radical tradition, the bearer of the true America.
Radicals stress that each person must join the community
himself; his willingness to resist demonstrates his commitment to freedom, peace and democracy.   The national draft
card turn-ins presented the government with the evidence to
send the resister to jail for five years.   Understandably
enough, those who made such a decision felt bonded to their
comrades who also had taken such a radical step.   They felt
they had indeed moved from protest to resistance.

         Eugene McCarthy called 1968 "the hard year."   The
year opened with the indictment of Spock, Ferber, Goodman,
Coffin, and Raskin for conspiring to counsel, aid and abet
violations of the Selective Service law and to hinder administration of the draft.   It was but the beginning of the trials of
the Resistance.   McCarthy entered the Presidential primaries,
and attracted a large following of anti-war youth.   Oglesby
and other sectarian leaders questioned such a tactic.   In
April, Martin Luther King was shot, and riots erupted.   Columbia went on strike.   In May, the Ultra-Resistance emerged,
with the Catonsville Nine destroying draft files.   They blazed
the path for twelve like-minded groups, who in the following
year destroyed thousands of draft records all across the
country.   In June, Kennedy was assassinated.   July saw the
Cleveland riots.   In August was the siege of Chicago.   Nixon
was elected in November.   With his election, Attorney Gen-

eral Ramsey Clark, who was somewhat sympathetic toward
the sectarians who were set upon by the police in Chicago,
was isolated.   The grand jury was convened, and as soon as
John Mitchell was in office he authorized the prosecution of
the Conspiracy.

The Ultra-Resistance, the Columbia strike and the
conspiracy trials exemplify the increasing violence of the
battle between sectarians and the established type.   The
trial of the Chicago Eight served as the occasion for the
Weathermen "Days of Rage" in Chicago.   The conflict between
Bobby Seale and Judge Hoffman in that same trial also helped
create the atmosphere in which the Chicago police could
ambush Black Panthers Fred Hampton and Mark Clark without
great public outcry.   Throughout 1969 and into 1970 the confrontation between sectarians and established types grew more
and more bitter.   A brief look at four sectarian responses to
events outlines the desperateness of the struggle: First, the
rejection of McCarthy's campaign by the sectarian leadership;
second, the escalation of violence by the Ultra-Resistance;
third, the escalation of campus conflict as typified by the
Columbia strike and fourth, the trial of the Chicago Eight as
an archetype of the conspiracy trials.

In "An Open Letter to the McCarthy Supporters" (1968),
Carl Oglesby asks if McCarthy is the pay-off of the years of
protest, the partial fruition of the attempt to build a movement to change America.   When he examines McCarthy's
record, he sees that McCarthy is a latecomer to the anti-
war position, and still sets his own opposition within the
context of a general acceptance of American foreign policy.
Therefore his record is ambiguous and his present policies
do not quite hit the nail on the head, even though he opposes
the war in Vietnam.   Further, he is not a man of power; it
is unlikely he will win.   Why then do so many young radicals
and young liberals support him?   Oglesby argues that support
springs from illusion, reality, and failure of nerve: First
there is the illusion.   McCarthy is visualized as a man in
the process of change.   It is believed that he will become
what the New Left knows he must be if America is to be
renewed.   Second, there is the reality.   Left politics in
America is hard.   Not much is possible.

> Don't demand the final salvation of the whole world
> tomorrow.   Demand, instead, the end of the War
> today.   Don't demand for tomorrow that real
> democracy establish itself in our society.   Demand,

>instead, that the old elites start at once behaving
>better [ibid., p447].

But Oglesby asks, does such realism really commend itself
to sectarians when McCarthy himself claims his overriding
objective is defense of the same American Empire which the
New Left so passionately opposes? McCarthy's campaign is
important as a manifestation of the breakdown of the liberal
coalition and the emergence of a newly politicized "grass
roots" constituency. But the practicality, the realism of his
policy is a withdrawal from a "mistake" in Vietnam and a
continuance of the Truman-to-Johnson cold war mission of
America.

>No question: Such a policy is "practical," "pos-
>sible," and "realistic." We've had it for years
>[ibid., p448].

Third, Oglesby says, there is failure of nerve. Almost
every young supporter of McCarthy is well to the left of the
candidate. Almost no one thinks there is more than one in
one hundred chances of his winning.

>We think you are afraid of your own politics, and
>that you are employing the McCarthy campaign as
>a means of making your dissent look respectable
>and "legitimate" [ibid.].

Oglesby urges the New Left not to borrow others'
causes because of the difficulty of its own, and not to under-
estimate its own importance. The battle is one that the
young radicals have begun; only the young ones will be loyal
to it. Others will seek to use it for their own purposes,
noble or ignoble. But this generation must be faithful to
itself.

>We think that the present stakes are immense.
>What we think is happening, in all this confusing
>and frightening disorder, is the unfolding of a new
>stage of human history, the writing by a new
>generation of a new human agenda--old in its es-
>sential hopes, new in the possibility of their reali-
>zation [ibid., p449].

The first task of radical politics, according to Oglesby, is
to clarify the main issues of the world we live in: American imperialism, racism, poverty, and the struggle for

liberation of people worldwide.   Political institutions designed
to perpetuate an elite in power will never transform imperialism.   Radicals must seek not only to stop the war in Vietnam
but the system that begot it.   Political deals with the elite of
that system are not the means of changing America.   No,

> You will have to go outside the system for the
> preparation of your means.   You will have to go
> inside yourself first to rediscover the feeling of
> your own possible freedom, and from there to the
> feeling of the possible freedom of others.
> Pride and Communion.
> That's what the Movement is about.   That's what
> we think you should be about [ibid. , p450].

Although sectarian leaders rejected McCarthy, electoral
politics was still attractive to a great many radicals.   Thousands did join the McCarthy campaign, hoping to force the
Administration to end the war.   Other sectarians entered
electoral politics by creating their own parties.   The Peace
and Freedom Party in California was an archetype of radical
electoral politics.   It was the reincarnation of the politics of
Eugene Debs.   The purpose was not so much to gain votes
as to articulate the issues and educate the people.   The
Founding Convention of the Party declared

> The main task of the Peace and Freedom Movement
> is to organize people to begin to gain real and
> concrete power over the institutions which control
> their everyday lives.   One important way to ac-
> complish this is to project into the electoral arena
> the voices of people fighting for human dignity, to
> make it clear that the demand for human dignity is
> at root a demand for power--and that the people
> will have this power only when we all can democrat-
> ically assure that our economy works to fulfill
> human needs rather than to increase the power and
> profit of a small minority.   The function of Peace
> and Freedom candidates is to act as the tribunes
> of Americans who have begun to fight back [Teodori,
> 1969, p443].

Some radical candidates, such as Robert Scheer,
editor of Ramparts, also entered Democratic primaries.
When they did not win they were not disappointed, for they
were convinced that

> We didn't lose, because our first concern was to
> raise the issues in the community.... For the
> first time, they had to take a stand on the war in
> Vietnam, and live with the implications of that
> stand, which I spelled out very closely. We suc-
> ceeded in putting the voter on the spot. That was
> our prime objective. In that sense, we won
> [Scheer, 1968, p44].

But many sectarians agreed with Oglesby's argument,
"You will have to go outside the system for the preparation
of your means." Many radicals felt the time for electoral
politics had passed. The Administration was unwilling to
end the war. The people were unwilling to change Administrations. Sectarians began to seek new avenues of action to
force a change, to create a new America.

The Ultra-Resistance consisted of sectarians who
chose the means of violence against government property to
dramatize their opposition to the war and at the same time to
physically interfere with the recruitment of men to fight the
war. For the Ultra-Resistance, who were primarily Roman
Catholics, both lay and clergy, the decision to employ violence
was an agonizing one. But the war continued to escalate.
Words fell on deaf ears. Children continued to be napalmed.
Villages were destroyed by fire-fights. In an exquisite mixture
of despair and hope, the Ultra-Resistance turned to violence
against property. Their violence was a sign of despair. In
the name of America, the Administration continued to murder
the innocent. Yet their violence was a sign of hope: a
renewal of America could be forced. By such dramatic
forceful action, those who sat in the seats of judgment would
be judged. The conscience of America would be awakened.
The war would end. But yet there was doubt. Perhaps not
so much would happen. Then at least resisters across the
nation would take heart. Draft files would be destroyed. The
odious war machine would grind to a halt. Perhaps. Nonetheless, a person must act.

In October 1967, the Baltimore Four poured blood
over the files in the Selective Service offices in the Baltimore
Customs House. The Catonsville Nine, including the Berrigans and seven other Catholic priests and laymen, attracted
wide publicity in May 1968 with the destruction of 378 draft
files with napalm they manufactured from a recipe in the
Special Forces Handbook. The Boston Two in June, and the
Milwaukee Fourteen in September destroyed over ten thousand

draft files.   The D. C. Nine burned files of the Chemical
Company in March 1969.   The Pasadena Three, the Silver
Springs Three and the Chicago Fifteen destroyed over twenty
thousand draft records in May of 1969.   Five other groups
raided various draft boards the same year; the most prolific
draft record mutilators were the Boston Eight, who struck
four draft boards, destroying over one hundred thousand files.
The East Coast Conspiracy to Save Lives was responsible for
the destruction of thousands of draft files in Philadelphia.

In his poetry Daniel Berrigan sums up the perspective
of the Ultra-Resistance.

> The time is past when good men may be silent
> when obedience
> can segregate men from public risks
> when the poor can die without defense
> How many indeed must die
> before our voices are heard
> how many must be tortured dislocated
> starved maddened?
> How long must the world's resources
> be raped in the service of legalized murder?
> When at what point will you say no to this war?
> We have chosen to say
> with the gift of our liberty
> if necessary our lives:
> the violence stops here
> the death stops here
> the suppression of the truth stops here
> this war stops here
> Redeem the times!
> The times are inexpressibly evil ...
> And yet and yet the times are inexhaustibly good ...
> In a time of death some men
> the resisters   those who work hardily for social
>   change
> those who preach and embrace the truth
> such men to overcome death
> their lives are bathed in the light of the resurrec-
>   tion
> the truth has set them free
> in the jaws of death
> they proclaim their love of the brethren
> We think of such men
> in the world   in our nation   in the churches
> and the stone in our breast is dissolved
> we take heart once more [Berrigan, 1970(a), pp94-
> 95].

Although convicted, only half of the Catonsville Nine
turned themselves in to be imprisoned.   Free while appeals
were made, they went underground when the appeals were
denied.   After two weeks, Phil Berrigan was seized by the
F. B. I. in a rectory in New York.   Dan Berrigan remained
free for four months, during which period he made a variety
of public appearances, in both churches and colleges.   The
conviction was growing amongst the Ultra-Resistance that if
it was right to resist an illegal law, it was right to resist
an illegal imprisonment.

In a letter to the Weatherman underground, Daniel
Berrigan suggests that the underground must come to see
itself as a mobile, internal revival community--the definition
of the future for radicals.   The movement must think seriously about what it means to have nowhere to go in America.

> It must mean to us--let us go somewhere in Ameri-
> ca, let us stay here and play here and love here
> and build here, and in this way join not only those
> who like us are recently kicked out also, but those
> who have never been inside at all, the blacks and
> the Indians and Puerto Ricans, and Chicanos, whose
> consciousness has gone far under the rock [Berri-
> gan, 1970(b), p187].

Thus, the underground must not be seduced into violence
against persons, for that way could only conclude in despair.
No longer would the radical hope of giving birth to the new
man be alive, but the movement would imbibe the bellicose
spirit of the army, the plantation, the corporation and the
diplomat.   The movement must still strive to be nonviolent.

> If there's any definition of the new man, the man
> of the future, it seems to me that we do violence
> unwillingly, bar exception, as instrument, knowing
> that destruction of property is only a means and
> keeping the end as vivid and urgent as alive to us
> as are the means so that the means are judged in
> every instance by their relation to the end [ibid.].

Berrigan also preached at the First Methodist Church
of Germantown, Pennsylvania, while underground.   He read
the text from Hebrews which praises men of old for the
faithfulness to the truth.   He then asked the church members
how such a text is to be translated in their lives in terms of
the bombing of helpless cities, the millions of Vietnamese

peasants perishing, the 50,000 children napalmed or the mil-
lionth refugee rounded up. Perhaps, he suggested, the moral
equipment of good obedient Americans was like that of good
obedient German Christians under the Nazis, allowing no
limit to the death of the innocent. He urged them to choose
truth.

> ... for my brother and myself, the choice is al-
> ready made. We have chosen to be powerless
> criminals in a time of criminal power. We have
> chosen to be branded as peace criminals by war
> criminals.... This is how we have tried to read
> and translate and embody in our lives the will of
> God, to respond to the voice of those great men
> and women who speak to us out of eternity, out of
> the past but most of all out of today, out of today's
> prisons and exile and underground and death itself
> [Berrigan, 1970(b), p187].

After he was seized by the F.B.I., Berrigan wrote from
prison of his sense of isolation and futility. The war was
going on, and it seemed that he and his brother had made
witness to no avail. Not only the struggle to change America,
but the struggle against hopelessness became part of the life of the
Berrigans, and other activists, as the sense of futility spread
throughout the movement.

Violence also escalated on the campus. In April of
1968, the S.D.S. at Columbia called a demonstration to protest University ties with the Institute of Defense Analysis and
the suspension of six students who had conducted an indoor
demonstration. The S.D.S. issued an eight-page newspaper
and a rallying call for the demonstration, "Up Against the
Wall." Mark Rudd, newly elected president of S.D.S.,
authored the lead article, which was an open letter to Grayson Kirk, the president of Columbia.

In the open letter, Rudd replies to Kirk's charge that
students "have taken refuge in a turbulent and inchoate
nihilism whose sole objectives are destruction." Rudd rejects
the contention that radicals are nihilistic. Rather, the conflict
between the students and the ruling generation is over values.
The generation that Kirk represents is the generation that
involves America in wars like Vietnam, drafts young men to
use for cannon fodder, and creates ghettoes by racist university expansion policies, labor practices, city government
and police. Specifically, Kirk runs a university which prides

itself in training youth to be lawyers and managers of such
a system.   Kirk's cry of nihilism represent's his inability
to understand the values of students.

> We do have a vision of the way things could be:
> how the tremendous resources of our economy
> could be used to eliminate want, how people in
> other countries could be free from your domination,
> how a university could produce knowledge for
> progress, not waste consumption and destruction
> (IDA), how men could be free to keep what they
> produce, to enjoy peaceful lives, to create.   These
> are positive values, but since they mean the
> destruction of your order, you call them "Nihilism"
> [Avorn, 1968, p26]. *

Rudd agrees with Kirk that the situation is "potentially
dangerous. "   Students will fight, even violently, to end war,
racism, and mis-education.   While Kirk argues that the
war in Vietnam was an accident, a well-intentioned mistake,
students know it is the fruit of a sick society.

> You call for order and respect for authority; we
> call for justice, freedom and socialism.   There
> is only one thing left to say.   It may sound nihilis-
> tic to you, since it is the opening shot in a war of
> liberation.   I'll use the words of LeRoi Jones,
> whom I'm sure you don't like a whole lot   "Up
> against the wall, motherfucker, this is a stick-up"
> [Ibid. , p27].

The point of confrontation politics, as far as Rudd
was concerned, was that it did put the "enemy up against
the wall" and force him to define himself.   By the takeover
of a building or a blockade, the university was forced to
either move to police--whose tactical squads were unusually
physical--or give in to the demonstrators.   It also put the
individual up against the wall: he could no longer be a sun-
shine radical, loving debate, hating the commitment of action.
He who shared the radical view of society would be forced to
share the struggle for a new order, or be disgraced in the
eyes of his fellow radicals.

*J. L. Avorn, et al., Up Against the Ivy Wall.   New York:
Atheneum, 1969.   Excerpts reprinted by permission of the
publisher.

The demonstration was chaotic, traveling from the
Sundial in the center of the campus, to the library which
was locked, to the site of the new gym and back to the
Sundial.   At the Sundial the decision was made to seize
Hamilton Hall and hold the Dean of Columbia College hostage.
It was done.   Black students notified black groups in Harlem.
Later in the evening blacks from Harlem entered Hamilton
Hall, thanked the students for "taking the first steps in the
struggle, " and announced they were taking over.   Students
opposing the demonstration, who were still at the Dean's
door continuing the debate, were forcibly evicted by the
blacks from the community.   The Vice President, urged by
Kirk to call police, suggested waiting the evening out.   During
the night, the blacks suggested whites leave Hamilton Hall,
and Rudd agreed.   Blacks had determined to barricade and
defend the building, perhaps with guns.   White students went
to the President's office, forced entry and sat in.   With the
fear of physical harm to Dean Coleman stalemating the
Administration, students continued to "occupy" and barricade
buildings for the next four days.   Five buildings were occupied.   Columbia was on the map of student revolutions.

The demands of the demonstrators--that Columbia
sever its ties with the Institute of Defense Analysis and that
the University not build the gymnasium--now included the
question of amnesty.   Kirk agreed to amnesty from criminal
prosecution but not amnesty from University discipline.   The
editors of the student paper reported

> Kirk took a John Foster Dulles stance: if the
> administration gave in at Columbia, students
> throughout the country would be encouraged to
> attempt similar takeovers at their universities
> and expect to win.   This domino theory accounted
> for a large measure of the intransigence of both
> the administration and the students.   Each side
> viewed the University as a miniature version of
> a full scale national revolution [ibid., p72].

The administrators perceived their actions as expressing the
necessity that social order be maintained in the face of
anarchy.   The student leaders saw themselves as the vanguard of the coming revolution.

In the buildings the radicals were discovering the
community they had often hoped to establish.   They had
brought the University to a halt.   What were to them the

real issues, the fundamental issues of society were being
discussed.

> Collective action against common oppressors broke
> down the inbred isolation of the individual; human
> creativity was expressed and acted upon by people
> united by their common goals. The potential for a
> society based on a communitarian ethic--communism,
> if you will--was being directly experienced by the
> people in the building [Halliwell, 1969, p212].

Radicals were sure that the basic principle of the radical
student movement--that the campus movement can change
society only if it relates to off-campus issues and groups--
was being experienced. Harlem was joining the students
because the students cared about the gym. The insurgency
among the poor and oppressed of America and the world was
strengthened as the battle broke out at Columbia. Soon the
fires of revolution will burn "on the many institutional fronts
of America [and] the harvest of the Columbia revolt and the
rest of the student movement will be reaped" (ibid., p213).

Faculty attempts at conciliation failed, first, because
the faculty was divided but more importantly because the
administration refused to grant the faculty power to deal with
the crisis. The trustees of Columbia invested that power in
the President. He exercised his power by calling the police.
Over a thousand police arrested and evicted seven hundred
demonstrators. Only the blacks of Hamilton Hall filed out
peacefully upon request of the police. Fierce battles broke
out at all other buildings. Hundreds of students and a score
of police were injured. The severity of the police attack
brought the condemnation of a majority of faculty and students.
A University wide strike resulted.

In the period of the strike, the communes which had
formed in the occupied buildings continued to be the center
of radicals' existence. The communes issued a statement
"On Solidarity."

The statement opens by quoting Camus' belief that the
purpose of revolution is to make the world safe for Man.
America is not safe for Man. The young are sent to die in
senseless war. The poor are wretched and exploited. The
University is not safe for Man, for it orders a thousand club-
swinging fascist cops against its own students and applauds
their action. But, the young, the poor, the students have

discovered a solidarity through this experience.

> This solidarity is growing; We will free Columbia
> of the company men and profiteers and the cake-
> eaters who control its future and direct its partici-
> pation in the death industries. Our weapon is
> solidarity.   Together we support the strike and
> paralyze this massive institution until Columbia is
> made safe for Man [Avorn, 1968, p224].

However, the professional and business schools of the
University soon returned to normal.   The faculty voted to
allow professors to work out with individual students a pass,
a grade or an incomplete.   Few professors resumed classes
as the end of the term was near.   Many students took a
pass and left campus for the summer vacation.   With the
feeling of revolution dissipating, open ideological controversy
erupted in the Strike Coalition between radicals and moderates
The radicals, determined to force the University to recognize
the legitimacy of their demands, reoccupied Hamilton Hall.
Kirk ordered the police to arrest them.   As the confrontation
following the arrests was diminishing, Kirk ordered the campus cleared by police.   The sweep resulted in nearly seventy
serious injuries and sustained police violence.   Kirk followed
this action with the suspension of seventy-three students.
The students were evicted from their rooms; draft boards
were informed that the students were now eligible for the
draft, and the state informed that the students no longer
qualified for scholarship assistance.

In reflecting on the strike, Mark Rudd argues that with
the communes the experience of participatory democracy became real to hundreds of students.   The decision making
process of the Strike Committee was therefore excruciatingly
slow, but each person participated in the decision in his
commune, which then sent its representative back to the
Strike Committee.   The press, Rudd believes, created the
strike leader as the symbol of the strike, and thus, completely missed the mass nature of the strike.   Mass media
naturally focus on spokesmen, but spokesmen do not create
mass movements.   Rudd claims that only in the minds of
people like Grayson Kirk, Drew Pearson and J. Edgar Hoover
is the individual conspiracy theory a reality.   They think in
terms of their own experience of power-brokering behind
scenes.   Such manipulation is precisely what radicals stand
against.   But

> more fundamentally, those in power cannot conceive
> of individuals directly acting in their own interest--
> against racism, the gym, the war in Vietnam, the
> arbitrary power of the University [ibid., p296].

But most of all, Rudd argues the power structure could not
grasp that students were fundamentally against the interests
of those they were fighting.   Thus, the violent seizure of
property and the demand that students control policy meant
to force the administration to capitulate or fight.   Fight they
did, Rudd says, with lies, slander, threats, police, violence,
suspensions, courts, liberal cooperation and all the organizational resources they could command.   Yet the radical movement grew.   It grew because students believed they were
fighting those who willingly (even gladly) executed

> policies which were criminal in themselves--Colum-
> bia's expansion into the community, her support of
> the war in Vietnam. Who ever measured the vio-
> lence done the victims of Columbia's policies?
> How can you weigh that violence against the act of
> seizing a few buildings? Depriving a few individuals
> of their "right" to an education (i.e., "I paid my
> $1,900") is certainly a lesser evil than allowing
> Columbia to continue its policies [ibid., p297].

The Ultra-Resistance and the Columbia strike indicate
the shift of mood that took place in the movement.   In the
beginning, the anti-war activists and the students were appealing to the conscience of those with whom they disagreed.
Although they were sectarians opposed to established types,
the common bond of the American civil religion was still
very evident.   But, in the later sixties, the sense of conflict
is pre-eminent.   Sectarians no longer believe the issue is
merely that the established type has wrong priorities; it is
apostate.   The established type has betrayed the ideals of
the founding Fathers, and seeks to perpetuate an autocratic,
imperialist society.   The sectarians are certain that the
established type purposefully oppresses the poor, the blacks,
the students and the third world.

This deepening radicalism is the reason that coalition
politics of the McCarthy type are rejected by the sectarian
leadership.   It is not simply that McCarthy cannot win, but
rather that he is part of the problem, not part of the solution.
The growing distance between sectarians and the established
types is dramatized in the action of the Berrigans; draft files

are burned to stop the system.   Daniel Berrigan publicly
states that he does not mean this to be only a symbolic act,
but a call to arms (against property) to men of conscience in
every community.   The fact that thousands of draft records
are burned in response to the Catonsville action is evidence
of the growing alienation.   The Berrigans continue to dramatize the sectarian opposition.   At first they accepted the
legitimacy of the public order by remaining to be arrested.
Soon the contradiction of that action became apparent to them.
Why should men committed to peace and freedom be jailed
by war criminals?   Those who know that their policies have
created the Land of Burning Children and yet still continue
such policies are not misguided; they are murderers.   They
have not a shred of moral legitimacy by which to rule; only
power maintains their position.   No longer do the sectarians
"love the sinner but hate the sin. "   The two are indistinguish-
able.   The apostate establishmentarians are destroying both
the soul and body of America.   Since their consciences are
scarred, they must be resisted, even to the destruction of
the property which is the instrument of their evil.

        Perhaps the two great religious gurus of the movement,
Martin Luther King, Jr. , and Daniel Berrigan represent in
personal profile the deepening radicalism.   King never failed
to emphasize the importance of redeeming his opponent by the
power of love.   Inherent in such a perspective was the faith
that the established type could be redeemed, not in some
future judgment, but now, by the power of love.   Although
King's faith in the power of love to change men might have
been greater than Berrigan's, still the primary difference
that emerges from their public statements is this: King has
a greater faith that the established type can be redeemed.

        Berrigan, on the other hand, finds his soul seared by
the napalm that ignites the flesh of little children.   He cannot escape the enormous deformity of this deed.   The stench
of burning flesh clings to the persons of the policy makers.
For him, the moral revulsion is so great that society is
sundered.   Idolators, "by nuclear liturgies, by racism, by
support of genocide/They embrace their society with all their
heart and abandon the cross. "   Because of them, the times
are inexpressibly evil.   The hope lies wholly with the sectarians.   The times are inexhaustibly good because "in a
time of death some men/the resisters/those who preach and
embrace the truth" are able to overcome death.   The lives
of resisters, not the life of the whole society, is bathed in
the light of the resurrection.   The resisters are those who,

with the violence against the property of the war makers
mean to cleanse the temple of America. For that action
they may be crucified, but ultimate victory will be theirs.

The same shift of mood is marked on campus. Mario
Savio at Berkeley believed he could convince and compel the
conscience of those who opposed him. To be sure, power
must be used, but the power was to be non-violent. There
was a bond of commonness, even a sense of community.
But at Columbia, the rallying cry was "Up against the wall,
motherfucker!" Sectarians believed that compared to the
enormous injury done to persons as a result of Columbia's
criminal policies, the violence done to property was nothing.
From the beginning, the students perceived themselves to be
fundamentally against the interests, not just the policies, of
those they were opposing. The goal was to make the criminal actions of the established type emerge from the shadows
of secret files. Students scarcely expected to "win." At
times in the strike as sectarians made the coalitions, they
hoped for amnesty. But amnesty, for radicals, was tactical.
It was the opportunity to renew the struggle within the same
institution.

The black-white split is also a marked difference in
the student movements of the late sixties. At Columbia,
blacks continually pushed whites to be more radical. Whites
often responded, suffering heavy beatings from the police.
Blacks, however, surrendered peacefully. The class nature
of the black movement took black students in one direction
while the anarchist tendencies of the white students carried
them in another. The black students continually looked over
their shoulder at Harlem, and raised the question of how to
improve the life of black people. Blacks in Hamilton Hall
were meticulous in cleaning the hall, rigging showers, and
publishing the fact that they were maintaining the premises
in the excellent condition in which they were found. They
were opposing definite racist policies of the Administration:
the gym and the tenements owned by Columbia.

Whites, on the other hand, believed that forcing the
Administration to violent reaction would expose its corrupt-
ness. Students who were on the fence would be radicalized.
Columbia could not be changed, radicals felt, without changing
the whole society, but if each radical would work within his
own institutional setting to light the fires of revolution, soon
"the harvest of the Columbia revolt and the rest of the student movement will be reaped." The F. S. M. at Berkeley,

having negotiated specific goals, disbanded, believing the community had been somewhat reformed. The radicals at Columbia never had such a goal nor hope, although many of the moderates who joined them shared the Berkeley vision. For the sectarians, the Administration was peopled with the Eichmanns of the sixties. As President Kirk's files were opened, revealing the estensive relationship Columbia maintained with the defense establishment, the elegant offices were filled with the stench of charred flesh from the Land of Burning Children. Who could speak of community or of reform? To the sectarians, the man was a murderer.

In Trial, Tom Hayden (1970) writes that the conspiracy trial brings the lessons of the Pentagon, Columbia and Chicago into focus: the democratic pragmatism of America is hardening into an inflexible fascist core. Radicals are surprised by this development, for their principal enemy in the sixties has been the danger of being co-opted by the liberals. But liberals proved not to be omnipotent. Counterrevolution is costly. The pursuit of imperialism abroad demands repression, even fascism, to stabilize the home front. The antiriot law passed before the Convention is a national policy commitment aimed to end a decade of protest. The irresponsible argument of Southern sheriffs, that "outside agitators" are responsible for all our troubles, is now endorsed as a national philosophy.

Hayden disagrees with the Walker Report that claims the Chicago police riots were spontaneous. Police take a hard line not because of a military threat posed by demonstrators, but to make a political point. Demonstrators are to be intimidated. The nation at large is to be shown that the Democratic party believes in law and order, not permissive liberal handwringing. Conservative attitudes on law and order are in the ascendancy. Liberal politicians who do not accept repressive domestic policies, such as Ramsey Clark and Eugene McCarthy, are increasingly isolated. As major politicians of differing parties developed a common foreign policy, so they also now share a common attitude toward sectarians.

> It was an unexpected but appropriate irony that
> Nixon and Humphrey, the conservative and liberal
> architects of the bipartisan cold-war strategy of
> the late forties, became in 1968 the leaders of a bipartisan coalition to bring the cold war home [ibid.,
> p20].

Hayden, with his co-defendants, is convinced that one of the reasons for charging that particular group of sectarians with conspiracy is that in the mind of the Justice Department they were responsible for much of the turmoil of the sixties. The Justice Department image of a radical is a behind-the-scenes manipulator of power and people. The Department apparently believes one of its own memos which traces the beginning of the anti-war movement to a meeting between David Dellinger and Ho Chi Minh in 1967.

The Justice Department, Hayden says, sought to prove that the sectarians were "ideological criminals, " i. e. , that they had a revolutionary state of mind. Therefore, the public and where possible, private speech of sectarians was considered as evidence against them, for it abundantly testified to their rebellious state of mind. Since they shared a common language and thus a common state of mind, it was obvious to Justice that they could be convicted of conspiracy.

The common state of mind that is considered criminal, as Hayden sees it, is first of all that the sectarians are internationalists.

> The world we see is one in which a decadent and super-rich American empire, with its principles of racial superiority, private property, and armed might, is falling apart. We want to join with the new humanity, not support a dying empire [ibid. , p33].

Underlying this internationalism is the fact that the defendants were beginning to live a new life style beyond that of capitalist America. Hair, clothes, language, demeanor, gravity before the judge are all part of what is prescribed in a courtroom. The defendants were obviously revolutionary in that they did not comply with the roles that society required of defendants. Therefore, since it is an ideology that is on trial in such a case, the court became a political trial.

The ritual of a courtroom in America is almost a holy ritual, Hayden believes. The judge acts like a high priest, wearing robes, interpreting obscure scriptures, and holds a gavel like a cross. The atmosphere suggests the court is above politics. The truth, of course, is that the court is political. Judges are elected or appointed by politicans; they are white, middle class, conservative males, and men of political motivation. Therefore, when on trial radicals must

treat a trial politically, i. e. , deal with the courtroom the
way it is, not the way it is ritualized.   Hayden lists seven
general guidelines.

"1.   We are political prisoners, not criminals" (ibid. ,
p98).   Sectarians must publicize the fact that Americans are
being tried and jailed for their political attitudes.

"2.   The people are the judge" (ibid.).   The final
courtroom for a political trial must be the opinion of the
public.   Political trials should therefore be tried in the
media.

"3.   Our politics must be carried into the courtroom"
(ibid. , p99).   Illegitimate authority that is resisted in the
streets must be resisted in the courtroom.   The government
is attacking radical politics.   Radicals must defend their
politics.

"4.   Internationalize the issue of repression" (ibid.).
This embarrasses the American public relations men and
encourages those who are opposing imperialism on their own
soil.

"5.   Battle even within the system" (ibid.).   A jury,
no matter how unrepresentative, is not completely under the
control of the government.   Appeals courts do sometimes
reverse.

"6.   Do not fear repression" (ibid. , p100).   Repression can be exposed and the people educated to understand
the existence of political prisoners.   Jail cannot always be
avoided; therefore use it to organize.

"7.   Use the trial to advance the general goals for
which you were indicted" (ibid.).   Since legal repression
seeks to place the movement on the defensive by deflecting
energy from the basic programs of ending the war and
racism, use the courtroom as a new front for the struggle.

Hayden concludes that in the midst of such a struggle,
effort often seems fruitless, hopeless.   The radicals are so
fragmented: youth, whites, blacks, women, students, workers
and so on and on.   Each group struggles toward its own goal.
But the fact that there are so many involved in the struggle is
a sign not for despair but for hope.

Again, the compression of experience in the anti-war
movement is evident. The Spock conspiracy trial found the
defendants quietly accepting the roles into which they were
cast by the court. Their struggle to prove themselves legally
innocent involved them in such contradictions that radicals
became thoroughly disgusted. Coffin's lawyer, in his closing
arguments, bore down heavily on Coffin's good character,
including the fact that he had been a stalwart worker for the
C. I. A. in days gone by. The reporters for Ramparts groaned
audibly at this (Mitford, 1970, p180). But a year later, the
Chicago Eight and their lawyers were seizing every opportunity
to speak of the meaning of their actions. No longer were the
defendants like the Berkeley students in the early sixties,
hoping to sway the consciences of the established type. Now,
even in the court, sectarians were attacking the legitimacy of
the proceedings. The exchange between Dellinger and Hoffman is instructive.

> The Court: ... I don't want you to talk politics.
> Dellinger: You see, that's one of the reasons I
> have needed to stand up and speak anyway, because
> you have tried to keep what you call politics, which
> means the truth, out of this courtroom, just as the
> prosecution has....
> The Court: I will ask you to sit down....
> Dellinger: Therefore it is necessary....
> The Court: I won't let you go any further....
> Dellinger: You wanted us to be like good Germans,
> supporting the evils of our decade, and when we
> refused to be good Germans, and came to Chicago
> and demonstrated, despite the threats and intimida-
> tion of the Establishment, now you want us to be
> like good Jews going quietly and politely to the
> concentration camps while you and this court sup-
> press freedom and truth. People will no longer be
> quiet, people are going to speak up. I am an old
> man, and I am just speaking feebly and not too
> well, but I reflect the spirit that will echo ...
> The Court: Take him out.
> Dellinger: ... throughout the world.
> (Disorder in the court) [Hayden, 1970(b), pp63-64].

The class of political prisoner was established by the
sectarians, and the courts and prisons became one more
institution in which to carry on the struggle for liberation.
Within the court as in the streets and in the university, the
sectarian opposition to empire was reaffirmed. The solidarity

of the sectarians with the lowest classes, the poor and blacks, was reiterated in testimony and summation. The appeal was made to the Founding Fathers but even more now to the basic principles of humanism upon which the Founding Documents rest. The imperial ambitions of the established type were denounced as betraying basic human aspirations. Hayden's call to courage, "Do not fear repression," exemplified the ever new commitment to freedom and brotherhood. The very instruments of repression themselves, the court and prison, became to the sectarians the means by which the new order will be ushered in.

Shortly after the trial of the Chicago Eight opened the Weatherman staged its "Days of Rage" in Chicago. In the June National Convention the S. D. S. had split. Weatherman supporters were elected to control of the S. D. S. national office, with Mark Rudd of Columbia serving as one of the top officers. The Weatherman was a group equipped for and intending to destroy as much property as possible. Shin'ya Ono described the purpose:

> ... White revolutionaries who understand that US imperialism is really a paper tiger, that the oppressed people of the world are really fighting and winning, that this imperialist mother is going to come down within our generation, must form themselves into a disciplined fighting force ... to ... fight not primarily for this specific demand or for that particular reform, but to disrupt the functioning of this imperialist country, and to smash it [Shin'ya Ono, 1969, p235].

Fred Hampton of the Chicago Black Panthers condemned the destruction as senseless and only tempting the Man to more vigorous repression. Many in the Weatherman went underground, refusing to appear in court. In March of 1970 three Weatherman members were killed in a New York townhouse explosion, presumably manufacturing bombs. In June, Weatherman took credit for bombing the New York City police headquarters. In July, Weatherman claimed to have been those who bombed a branch of the Bank of America in New York City. In September, Weatherman aided Dr. Timothy Leary to escape from prison.

But in December 1970, Weatherman issued a declaration entitled "New Morning--Changing Weather." Signed by Bernardine Dohrn and the Weather Underground, the statement reports that the death of their three friends in the townhouse ended the military conception of Weatherman. Weatherpeople remember now that they had not been turned on to the possibility of revolution by armed struggle. To believe that bombing or picking up the gun is the only action that can be considered revolutionary is to be involved in the "military error." It is better to seek to change and shape the cultural revolution. It is better to seek to change people where they live. "People become revolutionaries in the schools, in the army, in prisons, in communes and on the streets. Not in an underground cell" (Dohrn, 1970, p22). Groups of outlaws are isolated from the youth communities and cannot influence large numbers of people. Twos and threes are not a good form for revolution. It is time to organize, leaflet, convince and demonstrate again.

> We are so used to feeling powerless that we believe
> pig propaganda about the death of the movement, or
> some bad politics about rallies being obsolete and
> bullshit. ... The demonstrations and strikes fol-
> lowing the rape of Indochina and the murders at
> Jackson and Kent last May showed real power and
> made a strong difference. New People were reached
> and involved--and the government was put on the
> defensive [ibid., p23].

The action of the Weatherman had not been accepted in the movement. It was rejected by such persons as Hampton, Hayden and Berrigan, and of course, by pacifists such as Dellinger. With the Berrigans in jail and the Weatherman experiencing a change of heart, the movement began a withdrawal from violence. Once again the discussion of organizing in the schools, the army, the prisons, the communes and the streets was the focus of the movement.

The sectarians had been tempted to violence by the tenets of their faith that demanded ever new actions which expressed their commitment to freedom, brotherhood and democracy. The radical view that the Vietnamese were the vanguard of the world struggle for freedom against the oppression of the "U. S. ruling circles" encouraged expressions of solidarity with the Vietnamese. At first those expressions were limited to the carrying of the North Vietnamese flag. But inherent in such an identification was a dynamic which pulled American radicals toward "guerrilla warfare." As Cleaver put it, "if those little cats can do it, why not big studs like us?" Not only would violent actions against the

establishment express solidarity with the revolutionaries of
Vietnam, but sectarians believed it would hasten the day of
revolution in America. As Ferber observed, the movement,
feeling frustrated that America was not changing, turned
more and more to apocalypticism. Sectarians told one another
that the day of Revolution was drawing near. All that was
needed was one great courageous uprising to force the new day
and topple the corrupt regime. Then would be established the
new, pure America on the ashes of the old, corrupt, oppressive society.

But other tenets of the faith opposed the tendency to
violence. First of all, sectarians were powerfully attracted
by the basic principles of humanism upon which the Founding
Documents rest. Violence against persons would betray those
principles. So the Ultra-Resistance specifically limited its
violence to property. The experience of Dan Berrigan in
North Vietnam created in him a passionate sense of identity
with the North Vietnamese and their suffering--suffering that
was inflicted by the U.S. government. Out of this sense of
identification came the willingness to suffer years of prison
in order to bear witness against the war. But the violence
of his witness was restrained by the principles of humanism.
There would be no attempt to extract an eye for an eye, a
tooth for a tooth.

The Weatherpeople were less kindly disposed toward
the established types that might be killed by their bombs,
although they attempted to telephone warnings ahead. But
the townhouse explosion that killed three of their friends, and
the consequent realization that terror tactics were creating
Weatherpeople who were as full of guilt and fear as establishmentarians, turned Weatherman away from the violent
revolution. There was no point in a revolution that fashioned
uptight, guilty, fear-ridden people.

The commitment to democracy also turned the sectarians back from violence. Both the Black Panthers and the
Weatherman discovered that the people were not with them,
but rather feared and hated them. Violence did not create
revolutionaries, but revolutionaries were created by patient
organizing in the schools, the army, the prisons, the communes and the streets. The sectarian faith demanded that
its adherents take seriously the slogan "Serve the people."
Until the people were ready for armed revolution, the violence
of the sectarians was counterrevolutionary. The Vietnamese
experience could not be transplanted to America. American

sectarians were required to work within the context of the American civil religion.

In the years of their violent activity, the Weatherman received much of the publicity outside of the movement and were the focus of much of the discussion within the movement. But they were only a small part of the demonstrations which sectarians mounted against the war following Chicago. The Moratorium in the fall of 1969 attracted thousands in hundreds of rallies all across the nation in October, and thousands more in a mammoth march on Washington on November 15. The invasion of Cambodia triggered the first nationwide student strike in American history.

At Kent State, in the Spring of 1970, Chris Plant, a history graduate student, and six friends had created a protest organization after listening to Nixon's speech. (The organization was named World Historians Opposed to Racism and Exploitation--WHORE.) The students leafleted the campus announcing a noon rally on Friday, May 1, to bury the U.S. Constitution. Plant planted the Constitution with the words, "We inter the Constitution because it has been murdered by the chief executive of the United States." About 500 students witnessed the burial. Later fifty black students staged a protest of their own. That night there was a mini-riot in downtown Kent outside the town's strip of bars. Saturday, students burned the R.O.T.C. building. The National Guard was called on campus. On Sunday, Governor Rhodes changed the mission of the Guard from one of protecting lives and property to one of breaking up any assembly on campus, peaceful or otherwise. The Governor declared

> We're going to employ every force of law that we
> have under our authority.... We are going to
> employ every weapon.... I think we are up against
> the strongest, well trained militant group that has
> ever assembled in America. We are going to
> eradicate the problem--we're not going to treat the
> symptoms. There is no sanctuary for these people
> to burn buildings down.... It's over in Ohio [Stone,
> 1970, p114].

On campus, students reacted to Rhodes' outburst with ridicule, although some were shocked. Most accepted that Rhodes' tough talk was part of the Senate election campaign in which he was involved.

On Sunday night, about 200 students sat down at Pren-
tice Gate and were dispersed by the Guard's tear-gas.   On
Monday, May 4, there was no rioting on campus.   But from
8:30 to 12:25 various groups of persons gathered on campus.
The guard was under orders to disperse even peaceful as-
semblies.   Some students began following the Guard units as
they marched about the campus.   At 12:25 the Guard fired a
minimum of fifty-four rounds at the students.   Four students
were killed and nine were wounded (ibid., pp73-83).

The killing of the students intensified the demonstrations.   The strike swelled.   Attention was called to the
shooting of students at Jackson State.   There were militant
but non-violent demonstrations at draft boards and army bases
across the country.   The draft resistance movement had a
resurgence of its own.   During the first two weeks in May
more than ten thousand draft cards and card-pledges were
turned in around the country.   A new multi-tactic umbrella
group called Union for National Draft Opposition (U. N. D. O.)
enlisted three thousand charter members.   U. N. D. O. received office space, computer services and money from
Princeton University and began to coordinate fifty U. N. D. O.
chapters throughout the nation.   At a convocation at Princeton
U. N. D. O. projected a goal of ten thousand draft cards to be
turned in by June 10th.   As of November, 1970, close to
25, 000 were estimated to have turned in their draft cards or
signed the U. N. D. O. pledge (Ferber & Lynd, 1971, pp291-
293).

In an extensive interview in the November 9, 1972,
issue of Rolling Stone, Tom Hayden, along with Richard
Flacks, reflects on the radical movement since 1968.   Hayden
believes that there was a feeling that Chicago was going to be
some kind of "showdown. " Not that the Revolution would come
and the government be overthrown, or that the Left be
destroyed,

> but another kind of showdown, a liturgical showdown
> that everyone would participate in and be affected
> by in the whole country, in the whole world.   And
> out of that came a lot of things I think that still
> aren't understood [Hayden, 1972, p28].

Some of the things coming out of Chicago are the reform of
the Democratic Party, the necessity of change of policy to
make governing possible in America, the eighteen-year-old
vote, but also the end of S. D. S. and the creation of Weatherpeople.

Hayden considers the Weatherpeople the natural and final generation of S. D. S. , "the true inheritors of everything that had happened from 1960 on" (ibid. , p29). All the dis-illusionment, the failures, had ended in the blood of the reformers. Somehow Chicago crystallized all that, and Weatherpeople are convinced that time is running out, and the life and death struggle of the revolution is upon us. Hayden opposes this point of view, even though he understands why it has gripped the Weatherpeople. Hayden knows they would say he was not seizing the time, not willing to risk every-thing in order to force the revolution now. But Weatherpeople are learning that there is no short circuit to revolution, but radicals emerge in the same, slow, step-by-step process by which they themselves became radicalized.

But Weatherman, Hayden says, is not the principal result of Chicago: the principal result is that alternative ways of relating to people began to be searched out more seriously--not just alternative ways of relating to the establishment, but relating to people within the movement. Woodstock, the Moratorium, the Cambodian uprisings all demonstrate that the student movement did not die, but that the time had passed for a movement whose organization itself was oppressive. The women's liberation movement is per-haps the best example of the new direction.

The same reaction is also on the cultural side of the movement, Hayden points out. People are alienated by the absorption of rock music into the commercial culture. In both political and cultural ways, movement people are re-pressed within their own movement by the enormous power of the media. The media creates leaders, and the leader becomes a caricature of himself as portrayed by the media. But secondly, and more importantly, the leader becomes mythical--there is no way for just plain people to be like the leader. Therefore, people feel oppressed by the fact that the movement leadership, both political and cultural, is no longer like them. Leaders become addicted to and define themselves in relation to media and crowds. None of the movement leadership has been able to resolve the personal and political problems that emerge from this style of media co-optation.

The important thing to emphasize in the movement, Hayden believes, is that every creative turning point has been accomplished by some group no one has heard of, be-cause the energy really comes from the people and not the

leaders.   The function of leadership and organization is to
create continuity from one radical generation to the next.
The way the establishment maintains its rule is to erase
from human memory the consciousness of resistance.   Therefore, the counter-institutions in the established fields of
journalism, education, labor and other forms of work must
be maintained.   There is no such thing as working inside or
outside the movement, for the consciousness of resistance
must be kept alive everywhere.

Hayden thinks such a consciousness of resistance is
much different from Reich's idea of the "greening of America. "   Greening is a process through which, according to the
establishment, revolution will be accomplished by personal
growth.   Everyone will touch each other with personal growth.
The establishment favors that view, because without radical
institutions and radical organizing the consciousness of
resistance fades.   Such radical work is much more difficult
because of the experience of the last decade, because of the
leadership problem, and because of oppressive relationships
in the movement itself.

But what is encouraging about the radical movement,
according to Hayden, is that time is on the side of the
radicals.   When people are exposed again and again to truth,
they do change.   From the point that the movement and the
system joined the conflict, the government began losing
popular support, and the movement began to gain the confidence of the people.

> That's what I mean by saying that time is on our
> side, because as long as that process remains
> continuous, it's predictable, not accidental, that
> we would discover everything.   We will discover
> the entire history of America just as we've dis-
> covered in gruesome detail the entire history of
> My Lai.   We will discover the entire history of
> America, the good and the bad, the truth and the
> lies [ibid. , p34].

Therefore, Hayden believes, radicals can now enter
electoral politics with confidence, not in the candidates, but
in themselves, the issues and the people.   For example, the
McGovern worker can focus peace sentiment.   McGovern is
a creation of the movement, even though an establishment
person.   His personality will not get him elected.   But radicals can work in his campaign to raise the political consciousness of the country.

> If they do it with confidence in themselves, rather
> than illusions about McGovern, then they'll be really
> progressive and a powerful force in American life
> in the seventies without having to go through the
> illusions and traumas and frustrations that the peo-
> ple of my generation did from '60 to '64. They're
> going through it with their eyes open [ibid.].

Hayden feels that radicals must be aware that a long,
difficult and complicated period lies ahead. Little fundamental
change will happen immediately because of electoral reforms.
Berkeley is a good example. There is a new climate of
opinion growing in the city, but little real change. Therefore, the need for a vital, active independent radical movement, based in a variety of localities and institutions, must
be stressed. The Berkeley city council would not have
opened up without ten years of revolutionary cultural growth
in Berkeley. But radicals will probably forget that, turn to
electoral politics, get elected and discover they are powerless
in office.

But, if the movement stays alive as a critical and
independent force, then there will be a showdown between the
public sphere and the private sphere as radicals come to
dominate the public offices. Radicalism, once supposed to
be alien to American society,

> is going to be a force in the center of society,
> insisting on its democratic liberties, insisting on
> the enforcement of the Constitution, insisting on
> its right for the radicals who are duly elected to
> hold office, insisting on the right of the people to
> decide on the distribution of wealth, the control of
> polluters, the control of corporate investment, the
> control of a foreign policy [ibid., p36].

The response of the established type, according to
Hayden, will be to coopt by concessions and to maintain
power by making more and more decisions secretly. The
concessions will be like those in Vietnam. When finally the
people know too much about it and are sick of it, the establishment will yield on that issue, but only that issue. The
Pentagon Papers taught the public what the process is like,
but it also had taught the establishment of the need for
stricter security. Decisions will be made by fewer people.
Secrecy will be more rigidly maintained. But on this issue,
as on many others, the people are going to side with the

movement. There will be an increasing polarization around
the question of democratic rights and the need of the people
for peace.

> Those are issues that the majority of people are
> going to side with the Movement on. I see, really,
> hundreds and perhaps thousands of city councils af-
> fected by that, thousands of labor locals, thousands
> upon thousands of schools feeling this polarization
> ... all professional institutions. Anything but the
> military and corporations. And that's a struggle
> in which time is only on our side. We have to
> seize it, of course [ibid.].

Hayden still reflects the classic sectarian position.
He harks back to the Founding Documents. He demands
purity. Sectarians can never merge with the whole population, but the movement must be independent, critical, for
radicals must prove anew their commitment to true democracy.
The struggle is still on behalf of the people, who are the
oppressed, against the powerful, who are represented by the
military and the corporations. But now, as Troeltsch noted,
secular institutions are tolerated. Radicals are to live in
them as an alien environment. But sectarians are nevertheless, to be confident that time is on their side, for the
destruction of the oppressor is sure.

Other radicals are less certain. Andrew Kopkind,
writing on "The Sixties and the Movement" in Ramparts
(February 1973) believes that it is apparent there was no
broad base for revolution in America in the late sixties, but
radicals acted as if there were. They were certain that
the suburbs, "brimming with Marcusian contradictions," would
erupt any day. Students would flee schools and intellectuals
desert professions to join the revolution. "Surely, someone
must be organizing the working class, the blacks, the Chi-
canos; it would all come together" (ibid., p32). But to
Kopkind, the Greenwich Village townhouse explosion signaled
the end of the logical progression of New Left movements.
Kent State/Cambodia, May Day, 1971, are somehow different;
they are no longer really part of a movement. Coalitions
keep forming and dissolving, making gains or losses, somehow keeping alive both in the illusion and reality of the Left.
Kopkind details how he himself went from street fighting to
a rural commune, from reading Marxism to reading mysti-
cism. But now, he writes,

> I find myself back in a city, going to demonstra-
> tions, writing, poking around organizing projects,
> hoping. The New Left and the movements that it
> spawned did not change America--yet--in most of
> the ways it would have wanted; but it did provide
> the groundwork for a culture in which its members
> could exist. Life in that culture is not entirely
> satisfactory, which encourages us to perfect it.
> There is an infrastructure of institutions based on
> Left consciousness which lets us do that work:
> media, political organizations, educational institu-
> tions, living places.... People wait for a new
> organization, a pre-party, a party to appear, as
> the strikers waited for Lefty, or as they waited
> for Godot [ibid., p34].

The vacillation that Troeltsch argued was characteristic
of sectarians appeared in the latter half of the sixties. On
the one hand there was the attempt to restore the national
purity by violence, which was a contradiction. On the other
hand, there was renunciation of such universalist concerns
and a withdrawal to the pure community of sectarians. Both
black and white sectarians were tempted by violence. Such
a temptation was inherent in the sectarian doctrines which
demanded ever new actions that expressed a basic commitment to freedom. But the sectarian devotion to humanism
and democracy channeled such actions away from violence
and back to community organizing.

The organizing, however, was done from a new perspective. There was no more coalition politics in the sense
of seeking to influence liberals. Instead there was an attempt to fashion a truly independent power base for radicals.
The attempt was made politically in a variety of ways.
Where sectarians were concentrated, such as in university
communities or black communities in the South, radicals
ran for political office. Where the concentration of sectarians was not high enough to elect radicals, community
organizing was seen as important. All the reformist
measures which had attracted the energies of the charities
in America for one hundred-fifty years were now employed
by radicals. The purpose was not reform, however. The
sectarians meant revolution. The political consciousness of
the people would be raised, and a radical power base built.
Whether revolution would be within the system would now
depend on the people. Sectarian leadership would no longer
seek to force the revolution, but would serve the people.

In addition to the political arena, sectarians also sought to establish power bases in professional organizations. Again the characteristic sectarian vacillation appeared. At first there was the attempt to force the whole organization to deal with sectarian concerns. But later sectarians accepted the establishment of a sub-society within the parent group where sectarian persons and concerns were nurtured.

Sectarians continued to oppose the work ethic by denying worldly goods and achievements as determining the worth of man. Bobby Seale's description of the dedication of a Black Panther was perhaps the most striking example. But the struggle of Hayden and the movement leadership not to oppress the people of the movement by the style of their leadership also reflected the unwillingness of sectarians to exploit personal achievement.

The increased consciousness of sectarians concerning the relation of men and women testified to the continuing power of the sectarian concern for the oppressed. Both black and white radicals accepted the point made by the women's liberation movement: Males in the movement oppressed women as surely as did the establishmentarian types. Sectarians attempted to reduce both the reality and the sense of sexist repressors.

Throughout the sixties the opposition of sectarians to the cold war understanding of the American mission to the world remained firm. By the end of the sixties, the only means by which America could give encouragement to the world, according to sectarians, would be if the Revolution would succeed in the bastion of imperialism. But in the realistic light of the seventies, few sectarians believed the Revolution was at hand. Instead, they turned to the work that was possible. Some were still optimistic, certain that they were involved in a struggle in which time was on their side. The enormous outpouring of sectarian sentiment in 1970 continued to impress some radicals. They were certain that if the movement focused on the real needs of the people, the people would respond. The year 1970 exemplified such a hope. That did not mean that sectarian leadership could force the Revolution. Elitist tactics could scarcely hope to bring the downfall of an elitist order. Instead, sectarians reminded one another that they must serve the people. Thereby the sectarian presence would be maintained, and when the people were ready, America would be renewed.

Other sectarians were not so hopeful. They continued to work in the infrastructure of institutions based on Left consciousness. Such work was an inner necessity. But to hope for the renewal of America seemed much like waiting for Lefty, or waiting for Godot.

V

CONCLUSION

Troeltsch summarizes his argument for his typology in
these words:

> Thus, in reality we are faced with two different
> sociological types. This is true in spite of the
> fact (which is quite immaterial) that incidentally
> in actual practice they may often impinge upon
> one another. If objections are raised to the terms
> "Church" and "Sect, " and if all sociological groups
> which are based on and inspired by monotheistic,
> universalized, religious motives are described (in
> a terminology which is in itself quite appropriate)
> as Churches, we would then have to make the
> distinction between institutional churches and
> voluntary churches. It does not really matter
> which expression is used. The all important
> point is this: that both types are a logical result
> of the Gospel, and only conjointly do they exhaust
> the whole range of its sociological influence, and
> thus also directly of its social results, which are
> always connected with the religious organization
> [Troeltsch, 1960, pp340-341].

This study has demonstrated that the established and sectarian
types are as characteristic of the American civil religion as
of the "Gospel. " In actual practice the types of civil religion
impinge upon one another. All members of both types are
born into the ethos of the nation. The majority accept the
"standard" institutional expressions of that ethos. However,
sectarians must choose the radical experience. So perhaps
institutional and voluntary types might be as good a label.
But as Troeltsch says, it does not really matter what label
is used. The important point is that both types are a logical

result of the American experience.   Only together do they
exhaust the whole range of the sociological influence of the
civil religion.   Only by examining the action and interaction
of the types can their social results be adequately grasped,
and the dynamic of the national life fully understood.

In the postwar period, and especially in the sixties,
the difference between the context into which common experiences were placed by established and sectarian types was
marked.   Sectarian and established types had differing socially constructed worlds and therefore differing views of reality
within the national ethos.   For each type its contextuating
orientation was costly to establish and therefore costly to
amend.   When at first it seemed as if sectarians only sought
to change a "bit" in the contextuating orientation, the reaction
of the established type was relatively mild.   But as the
decade progressed, it became more and more apparent that
for sectarians a bit was not sufficient.   They meant to change
the whole contextuating orientation.   America, sectarians felt,
must become a new nation.   Under such an impact, the
resistance of the established type stiffened.   Conflict escalated.

The central bit in the contextuating orientation of the
established type was the mission of America to the world.
During the postwar period this mission was articulated in
both cold war and universalist language.   The poetry of
Kennedy escalated the commitment to the universal mission
of America, promising that "the energy, the faith, the
devotion which we bring to this endeavor will light our
country and all who serve it, and the glow from that fire
can truly light the world" (Kennedy, 1962, p10).   The actions
of Lyndon Johnson escalated the cold war into a hot one in
Vietnam, with the purpose of demonstrating that "because we
fight for values and we fight for principle, rather than territory or colonies, our patience and our determination are
unending" (Johnson, 1965, p346).   The principle was that
all peoples everywhere be free to choose the democratic way
of life as understood by the established type.   The faith was
that if peoples were truly free they would indeed choose a
form of government like America's, and join America in
helping to guarantee the freedom of all nations.

In opposition to the desire of the established type to
make universal the mission of America, sectarians focused
primarily on the purity of America herself.   Sectarians
wanted the power of mutuality to replace the power of domi-

nation. The sectarians urged that each person and group make his or her values explicit. The demand was for values that attach to the intimacy of fellowship. Love and justice, sectarians argued, can prevail only where they are supported by the presence of brotherly responsibility. Such brotherhood and responsibility can only exist in a community which truly practices participatory democracy. Sectarians demanded that America renew her own soul by the power of such a vision. Only then, and only by the power of her example, would it be possible for America to be a light to the nations. But in face of the tremendous effort needed to renew America now, sectarians had little energy to expend in speculating on what America's mission to the nations might be once she was purified. Instead, sectarian energies were demanded by the work of purifying the nation, which included calling the nation back from seeking to refashion the world by force of arms.

The established type has historically articulated the definitive doctrines of the civil religion for the large majority of persons in the nation. These doctrines accord with the interests of the upper classes. They are promulgated by those who exercise power in society. Throughout the sixties, when societal conflict became bewilderingly intense, the established type appointed commissions to study a particular aspect of the conflict and publish reports. Since the commissions were composed of persons of the established orientation, it was not surprising that the reports were set within the context of the established orientation.

Little legislation resulted from the work of the commissions. Rather, they had the purpose of interpreting the meaning of events. While the media reported the actions of the sectarians during the sixties, the interpretation of those actions were perhaps even more important. The interpretation that reached the wider public was nearly unfailingly of the established type. Only those few sectarians, such as Martin Luther King, Jr., who could command space in national media such as Look magazine, reached the wider public directly. But the vast majority of the newspapers and magazines, which bore the weight of the interpretive response, was of the established type.

Sectarians, in characteristic fashion, were closely identified with those who were oppressed by the established order. Amongst those who were oppressed, the sectarian interpretation of the meaning of the events of the decade was widespread. The black church, the teach-ins, the proliferating radical publications, and the omnipresent "organizing" all served as vehicles of sectarian interpretation.

Thus not only were events set into differing contexts by the established and sectarian types as they happened, but the sectarian interpretation of those events was not heard by the established type. Sectarians did not credit the established interpretation. Each type therefore reinforced by its interpretation of events its own perception of reality, which came to expression in the differing images of the American civil religion.

The asceticism of the established type, as Troeltsch noted, is on good terms with the world. It is a method of acquiring virtue and special achievements by discipline. The work ethic affirmed, according to the established type, that the door of achievement was open to all in America who would discipline themselves to step through that door. As with the Calvinists of old, the evidence of virtue was therefore worldly success. But this ethic often suggested the corollary belief that those who were not successful were those who chose the path of indolence and sloth.

In the sixties, Lyndon Johnson struggled against that corollary from the standpoint of the established type. He argued that in fact America had not allowed the work ethic its full range of creativity, for America denied true opportunity to black people. Therefore if America would open the door of the "special American justice" to blacks, the work ethic would come to be valid for all Americans.

But the meaning of "true opportunity" was worlds apart for sectarians and establishmentarians. The established type meant to provide the opportunities through such programs as Headstart for the poor black to compete in the established system. The sectarians understood "true opportunity" in terms of the poor being in control of the systems that governed their lives. Sectarians did not gain control, and lashed out in anger. Established types believed sectarians to be ingrates and subversives. Sectarians were certain that established types were tyrants.

The sectarian certainty was strengthened by the sectarian rejection of the work ethic. Sectarians denied that worldly goods and achievements determined the worth of a man. They denied that worldly success was evidence of personal discipline and virtue. Personal traits that were

valued by sectarians were those that strengthened the bonds
of brotherhood. Thus the lifestyle issue was a political as
well as a personal issue throughout the sixties. Aggressive,
competitive lifestyles were scorned by sectarians. Lifestyles that expressed solidarity, community and mutual support were valued. Radical politics hoped to incarnate radical
lifestyles. As Hayden, Rubin and other movement leaders
discovered, such a blending of lifestyle and politics was
nearly an impossibility. Nonetheless, the attempt continued.

In the sixties, as throughout American history, the
mainstream of development of the nation flowed along the
established type of the civil religion, precisely because the
nation is the institutional structure of the civil religion. Yet
the appeal of the sectarians to the basic values of the American Revolution, and the sectarian demand that these values
be actualized in the life of the nation, had an important impact upon the direction of national life in the sixties. The
dynamic of this interaction answers the first question that
was raised in the introduction: What has been the result of
the resurgence of political activity by the sectarians during
the 1960's?

Troeltsch argued that the church type was itself partially dependent upon the renewing energy of the sect.

> The Protestant Church-type, therefore, has per-
> sisted with the aid of sectarian ideas and the
> relativism of idealism and mysticism.... More
> and more the central life of the Church-type is
> being permeated with the vital energies of the
> sect and of mysticism; the history of Protestantism
> reveals this very clearly [Troeltsch, 1960, p1009].

In the 1960's, the vital energies of the sectarian type
of the civil religion permeated the established type. The
issues of racism, poverty and war were raised by sectarians.
The basic values underlying the Founding Documents and the
language of those Documents themselves were invoked to
demand the renewal of American society. The sectarian call
to renew America according to the vision of the Founding
Fathers touched the "mystic chords of memory." Although
the initiative belonged to the sectarians, the response was
not in accordance with radical demands. The concerns of
the established type dictated the way in which the sectarian
demands were actualized in societal structures.

First, it must be emphasized that the established type accepted the fact that America ought to be more just toward blacks and other minorities, that persons in poverty ought to have the opportunity to be free from economic bondage, and that peace is essential for the sake of all mankind. Kennedy began the decade by declaring that America was renewing her ancient commitment to human rights, both at home and around the world. Lyndon Johnson made civil rights and the War on Poverty twin pillars of his Great Society, and declared, "We shall overcome." By the end of the sixties President Nixon was speaking of the New American Revolution. He declared in his second inaugural address

> We have the chance today to do more than ever before in our history to make life better in America ... to ensure the God-given right of every American to full and equal opportunity [Nixon, 1973, p10].

But the established type moved to actualize the values in the appropriate way. The appropriate way was, of course, according to the doctrines of the established type of the American civil religion: within the context of the cold war, in close connection with the upper classes, in accordance with the work ethic, under the control of the established type and within the organization structures of the system. Many of the established types were genuinely convinced that they were truly accomplishing the task about which sectarians talked.

But to the sectarians such an attempt to actualize basic American values distorted those values beyond recognition. Sectarians turned the statement that Niebuhr made concerning the Communists against the established type.

> ... We have to deal with a vast religious-political movement which generates more extravagant forms of political injustice and cruelty out of the pretensions of innocency that we have ever known in human history [Niebuhr, 1952, p22].

For established types to suggest that they were wholly committed to justice made sectarians want to vomit. To compromise the true values of justice, democracy, freedom and peace by seeking to realize them without disturbing the basic structure of American society was to so warp their meaning that the values became demonic, according to sectarians.

The established type perceived its role as a balancing of pressure groups.   Since F. D. R. and the New Deal the federal government had been responsive to those sectors of American society which were able to organize themselves to demand redress of grievances.   Established types in the university, such as Clark Kerr, also understood their function to be mediators of diverse demands.   But sectarians could not accept the fact that their demand for true justice and freedom was reduced to just one more demand amongst the many which established types adjudicated.   To sectarians, the notion that truth could be reduced to the ignominy of one amongst many pleaders of special interest was blasphemous.

Although sectarians were not impressed by the changes, American society did reform somewhat under the impact of the sectarian demand.   The results of the sectarian political activity were seen in three areas.   First, the understanding of the mission of America to the world was refashioned.   American involvement in the war was ended.   The Nixon Administration accepted a world divided into spheres of influence.   New relationships were established with the Communist powers.   Presumably these relationships were meant to solidify mutually acceptable spheres of influence in the seventies.   The decision was made that no longer would America intervene militarily in the affairs of other nations, except where that intervention would be decisive.   Those responsible for the Vietnam debacle were exiled from the seats of power.   The Senior Advisory Group lost its vast influence over the construction of a bi-partisan foreign policy.   New advisors and new visions were sought.   The cold war perspective changed.

The change of the established type in this regard was not wholly due to the influence of the sectarians.   The failure of the policy was important.   After twenty years, the Vietnamese were still willing to continue the struggle against overwhelming technological superiority.   Their willingness to continue the war was responsible for escalating the costs beyond what the established type was willing to bear.   Thus sectarian resistance to the war was an important but secondary factor in the reversal of the Vietnam policy.

But sectarian activity was perhaps more influential in the re-evaluation of the total cold war policy.   The domestic effects of the war were a result of sectarian protest.   The draft was ended.   A vast pool of young men was therefore no longer available to man the outposts of empire.   The threat of mobilizations, draft resistance, campus insurrections and critical media reviews gave the planners of U. S. policy pause. The Nixon Doctrine proclaimed that American troops would no longer fight for the freedom of other nations. This, of course, was not the sectarian point. Sectarians saw the military-industrial character of the American mission to the world as evil, and demanded that America renounce empire. The Nixon Doctrine was the response of the established type. The new perspective was still an established one. A final result of sectarian protest against the war was that amnesty began to be debated within the established type. The sectarian emphasis on amnesty as a right modified the established tendency to regard desertion as betrayal.

The second major area in which sectarian political activity had concrete result was the arena of racism. At the outset of the sixties, racism was institutionalized in the legal system of the South. By the end of the decade, federal legislation had swept away the legal basis of the Southern regional form of the civil religion. The number of black officials elected in the South increased dramatically. Another concrete evidence of change was the significant increase of blacks and other minorities recruited by the universities of the nation. A broader range of scholarship aid was made available to these students than ever before. The income level of blacks and Mexican-Americans increased. Greater percentages of both groups moved into the middle class. More serious efforts were made to meet and enforce the laws requiring equal opportunity in hiring.

Again, these reforms were wholly within the control of the established type. The income gap between blacks and whites remained about the same. Racism was still a reality across the whole country. The federal government bought trainloads of lettuce and grapes in an attempt to support the corporate farms of California in their struggle against the migrant workers. Like Mailer, the Nation became weary of Black, Chicano and American Indian demands. The media turned its attention to other crises, such as Watergate. The reform was far from that which the sectarians had demanded. It did not usher in a society of freedom and justice for all. But the established type had attempted to right the ancient evil of racism with an energy unprecedented in any other decade of American history.

The third area was the struggle to eradicate poverty in America. The sectarian demand for a restructuring of the American economic system received short shrift. The work ethic was far too strong a doctrine, especially in the hands of the moneyed classes. It was not easily modified. The established response to the sectarian demand was the War on Poverty. It was long on rhetoric but short on funding. The debates of the nineteenth century over whether the poor were the authors or victims of their condition were rehearsed. Old solutions were given new names. There were some successes. Mostly hopes were raised only to be dashed. The established type did little. By 1973 the Office of Economic Opportunity was being declared Marxist by the Nixon Administration and was rapidly dismantled.

The sectarians were unable to dramatize the issue of poverty and to bring it before the American conscience in as effective a way as they did the issues of war and racism. This was partly because masses of the oppressed did not themselves demand redress. The March on Washington for Jobs and Freedom in 1963 appeared to most observers to be made up of the middle class. Civil rights, not poverty, was the image of the March. Throughout the Nation, blacks marched and rioted to protest racist social structures. Students marched, resisted and burned draft cards and files to protest the war and the draft. But the poor remained largely invisible. Sectarian organizers of the poor soon found themselves unable to elicit even the smallest of responses from City Hall. The homeliness of the demands--to enforce the code requiring toilets to be in working order--did not excite media attention. By 1967, Tom Hayden, one of the most celebrated of the radical organizers of the poor, had left Newark. The Poor Peoples March received little sympathy and effected less change. Twentieth-century America still believed that the poor who really wanted to could work their way out of the slums. Sectarians were unable to win Americans from that faith.

The sect, in its turn, reacted to the response of the established type. Sectarians felt the values they had urged upon America had been co-opted and distorted by the established type. Therefore sectarians redoubled their efforts. The action-reaction pattern of the sixties is perhaps best described by the systems concept. The systems concept postulates that there is a constant action-reaction between associated things. The closer the association, the more obvious is the action-reaction. The resurgence of political

activity by sectarians at the opening of the sixties brought
them into the most intimate association with the established
type.   The sect would act, providing a stimulus to the
established type.   The established type would respond.   The
sectarians would react to the response.   This feedback provided a stimulus for the established type.   The system would
recycle, but at another level.

The sectarians therefore moved from one style of
politics to another as the system cycled.   At first they hoped
to renew America by appeal to conscience.   In some cases,
such as Greensboro, this appeal was successful.   This gave
hope and impetus for the movement to continue.   But in most
places throughout the South, the regional form of the established type of the civil religion opposed any reforms.   Sectarians reacted to the negative response by coalition politics.
Rather than a pure appeal to conscience and a direct confrontation between oppressor and oppressed, a mixture of
tactics was used.   Coercion by federal law was added.   The
South resisted more fiercely.   The response of the established type in the federal government was by means of the
excruciatingly slow and ambiguous processes of federal legislation.   The sectarian reaction was "Freedom now!"   Coalition politics was abandoned.   It was time, sectarians cried,
to throw themselves upon the gears of the oppressive machine
and bring it to a halt.   The established type responded to
most mass demonstrations as if they were riots.   Repression
was the rule.   The overreaction of the established type carried sectarians in a variety of directions.   Many who were
on the fringes of the sectarian movement became deeply
committed to change.   Some turned to violence, the underground, and revolutionary actions.   Some turned to the new
politics, convinced that they must build a radical political
base to elect radicals to office, for political office was the
surest way to power for sectarians.   Blacks in the South
and black and white radicals in Berkeley succeeded.   Yet
other sectarians turned to communes.   Some found a home in
the radical institutions they had created across the sixties
and waited for Godot.

In short, the vital energies of the sectarians forced
the established type to respond to sectarian priorities.   But
the response was in accordance with the establishmentarian
patterns.   Sectarians demanded that American society correspond to the ideals of the Founding Fathers.   The demand
somewhat altered the character of American life, but the
mainstream still flowed along the channel fashioned by the
established type.

The final difference in the contextuating orientations of the established and sectarian types was the polarity of organizational effort versus personal action. Established types stressed the importance of an organized system which sought to actualize American values. Yet at the same time, the actualization of those values was considered to be the goal of whatever system was constructed. This orientation led to some ironical policies and beliefs: Mideast oil wells owned by American companies were bound to pump freedom into the life of those countries, whereas under the British they had only been used to exploit the people. American universalism and the Monroe Doctrine could co-exist within the same foreign policy because both had the same intention: the establishment of freedom and democracy for people everywhere. The free-fire zone, the defoliation, the cratering of farmland and the resettlement of populations was good for South Vietnam because freedom and peace were the ultimate purpose of the actions. Great welfare bureaucracies, providing jobs for millions of college educated middle class persons, were good for the poor because the final end of such activity was to open the door of opportunity to the disadvantaged. Such beliefs and policies are evidence that truth was objectified for the established type. America possessed the truth, and it was enshrined in the organization and action of the American national life.

Sectarians appealed to ever new actions of the individual which would express and demonstrate his or her commitment to freedom, brotherhood, peace and democracy. The idea of the established type that the individual actions of particular persons in various positions of authority, or the wrong directions of particular policies could be overlooked because the intent was benevolent, was heresy to sectarians. To the radical, actions express intentions. If the institutions of American society oppress the black and exploit the poor, it is because the established type intends to oppress the black and exploit the poor. The individual person either participates in or opposes such action. There is no neutrality.

The sectarian equating of intent and act led to a deep suspicion of all organized activity. As Weber notes, bureaucracy is inherently oppressive; it serves the interests of the in-group at the expense of the out-group. Sectarians thus found themselves in a double bind: in order to be successful in renewing American society it was necessary that they organize to present their demands in a powerful and effective manner. The structure and values of American society encouraged such action. But almost as soon as sectarian organization emerged, it fractured. The bureaucratic oppression of organization offended the sectarian mentality. Believing that oppression was not happenstance but purposeful, splinter sects would attack the parent group. Women felt particularly ill used in the movement, purposefully reduced to the role of secretaries, janitors, cooks and sex objects. But wherever the leadership of the sectarian groups became elitist--as it often did under the impact of the media-- the rank and file would feel oppressed. The value questions of the meaning of true democracy, true freedom, true peace, true brotherhood would emerge against the leaders of the group as well as against the structures of the established society.

As the vital energies of some sectarian groups diminished, and the group became more established, such as in the case of S. C. L. C. , the passionate commitment to true values would spark a new movement, such as Jesse Jackson's "Operation Breadbasket" in Chicago. As Troeltsch argues, the ideal of a perfect society apparently has the power to energize endlessly the actions of sectarians. Perhaps the source of such energy is the life instinct itself, which seeks to mitigate the suffering that is common to human society. Thus the dynamic of the sect is such that society is never allowed to rest content with its present structures. The sect will demand change. It will be either aggressive or passive. It will either demand that the whole society conform to the sectarian image of the true society, or it will recruit members from the host society to join the sect in withdrawing to the pure sectarian group.

The second question raised in the introduction, "What will now become of the radical movement?" can be answered in light of this church-sect dynamic. Since 1968 commentators have been speaking of the demise of the radical movement. But if the movement is seen from the perspective of the sectarian type of the civil religion, it is clear that it will endure as long as the nation itself has meaning for Americans. Sectarians have been active since the founding of the Republic. Their political activity in the sixties has been traced in detail. Troeltsch points out that the social position of the sects and the varying conditions "within the fundamental elements in life" are the hidden reasons for the sudden changes in sectarian thought and activity (Troeltsch, 1960, p1003). It was the social position and varying conditions within the lives of students and blacks that interacted

with the American civil religion to create the issues and
leadership of the movement in the sixties.

In the short run, at least through the mid-seventies, the
sectarian task continued to be outlined by the major issues that
gave it form. The movement was not as visible, for it did not
again ignite the magnitude of protest that it did in 1970. The draft
ended, and thus the personal stake in the sectarian movement diminished for a great number of students. Since
the sectarian dynamic requires this personal involvement,
the number of persons open to radicalization was
drastically reduced. However, sectarians continued to press
the issues of racism, exploitation of the poor, amnesty and
participatory democracy. A variety of experimental lifestyles,
both urban and rural, continued. The black freedom
movement focused primarily on class issues, seeking to
bring black people into fuller participation in the economic
life of society.

In the long run, it is reasonably certain that sectarians will turn again to widespread political activity. Such
activity will be directed in part against the sectarians of
the sixties as well as against the established type. Such is
the sectarian dynamic. For at present, radicals command
wider resources than did the radicals of the fifties. As
Kopkind observes, radicals in the sixties created their own
institutions or sub-institutions within established ones. Thus
the New Left is likely to experience even more forcefully
than did the Old Left the pains attendant upon bureaucratization. The next wave of sectarian protest will discover that
the radical institutions that endured from the sixties are
"not to be trusted. "

Yet some individuals will be trusted, even as Muste
and Dellinger were relied upon by the radicals of the sixties.
These sectarians will be the ones who have kept alive the
"sense of resistance. " Such men ensure that the sectarian
vision will flame again. Another Great Awakening will
sweep the country. Americans will be summoned to renew
their heritage. Ancient evils will be exposed. Sectarians
will demand that society be purified anew. The battle
between the established type and the sectarian type will be
joined once more.

Opposing this view are those who suggest that all
religion is on the wane. The sixties witnessed the death of

God, the decline of the church and the continuing secularization of American society. Yet the sixties were also surely a period of a Great Awakening in America. It was a Great Awakening of the sectarian form of the civil religion. These apparently conflicting trends can be interpreted in two ways.

First, Werner Stark suggests that our age is not less religious, but that religion is now flowing into newer forms. The newer liturgies are more difficult to perceive, for their symbols are so familiar and their perspectives so comfortable. The civil religion uses just such familiar symbols and perspectives. The majority of Americans accepted the involvement of America in one of the most destructive wars in history when the necessity of the war was expressed in the language of the civil religion.

Second, the language of the civil religion conforms readily to our age. The Founding Fathers early cast the Calvinist symbols into the rational language of the Enlightenment. It is this translation that the "secular" age of the sixties adopted. As the decade wore on and sectarians became more and more uneasy with rationalist categories, a variety of religious languages flourished. But the dominant one was the language of the American civil religion.

Religious symbolizations do not disappear, but do change forms. It is the nature of man to be reflective. A search for meaning is part of that process of reflection. Perhaps, as Weber argues, the reason for the search is to mitigate the suffering that is common to man. But since until the day of the Revolution or the Revelation, suffering will continue, religion will continue to flow into forms appropriate to each age.

Finally, is such a study useful for ethical decision making? Rawls believes that

> Justice is the first virtue of social institutions, as truth is of systems of thought. A theory however elegant and economical must be rejected or revised if it is untrue; likewise laws and institutions no matter how efficient and well-arranged must be reformed or abolished if they are unjust [Rawls, 1971, p3].

He goes on to argue that justice and goodness are congruent in a well ordered society (ibid. , pp513-597). Both estab-

lished and sectarian types would agree.   But their views of
what constitutes justice and goodness are divergent.   Is it
possible to resolve the conflict between the established and
sectarian views so as to choose the good rather than the
partisan doctrine of the good?

Troeltsch believes that the church type is superior to
the sect type so far as the form of organization is concerned.
The church type alone is connected with the unbroken unity
of an instinctive world-outlook of the great masses of people.
It is able to give coherence and meaning to life by binding
together cult, symbols, beliefs and behavior in a manifest
way for a wide community.   The church type organizes the
community, celebrating the creative and encouraging the
expansive energies within it.   Yet it remains in touch with
the actual conditions of life, tempering its enthusiasms with
the knowledge of what is possible.   While it must be admitted
this tempering becomes in fact a far-reaching adjustment and
compromise of the original ideals, yet the church type is at
least somewhat open to the fresh winds of the spirit that are
generated by the sect.   The church type is able to accept
criticism of its compromises.   It attempts to reorganize the
community in a closer harmony with the ideal.   Such compromise, Troeltsch suggests, is creative, for it enhances
the quality of life for the whole of society.   Sect types still
are necessary for the purification of the church type, but
"although they will render indispensable services and they
will develop profound energies, ... they will never fully
realize their actual ideal intention within the sphere of our
earthly struggle and conflict" (Troeltsch, 1960, p1013).
Therefore, Troeltsch concludes the church type is our best
hope, for

> Nowhere does there exist an absolute Christian
> ethic, which only awaits discovery; all that we
> can do is learn to control the world-situation in
> its successive phases just as the earlier Christian
> ethic did in its own way.   There is no absolute
> ethical transformation of material nature or of
> human nature; all that does exist is a constant
> wrestling with the problems which they raise
> [ibid.].

Troeltsch's arguments apply with equal force to the
established type of the civil religion.   Only the established
type can bind together as diverse and extended a community
as the people of a country into a nation.   Only the estab-

lished type can effect the compromises necessary so that
citizens from a great variety of backgrounds and possessing
a wide diversity of views feel bound into the nation. Only
the established type commands the broad resources necessary
to improve the quality of life for the whole of a society.

Further, as Merleau-Ponty (1969) suggests, the sectarian position is nearly untenable once sectarians embark
on the seas of politics. It is the curse of politics that it
must translate values into action. Political action is by
nature impure, because it is the collective action of one
group of persons upon another group. The sectarian desire
for a pure humanism is no longer a possibility. Coercion
and violence are again a necessity.

But such arguments, while forceful, are in the final
analysis structural arguments. They are useful in calling
attention to the fact that most persons are born into the
established type. Most persons perceive, not the purity of
sectarian values, but the coercion and violence that attends
the attempt to translate those values into political action.
To persons within the established type, the coercion and
violence that maintains the established órder is often not as
evident, both because it accords with their values and because it usually is not experienced as directed toward them.
Therefore for the majority of persons within a society, sectarian political action often appears to have the goal of disruption rather than renewal. For such persons, the sectarian path is not a real option.

But for those for whom the sectarian orientation becomes a possibility, it also becomes a risk. Yet at such
a point to remain within the established orientation becomes
a decision as well. Historically, both paths have led to
good and evil. Further, the individual both chooses and is
chosen. He chooses particular actions which tend to place
him within the orbit of one or the other of the differing
communities. In some ways, then, a person decides in
favor of one orientation and one faith. On the other hand,
once within the range of a particular faith, a person finds
that life is interpreted in terms of the symbols of that orientation. Nonetheless, intention and choice are still factors.

The choice between differing orientations rests first
of all on the judgment of whether the society is just. If the
society is unjust, and opposes reform, the sectarian orientation becomes the only possible ethical choice. But if society

seems reasonably just, and is apparently willing to reform
the injustices that remain, then the choice is not as clear-
cut. The latter is true of American society, according to
the established perspective.

The question then becomes, "Is it better to press for
reform from within the established perspective or to demand
total renewal of the society from within the sectarian orientation?" Since in both cases, the goal is to create a more just
society, the ends are equally as good. The means then become more important. Is there an ethical choice to be made
between the sectarian method of encouraging the oppressed
to act on their own behalf and the establishmentarian attempt
to make the good universal by organizational effort? Obviously, either of these alternatives alone tends to evil. If the
established type has no sectarian opposition, the bureaucratic
oppression of the out-group increases with a vengeance. If
only the sectarian means prevails, only those motivated by
the sectarian vision share in the new society.

The context in which the choice is made is therefore
of great importance. Where there is no sectarian movement,
a society is likely to oppress its out-groups. The attempt
to decrease that oppression by increasing bureaucracy will
be unsuccessful, for bureaucracy itself is inherently oppressive. For justice to emerge, there is therefore a need to
create a countervailing force where none exists. This suggests that in a context where sectarian political activity is
minimal, the ethical choice is to strengthen such activity.
Where there is a vigorous sectarian political agency, the
choice is more contextual and more ambiguous.

Now we may answer the question, Can the good be
chosen, or only the partisan doctrine of the good? Yes,
the good may be chosen. One action or one choice is more fitting
than another. Even though persons are shaped by their participation in particular communities, still it must be affirmed that
action which is responsible is action taken in the light of the
universal community (Niebuhr, 1963, pp69-89).

The good is chosen when, after serious consideration
of the context, a sense of obligation to those of the differing
orientation is maintained even in the midst of a passionate
espousal of one's own faith (Rawls, 1971, pp376, 377). The
questions of whether a person seeks reform from within the
established perspective or renewal from the sectarian stance
and whether the ties to those persons holding the opposing

faith are maintained are both important. Such a judgment is rooted in the humanistic values common to both types of the civil religion.

Looking back across the sixties, we can see how difficult it is to maintain genuine contact with persons of the opposite perspective. The dynamics of the established-sectarian conflict make such attempts precarious. Martin Luther King, Jr. was convinced that established types were worth loving. By the time of his death, many left wing sectarians were ridiculing him. Although King still commanded great respect amongst the masses of black people, amongst sectarians his influence had declined. Robert Kennedy, of the established type, not only visited in established manner the slums, barrios and migrant worker camps of America. He also entered into personal dialogue with those who were most fiercely opposed to him--the S. N. C. C. workers and the Black Panthers. But the intense pressure generated by his need for the political support of the established type often muted his passion for reform. The political strength of both established and sectarian leadership lies in the centrist position of each type. In turn, the expressions of the leaders tend to establish the centrist position. As the tension between types increases, the central positions of the types move increasingly further apart. It is difficult to maintain genuine public contact with persons of differing perspectives. But the civil religion requires Americans to accept those of differing contextuating orientations as persons with the full rights that all humanity exercises.

The basic argument of this study has been that the established and sectarian types are characteristic of the American civil religion. Only by examining the action and interaction of the types can the dynamic of the national life be fully understood. The radical movement of the sixties was neither a wholly new experience for America nor the perennial generational revolt. It was one more of the periods of sectarian political activity, with roots deep in the American experience, nourished by the Abolitionists, the Progressive Movement, the Socialists, and the centuries old struggle of the American blacks to be free indeed. As surely as the potent mixture of great suffering and great hope is compounded again, sectarian political activity will flame across the land. Once again Americans will demand that the nation bring at once to full fruition the Declaration

We hold these truths to be self evident, that all men are created equal; that they are endowed by their creator with certain unalienable rights; that among these are life, liberty, and the pursuit of happiness. . . .

REFERENCES

Abell, A. I. American Catholicism and Social Action: A
Search for Social Justice. Notre Dame: University of
Notre Dame, 1960.

Adelson, A. SDS. New York: Scribner's, 1972.

Adler, M. J. The Negro in American History: I. Black
Americans: 1928-1968. London: Encyclopaedia
Britannica, 1969.

Ahlstrom, S. E. "The American National Faith: Humane,
Yet All Too Human." In J. M. Robinson (ed.),
Religion and the Humanizing of Man. Riverside, Cal.:
Council on the Study of Religion, 1972(a).

Ahlstrom, S. E. A Religious History of the American
People. New Haven: Yale University Press, 1972(b).

Alinsky, S. "The War on Poverty--Political Pornography."
Journal of Social Issues, 21 (1). In C. Waxman (ed.),
Poverty: Power and Politics. New York: Grosset &
Dunlap, 1968.

Alinsky, S. Rules for Radicals: A Practical Primer for
Realistic Radicals. New York: Random House, 1971.

Alperovitz, G. Cold War Essays. Garden City, N. Y.:
Doubleday, 1970.

American Friends Service Committee. The U. S. and the
Soviet Union: Some Quaker Proposals for Peace. New
Haven: Yale University Press, 1949.

American Friends Service Committee. Steps to Peace: A
Quaker View of U. S. Foreign Policy. New York:
Author, 1951.

American Friends Service Committee. Speak Truth to Power: A Quaker Search for an Alternative to Violence. New York: Author, 1955.

Anthony, E. Picking up the Gun. New York: Pyramid Books, 1971.

Apter, D. E. and Joll, J. Anarchism Today. Garden City, N. Y.: Doubleday, 1972.

Arendt, H. "Reflections on Violence." The New York Review of Books, Feb. 29, 1969, pp. 28-32. Cited by Fogelson, R. M. Violence As Protest: A Study of Riots and Ghettos. Garden City, N. Y.: Doubleday, 1971. P. 153.

Arendt, H. Crises of the Republic. New York: Harcourt & Brace, 1972.

Avorn, J. L., et al. Up Against the Ivy Wall: A History of the Columbia Crisis. New York: Atheneum, 1969.

Aya, R. and Miller, N. (eds.) The New American Revolution. New York: Free Press, 1971.

Babcox, P., et al. The Conspiracy. New York: Dell, 1969.

Baker, R. K. The Los Angeles Times, February 4, 1973.

Balagoon, K., et al. Look for Me in the Whirlwind: The Collective Autobiography of the New York 21. New York: Random House, 1971.

Baldwin, James. "A Negro Assays the Negro Mood," The New York Times Sunday Magazine, March 12, 1961, pp. 25, 103-105.

Baritz, L. The American Left: Radical Political Thought in the 20th Century. New York: Basic Books, 1971.

Barnet, R. J. Roots of War. New York: Atheneum, 1972.

Bates, D. The Long Shadow of Little Rock. New York: McKay, 1962.

Bell, D. The End of Ideology. New York: Free Press, 1962.

Bellah, R. **Beyond Belief.** New York: Harper & Row, 1970.

Berger, P. L. and Luckmann, T. **The Social Construction of Reality.** Garden City, N. Y.: Doubleday, 1967.

Berger, P. L. **The Sacred Canopy: Elements of a Sociological Theory of Religion.** Garden City, N. Y.: Doubleday, 1969.

Berger, P. L. **A Rumor of Angels.** Garden City, N. Y.: Doubleday, 1970(a).

Berger, P. L. and Neuhaus, R. **Movement and Revolution.** Garden City, N. Y.: Doubleday, 1970(b).

Berman, R. **America in the Sixties: An Intellectual History.** New York: Harper & Row, 1968.

Berrigan, D. **The Trial of the Catonsville Nine.** Boston: Beacon Press, 1970(a).

Berrigan, D. "Things Hoped For." **Christianity and Crisis,** 1970(b), 30, 186-188.

Berrigan, D. **The Dark Night of the Resistance.** New York: Bantam, 1971(a).

Berrigan, D. and Coles, R. **The Geography of Faith.** Boston: Beacon Press, 1971(b).

Berrigan, D. "Letter to the Weatherman." In Salisbury, H. E. (ed.), **The Eloquence of Protest: Voices of the 70's.** Boston: Houghton Mifflin, 1972.

Blaustein, A. P. and Zangrando, R. L. (eds.) **Civil Rights and the American Negro: A Documentary History.** New York: Trident Press, 1968.

Bond, J. **A Time to Speak, A Time to Act: The Movement in Politics.** New York: Simon & Schuster, 1972.

Bowen, H. R. Inaugural Address. University of Iowa, December 5, 1964. In Weaver, D. A. (ed.), **Builders of American Universities: Inaugural Addresses of College and University Presidents.** Vol. III. Southwest Baptist College, 1964.

Brewster, K. Inaugural Address. Yale University, April 11, 1964. In Weaver, D. A. (ed.), Builders of American Universities: Inaugural Addresses of College and University Presidents. Vol. III. Southwest Baptist College, 1964.

Carmichael, S. and Hamilton, C. V. Black Power and the Politics of Liberation in America. New York: Random House, 1967.

Carmichael, S. Stokely Speaks: Black Power Back to Pan-Africanism. New York: Random House, 1971.

Cherry, C. (ed.) God's New Israel: Religious Interpretations of American Destiny. Englewood Cliffs, N. J.: Prentice-Hall, 1971.

Clark, K. Dark Ghetto: Dilemmas of Social Power. New York: Harper & Row, 1965.

Cleaver, E. Soul on Ice. New York: Dell, 1968.

Cleaver, E. "The Fascists Have Already Decided in Advance to Murder Chairman Bobby Seale in the Electric Chair: A Manifesto." In Foner, P. S. (ed.), The Black Panthers Speak. Philadelphia: Lippincott, 1970.

Coffin, W. S., Jr. Sermon in Arlington Street Church, October 16, 1967. In Mitford, J. The Trial of Dr. Spock, the Rev. William Sloane Coffin, Jr., Michael Ferber, Mitchell Goodman and Marcus Raskin. New York: Random House, 1970.

Cohen, M. and Hale, D. (eds.) The New Student Left: An Anthology. Boston: Beacon Books, 1967.

Commager, H. S. "America's Defeat?" The New York Review of Books, 1972, 19 (5), 7-13.

Cone, J. H. A Black Theology of Liberation. New York: Lippincott, 1970.

Congressional Quarterly. Revolution in Civil Rights: 1945-1968. Washington, D. C.: Author, 1970.

Congressional Quarterly. Civil Rights: Progress Report,
    1970. Washington, D. C. : Author, 1971.

Conzelmann, H. , et al. Das Neues Testament Deutsch: Die
    Kleineren Briefe Des Apostles Paulus. Gottingen:
    Vandenhoeck & Ruprecht, 1962.

Cooper, C. L. The Lost Crusade: America in Vietnam.
    New York: Dodd, Mead, 1970.

Daniels, J. The Man of Independence. Philadelphia: Lip-
    pincott, 1950.

Davis, A. Y. (ed.) If They Come in the Morning. New
    York: The New American Library, 1971.

Day, D. Loaves and Fishes. New York: Harper & Row,
    1963.

Debs, E. V. Writings and Speeches. New York: Heritage
    Press, 1948.

Dellinger, D. Revolutionary Nonviolence. Garden City,
    N. Y. : Doubleday, 1971.

Dobbins, C. G. and Lee, C. Whose Goals for American
    Higher Education? Washington, D. C. : American
    Council on Education, 1968.

Dohrn, B. "New Morning--Changing Weather. " In Salisbury,
    H. E. (ed.), The Eloquence of Protest: Voices of the
    70's. Boston: Houghton Mifflin, 1972.

Domhoff, G. W. Who Rules America? Englewood Cliffs,
    N. J. : Prentice-Hall, 1967.

Domhoff, G. W. The Higher Circles: The Governing Class
    in America. New York: Random House, 1970.

Dulles, J. F. "Freedom's New Task. Vital Speeches of the
    Day, March 15, 1956. " In Cherry, C. (ed.), God's
    New Israel: Religious Interpretations of American
    Destiny. Englewood Cliffs, N. J. : Prentice-Hall, 1971.

Dunne, J. G. Delano: The Story of the California Grape
    Strike. New York: Farrar, Straus & Giroux, 1967.

Durkheim, E. The Elementary Forms of the Religious Life.
    London: Allen & Unwin, 1915.

Einstein, A. (Collected Writings). In Natha, O. and
    Nordern, F. (eds.), Einstein on Peace. New York:
    Schocken Books, 1968.

Eisenhower, D. D. Mandate for Change. Garden City,
    N. Y.: Doubleday, 1963.

Eisenhower, D. D. Waging Peace. Garden City, N. Y.:
    Doubleday, 1965.

Etzioni, A. The Active Society. Glencoe: Free Press,
    1968.

Evans, R. , Jr. and Novak, R. Nixon in the White House:
    The Frustration of Power. New York: Random House,
    1971.

Fanon, F. The Wretched of the Earth. New York: Grove
    Press, 1963.

Farber, J. The Student as Nigger. New York: Simon &
    Schuster, 1969.

Farmer, J. Freedom When? New York: Random House,
    1966.

Ferber, M. "A Time to Say No. Arlington Street Church,
    October 16, 1967. " In Mitford, J. The Trial of Dr.
    Spock, the Rev. William Sloane Coffin, Jr., Michael
    Ferber, Mitchell Goodman and Marcus Raskin. New
    York: Random House, 1970.

Ferber, M. and Lynd, S. The Resistance. Boston: Beacon
    Press, 1971.

Feuer, L. The Conflict of Generations: The Character and
    Significance of Student Movements. New York: Basic
    Books, 1969.

Finn, J. Protest Pacifism and Politics. New York:
    Random House, 1968.

Fitzgerald, F. "Can the War End?" The New York Review
    of Books, 1973, 20 (2), 13-15.

Flacks, R. "SDS Working Paper, June, 1965." In Jacobs,
    P. and Landau, S. (eds.), The New Radicals: A
    Report with Documents. New York: Random House,
    1966.

Flacks, R. Youth and Social Change. Chicago: Markham,
    1971.

Fogelson, R. M. Violence as Protest: A Study of Riots and
    Ghettos. Garden City, N.Y.: Doubleday, 1971.

Foner, P. S. The Black Panthers Speak. Philadelphia:
    Lippincott, 1970.

Franklin, B. From the Movement Toward Revolution. New
    York: Van Nostrand Reinhold, 1971.

Friedman, L. (ed.) The Civil Rights Reader: Basic Docu-
    ments of the Civil Rights Movement. New York:
    Walker & Co., 1967.

Friedman, L. The Wise Minority. New York: Dial Press,
    1971.

Fulbright, J. W. The Arrogance of Power. New York:
    Random House, 1966.

Gabriel, R. H. The Course of American Democratic Thought.
    (2nd ed.) New York: Ronald Press, 1956.

Gardner, L. C., Schlesinger, A., Jr., and Morgenthau, H.
    J. The Origins of the Cold War. Waltham, Mass.:
    Ginn & Co., 1970.

Gettleman, M. E. and Mermelstein, M. (eds.). The Great
    Society Reader: The Failure of American Liberalism.
    New York: Random House, 1967.

Gettleman, M. E. (ed.) Vietnam: History, Documents and
    Opinions. New York: New American Library, 1970.

Gitlin, T. "The Radical Potential of the Poor." Interna-
    tional Socialist Journal, 1965, 24 (24). In Teodori,
    M. (ed.), The New Left: A Documentary History.
    New York: Bobbs-Merrill, 1969.

Golden, H. Mr. Kennedy and the Negroes. Greenwich:
    Fawcett Publications, 1964.

Goldman, E. F. The Crucial Decade--and After. New York:
Random House, 1960.

Goodman, P. Growing Up Absurd. New York: Random
House, 1960.

Goodman, P. New Reformation: Notes of a Neolithic Conservative. New York: Random House, 1970.

Graham, H. D. and Gurr, T. R. Violence in America:
Historical and Comparative Perspectives. New York:
New American Library, 1969.

Grant, J. Black Protest: History, Documents and Analyses
1619 to the Present. Greenwich: Fawcett Publications,
1968.

Graubardi, S. R. and Ballotti, V. The Embattled University.
New York: George Braziller, 1970.

Gravel, M. The Pentagon Papers: The Defense Department
History of the U.S. Decisionmaking on Vietnam. Vols.
I, II, III, & IV. Boston: Beacon Press, 1971.

Grier, W. H. and Cobbs, P. M. Black Rage. New York:
Bantam, 1968.

Halberstam, D. The Best and the Brightest. New York:
Random House, 1972.

Halle, L. J. The Cold War as History. New York: Harper
& Row, 1967.

Halliwell, S. "Columbia, an Explanation." In Long, P.
(ed.), The New Left: A Collection of Essays. Boston:
Porter Sargent, 1969.

Harrington, M. The Other America. Baltimore: Penguin
Books, 1963.

Harrington, M. Toward a Democratic Left. Baltimore:
Penguin Books, 1968.

Hayakawa, S. I. "Education in Ferment." Speech to the
Commonwealth Club of San Francisco, January, 1969.
In McEvoy, J., & Miller, A. (eds.), Black Power and
Student Rebellion. Belmont, Cal.: Wadsworth, 1969.

Hayden, T. "Letter to the New (Young) Left." The Activist, Winter, 1961. In Cohen, M. and Hale, D. (eds.), The New Student Left: An Anthology. Boston: Beacon Books, 1967.

Hayden, T. and Wittman, C. "An Interracial Movement of the Poor." S. D. S. Working Paper, 1963. In Cohen, M. and Hale, D. (eds.), The New Student Left: An Anthology. Boston: Beacon Books, 1967.

Hayden, T. Rebellion and Repression. New York: World, 1970(a).

Hayden, T. Trial. New York: Holt, Rinehart & Winston, 1970(b).

Hayden, T. "An Interview with Tom Hayden." Rolling Stone, 121 (November 9, 1972), 28-36.

Heirich, M. The Spiral of Conflict. New York: The Columbia University Press, 1971.

Hentoff, N. Peace Agitator: The Story of A. J. Muste. New York: Macmillan, 1963.

Herberg, W. Protestant, Catholic, Jew. (2nd ed.) Garden City, N. Y.: Doubleday, 1960.

Hilsman, R. To Move a Nation. Garden City, N. Y.: Doubleday, 1967.

Hoopes, T. The Limits of Intervention. New York: David McKay, 1969.

Hopkins, C. H. The Rise of the Social Gospel in American Protestantism 1865-1915. New Haven: Yale University Press, 1967.

Horowitz, I. L. and Friedland, L. The Knowledge Factory: Student Power and Academic Politics in America. Chicago: Aldine, 1970.

Howe, I. (ed.) The Radical Papers. Garden City, N. Y.: Doubleday, 1966(a).

Howe, I. Steady Work: Essays in the Politics of Democratic
    Radicalism 1953-1966. New York: Harcourt, Brace &
    World, 1966(b).

Ianniello, L. (ed.) Milestones Along the March: Twelve
    Historic Civil Rights Documents from WW II to Selma.
    New York: Praeger, 1965.

Jackson, G. "Towards the United Front." In Davis, A.
    (ed.), If They Come in the Morning. New York: New
    American Library, 1971.

Jacobs, H. (ed.) Weatherman. San Francisco: Ramparts
    Press, 1970.

Jacobs, P. and Landau, S. The New Radicals: A Report
    with Documents. New York: Random House, 1966.

Johnson, B. "Church Sect Revisited." Journal for the
    Scientific Study of Religion, 1971, 10, 124-138.

Johnson, L. B. "To Fulfill These Rights." Speech at
    Howard University, June 4, 1965. In Gettleman, M.
    E. and Mermelstein, M. (eds.), The Great Society
    Reader: The Failure of American Liberalism. New
    York: Random House, 1967(a).

Johnson, L. B. "American Policy in Viet-Nam." Speech at
    Johns Hopkins University, April 7, 1965. In Raskin,
    M. G. and Fall, B. B. (eds.), The Viet-Nam Reader:
    Articles and Documents on American Foreign Policy
    and the Vietnam Crisis. (2nd ed.) New York: Random
    House, 1967(b).

Johnson, L. B. The Vantage Point: Perspectives of the
    Presidency, 1963-1969. New York: Holt, Rinehart &
    Winston, 1971.

Kahn, T. "The Political Significance of the Freedom Rides."
    Address at SDS Conference on Race and Politics,
    University of North Carolina, 1962. In Cohen, M.
    and Hale, D. (eds.), The New Student Left: An
    Anthology. Boston: Beacon Books, 1967.

Kalb, M. and Abel, E. Roots of Involvement: The U. S. in
    Asia 1784-1971. New York: Norton, 1971.

Kaufman, A. S. The Radical Liberal. New York Simon &
     Schuster, 1968.

Keniston, K. Young Radicals: Notes on Committed Youth.
     New York Harcourt & Brace, 1968.

Kennan, G. F. , et al. Democracy and the Student Left.
     New York Bantam Books, 1968.

Kennedy, J. F. Profiles in Courage. New York Harper &
     Row, 1955.

Kennedy, J. F. Public Papers, 1961. Cited in Walton, R.
     S. Cold War and Counterrevolution: The Foreign
     Policy of John F. Kennedy. New York Viking Press,
     1972.

Kennedy, J. F. To Turn the Tide: A Selection from Presi-
     dent Kennedy's Public Statements from His Election
     Through the 1961 Adjournment of Congress. New York
     Harper & Row, 1962.

Kennedy, J. F. Public Papers, 1963. Cited in Walton,
     R. S. Cold War and Counterrevolution: The Foreign
     Policy of John F. Kennedy. New York Viking Press,
     1972.

Kennedy, R. F. To Seek a Newer World. New York
     Bantam Books, 1968.

Kennedy, R. F. Thirteen Days: A Memoir of the Cuban
     Missile Crisis. New York Norton, 1969.

Kerr, C. The Uses of the University. Cambridge: Harvard
     University Press, 1963.

Kerr, C. "Governance and Functions. " In Graubardi, S.
     R. , & Ballotti, V. The Embattled University. New
     York George Braziller, 1970.

King, M. L. , Jr. Stride Toward Freedom: The Montgomery
     Story. New York Harper & Row, 1958.

King, M. L. , Jr. "I Have A Dream. " Address at the
     March on Washington, 1963. In Meier, A. , et al. ,
     Black Protest Thought in the Twentieth Century.
     Indianapolis: Bobbs, Merrill, 1971.

King, M. L., Jr. Where Do We Go From Here: Chaos or Community. New York: Harper & Row, 1967.

King, M. L., Jr. "We Still Believe in Black and White Together." Look, 1968, 32. In Meier, A., et al., Black Protest Thought in the Twentieth Century. Indianapolis: Bobbs, Merrill, 1971.

Kissinger, H. A. American Foreign Policy. New York: Norton, 1969.

Kolko, G. The Politics of War. New York: Random House, 1968.

Kolko, G. The Roots of American Foreign Policy. Boston: Beacon Press, 1969.

Kopkind, A. "The Sixties and the Movement." Ramparts, 1973, 11 (8), 29-34.

Kotz, N. Let Them Eat Promises: The Politics of Hunger in America. Englewood Cliffs, N. J.: Prentice-Hall, 1969.

Kruytbosch, C. E. and Messinger, M. (eds.) The State of the University: Authority and Change. Beverly Hills, Cal.: Sage Publications, 1970.

Lasch, C. The New Radicalism in America: 1889-1963. New York: Random House, 1965.

Lasch, C. The Agony of the American Left. New York: Random House, 1969.

Lawson, J. M., Jr. "From a Lunch-Counter Stool." Address at SNCC Conference, Raleigh, N. C., April, 1960. In Meier, A., et al. (eds.), Black Protest Thought in the Twentieth Century. (2nd ed.) Indianapolis: Bobbs, Merrill, 1971.

Lens, S. Radicalism in America. New York: Crowell, 1969.

Lenski, G. The Religious Factor. New York: Doubleday, 1963.

Leuctenburg, W. E. Franklin D. Roosevelt and the New Deal. New York: Harper & Row, 1963.

Lewis, A. Portrait of a Decade: The Second American Revolution. New York: Bantam Books, 1971.

Lewis, D. L. King: A Critical Biography. New York: Praeger, 1970.

Lewis, J. "March on Washington." Speech at March on Washington, August 28, 1963. In Grant, J., Black Protest: History, Documents and Analyses 1619 to the Present. Greenwich: Fawcett Publications, 1968.

Liberation. Editorial, Tract for the Times. 1, March, 1956.

Lincoln, C. E. The Black Muslims in America. Boston: Beacon Press, 1961.

Link, A. S. and Catton, B. A History of the U.S. since the 1890's. (3rd ed.) New York: Knopf, 1963.

Lippmann, W. "U.S. Foreign Policy: Shield of the Republic." New York Times, August 19, 1942, p. 53. Cited in Wittner, L. S., Rebels Against War: The American Peace Movement, 1941-1960. New York: Columbia University Press, 1969.

Lipset, S. M. The First New Nation: The United States in Historical and Comparative Perspective. Garden City, N.Y.: Doubleday, 1967.

Lipset, S. M. Revolution and Counterrevolution: Change and Persistence in Social Structures. Garden City, N.Y.: Doubleday, 1970.

Lipset, S. M. and Schaflander, G. M. Passion and Politics: Student Activism in America. Boston: Little, Brown, 1971.

Little, D. American Foreign Policy and Moral Rhetoric: The Example of Vietnam. New York: Council on Religious and Foreign Affairs, 1969.

Long, P. (ed.) The New Left: A Collection of Essays. Boston: Porter Sargent, 1969.

Los Angeles Times. Thursday, September 21, 1972.

Luckmann, T. The Invisible Religion: The Problem of Religion in Modern Society. London: Macmillan, 1967.

Lunsford, T. F. "Authority and Ideology in the Administered University." In Kruytbosch, C. E. and Messinger, M. (eds.), The State of the University: Authority and Change. Beverly Hills, Cal.: Sage Publications, 1970.

Lynd, S. Intellectual Origins of American Radicalism. New York: Random House, 1969.

McCarthy, E. J. The Year of the People. Garden City, N.Y.: Doubleday, 1969.

McEvoy, J. and Miller, A. Black Power and Student Rebellion. Belmont, Cal.: Wadsworth, 1969.

McKissick, F. Three-fifths of a Man. London: Macmillan, 1969.

Maclear, J. F. "The Republic and the Millennium." In Smith, E. A. (ed.), The Religion of the Republic. Philadelphia: Fortress, 1971.

Mailer, N. The Armies of the Night. New York: New American Library, 1968(a).

Mailer, N. Miami and the Siege of Chicago: An Informal History of the Republican and Democratic Conventions of 1968. New York: World, 1968(b).

Malcolm X. The Autobiography of Malcolm X. New York: Grove Press, 1965.

Marcuse, H. An Essay on Liberation. Boston: Beacon Press, 1969.

Marx, G. T. Protest and Prejudice: A Study of Belief in the Black Community. New York: Harper & Row, 1967.

Mauss, A. L. (ed.) "The New Left and the Old." Journal of Social Issues, 1971, 27 (1), 1-20.

May, H. F. Protestant Churches and Industrial America. New York: Harper & Row, 1967.

Mead, S. E. The Lively Experiment: The Shaping of Christianity in America. New York: Harper & Row, 1963.

Meier, A. and Broderick, F. Negro Protest Thought in the 20th Century. New York: Bobbs-Merrill, 1965.

Meier, A. , et al. Black Protest Thought in the 20th Century. (2nd ed.) New York: Bobbs-Merrill, 1971.

Merleau-Ponty, M. Humanism and Terror: An Essay on the Communist Problem. Boston: Beacon Press, 1969.

Michaelson, R. "The Public Schools and 'America's Two Religions. ' " A Journal of Church and State, Autumn, 1966, pp. 380-400. Cited in Cherry, C. (ed.), God's New Israel: Religious Interpretations of American Destiny. Englewood Cliffs, N. J.: Prentice-Hall, 1971.

Mills, C. W. The Power Elite. Oxford: Oxford University Press, 1956.

Mills, C. W. Listen Yankee. New York: McGraw-Hill, 1960.

Mills, C. W. Power, Politics and People: The Collected Essays of C. Wright Mills. Oxford: Oxford University Press, 1963.

Mitford, J. The Trial of Dr. Spock, the Rev. William Sloane Coffin, Jr. , Michael Ferber, Mitchell Goodman, and Marcus Raskin. New York: Random House, 1970.

Moore, B. Reflections on the Causes of Human Misery and Upon Certain Proposals to Eliminate Them. Boston: Beacon Press, 1972.

Morgan, R. (ed.) Sisterhood Is Powerful: An Anthology of Writings from the Women's Liberation Movement. New York: Random House, 1970.

Morgenthau, H. J. "Origins of the Cold War. " In Gardner, L. C. , Schlesinger, A. , Jr. and Morgenthau, H. J. , The Origins of the Cold War. Waltham, Mass.: Ginn & Co. , 1970.

Morison, S. E. Oxford History of the American People. Oxford: Oxford University Press, 1965.

Moses, B. "Questions Raised by Moses." Talk at the Fifth Anniversary of SNCC, 1965. In Jacobs, P. and Landau, S. The New Radicals: A Report with Documents. New York: Random House, 1966.

Moynihan, D. P. "The Negro Family: The Case for National Action, 1965." In Rainwater, L. and Yancey, W. L. (eds.), The Moynihan Report and the Politics of Controversy. Cambridge, Mass.: M. I. T. Press, 1967.

Moynihan, D. P. (ed.) On Understanding Poverty: Perspectives from the Social Sciences. New York: Basic Books, 1969.

Moynihan, D. P. Maximum Feasible Misunderstanding: Community Action in the War on Poverty. New York: Free Press, 1970.

Muse, B. Ten Years of Prelude: The Story of Integration since the Supreme Court's 1954 Decision. New York: Viking Press, 1964.

Muste, A. J. "The Workability of Nonviolence." In Weinberg, A. and Weinberg, L. (eds.), Instead of Violence. New York: Grossman, 1963.

Muste, A. J. The Essays of A. J. Muste. Edited by Nat Hentoff. New York: Bobbs-Merrill, 1967.

National Advisory Commission on Civil Disorders. Report. New York: Bantam Books, 1968.

Neary, J. Julian Bond: Black Rebel. New York: William Morrow, 1971.

Newfield, J. Robert Kennedy: A Memoir. New York: Dutton, 1969.

Newfield, J. A Prophetic Minority. New York: New American Library, 1970.

Newfield, J. Bread and Roses Too. New York: Dutton, 1971.

Newfield, J., & Greenfield, J. A Populist Manifesto: The Making of a New Majority. New York: Praeger, 1972.

Newton, H. "Huey Newton Talks to the Movement." Chicago: SDS, 1968." In Meier, A., et al (eds.), Black Protest Thought in the 20th Century. (2nd ed.) New York: Bobbs-Merrill, 1971.

Newton, H. To Die for the People. New York: Random House, 1972.

Niebuhr, H. R. The Responsible Self. New York: Harper & Row, 1963.

Niebuhr, R. The Irony of American History. New York: Scribner's, 1952.

Niebuhr, R. Love and Justice: Selections from the Shorter Writings of Reinhold Niebuhr. New York: World, 1967.

Nisbet, R. A. The Degradation of the Academic Dogma: The University in America, 1945-1970. New York: Basic Books, 1971.

Nixon, R. M. "Television and Radio Address to the Nation, November, 1969." In Gettleman, M. E. (ed.), Vietnam: History, Documents and Opinions. New York: New American Library, 1970.

Nixon, R. M. "Television Address to the Nation, April 30, 1970." In Gettleman, M. E. (ed.), Vietnam: History, Documents and Opinions. New York: New American Library, 1970.

Nixon, R. M. "Second Inaugural Address." Los Angeles Times, January 21, 1973.

Novak, M. A Theology for Radical Politics. New York: Herder & Herder, 1969.

Nye, R. B. This Almost Chosen People. East Lansing, Mich.: Michigan State University Press, 1966.

Oglesby, C. "Let Us Shape the Future." Speech to March on Washington to End the War in Vietnam, November 27, 1965. In Cohen, M. and Hale, D. (eds.). The New Student Left: An Anthology. Boston: Beacon Books, 1967.

Oglesby, C. and Shaull, R. Containment and Change. London: Macmillan, 1967.

Oglesby, C. "An Open Letter to McCarthy Supporters" (1968). In Teodori, M. (ed.), The New Left: A Documentary History. New York: Bobbs-Merrill, 1969.

O'Neill, W. C. Coming Apart: An Informal History of America in the 1960's. Chicago: Quadrangle, 1971.

Perkins, James A. Inaugural Address, Cornell University, Oct. 4, 1963, in Weaver, D. A. (ed.). Builders of American Universities: Inaugural Addresses of College and University Presidents. Vol. III. Southwest Baptist College, 1969.

The President's Commission on Campus Unrest: Report. Washington, D. C.: U. S. Government Printing Office, 1970.

Rainwater, L. and Yancey, W. L. (eds.). The Moynihan Report and the Politics of Controversy. Cambridge, Mass.: M. I. T. Press, 1967.

Raskin, M. G. and Fall, B. B. (eds.) The Viet-Nam Reader: Articles and Documents on American Foreign Policy and the Vietnam Crisis. (2nd ed.) New York: Random House, 1967.

Rauschenbusch, W. Christianity and the Social Crisis. New York: Harper & Row, 1907.

Rawls, J. A Theory of Justice. Cambridge, Mass.: Harvard University Press, 1971.

Reich, C. A. The Greening of America. New York: Random House, 1970.

Reist, B. A. Toward a Theology of Involvement. Philadelphia: Westminster, 1966.

Reynolds, E. The Forbidden Voyage. New York: David McKay, 1961.

Robinson, J. M. (ed.) Religion and the Humanizing of Man. Riverside, Cal.: Council on the Study of Religion, 1972.

Roosevelt, F. D. "Annual Message to Congress, 1942." In Cherry, C. (ed.), God's New Israel: Religious Interpretations of American Destiny. Englewood Cliffs, N. J.: Prentice-Hall, 1971.

Rostow, E. Law, Power and Pursuit of Peace. New York: Harper & Row, 1968.

Roszak, T. The Making of a Counter Culture. Garden City, N. Y.: Doubleday, 1969.

Roszak, T. Where the Wasteland Ends: Politics and Transcendence in Postindustrial Society. Garden City, N. Y.: Doubleday, 1972.

Rothstein, R. "Evolution of the ERAP Organizers." Radical America, 1968, 2 (2). In Long, P. (ed.), The New Left: A Collection of Essays. Boston: Porter Sargent, 1969.

Rubin, J. We Are Everywhere. New York: Harper & Row, 1971.

Ruether, R. R. The Radical Kingdom: The Western Experience of Messianic Hope. New York: Harper & Row, 1970.

Rustin, B. Down the Line: The Collected Writings of Bayard Rustin. Chicago: Quadrangle, 1971.

Salisbury, H. E. (ed.) The Eloquence of Protest: Voices of the 70's. Boston: Houghton Mifflin, 1972.

Sampson, E. E. and Korn, H. A. (eds.) Student Activism and Protest. San Francisco: Jossey Bass, 1970.

Savio, M. "An End to History." Speech at Berkeley, December, 1964. In Jacobs, P. and Landau, S., The New Radicals: A Report with Documents. New York: Random House, 1966.

Scheer, R. "Scheer Speaks for Himself." Excerpt from Lang, S., The Scheer Campaign, 1967. In Teodori, M. The New Left: A Documentary History. New York: Bobbs-Merrill, 1969.

Schlesinger, A. M., Jr. A Thousand Days: John F. Kennedy in the White House. Boston: Houghton Mifflin, 1965.

Schlesinger, A. M., Jr. "Origins of the Cold War." In
    Gardner, L. C., Schlesinger, A. M., Jr., and
    Morgenthau, H. J., The Origins of the Cold War.
    Waltham, Mass.: Ginn & Co., 1970.

Seale, B. Seize the Time: The Story of the Black Panther
    Party and Huey P. Newton. New York: Random
    House, 1970.

Searle, J. R. The Campus War: A Sympathetic Look at the
    University in Agony. New York: World, 1971.

Shafer, H. B. "Editorial Research Reports." Daily Pilot,
    December 16, 1972.

Sheehan, N., et al. The Pentagon Papers. New York:
    Bantam Books, 1971.

Shin'ya Ono. "A Weatherman: You Do Need a Weatherman
    to Know Which Way the Wind Blows." Leviathan,
    December, 1969. In Jacobs, H., Weatherman. San
    Francisco: Ramparts Press, 1970.

Silverman, H. J. (ed.) American Radical Thought: The
    Libertarian Tradition. Lexington: Heath, 1970.

Simmer, E. (ed.) Pain and Promise: The Chicano Today.
    New York: New American Library, 1972.

Smith, E. A. (ed.) The Religion of the Republic. Phila-
    delphia: Fortress, 1971.

Smith, G. K. (ed.) The Troubled Campus: Current Issues
    in Higher Education. San Francisco: Jossey Bass,
    1970.

Smith, J. W. and Jamison, A. L. The Shaping of American
    Religion. Princeton: Princeton University Press,
    1961.

Smith, T. L. Revivalism and Social Reform. Nashville:
    Abingdon, 1957.

Smylie, J. E. "National Ethos and the Church." Theology
    Today, October, 1963, pp. 313-17. Cited by Cherry,
    C. (ed.), God's New Israel: Religious Interpretations
    of American Destiny. Englewood Cliffs, N.J.: Pren-
    tice-Hall, 1971. p. 13.

Sorensen, T. C. Kennedy. New York: Harper & Row, 1965.

Stahr, E. J. Inaugural Address. Indiana University, November 19, 1962. In Weaver, D. A. (ed.), Builders of American Universities: Inaugural Addresses of College and University Presidents. Vol. III. Southwest Baptist College, 1964.

Stark, W. The Sociology of Religion. New York: Fordham University Press, 1966. 5 vols.

Steel, Ronald. Pax Americana. New York: The Viking Press, 1967.

Stoltz, M. Politics of the New Left. Beverly Hills: Glencoe, 1971.

Stone, I. F. The Killings at Kent State. New York: Random House, 1970.

Sundquist, J. L. On Fighting Poverty: Perspectives from Experience. New York: Basic Books, 1969.

Sutherland, E. (ed.) Letters from Mississippi. New York: McGraw-Hill, 1965.

Swomley, J. M., Jr. American Empire: The Political Ethics of Twentieth Century Conquest. London: Macmillan, 1970.

Teodori, M. (ed.) The New Left: A Documentary History. New York: Bobbs-Merrill, 1969.

Thoreau, H. D. Walden and On the Duty of Civil Disobedience. New York: Rinehart, 1953.

Trewhitt, H. L. McNamara. New York: Harper & Row, 1971.

Troeltsch, E. The Social Teachings of the Christian Churches. Translated by Olive Wyon. New York: Harper & Row, 1960. 2 vols. (Orig. ed.: New York: Macmillan, 1931.)

Truman, H. S. Memoirs. Vol. 1. Year of Decisions. Garden City, N.Y.: Doubleday, 1955.

Truman, H. S. Memoirs. Vol. 2. Years of Trial and Hope. Garden City, N. Y.: Doubleday, 1956.

Tyler, A. F. Freedom's Ferment. New York: Harper & Row, 1944.

U. S. President's Committee on Civil Rights. To Secure These Rights: The Report of the President's Commission on Civil Rights. New York: Simon and Schuster, 1947.

Walker, D. Rights in Conflict. New York: Bantam, 1968.

Walton, R. J. Cold War and Counterrevolution: The Foreign Policy of John F. Kennedy. New York: Viking Press, 1972.

Watters, P. Down to Now: Reflections on the Southern Civil Rights Movement. New York: Pantheon Books, 1971.

Waxman, C. (ed.) Poverty, Power and Politics. New York: Grosset & Dunlap, 1968.

Weaver, David A. (ed.) Builders of American Universities: Inaugural Addresses of College and University Presidents. Vol. III. Southwest Baptist College, 1969.

Weber, M. From Max Weber: Essays in Sociology. Edited by Gerth, H. H., & Mills, C. W. New York: Oxford University Press, 1946.

Weber, M. The Protestant Ethic. New York: Scribner's, 1958.

Weber, M. The Sociology of Religion. Boston: Beacon Press, 1963.

Weinstein, J. The Decline of Socialism in America. New York: Monthly Review Press, 1967.

Williams, W. A. The Roots of Modern American Empire. New York: Random House, 1969.

Williams, W. A. The Tragedy of American Diplomacy. New York: Dell, 1972.

Wilson, J. F.   "The Status of Civil Religion in America."
    In Smith, E. A. (ed.), The Religion of the Republic.
    Philadelphia: Fortress, 1971.

Wittman, C.   "Students and Economic Action."   SDS Pamphlet,
    April, 1964.   In Teodori, M. (ed.), The New Left: A
    Documentary History.   New York: Bobbs-Merrill, 1969.

Wittner, L. S.   Rebels Against the War: The American
    Peace Movement, 1941-1960.   New York: Columbia
    University, 1969.

Wolf, W. J.   The Religion of Abraham Lincoln.   New York:
    Seabury Press, 1963.

Wolff, M.   Lunch at the Five and Ten: The Greensboro
    Sit-In.   New York: Stein & Day, 1970.

Wright, N., Jr.   "Black Power and Urban Unrest."   Address
    at the Abyssinian Church in Harlem, New York
    October 23, 1966.   In Cherry, C. (ed.), God's New
    Israel: Religious Interpretations of American Destiny.
    Englewood Cliffs, N. J.:   Prentice-Hall, 1971.

Yinger, J. M.   Religion, Society and the Individual.   New
    York: Macmillan, 1962.

Young, W. M., Jr.   Beyond Racism: Building an Open
    Society.   New York: McGraw-Hill, 1969.

Zinn, H.   SNCC: The New Abolitionists.   Boston: Beacon
    Press, 1965.

INDEX